ALASTAIR SAWDAY'S
SPECIAL PLACES TO STAY

I0628065

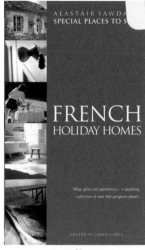

FRENCH HOLIDAY HOMES

Villas, gîtes and apartments – a sparkling collection of over 360 gorgeous places.

EDITED BY EMMA CAREY

£12.99/$23.95

FRENCH BED & BREAKFAST

A book without equal – bustling with characters and beautiful places.

EDITED BY EMMA CAREY

£15.99/$23.95

ALASTAIR SAWDAY'S
SPECIAL PLACES TO STAY

PARIS HOTELS

Paris is too magical for you to waste a moment in the wrong hotel.

EDITED BY SUSAN SCARESCI

£9.99/$17.95

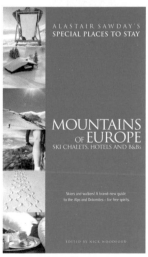

ALASTAIR SAWDAY'S
SPECIAL PLACES TO STAY

MOUNTAINS OF EUROPE
SKI CHALETS, HOTELS AND B&Bs

Skiers and walkers! A brand-new guide to the Alps and Dolomites – for free spirits.

EDITED BY NICK WOODFORD

£9.99/$17.95

Credit card orders (free p&p) 01275 464891
www.specialplacestostay.com

In US: credit card orders (800) 243-0495, 9am-5pm EST,
24-hour fax (800) 820-2329 www.globepequot.com

Fourth edition
Copyright © October 2005
Alastair Sawday Publishing Co. Ltd
Published in October 2005
Alastair Sawday Publishing Co. Ltd
Yanley Lane
Long Ashton
Bristol BS41 9LR
Tel: +44 (0)1275 464891
Fax: +44 (0)1275 464887
E-mail: info@specialplacestostay.com
Web: www.specialplacestostay.com

The Globe Pequot Press
P. O. Box 480, Guilford,
Connecticut 06437, USA
Tel: +1 203 458 4500
Fax: +1 203 458 4601
E-mail: info@globepequot.com
Web: www.globepequot.com

Design:
Caroline King

Maps & Mapping:
Maidenhead Cartographic Services Ltd

Printing:
Butler & Tanner, Frome, UK

UK Distribution:
Penguin UK, 80 Strand, London

US Distribution:
The Globe Pequot Press, Guilford,
Connecticut

All rights reserved. No part of this
publication may be used other than
for the purpose for which it is intended
nor may any part be reproduced, or
transmitted, in any form or by any
means, electronically or mechanically,
including photocopying, recording or any
information storage or retrieval system
without prior written permission from
the publisher. Request for permission
should be addressed to: Alastair Sawday
Publishing Co. Ltd, Yanley Lane, Long
Ashton, Bristol BS41 9LR in the UK; or
The Globe Pequot Press, P.O. Box 480,
Guilford, Connecticut 06437 in North
America.

A catalogue record for this book is
available from the British Library.

This publication is not included under
licences issued by the Copyright Agency.
No part of this publication may be used
in any form of advertising, sales
promotion or publicity.

**Alastair Sawday has asserted his right
to be identified as the author of this
work.**

ISBN 1-901970-63-9
    978-1-901970-63-0

Paper and Printing: We have sought the lowest
possible ecological 'footprint' from the
production of this book, using super-efficient
machinery, vegetable inks and high
environmental standards. Our printer is ISO
14001-registered.

The publishers have made every effort to
ensure the accuracy of the information
in this book at the time of going to
press. However, they cannot accept
any responsibility for any loss, injury
or inconvenience resulting from the
use of information contained therein.

ALASTAIR SAWDAY'S
SPECIAL PLACES TO STAY

FRENCH
HOTELS
CHÂTEAUX & OTHER PLACES

Contents

Guide entries

Back

Index by département

Photo Le Château de Mazan, entry 348

Alastair Sawday Publishing

We are the faceless toilers at the pit-face of publishing but, for us, the question of who we are and how we inter-react is important. For who we are shapes the books, the books shape your holidays, and thus are shaped the lives of people who own these 'special places'. So we are trying to be a little more than 'just a publishing company'.

New eco offices

By the end of 2005 we will have moved into our new eco offices. By introducing super-insulation, underfloor heating, a wood-pellet boiler, solar panels and a rainwater tank, we will have a working environment benign to ourselves and to the environment. Lighting will be low-energy, dark corners will be lit by sun-pipes and one building is of green oak. Carpet tiles are leased: some of recycled material, most of wool and some of natural fibres. We will sail through our environmental audit.

Environmental & ethical policies

We combine many other small gestures: company cars run on gas or recycled cooking oil; kitchen waste is composted and other waste recycled; cycling and car-sharing are encouraged; the company only buys organic or local food; we don't accept web links with companies we consider unethical; we use the ethical Triodos Bank for our deposit account.

We have used recycled paper for some books but have settled on selecting paper and printer for their low energy use. Our printer is British and ISO14001-certified and together we will reduce our environmental impact.

Thanks partially to our Green Team, we recently won a Business Commitment to the Environment Award – which has boosted our resolve to stick to our own green policies. Our flagship gesture, however, is carbon offsetting; we calculate our carbon emissions and plant trees to compensate as calculated by Future Forests. In 2006 we will support projects overseas that plant trees or reduce carbon use; our money will work better by going direct to projects.

Ethics

But why, you may ask, take these things so seriously? You are just a little publishing company, for heavens sake! Well, is there any good argument for not taking them seriously? The world, by the admission of the vast majority of scientists, is in trouble. If we do not change our ways urgently we will doom the planet and all its creatures – whether innocent or not – to a variety of possible catastrophes. To maintain the status quo is unacceptable. Business does much of the damage and should undo it, and provide new models.

Who are we?

Pressure on companies to produce Corporate Social Responsibility policies is mounting. We are trying to keep ahead of it all, yet still to be as informal and human as possible – the antithesis of 'corporate'. (We even have unofficial 'de-stress operatives' in the shape of several resident dogs.)

The books – and a dilemma

So, we have created fine books that do good work. They promote authenticity, individuality, high quality, local and organic food – far from the now-dominant corporate culture. Rural economies, pubs, small farms, villages and hamlets all benefit. However, people use fossil fuel to get there. Should we aim to get our readers to offset their own carbon emissions, and the B&B and hotel owners too? That might have been a hopeless task a year or so ago, but less so now that the media has taken on board the enormity of the work ahead of us all.

We are slowly introducing green ideas into the books: the Fine Breakfast Scheme that highlights British and Irish B&B owners, who use local and organic food; celebrating those who make an extra effort; gently encouraging the use of public transport, cycling and walking. Next year we are publishing a book focusing on responsible travel and eco-projects around the globe.

Our Fragile Earth series

The 'hard' side of our environmental publishing is the Fragile Earth series: *The Little Earth Book, The Little Food Book* and *The Little Money Book*. They have been a great success. They consist of bite-sized essays, polemical and hard-hitting but well researched and methodical. They are a 'must have' for people from all walks of life – anyone who is confused and needs clarity about some of the key issues of our time.

Lastly – what is special?

The notion of 'special' is at the heart of what we do, and highly subjective. We discuss this in the Introduction. We take huge pleasure from finding people and places that do their own thing – brilliantly; places that are unusual and follow no trends; places of peace and beauty; people who are kind and interesting – and genuine.

We seem to have touched a raw nerve with thousands of readers; they obviously want to stay in special places rather than the dull corporate monstrosities that have disfigured so many of our cities and towns. Life is too short to be wasted in the wrong places. A night in a special place can be a transforming experience.

Alastair Sawday

Acknowledgements

When Susan began this job she was very much on her own, sailing close to the wind in choppy seas. But now, thanks to her own efforts with previous editions, she has a fair wind behind her. Hotel owners are delighted to see her and have learned to appreciate the travellers who so enjoy their special places. But her job is nevertheless a challenging one – sometimes frustrating. She is a real 'trooper' and a delight; her relentless quest for high quality and 'specialness' have made this book the success it is.

Alastair Sawday

Susan would like to offer...
Special thanks to our anonymous inspectors who shall remain anonymous, and to Europcar.

And gratitude to my mentor Ann Cooke-Yarborough and to Jackie King who meets my frazzle and dazzle with more serenity than my yoga teacher.

Editor Susan Herrick Luraschi

Series Editor Alastair Sawday

Editorial Director Annie Shillito

Managing Editor Jackie King

Production Manager Julia Richardson

Web & IT Russell Wilkinson, Chris Banks, Brian Kimberling

Production Paul Groom, Allys Williams, Philippa Rogers

Copy Editor Jo Boissevain

Editorial Maria Serrano, Rebecca Stevens, Danielle Williams,

Sales & Marketing & PR Siobhan Flynn, Andreea Petre Goncalves, Sarah Bolton

Accounts Sheila Clifton, Bridget Bishop, Christine Buxton, Jenny Purdy, Sandra Hassell

Writers Susan Herrick Luraschi, Ann Cooke-Yarborough, Jo Boissevain, Viv Cripps, Helen Pickles, Allys Williams

Inspections Susan Luraschi, Richard & Linda Armspach, Helen Barr, Alyson & Colin Browne, Elizabeth & Neil Carter, Jill Coyle, Meredith Dickinson, Sue Edrich, John & Jane Edwards, Valerie Foix, Georgina Gabriel, Denise Goss, Diana Harris, Miranda Jane Perryman Menist, Jo-Bell Moore, Peter & Clarissa Novak, Elizabeth Yates

And many thanks to those people who did just a few inspections.

A word from Alastair Sawday

From the great, squat, massiveness of Brittany's châteaux to the sky-scraping elegance of their turreted Loire cousins, the buildings in this book are as spectacularly lovely as their owners. The book's reach is impressive – it covers every corner of France and reveals to you some of the loveliest hotels imaginable. So it is no surprise that it has been such a success.

Whenever I am asked to write these pieces I go back to the books and re-read them, and am struck again and again by the spirit-lifting, honest enterprise manifest within the pages. Here, with French Hotels, there are hundreds of people devotedly defending their way of looking at the world, pouring their energies into maintaining and displaying these astonishing buildings. Each hotel differs from its neighbour; each owner has his or her own style. It is fun to hear of such differences and exhilarating to experience them – as you will discover when you do your travelling.

You will meet wine-makers, farmers, craftspeople, intellectuals, sportsmen, musicians, artists, aristocrats, merchants, writers and poets. They will spoil you rotten or leave you alone, encourage you to get under the skin of their local culture or let you do your own thing. You can loaf all day beside the stream, fish in lakes, walk in ancient parkland – all this within the grounds of these places. There are few, if any, countries with such a sparkling variety of special places to stay and such inspired professionalism in running them.

Let us know how you enjoy it all.

Alastair Sawday

Introduction

WE LIKE THEM SMALL, WE LIKE THEM FAMILY-RUN, WE LIKE CHÂTEAU-CHIC AND TRULY TRAD AND ALL THOSE IN BETWEEN

On 29 May 2005, with a 69% turnout, the French voted *'non'* in their referendum on the European constitution; the Netherlands soon followed suit. Some predicted that 'Europe' would now be on the back burner. However, from our vantage point, it appears that Europe is taking baby steps in directions unthinkable four or five years ago. Behind the big headlines from Brussels announcing this proposition or that decree, there is a dynamic cross-cultural revolution going on right in front of our eyes and we, as close observers, take delight in it.

As far as the hospitality business goes, British, Dutch, Belgian, Italian, American and German nationals have thrown their hats in the ring, ferreted out attractive properties, completed renovations with style and panache and launched themselves into their enterprises. Some of them are very good at it.

We waited awhile to see whether this was just a fashion or a passing fancy and to see if they had real staying power. We waited for historic reasons; we, of course, were writing guides for the British traveller that they might exchange and 'converse' with the French. We also waited to see if these interlopers were only catering to travellers of their own cultures, in a sort of ghetto mentality where only a light French dusting was allowed to filter through, a safe Hilton-to-Hilton type of travel perfected by some Americans.

Our fears have been unfounded, so we have taken a leap; this fourth edition includes a good sprinkling of non-French owners settling in and setting up. Some are escaping stressful career paths, some are running from urban claustrophobia, some thrive in a change of culture, some have suitable experience in their own countries. However, we can assume that they all are following the universal dream of 'having a place of one's own and living in France', and are passionate about food.

Photo left Hostellerie Le Castellas, entry 282
Photo right Jardins Secrets, entry 280

Introduction

What is it about the French and their France?

What exactly is the attraction? How do they inspire both admiration and frustration? On one hand they alienate much of the world with their posturing, and on the other they generate admiration – even devotion – for they way they, for example, break their bread, choose their wines and conduct themselves at table. And bring their children up in the same attitudes. One isn't lured to a new country just by its physical beauty, its miles of coastline, its landscapes and architecture (although they help).

Can it be nostalgia for the 'village'? That France has largely managed to keep post offices, bakeries, schools, grocery shops, butchers – and, if you are lucky – at least one café in the larger villages and that even the smallest are visited by the roving butcher, baker and grocer with a wide choice of fresh produce?

There are many subtleties and intangibles to the French lifestyle. I was converted by my first meal in a student restaurant. There it was, the humble hard-boiled egg and mayonnaise. But there also was the slice of red tomato, a crispy green leaf and such an artistic powdering of parsley, I almost wept at the beauty of it. Now I haunt the markets. My fishmonger tells me that his family has had the same place in the market for 60-odd years, that his grandfather used to bring the catch in a horse and cart. There is an old postcard in the café across the road that shows just that.

Ah, the French Touch. Of course, I'm prejudiced. I think people come – and stay – because the French 'do it' best: they have excellent hotel and cookery schools; they are rigorous yet flexible; they have a fine aesthetic sense; they have a history of hospitality, not to mention cuisine. Not so long ago, France was the only European country where you could find a decent independently-run, medium-priced hotel. In most of the other countries, it was either a palace or a hostel.

Our wish is that the new arrivals make a go of it, that they integrate into their communities and that Europe benefits from them. For the next generation will probably, and happily, be French.

Photo Hostellerie du Manoir de Saint Jean, entry 264

How we choose our Special Places
Special Places are just that –
special. We select them for their
fascination and character. But also
for the people who run them. We
like them small, we like them
family-run, we like château-chic
and truly trad and all those in
between. We know you like them
because you tell us so.

Passion is a word not normally
associated with the world of
hospitality, but passion – and
commitment – are important to us.
And flair? We see it in a carved door
lovingly restored or a beautiful
antique in just the right corner, in
the taste of the freshest scallop or
the tenderest veal medallion… and
we are very happy when we learn
that the owner will serve breakfast
until noon.

We visit every property.
Atmosphere, welcome and value for
money are key; each place is judged
on its own merit, not by
comparison. But do not expect the
same service and comfort from a
€60-a-room inn as from a €250-a-
room hotel. Friendly staff are more
important to us than jacuzzis, a
bowl of fresh flowers more
important than a satellite TV. (And
we are earnestly trying to let our
owners know that a cup of (decent)
tea at the right moment is an
important goal to reach.)

Photo Le Mas de Peint, entry 323

We have a Pullman car in Pas de
Calais, a troglodyte room in the
Bouche du Rhône, mills and manors,
auberges and hotels, towers, turrets
and bastides and classy bed &
breakfasts. France is blessed with
great food and a richness of scenery
and rural living that is hard to beat.
Our owners have originality, energy
and independence and give more
than a passing nod to tradition and
regional differences.

Do plan to stay more than one
night on your travels; some of our
hoteliers feel that 'zapping' has now
entered their world and they miss
the complicity (and serenity) of
longer visits.

Introduction

What to expect

These places range from the small and intimate to the grand and gracious. Those which are small and owner-run don't have lifts or porters so do call ahead and book that ground floor room if you foresee a problem. Expect to feel a privileged guest in your chosen house and to gain a fascinating glimpse of a French way of life.

We specify in the Quick Reference indices at the back of the book if the dinner is hosted and taken at a communal table: *table d'hôtes*. This is usually a wonderful opportunity to get to know your hosts and to make new friends among the other guests. This means the same food for all and absolutely must be booked ahead. If you normally flee from dining with strangers, we urge you to try it - just once! Many places do both so you can check when booking. If a late arrival is unavoidable, some hosts will prepare a cold meal if given advance notice. Remember these are not hotels with full staff.

For the hotels we have ignored the 'star' system. This is because it uses criteria different from ours. A hotel that we think the world of may be near the bottom of the official 'star' list simply because it has no lift. Other owners, unwilling to be swept into a bureaucratic system or to partition an 18th-century bedroom to create a bigger bathroom, refuse to apply for a star rating. The system is technical and incapable of accounting for character, style or warmth of welcome, the very things that we rate most highly.

Photo above Bastide Saint Mathieu, entry 370
Photo right Villa Augusta Hôtel Restaurant, entry 313

Introduction

Traditional *hôtellerie* is thriving with its intricate wall-coverings, Régence, Louis XIV and XV furniture in harmony with the buildings themselves, classic cuisine in the kitchens. This is the image of France that many travellers have in mind – and it's hugely popular. One reader called such a place "a minimalist's nightmare": he absolutely loved it, in all its glory.

By contrast there is a growing number of boutique hotels represented by the minimalists who keep things bare, fresh and light, using colour schemes of white, cream and grey. There may be one or two pieces of exquisite furniture and the odd splash of colour, but nothing that jars the eye, just space and serenity. These places may have variations of nouvelle cuisine with a sprinkling of foreign spice. A meat-and-potatoes personality would not feel at home here.

At inns, or restaurants with rooms, food takes priority. Rooms are secondary, but they are comfortable and clean. Kitchen gardens have popped up all over the place and *le terroir* – seasonal, fresh and local food – is de rigueur. Be sure to book as the typical auberge can feed more people that it can sleep. Remember, too, that dinner is not served before 7.30pm and outside the larger towns, last orders may be taken no later than 9pm.

Choosing the right place for you
Read the descriptions carefully and pick out the places where you will be comfortable. If 'antique beds' sound seductively authentic, remember they are liable to be antique sizes too (190cm long, doubles 140cm wide). If in doubt, ask, or book a twin room, usually larger. A problem well defined is half-way solved: do discuss any problem with your hosts – they can usually do something about it on the spot. If you find anything we say misleading (things and people do change in the lifetime of a guide), or you think we miss the point, please let us know.

Photo Le Gué du Holme, entry 80

How to use this book

Bedrooms
- double: one double bed
- twin: two single beds
- triple: three single beds
- family room: mix of beds (sometimes sofabeds) for three or more people. A family room will always have a double bed.
- duplex: a room on two floors with a staircase
- suite: either one large room with a sitting area or two or more interconnecting rooms, plus one or more bathrooms
- apartment: similar to suite but sometimes with an independent entrance and possibly a small kitchen. If it comes after the '+' in the rooms description, it is categorised as 'self-catering' and has a kitchen.

Extra beds and cots for children, at extra cost, can be provided; ask when booking.

Bathrooms
Assume all bedrooms are 'en suite', either with bath or shower. We say if a bedroom has either a separate, or a shared bathroom. For simplicity we refer to 'bath'. This doesn't necessarily mean it has no shower; it could mean a shower only.

Prices
The first price range is for two people sharing a room: the lower price indicates the least expensive room in low season; the higher price, the most expensive room in high season. If breakfast is not included, we say so and give the price. Prices are given for 2006-2007 but are not guaranteed so please check when you book. If there are no single rooms, there will generally be a reduction for single occupancy of a double.

Half-board
Do look into attractive half-board terms and special prices for children. Half-board (*demi-pension*) includes breakfast and dinner. Full-board (*pension complète*) includes all three meals. Prices given are generally per person ('p.p.'). Ask about reduced rates when booking longer stays and out of season visits. And check www.specialplacestostay.com for up to date information and special offers.

Meals
The number and type of courses you will be offered for lunch and dinner varies. Some places have set menus at fixed prices. Most places serving lunch will have a good value menu during the week, changing the menu and the prices on the weekend. Many places offer a *table d'hôtes* dinner to overnight guests (see What to Expect). This may be dining at separate tables, but often the meal is shared with other guests at a communal table. These are

Introduction

sometimes hosted by Monsieur or Madame (or both). Advance notice is required for these and they may not be available every night. Make sure your meal is reserved on the first night, especially if you are staying deep in the countryside.

Closed

When given in months, this means for the whole of both months named. So, 'Closed: November-March' means closed from 1 November to 31 March.

Booking

It is essential to book well ahead for July and August and wise for other months. Most places now have web sites and email addresses. We have a booking form at the back of this book and on www.specialplacestostay.com. However, please remember that technology may be put aside at busy times and a small place may just not have the time or the personnel to respond quickly to email requests.

Some places require a deposit to confirm a booking. If you cancel you are likely to lose part, or all, of it. Check the exact terms when you book. A credit card number is the standard way to place a deposit. Be aware of some of the French holiday dates which can make booking difficult.

The French have 11 annual national holidays. In May there is a holiday nearly every week depending upon the dates of the 'moveable feasts' (see below). So be prepared for stores, banks and museums to shut their doors for days at a time. Booking hotels in advance becomes essential.

1 January	New Year's Day (*Jour de l'an*)
1 May	Labour Day (*Fête du premier mai*)
8 May	WWII Victory Day (*Fête de la Victoire*)
14 July	Bastille Day
15 August	Assumption of the Blessed Virgin (*Assomption*)
1 November	All Saints Day (*La Toussaint*)
11 November	Armistice Day (*Jour d'armistice*)
25 December	Christmas Day (*Noël*)
26 December	2nd day of Christmas (Alsace Lorraine only)

Moveable Feasts	2006	2007
Good Friday*	14 April	6 April
Easter (Pâques)	16 April	8 April
Easter Monday	17 April	9 April
Ascension (l'Ascencion)	25 May	17 May
Pentecost (la Pentecôte)	4 June	27 May
Whit Monday	5 June	28 May

*(Alsace Lorraine only)

When a holiday falls on a Tuesday

or Thursday, many people may take a longer break by including Monday or Friday (*faire le pont*). This is not official and does not apply to institutions such as banks but is sufficiently commonplace to cause difficulties in booking rooms or travelling.

Payment
MasterCard and Visa are generally welcome; American Express is often accepted in the upper range hotels. The few places that don't accept credit cards are indicated at the end of their description. Drawing cash is easy as virtually all ATMs in France take Visa and MasterCard.

Taxe de séjour
A small tax that local councils can levy on all visitors may be charged; you may find your bill increased by €0.50-€2 per person per day.

Tipping
Almost all restaurants include tax and a 15% service charge (*service compris*) in their prices. If a meal or service has been particularly good, leaving another €1.50 (or 2%-3%) is customary, as is leaving the waiter the small change from your bill if you pay in cash. If service is not included (*service non compris*), a 15% tip is appropriate.
In hotels tip porters €1.50 for each

Photo Hôtel Le Cavendish, entry 368

bag and chambermaids €1.50 a day. Taxi drivers should receive 10%-15% of the metered fare. Small tips of about €1 are reasonable for cloakroom attendants, ushers and museum tour guides.

Electricity
You will need an adaptor plug for the 220-volt 50-cycle AC current. Americans also need a voltage transformer (heavy and expensive).

Symbols
Pets
Even though a place may be listed as accepting animals, some will only take small dogs; others will limit the number of animals staying at the same time. Do check ahead. There is always a supplement to pay.

Smoking
Non-smoking means no smoking is allowed anywhere in the building.

Introduction

Internet

Our web site (www.specialplacestostay.com) has online pages for all of the places featured here and from all our other books – around 4,500 Special Places in Britain, Ireland, France, Italy, Spain, Portugal, India, Morocco, Turkey and Greece. There's a searchable database, a taster of the write-ups and colour photos. For more details see the back of the book.

Disclaimer

We make no claims to pure objectivity in choosing our Special Places to Stay. They are here because we like them. Our opinions and tastes are ours alone and this book is a statement of them; we hope that you will share them.

We have done our utmost to get our facts right but apologise unreservedly for any mistakes that may have crept in. Feedback from you is invaluable and we always act upon comments. With your help and our own inspections we can maintain our reputation for dependability.

You should know that we do not check such things as fire alarms, swimming pool security or any other regulation with which owners of properties receiving paying guests should comply. This is the responsibility of the owners.

Quick reference indices

At the back of the book we direct you to places that serve *table d'hotes,* places where you can take cookery lessons or test your wine-tasting skills, go mushroom hunting or practice a craft... do take a look.

Subscriptions

Owners pay to appear in this guide. Their fee goes towards the cost of inspections (every single entry has been inspected by a member of our team before being selected), of producing an all-colour book and maintaining a sophisticated web site. We only include places and owners that we find positively special. It is not possible for anyone to buy their way into our guides.

Photo above Hostellerie du Val de Sault, entry 346
Photo right Hôtel Alba, entry 120

And finally

A huge 'thank you' to all of you who have taken the time and trouble to write to us about your experiences and to recommend new places. This is what we do with the correspondence we receive.

Feedback

- Owners are informed when we receive substantially positive reports about them.
- Recommendations are followed up with inspection visits where appropriate.
- Poor reports are followed up with the owners in question: we need to hear both sides of the story.

Really bad reports lead to incognito visits after which we may exclude a place from our web site and next edition of the guide. It is very helpful to us if you can let us know the date of your visit.

We love to hear from you and your comments make a real contribution to this book, be they on our report form, by letter or by email to info@sawdays.co.uk. Or you can visit our web site and write to us from there.

Bon Voyage!

Susan Herrick Luraschi

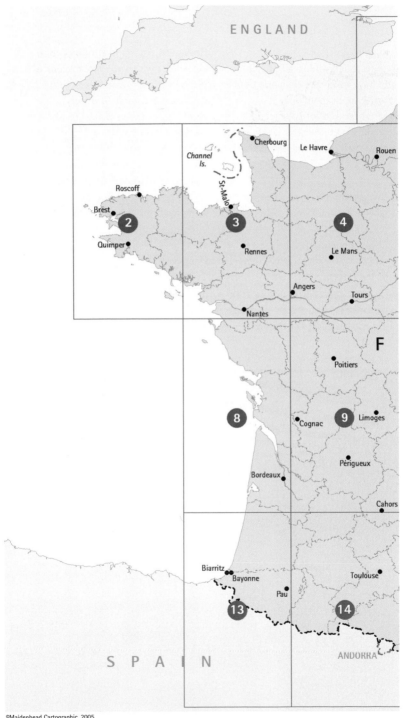

©Maidenhead Cartographic, 2005

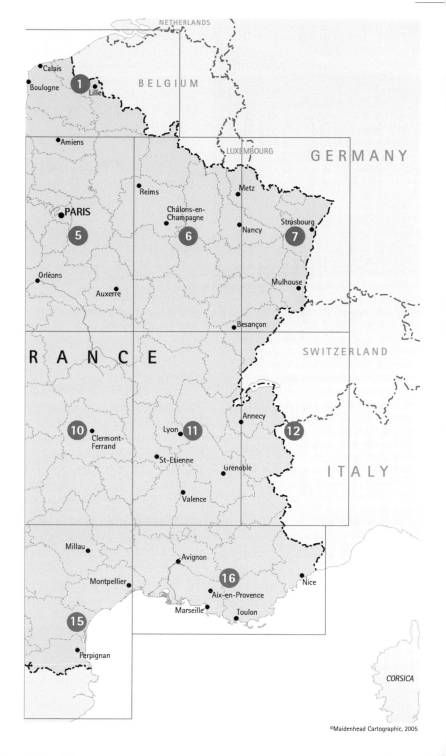

©Maidenhead Cartographic, 2005

Tips for Travellers

out private insurance.
To call French emergency services
dial 15: the public service called
SAMU or the Casualty Department –
Services des Urgences – of a
hospital. The private service is called
SOS MÉDECINS.

Other insurance
It is probably wise to insure the
contents of your car.

Roads & driving
Current speed limits are: motorways
130 kph (80 mph), RN national trunk
roads 110 kph (68 mph), other open
roads 90 kph (56 mph), in towns 50
kph (30 mph). The road police are
very active and can demand on-the-
spot payment of fines.

One soon gets used to driving on the
right but complacency leads to
trouble; take special care coming out
of car parks, private drives, one-lane
roads and coming onto roundabouts.

Directions in towns
The French drive towards a
destination and use road numbers
far less than we do. Thus, to find
your way à la française, know the
general direction you want to go, i.e.
the towns your route goes through,
and when you see *Autres Directions*
or *Toutes Directions* in a town,
forget road numbers, just continue
towards the place name you're
heading for or through.

Public holidays
Be aware of public holidays; many
national museums and galleries
close on Tuesdays, others close on
Mondays (e.g. Monet's garden in
Giverny) as do many country
restaurants, and opening times may
be different. Beware also of the
mass exodus over public holiday
weekends, both the first day –
outward journey – and the last –
return journey.

Medical & emergency procedures
If you are an EC citizen, have an
E111 form with you for filling in
after any medical treatment. Part of
the sum will subsequently be
refunded, so it is advisable to take

Map 1

27

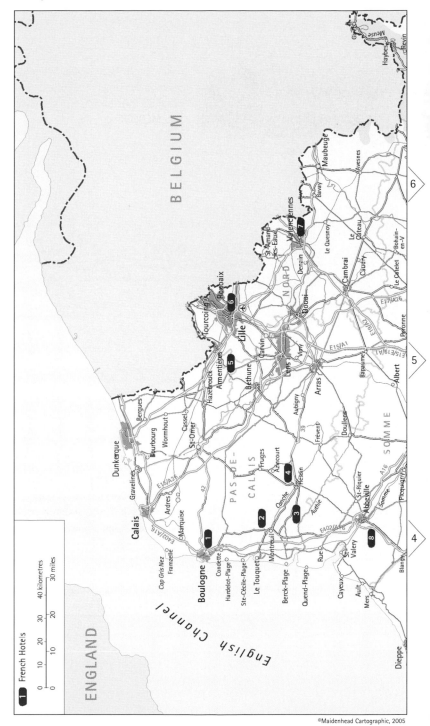

©Maidenhead Cartographic, 2005

Map 2

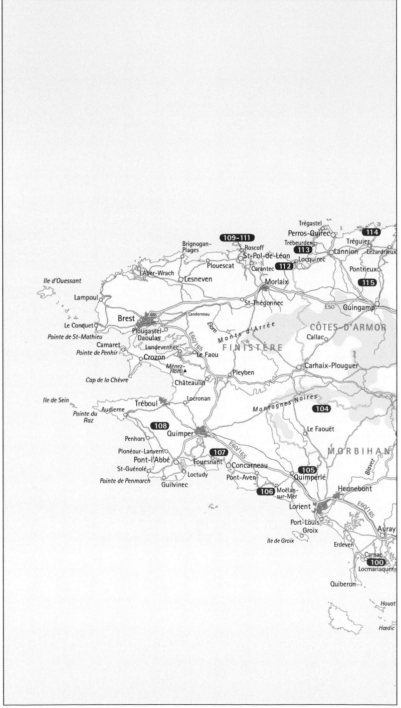

Map 3

29

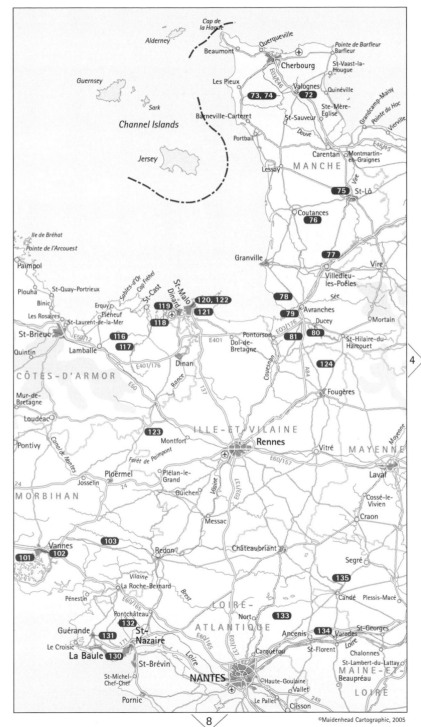

©Maidenhead Cartographic, 2005

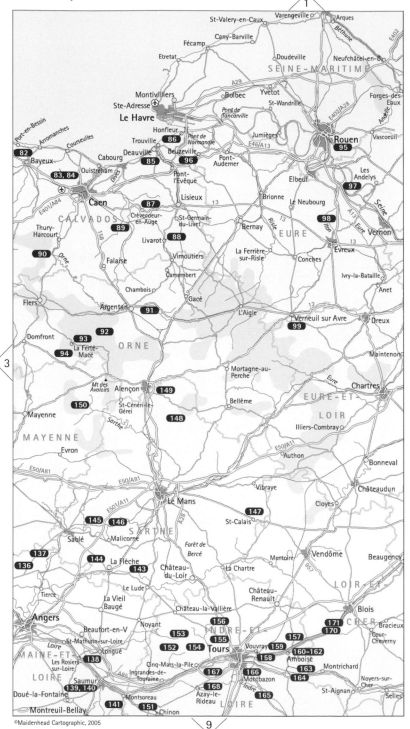

©Maidenhead Cartographic, 2005

Map 5

31

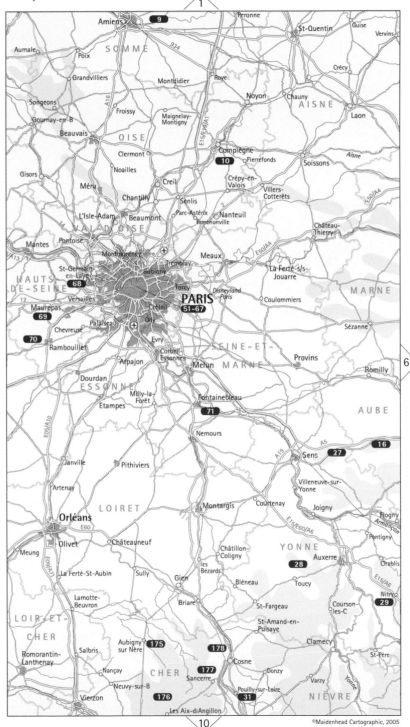

©Maidenhead Cartographic, 2005

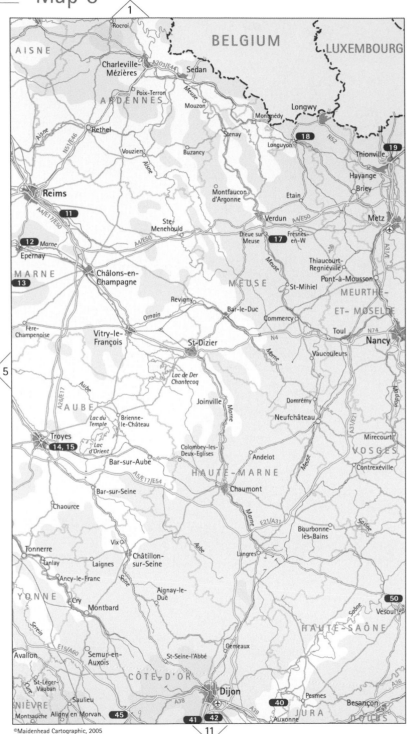

©Maidenhead Cartographic, 2005

Map 7

33

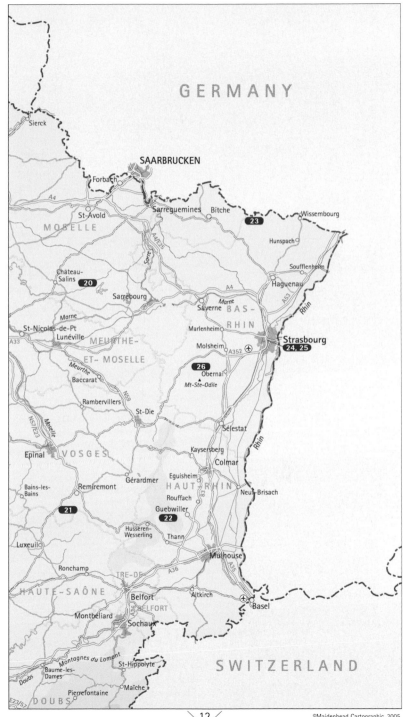

©Maidenhead Cartographic, 2005

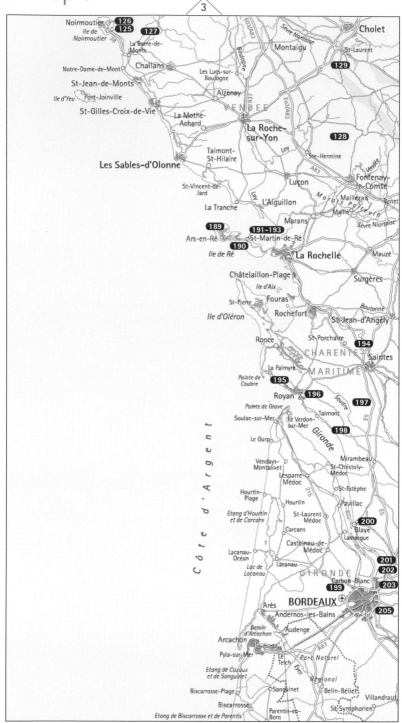

©Maidenhead Cartographic, 2005

Map 9

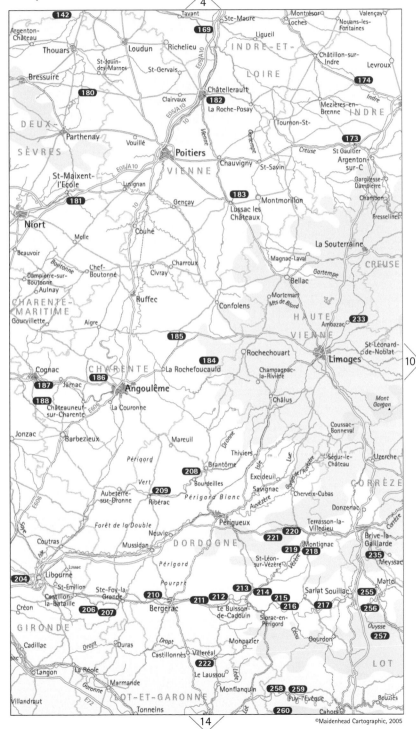

©Maidenhead Cartographic, 2005

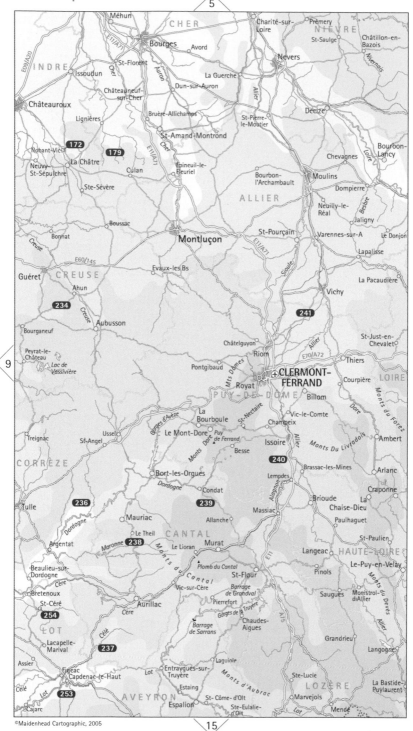

©Maidenhead Cartographic, 2005

Map 11

37

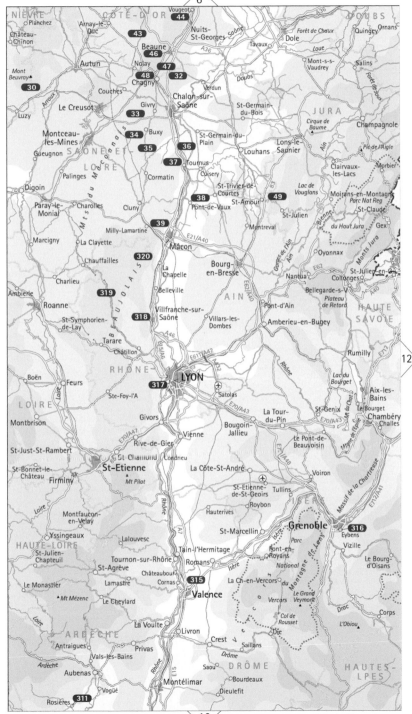

©Maidenhead Cartographic, 2005

7

DOUBS
Morteau
Mouthier
Doubs
Montbenoît
Pontarlier
Cluse de
Joux
Les Hôpitaux-Neufs
Mont d'Or
Chaux
Neuve

SWITZERLAND

Lausanne

E25/E62
Lac Léman (Lake Geneva)
Evian
Thonon
Sciez
Abondance
Geneva
305, 306
Morzine
Mt Salève
Bonneville
307
Cluses
308
HAUTE
SAVOIE
Argentière
Sallanches
Servoz
Chamonix
Annecy
Arve
Chamonix-Mont-Blanc
Thônes
Combloux
Le Fayet
309
Chaîne des Aravis
Mont Blanc
Tunnel du Mont-Blanc
St-
Jorioz
Lac
d'Annecy
Megève
Flumet
Mont Blanc
Les
Contamines
Ugine
310
Albertville
Conflans
Roignais
Bourg-St-Maurice
SAVOIE
Isère
Aiguebelle
Aime
Mt Pourri
Moûtiers
Val d'Isère
Grande
Casse
Parc National
Bonneval
de la Vanoise
Massif de la Vanoise
Bessans
La Chambre
St-Jean-de-Maurienne
Arc
Lanslebourg
Avrieux
Modane
Valloire

ITALY

La Grave
La Meije
Le Monêtier-les-Bains
ISÈRE
358
Chantemerle
Montgenèvre
Massif des Écrins
Mt Pelvoux
Briançon
Parc National
Abriès
des Écrins
Parc Nat Rég
Château-Queyras
Queyras
Vieux
Chaillol
du Queyras
Guillestre
HAUTES-ALPES
Vars
Les Claux
Gap
Embrun
Barrage de
Serre-Ponçon

©Maidenhead Cartographic, 2005

11

16

Map 13

39

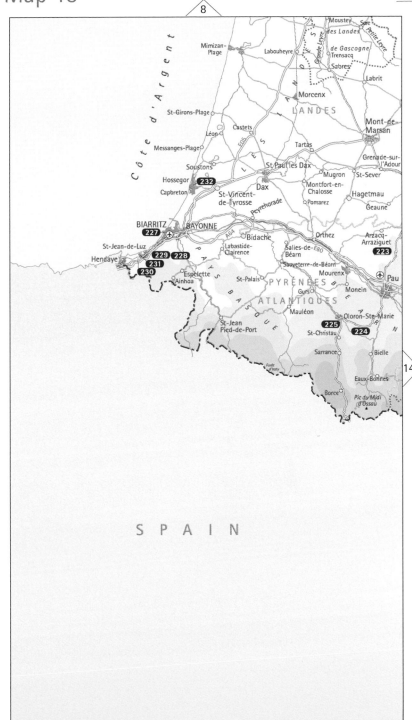

©Maidenhead Cartographic, 2005

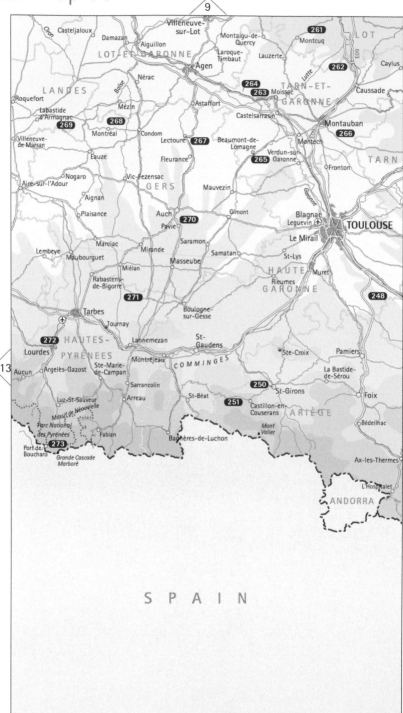

©Maidenhead Cartographic, 2005

Map 15

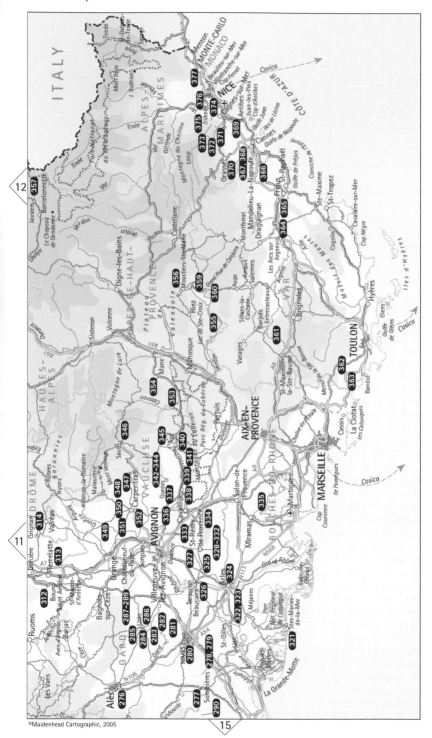

©Maidenhead Cartographic, 2005

How to use this book

① region

② write up
Written by us, after inspection.

③ rooms
Assume rooms are en suite;
unless we state otherwise.

④ price
The price shown is for two
people sharing a room.
Half-board prices are per
person. A price range
incorporates room/seasonal
differences.

⑤ meals
Prices are per person. If
breakfast isn't included we give
the price.

⑥ closed
When given in months, this
means for the whole of the
named months and the time in
between.

---

① Indre-et-Loire

The Cottage & The Farmhouse Loft
Le Grand Pressigny, Indre-et-Loire

② Civray is a tiny hamlet hidden away in the countryside: it would be hard to find anywhere more tranquil. And if you tire of walking, cycling, fishing – or swimming in the silky waters of the river – there are vineyards to visit, *fermes auberges* to discover and all the attractions of the Loire châteaux. Lovely Jill is half Australian, passionate about rural France and has restored this little cluster of ancient stone buildings with the lightest of hands. The Cottage is compact but has all you need: a living area with little pine kitchen, woodburning stove, sofabed, play equipment in the garden. Upstairs, under magnificent curving beams, a large double bedroom, simply and attractively furnished. It has its own rustic balcony overlooking farmland – not another building in sight. Wooden stairs wind down to the gardens, which have a haphazard charm; fresh home-grown vegetables and home-laid eggs are often available. Jill has also converted the Farmhouse Loft, a heavily timbered and imaginative space with three bedrooms and a big, jolly kitchen/living area, easy for families. *Bring own linen*

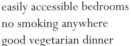

sleeps	Cottage 2-3 + cot. Farmhouse Loft 5 + cot. Can be booked together. **③**
rooms	Cottage: 1 double, 1 single sofabed; 1 shower room, 1 bathroom. Farmhouse Loft: 2 doubles, 1 single; 1 bathroom. **④ ⑤**
price	Cottage £150-£250. Farmhouse Loft £170-£305. Prices per week. **⑥**
closed	Winter. **⑦**

Jill Christie
tel +33 (0)2 47 94 92 02
fax +33 (0)2 47 94 92 02

⑨ Map 9 Entry 118

⑧

---

⑦ directions
Use as a guide and travel with a good map.

---

⑧ symbols
see the last page of the book for a
fuller explanation:

🕭	wheelchair facilities
🏃	easily accessible bedrooms
✗	no smoking anywhere
🍎	good vegetarian dinner options
🐕	guests' pets welcome

owners' pets live here

At least one bedroom has
air-conditioning.

pool

bikes on the premises to borrow
or hire

tennis on the premises

information on local walks

---

⑨ map & entry numbers

Photo Corel

champagne-ardenne
picardy
the north

Enclos de L'Evêché

6 rue de Pressy, 62200 Boulogne sur Mer, Pas-de-Calais

Up gracious steps you enter the 1850 mansion that almost rubs shoulders with Boulogne's basilica. The salons are splendidly panelled from top to toe, the immense 19th-century sideboards came with the house – this is no humble abode! All is polished parquet and hotel-like perfection, with the personal touch we so like. The charming young owners usher you up a majestic stair to bedrooms in independent wings. Each one is airy, uncluttered and large, and themed according to its name: Desvres (a porcelain town), pretty and serene, all white painted furniture and blue toile de Jouy; Godefroy de Bouillon (an 11th-century knight from Boulogne), rustic, with sand-blasted rafters and impeccably limewashed walls. Bathrooms are stocked with toiletries and towels, some have jacuzzis. There's a suntrapped courtyard for summer, a day room for TV, internet and the odd cigar, and a choice of tables for breakfast – be as convivial or as peaceful as you like. Pascaline and Theirry tell us that they will soon be opening their own restaurant: we are convinced that it wil be as elegant and special as the rest.

rooms	5: 2 doubles, 1 twins, 1 single, 1 family room for 4.
price	€70–€115.
meals	Many restaurants in town.
closed	Rarely.
directions	Follow signs to 'Vieille Ville' & to car park 'Enclos de l'Evêché'. House next to car park & cathedral.

	Pascaline & Thierry Humez
tel	+33 (0)3 91 90 05 90
fax	+33 (0)3 91 90 05 94
email	contact@enclosdeleveche.com
web	www.enclosdeleveche.com

Map 1 Entry 1

Auberge d'Inxent

La Vallée de la Course, 62170 Inxent, Pas-de-Calais

And, the lucky winner is… some people who collect bottle caps do win prizes. A sommelier in a large restaurant in Lille, Jean-Marc won the Perrier contest on the luck of a draw. Off he tripped with his young wife and two children to a most emerald green valley and claimed a whitewashed, geranium-boxed dream of an 18th-century country inn. Order a trout on their vine-covered terrace and back comes a live one in a bucket from their superb trout farm across the road on the banks of the river Course. Needless to say Jean-Marc's exceptional, reasonably priced wine list and creative use of local produce should lead to a prolonged stay, and the nearby ramparts of Montreuil Sur Mer are well worth a visit. Inside all is wonky wooden beams, low ceilings, a battery of copper pans behind the original zinc countertop, red-checked tablecloths and the warmth and cosiness of a country kitchen with burning fireplaces on chilly days. The beamed-ceiling bedrooms have been recently furnished with cherry wood copies of antiques and the walls papered to look ragged. Some of the best people win the best prizes.

rooms	5: 3 doubles, 2 twins (1 with terrace).
price	€62–€70.
meals	Breakfast €8. Lunch & dinner €14–€38. Restaurant closed Tuesdays & Wednesdays out of season.
closed	20 December–20 January; 1 week in July.
directions	From Boulogne N1 for Samer. After Samer at 5km head for Bernieulles, Beussent, Inxent.

	Laurence & Jean-Marc Six
tel	+33 (0)3 21 90 71 19
fax	+33 (0)3 21 86 31 67
email	auberge.inxent@wanadoo.fr

Map 1 Entry 2

Le Manoir

34 rue Maresquel, 62870 Gouy Saint André, Pas-de-Calais

Wrought-iron gates, a gravel drive, a spreading lime and afternoon tea on the terrace – gracious country living. Jennifer (English) and Helmut (German) – former Sawday hosts from Romney Bay House in Kent – run the 18th-century manor house with friendly professionalism and exacting attention to detail. So much space – three reception rooms, large bedrooms, 12 hectares of parkland… you can be as private or as gregarious as you like. The salon and sitting room are elegant with deep sofas and creamy walls; breakfasting under the chandelier in the dining room, all polished tables and rich reds, makes you feel truly pampered. The three carpeted bedrooms are civilised spaces of soft lighting, well-chosen antiques and pretty porcelain; you could be staying with a country-house friend. Throw open the windows in the morning: the views across manicured lawns, formal garden and orchard to countryside will put a big smile on your face. No evening meals but lots of excellent dining in Montreuil, and beaches, riverside walks and birdwatching in abundance.

rooms	3: 2 doubles, 1 twin.
price	€115.
meals	Breakfast €8.
	Good dining in Montreuil, 10km.
closed	2 weeks in June; Christmas.
directions	From A16 exit 25 for N39 Arras & Hesdin. Exit for Campagne les Hesdin. Look for Gouy St André; right at main crossroad; 1st iron gate on left.

	Jennifer & Helmut Gorlich
tel	+33 (0)3 21 90 47 22
fax	+33 (0)3 21 86 70 98
email	helmut.gorlich@wanadoo.fr
web	www.lemanoir-france.com

Map 1 Entry 3

Les Trois Fontaines
16 rue d'Abbeville, 62140 Marconne-Hesdin, Pas-de-Calais

Here is a long, low, plain Scandinavian style building dressed up to look like a typical French inn – and succeeding. With its half-length nets and flower boxes, it fits into the little market town (wonderful market on Thursday mornings) as if it had always been there and the pavement tables are well used by locals. So, of course, is the restaurant. Arnaud Descamps is friendly and anxious to please. He took over in 1999 and is concentrating on the quality of the food he serves in his panelled, chequer-floored dining room: menus change every day and there's a special one for children. Bedrooms are in separate buildings overlooking the fine garden: traditional French style with quiet wallpapers and candlewick bedcovers. In the new wing, twin rooms are very comfortable, simply and decently clad with good quality pine, dark blue carpet, good lighting and pristine bed linen. Each room has its own table and chairs for summer breakfasts facing the garden. It is, indeed, a very typical small French hotel; it's quiet, good value and well placed for cross-channel visitors and the great beaches of Le Touquet and Berck.

rooms	16 doubles.
price	€47-€67.
meals	Breakfast €7.
	Lunch & dinner €17-€32.
closed	20 December-5 January.
directions	From Calais for Arras. After Montreuil, N39 for Hesdin. Follow signs to Marconne centre. Hotel opposite the Mairie.

	Arnaud Descamps
tel	+33 (0)3 21 86 81 65
fax	+33 (0)3 21 86 33 34
email	hotel.3fontaines@wanadoo.fr
web	www.hotel-les3fontaines.com

Map 1 Entry 4

Station Bac Saint-Maur

La Gare des Années Folles, 77 rue de la Gare, 62840 Sailly sur la Lys, Pas-de-Calais

All aboard! Vincent, Chef de Gare, and his young crew of conductors man the bistro: an imaginatively converted, 1921 red-bricked railway station filled with vintage suitcases and trunks spewing old tourist brochures. There are miniature tin trains, a wind-up wooden telephone, hand-held lanterns, sepia etchings on the walls, old station wall clocks and a paraphernalia of reminders of the golden era of train travel. You dine in the station, then retire to your rooms in the carriage of an authentic 'PLM' that travelled the Paris, Lyon, Mediterranean lines. Let Valérie know in advance and you will be served in the elegant restaurant compartment with its warm mahogany walls inlaid with mother-of-pearl. Retire to your first-class *couchettes* (authentic, so narrow) to dreams of the Orient Express. As if on cue, a real train passes by every now and again adding its clanking to the authenticity. A full playground just outside, a children's menu and antique highchairs make this a super place for kids. Groups can take a tour along the La Lys aboard a barge; the lock is 400m from the station.

rooms	6 Pullman compartments each with 2 singles, all sharing 2 showers.
price	€35-€65.
meals	Breakfast €6.50. Lunch & dinner in station €8.50-€24; served on board €28-€70. Children's meals €6.50.
closed	23 December-5 January.
directions	From A25 exit 9 for Erquinghem to Sailly. At Bac St Maur, 2nd left immediately after Havet factory.

Vincent & Valérie Laruelle

tel	+33 (0)3 21 02 68 20
fax	+33 (0)3 21 02 74 37
email	chefdegare@wanadoo.fr
web	www.stationbacsaintmaur.com

Map 1 Entry 5

© Photo Eliophot – Aix-en-Provence

Hôtel Brueghel

5 Parvis Saint Maurice, 59000 Lille, Nord

A quick stroll from the train station along lively pedestrian streets, keeping your eye out for the spires of the Saint Maurice Church, will get you there in no time. How Danièle Lhermie achieves such a homely feel in such a big city hotel is a bit of a mystery. Could it be the restored 19th-century elevator with its clanking wrought-iron, see-through concertina doors, the warm wooden panelling of the reception desk or the cheery young staff? The Flemish grandmother in one painting is no relation but all the other objects in the lobby and breakfast rooms belong to her; she confesses her obsession with, and joy in, haunting the many local antique markets. There is even an annual three-day antique orgy, the first weekend of September, when all of Lille and the surrounding areas empty their attics and survive on chips, mussels and beer. The rooms are small and tastefully done: antique rattan chairs, 'distressed' desks, splashes of sea-blue in the bathrooms. If you come by car, public parking is just across the street in *Des Tanneurs*. but call ahead to avoid getting lost in the one-way pedestrian streets.

© Photo Eliophot – Aix-en-Provence

rooms	66: 53 doubles, 12 twins, 1 family room for 4.
price	€78-€120. Single occupancy €72.
meals	Breakfast €7.50. Fine restaurants in town.
closed	Never.
directions	In centre of town on pedestrian street, off Rue de Paris.

Danièle Lhermie

tel	+33 (0)3 20 06 06 69
fax	+33 (0)3 20 63 25 27
email	hotel.brueghel@wanadoo.fr
web	www.hotel-brueghel.com

Map 1 Entry 6

Auberge du Bon Fermier

64 rue de Famars, 59300 Valenciennes, Nord

Forget your high heels, for the cobblestones in the flowered courtyard penetrate into the bar, reception and restaurant of this 16th-century auberge. It is a maze of passageways, burnished beams and tiny staircases. A bright copper-bellied *lavabo* greets you at the top of the stairs leading to the rooms. Looking down from a glassed-in corridor, you can almost hear the clatter of hooves arriving in the courtyard, now a quiet terrace for afternoon tea and snacks. The rooms are delightful, one with tapestried curtains and walls, another with red bricks and wooden struts, all with baths and bathrobes. There are also two larger, lighter ground-floor rooms with post-modern lamps and tables. Downstairs a suit of armour guards a wooden reception dais and comes to life in the evenings when the main restaurant is lit only by candles. The passengers jostling between Paris and Brussels were probably delighted to have been delayed in this cosy staging inn. Monsieur Beine takes enormous trouble to create new menus with his chef.

rooms	16: 14 doubles, 2 singles.
price	€100-€126. Singles €81-€107.
meals	Breakfast €9. Lunch & dinner €23-€47.
closed	Rarely.
directions	From Cambrai A2 for Brussels, exit Valenciennes centre. Do not get off autoroute before. Continue for Valenciennes centre. Signed.

	Monsieur Beine
tel	+33 (0)3 27 46 68 25
fax	+33 (0)3 27 33 75 01
email	beinethierry@hotmail.com
web	www.bonfermier.com

Map 1 Entry 7

Château de Béhen
8 rue de Château, 80870 Behen, Somme

Horsy people and families will be in clover. There are donkeys to stroke, bicycles to hire and horses to admire and to ride. Surrounded by wooded parkland, the red-brick building with limestone trim started life as a summer residence. Later its ground floor was extended, then it was bombed and repaired. In the 1950s the Cuveliers moved in, adding paddocks, horses and a pond for swans. Today there are six large and lovely bedrooms for guests. Classically French, in sympathy with the style of the place, they have solid oak floors dressed with rugs, bedspreads plain or toile de Jouy and warm colours. Original panelling graces the first-floor rooms while those above have sloping ceilings and a beam or two. Bathrooms are hotel-perfect with double basins of mottled marble. Norbert-André, who managed stud pacers in Australia for ten years, has come home to cook, and he does a grand job. Four-course table d'hôtes, at single tables if preferred, may include salt-marsh lamb or fish in cream sauce. Cheeses are local, vegetables are fresh-picked, banquets can be arranged. An equestrian address, and a comfortable one, too.

rooms	6: 2 doubles, 1 twin, 1 suite for 2, 1 suite for 4, 1 family for 4.
price	€102-138. Suites & family room €144-€190.
meals	Dinner from €37, with aperitif & wine; book 2 days ahead.
closed	Rarely.
directions	Calais A16 to Abbeville exit 23; A28 to Rouen. Exit 3 Monts Caubert to D928; 800m, right to Behen. Behind church, then 200m beyond, on right.

	Cuvelier Family
tel	+33 (0)3 22 31 58 30
fax	+33 (0)3 22 31 58 39
email	norbert-andre@cuvelier.com
web	www.chateau-de-behen.com

Map 1 Entry 8

Le Macassar

8 place de la Republique, 80800 Corbie, Somme

Le Macassar is named after the rare ebony used in the drawing room panelling – one exquisite example of many intricacies here. This gem of an 19th-century townhouse was restyled in the Twenties and Thirties to please a pretty young wife – but it's more 'femme fatale' than blushing belle. The master suite is the epitome of Art Deco glamour, ash and bird's-eye maple furniture set off by turquoise velvet walls, a carved stone fireplace and fine contemporary art. The 'colonial' suite is more muted in white and cream, while the Louis XV style rooms have oriental carpets and painted panelling. All have CD players, feather duvets, extravagant bathrooms and masses of space. Downstairs are several luxurious corners in which to lounge rakishly: pluck a book from the Art Nouveau study and admire its collection of glass, savour the textures and tones of the Moroccan room, play a round of billiards in the old library. Outside, an Italianate courtyard, a splashing fountain and a haze of lavender. In spite of the gorgeousness, it's easy to feel at home. The hosts are charming, the town small and historic.

rooms	6: 3 doubles, 3 suites.
price	€130-€225.
meals	Hosted dinner with wine €35, book ahead.
closed	Rarely.
directions	A16 exit 20 Amiens Nord; after tollgate, right at r'bout onto ring road (Rocade). Exit 36a Corbie; follow signs into Corbie, then centre ville. On main square.

Miguel de Lemos
tel   +33 (0)3 22 48 40 04
email   info@lemacassar.com
web   www.lemacassar.com

Map 5 Entry 9

Auberge A La Bonne Idée

3 rue des Meuniers, 60350 St Jean aux Bois, Oise

Deep in the forest, the walled village is worth a visit and the Bonne Idée is where sophisticates from Paris and Brussels come to escape the excitement, knowing they will find a genuine welcome, country peace and superb food. The inn, once a woodcutters' dive, still has masses of old timber and tiling in what could be called romantic-rustic style. Start with a drink by the fire in the bar, move to an elegant table in the dining room where bread warms by the great fireplace, and enjoy a fine meal. A tour of the pretty garden will tell you that vegetables and poultry are home-grown, though the deer and wild sow are purely decorative reminders of the house's hunting-lodge past. Here are the summer terrace and space for children to play. Bedrooms, four in the main house, the rest in the converted stables, are gradually being renovated by the new owners in a bright, stylish contemporary fashion, nicely adapted to the fabulous hulk of the building. Some rooms and apartments have terraces. Ideal for walking, cycling, riding and relaxing; Compiègne and the great castle of Pierrefonds are very close.

rooms	23: 20 doubles, 3 apartments for 2-4 (without kitchen) .
price	€69-€75. Apartments €80-€150.
meals	Breakfast €8.50. Lunch €30-€65. Dinner €45-€65. Restaurant closed Sun evenings Jan-Mar & Mondays in winter.
closed	Mid-January-mid-February.
directions	A1 exit 9 for Verberie & Compiègne. Through Verberie, left on D332 for Compiègne for 5km; right on D85 for St Jean aux Bois.

	Yves Giustiniani
tel	+33 (0)3 44 42 84 09
fax	+33 (0)3 44 42 80 45
email	a-la-bonne-idee.auberge@wanadoo.fr
web	www.a-la-bonne-idee.fr

Map 5 Entry 10

Le Cheval Blanc

Rue du Moulin, 51400 Sept Saulx, Marne

In a sweet village of 500 souls, off the village square, a relaxing, family-run hotel in roaming riverside grounds. White plastic furniture sits under dainty parasols and Virginia creeper adds character to a plain façade. This is a scattered and surprising property, comprising a converted barn, cottages, outbuildings and a watermill. Bedrooms flaunt a variety of colours and styles, from floral-traditional to floral-modern... several glass-top tables, coordinating country cottons, satin chintz, glossy bathrooms, comfort and space. Many rooms have extremely nice garden views. Young Madame is fifth generation owner of this venerable business, her husband is chef de cuisine and the restaurant seating 100 has had a tasty reputation ever since Napoleon III's military camp passed by. Now, billowing curtains, fancy table linen and floral porcelain are a fitting accompaniment to the classic French gourmet menus, of which there are three. The wine list is equally fabulous – naturally – this is Champagne! Ask about special packages: cellar tours, mountain bike rides, boat trips and more.

rooms	24: 10 doubles, 9 twins/doubles, 4 suites, 1 apartment for 4.
price	€62–€118. Suites & apartment €158.
meals	Breakfast €11. Lunch & dinner €24–€58.
closed	February.
directions	Exit 26 Reims. N44 toward Chalons en Champagne for 24km. Left onto D37 at Les Petites Loges to Sept Saulx.

	Armelle & Fabien Abdalalim
tel	+33 (0)3 26 03 90 27
fax	+33 (0)3 26 03 97 09
email	cheval.blanc-sept-saulx@wanadoo.fr
web	www.chevalblanc-sept-saulx.com

Map 6 Entry 11

Le Clos Raymi

3 rue Joseph de Venoge, 51200 Epernay, Marne

What more seductive combination than champagne and culture? Easy to get to from both Reims Cathedral and the champagne vineyards, this enticing home has the added attraction of Madame Woda herself. Ever attentive to the comfort of her guests, she purrs with pride in her renovation of the Chandon (the other half of Moët) family house. The intricate, pale blue mosaic covering the entrance hall and the hardwood staircase were left alone but her artistic touch is everywhere: shades of cream, beige and extra pale grey; good beds dressed in vintage linens; attractive bathrooms with scented lotions; fresh flowers in every room; etchings and paintings from the 1930s; books of poetry on a shelf. Take a peek at the downstairs bathroom with its Cubist paintings and an interesting replacement for the usual sink. A champagne apéritif can be organised in a splendid little sitting room and, if weather permits, the buffet breakfast can be taken in the parasoled garden behind the house. Madame Woda will help organise champagne tastings and has her favourite people to recommend. Gracious living here.

rooms	7 doubles.
price	€100–€155.
meals	Breakfast €14.
	Lunch & dinner available locally.
closed	Rarely.
directions	From Paris A4 exit Château Thierry; N3 to Epernay.

	Madame Woda
tel	+33 (0)3 26 51 00 58
fax	+33 (0)3 26 51 18 98
email	closraymi@wanadoo.fr
web	www.closraymi-hotel.com

Map 6 Entry 12

Château d'Etoges
4 rue Richebourg, 51270 Etoges, Marne

Louis XIV himself was impressed by the beauty of the garden, fountains and ponds at Etoges, used as a stopover by various kings of France on journeys east. This moated château was built early in the 17th century and restored as a hotel in 1991 by the family who has lived here for over a century. If you enjoy waking up in beautiful sheets, this is for you. Rooms are all different and two have intriguing little mezzanine bedrooms over the bathroom – presumably originally for servants, now great fun for children. Many rooms have four-posters; all are furnished with antiques and are extremely French. If you fancy breakfast in bed, it will appear on a lace-covered table, with bread, croissants and a bowl of fruit. If you prefer to wander downstairs, choose from a buffet and sit on the terrace if it's warm. This could be a luxurious base for champagne tastings or simply a very pleasant break, convenient if you're heading for eastern France, like Louis XIV or, more likely, meandering south through Reims. It's easy country for cycling or you can try punting if you feel this is more in tune with the surroundings.

rooms	29: 26 twins/doubles, 3 suites.
price	€80–€200. Suites €200.
meals	Breakfast €12. Lunch & dinner €30–€65. Children's meals €12.
closed	22 January–16 February.
directions	From Paris A4 exit at Ferté sous Jouarre, follow signs for Chalons en Champagne. Château in centre of Etoges.

Madame Filliette-Neuville
tel	+33 (0)3 26 59 30 08
fax	+33 (0)3 26 59 35 57
email	contact@etoges.com
web	www.etoges.com

Map 6 Entry 13

Le Champ des Oiseaux

20 rue Linard-Gonthier, 10000 Troyes, Aube

Only the Museum of Modern Art stands between the cathedral and this amazingly pure group of 15th-century houses in the centre of lovely, unsung old Troyes. One is dazzled by the astonishing timbers, beams and rafters, inside and out, seduced by the simplicity of the beautifully jointed stone paving, the wooden floors, the softly luminous natural materials: the owners had their brilliant restoration done by craftsmen who knew the ancestral methods and made it look 'as good as new'… in 1460. Corridors twist around the creeper-climbed courtyard and the little internal garden, staircases change their minds, the place is alive with its centuries. Each bedroom has a personality, some soberly sandy and brown, others frivolously floral; they vary in size and status but all are warmly discreet in their luxury and good furniture. And, of course, bathrooms are perfect modern boudoirs. The unexpected salon, a long, white barrel vault of ancient stones, the original stonemason's craft lovingly revealed, was once a cellar. The Boisseau family can be justifiably proud of their contribution to medieval Troyes.

rooms	12: 9 doubles, 3 twins.
price	€90–€145.
meals	Breakfast €15.
	Great restaurants nearby.
closed	Never.
directions	In centre of Troyes, very close to the Cathedral.

	Madame Boisseau
tel	+33 (0)3 25 80 58 50
fax	+33 (0)3 25 80 98 34
email	message@champdesoiseaux.com
web	www.champdesoiseaux.com

Map 6 Entry 14

La Maison de Rhodes

18 rue Linard-Gonthier, 10000 Troyes, Aube

An exceptional find, a 16th-century timber-framed mansion that once belonged to the Templars. Monsieur Thierry's breathtaking renovation has brought a clean contemporary style to ancient bricks and mortar. Highlights include an interior courtyard of cobble and grass and heavy wooden doors under the coachman's porch that give onto the street. The house sits plumb in the old quarter of Troyes, on the doorstep of the cathedral. Bedrooms are bona fide jaw-droppers – expect the best in minimalist luxury. Huge beds are dressed in white linen, ancient beams straddle the ceilings. Walls are either exposed rough stone, or smooth limestone, or a clever mix. Bathrooms, too, are outstanding; most are enormous and have terracotta floors, big bath tubs, fluffy robes. Views are to the cathedral spires, the courtyard or the formal gardens of the Museum of Modern Art, directly opposite. A perfect blend of old and new, an exhilarating architectural landscape. Troyes is full of wonders, though the bibulous may be tempted to venture beyond the city walls. The region is quite well-known for its local tipple – champagne.

rooms	11: 8 doubles, 3 suites for 2-4.
price	€130-€180. Suites €200-€230.
meals	Breakfast €17. Dinner €30-€50. Restaurant closed Sundays.
closed	Never.
directions	In centre of Troyes, at the foot of the Cathedral.

	Thierry Carcassin
tel	+33 (0)3 25 43 11 11
fax	+33 (0)3 25 43 10 43
email	message@maisonderhodes.com
web	www.maisonderhodes.com

Map 6 Entry 15

Domaine du Moulin d'Eguebaude
10190 Estissac, Aube

The secluded old buildings house two owner-families, a restaurant, several guest rooms and 50 tons of live fish. Fishing folk gather on Sundays to catch trout in the spring water that feeds the ponds; groups come for speciality lunches. Four-course meals may include watercress soup, steamed trout with cider, a selection of local cheeses and cinnamon custard. For breakfast around the large table there are brioches, baguettes, croissants, yogurt, cottage cheese, fruit salad, cereals, apple juice and their own jams and honey. Created from an old mill 40 years ago, the compact bedrooms under the eaves are small-windowed, simply furnished and prettily decorated in rustic or 'grandmother' style. Futher rooms in the cottage across the driveway have been newly built in the regional half-timbered style. At one end of their shop – packed with cottage-industry goodies (charcuterie, honey, jams, wine and champagnes) is a wide floor of thick glass under which immense fish can be seen swimming to and fro between the water tanks. Fun for children, and good English spoken.

rooms	8: 5 doubles, 1 triple, 2 twins. (Triples & twins can sleep 4.)
price	€49-€70.
meals	Dinner with wine €20, book ahead.
closed	Christmas & New Year.
directions	From Paris A5 exit 19 on N60 to Estissac; right on to Rue Pierre Brossolette; mill at end of lane.

Edouard-Jean & Chantal Mesley

tel	+33 (0)3 25 40 42 18
fax	+33 (0)3 25 40 40 92
email	eguebaude@aol.com

Map 5 Entry 16

Photo Corel

alsace
lorraine

Hostellerie du Château des Monthairons
55320 Dieue sur Meuse, Meuse

If you fancy peace and quiet in beautiful grounds, or a spot of fishing, this would be a fine choice. Monthairons served as an American military hospital in the First World War but was a base for German troops in the Second. It is now run by three couples of the Thouvenin family, who bought it 20 years ago. One couple looks after the restaurant and food, the others run the hotel and grounds. Because of the personal touch, you'll feel at home here in spite of the size. Bedrooms are classic French and come in all sizes, with some duplex suites which would be perfect for families. Families who love exploring, swimming and canoeing would be in their element here; the Meuse meanders through the huge grounds. Apparently a former owner diverted the river especially and the nearby meadow is now known as the 'old river'. The restaurant is elegant and full of flowers – more for a special dinner than a quick bite with the children. Unusual actvities? Choose between an introduction to fly-fishing and a leisurely ride in a horse-driven carriage.

rooms	20: 13 twins/doubles, 4 duplexes for 2-3, 2 suites for 2-4, 1 family for 2-4.
price	€85-€155. Duplexes & family room €145-€180. Suites €200-€280.
meals	Breakfast €13-€14.50. Lunch weekdays €22. Dinner €32-€78.
closed	January-10 February.
directions	From A4 exit Voie Sacrée for St Mihiel on D34. Monthairons 2.5km on left after Ancemont.

	Thouvenin Family
tel	+33 (0)3 29 87 78 55
fax	+33 (0)3 29 87 73 49
email	accueil@chateaudesmonthairons.fr
web	www.chateaudesmonthairons.fr

Map 6 Entry 17

Le Mas & La Lorraine

Place de la Gare, 54260 Longuyon, Meurthe-et-Moselle

A proud building, solidly French, with flowers cascading from every window. The hotel is a nostalgic reminder of a lost era – the great days of steam trains. It stands across the square from the station and was built in 1925 to cater for the travellers the railway brought; the Italian Express stopped here. These days it is more of a restaurant-with-rooms, the emphasis clearly on the ambrosial food. Monsieur Gérard took over from his parents 35 years ago, yet still cooks with unwavering exuberance and flair; his *grandes soirées dégustation* are not to be missed. Course after course flies at you: coquilles Sainte Jacques, foie gras, fillet de veau, gratin d'ananas à la crème de coco. Meals are taken in a big rustic restaurant, a convivial room where an open fire roars in winter. Every now and then live music nights are held and you dine to the accompaniment of classical guitar or jazz piano. Downstairs, blue velvet armchairs and huge bay windows in the airy sitting room; upstairs, simply furnished bedrooms that are clean, functional and reasonably priced. Belgium and Luxembourg are within easy reach.

rooms	14: 5 doubles, 6 twin, 1 triple, 2 family rooms for 4.
price	€48-€58.
meals	Breakfast €8. Lunch & dinner €20-€62.
closed	January.
directions	From A4, exit 30 onto N3 then N18 to Longuyon. Hotel opposite railway station (yellow & blue).

	Gérard Tisserant
tel	+33 (0)3 82 26 50 07
fax	+33 (0)3 82 39 26 09
email	mas.lorraine@wanadoo.fr
web	www.lorraineetmas.com

Map 6 Entry 18

L'Horizon

50 route du Crève-Cœur, 57100 Thionville, Moselle

The house is only 50 years old but its arcading anchors it and Virginia has crept all over it, clothing its façade in lively warm character. Here is comfortable living in graceful surroundings, as in an elegant private house. A huge terrace envelops the ground floor – from here and from the smart restaurant you have plunging views over Thionville with an astounding, glittering cityscape at night. Some first-floor rooms give onto a balcony over the same view. Despite the surprising hall with its marbled flooring and glamorous tented ceiling, the bedrooms are classic French chic (though carpets may be a little worn here and there and some rooms are smaller than others) and bathrooms border on the luxurious. But above all, you will warm to your utterly charming hosts. Monsieur Speck is passionate about Second World War history: the Maginot Line is all around, Thionville is on the Liberty Road that is marked every kilometre from Cherbourg in Normandy to Bastogne in Lorraine. He is fascinating on the subject.

rooms	12 doubles.
price	€98–€145.
meals	Breakfast €11. Lunch & dinner €39–€53. Restaurant closed Saturdays & Monday lunchtimes.
closed	January.
directions	From A31 exit 40 to Thionville. Follow signs for Bel Air Hospital north of town. At hospital bear left up hill leaving town. Hotel 400m on left.

	Jean-Pascal & Anne-Marie Speck
tel	+33 (0)3 82 88 53 65
fax	+33 (0)3 82 34 55 84
email	hotel@lhorizon.fr
web	www.lhorizon.fr

Map 6 Entry 19

Château d'Alteville

Tarquimpol, 57260 Dieuze, Moselle

A house with more than a whiff of history. The château was built for one of Napoleon's generals, and the two paintings that hang in the Louis XVI salon were gifts from the Emperor. Monsieur's family has farmed here for five generations; he now welcomes guests with kindness and much attention. Bedrooms are solidly traditional with carved armoires, Voltaire armchairs and draped bedheads; parkland views float in through the windows. Bathrooms are functional but adequate. Downstairs is more stylish: a library/billiard room, a multi-fenestrated sitting room and a dining room where splendid dinners are eaten by candlelight in the company of your lively, intelligent hosts. Bigger parties are entertained in the trophy-lined *salle de chasse*. Recline on the sound-proofed terrace at the back and gaze on the château-esque grounds, or pull on your hiking boots and follow your nose though woodland, circumnavigating the odd lake. Madame, soul of the house, cooks with skill and fills the place with flowers.

rooms	6: 5 doubles, 1 twin.
price	€61–€77.
meals	Breakfast €7. Hosted dinner €31–€38, book ahead; wine €10.
closed	15 October–15 April.
directions	From Nancy N74 for Sarreguemines & Château Salins. At Burthecourt x-roads D38 to Dieuze; D999 south 5km; left on D199F; right D199G to château.

Livier & Marie Barthélémy
tel	+33 (0)3 87 86 92 40
fax	+33 (0)3 87 86 02 05
email	chateau.alteville@caramail.com

Map 6 Entry 20

Auberge de la Vigotte

1 La Vigotte, 88340 Girmont Val d'Ajol, Vosges

Young and enthusastic, Michel and Jocelyne have done up this 18th-century farmhouse overlooking valleys and conifer coated mountainsides. Michel is a passionate cook and Jocelyne teaches English in a local school. Rooms have carved or painted beds and all look out onto fantastic views. With tennis, volleyball and a children's play area, this is a perfect place for families. You can also ride, or swim in a lake in the grounds, while in the winter you can go cross-country skiing. Meals are a mix of very traditional and more contemporary: ranging from pigs' trotters to beef cheeks to tomatoes with cardamom. An hour from Mulhouse, 700m up, on the gentle slopes of the Vosges, the auberge is set in densely wooded countryside: total peace and quiet. In winter you will find a roaring fire and a warm welcome, in the summer you can swim in a private lake and round off your day with dinner out on the terrace. Although somewhat off the beaten track for English holidaymakers, this would make a good stopover, and could also be a great choice for an out-of-doors holiday.

rooms	20: 13 doubles, 6 twins, 1 family room for 3.
price	€55-€100. Half-board €55 p.p. with min. 3-night stay.
meals	Breakfast €7. Lunch & dinner €18-€38. Children's meals €10. Restaurant closed Tuesdays & Wednesdays.
closed	2 November-20 December.
directions	From Remiremont D23 then D57. Follow white signs to Auberge.

	Michel & Jocelyne Bouguerne-Arnould
tel	+33 (0)3 29 61 06 32
fax	+33 (0)3 29 61 07 88
email	courrier@lavigotte.com
web	www.lavigotte.com

Map 6 Entry 21

Hostellerie Saint Barnabé

53 rue de Murbach, 68530 Murbach, Haut-Rhin

It feels good here. The young owners of this angular, 100-year-old, flower-decked hotel are spontaneously smiley, chatty and attentive. He is the chef – trained with France's best and chef at Château d'Isenbourg for some years, so food is important here, and good. She is the perfect adviser on what to do between the Vosges hills and the Alsace plain: there are typical Alsatian villages and wine-growers to visit, bike rides and good fishing places (they also have mini-golf on the spot). The ferny woods are full of paths and burbling brooks and there's skiing in the snow season. There are two sorts of guest rooms: in the main house they are big, decorated with care and individuality (the yellow and white room has an iron-frame canopied bed, the red and white one twin head cushions and super-soft quilts), with smashing bathrooms and the odd balcony; in the separate building behind, they are smaller and more old-fashioned (and cheaper!) but are gradually being renovated. Here, bedroom doors all have typically Alsatian hand-painted, floral decoration. A great place for nature lovers and gourmets.

rooms	27 twins/doubles.
price	€80-€190.
meals	Buffet breakfast €14. Lunch & dinner €28-€58. Picnic on request.
closed	14 November-20 November; 3 days at Christmas; 9 January-10 February.
directions	From N83 (betwen Belfort & Colmar) D430 for Guebwiller & Lautenbach. D429 for Buhl then Murbach. Hotel on left.

	Clémence & Eric Orban
tel	+33 (0)3 89 62 14 14
fax	+33 (0)3 89 62 14 15
email	hostellerie.st.barnabe@wanadoo.fr
web	www.hostellerie-st-barnabe.com

Map 7 Entry 22

Hôtel Anthon

67510 Obersteinbach, Bas-Rhin

Smaller than mountains, grander than hills, the lushly wooded slopes are pure Vosges forest, the clear Steinbach snakes its way through pastures, red rocky outcrops emerge in forbidding contrast to such bucolic enchantment. This little hotel, in the same deep pinky-orange colour as the rocks, is in typical Vosges style. Inside, more warm wood, including a fine carved staircase, echoes the living forest. It is sweetly simple – not basic in any way, just pretty and uncluttered, with carved wardrobes and Vosges dining chairs, peachy-beige or muted turquoise-green paintwork and coir floors. Bedrooms are not big but, again, prettily done with gingham duvets, starched cloths on round tables, windows onto the quiet night. The first-floor breakfast room is delightful – immaculate white cloths and regional pottery – but the restaurant, definitely in a different class, is the heart of this place. In the big, embracing room with its refined table settings and service, delicious dishes await you – and Madame's huge collection of soup tureens is dazzling.

rooms	8: 3 doubles, 4 twins, 1 suite
price	€58. Suite €98.
meals	Breakfast €10. Lunch & dinner €24–€45; gourmet dinner €61. Restaurant closed Tuesdays & Wednesdays.
closed	January.
directions	From Haguenau D3 & D27 through Woerth to Lembach (25km); there, left to Niedersteinbach & Obersteinbach. Hotel in village centre.

	Danielle Flaig
tel	+33 (0)3 88 09 55 01
fax	+33 (0)3 88 09 50 52
email	info@restaurant-anthon.fr
web	www.restaurant-anthon.fr

Map 7 Entry 23

Hôtel du Dragon

2 rue de l'Ecarlate, 67000 Strasbourg, Bas-Rhin

In old Strasbourg's hub, looking over river and cathedral, the Dragon is grandly, solidly 17th century on the outside, sleekly, refreshingly 20th century on the inside. Built as a private mansion – where Louis XIV stayed on his way to visit Marie-Antoinette in Austria – it became a hotel 12 years ago. The little courtyard received a classically pedimented porch and potted shrubs: a pretty place for an evening drink. Inside, they took a deeply contemporary approach and it is sober, infinitely stylish and extraordinarily restful. Variegated grey and white are the basics: grey curtains on white walls, superb grey pinstripe carpeting, an arrestive pattern of grey and white tiles in the bathrooms, blue and green bedcovers for a dash of colour. And some good abstract paintings and sculptures here and there, displayed to great advantage. Some have river views and others see the cathedral's lovely spire. After 20 years as a mountain guide, Monsieur Zimmer has returned to his native Strasbourg and intends to make the Dragon as welcoming as it is elegant. He is quiet and gentle and has a predilection for English-speaking guests.

rooms	32: 30 twins/doubles, 2 apartments for 3 (without kitchen).
price	€79–€112. Apartments €135–€145.
meals	Breakfast €10. Many fine restaurants in town.
closed	Rarely.
directions	Across the river from Petite France, off Quai St Nicolas.

	Jean Zimmer
tel	+33 (0)3 88 35 79 80
fax	+33 (0)3 88 25 78 95
email	hotel@dragon.fr
web	www.dragon.fr

Map 7 Entry 24

Hôtel Cardinal de Rohan

17-19 rue du Maroquin, 67000 Strasbourg, Bas-Rhin

The atmosphere here is a rare combination: stylish and polite yet utterly friendly, plushly comfortable but not overwhelming. Standing in the historic centre, the solid building round its central courtyard in traditional 17th-century Strasbourg layout has been virtually rebuilt, with proper respect for its tall narrow neighbours, three rows of roof windows and tangles of geraniums down the façade. An 18th-century Gobelins tapestry graces the elegant sitting room; the breakfast room, pale and restful, feels like a country-house dining room: high-backed cane chairs, ivory cloths, antique chest of drawers. Top-floor rooms have pine-clad sloping ceilings and dormer windows; lower rooms are sober, masculine dark and pale blue or rich, warm ginger and cream or spring-fresh green. They come in 'rustic' or 'period' décor, have good velvet or thick contemporary fabrics, clean lines and rich French swag effects. There are gilt-framed mirrors, the occasional antique armoire and smart marble-and-tile bathrooms. Superb comfort, friendliness and attention to detail are the hallmarks here.

rooms	36: 32 twins/doubles, 4 triples.
price	€65-€129. Triples €109-€139. Child under 15 in parents' room, free.
meals	Breakfast €10. Dozens of restaurants within walking distance.
closed	Rarely.
directions	From ring road, exit Place de l'Etoile for Centre Ville & Cathedral to underground car park (Place Gutenberg). Book ahead for private car park.

	Claude Hufajen
tel	+33 (0)3 88 32 85 11
fax	+33 (0)3 88 75 65 37
email	info@hotel-rohan.com
web	www.hotel-rohan.com

Map 7 Entry 25

Relais des Marches de l'Est

24 rue de Molsheim, 67280 Oberhaslach, Bas-Rhin

Bénédicte and Sylvain wear two hats: sculptors and artists they are also welcoming hosts to their renovated farmhouse and restaurant. They originally intended only to provide a hiking stopover for walkers and riders on horseback in 1987; things just grew. Now there is a bistro dedicated to making *tartes flambées* (Alsatian pizza) with an oven they built themselves and two other dining rooms with large tables – one with a couple of armchairs – that feel more like sitting rooms in a home. Bénédicte has set out her palette of soft autumn colours for the bedrooms; browns, mossy greens, oranges and reds. A good choice of paintings and prints lights the walls and a fresco (Sylvain's, of course) decorates a room on the ground floor. More of his pieces are nicely placed in the passageways. The medium-sized to small bedrooms have good mattresses and look over the garden or street. Sylvain has a third hat: he can give you some hands-on courses in modelling, casting and stone-cutting. This is a homely, cosy place with gentle, pleasant company.

rooms	8: 5 doubles, 3 singles.
price	€43–€55. Half-board €50–€55 p.p.
meals	Breakfast €7–€9. Dinner €13–€25. Restaurant 50m.
closed	Rarely.
directions	From Strasbourg, A352 exit at Gresswiller to N420. D392 in Dinsheim for 7km towards Schirmeck, then right onto D218 to Oberhaslach. Hotel on left on main street.

	Bénédicte Weber & Sylvain Chartier
tel	+33 (0)3 88 50 99 60
fax	+33 (0)3 88 50 91 26
email	weber.benedicte@wanadoo.fr

Map 7 Entry 26

Photo Château de Villette entry 30

burgundy
franche comté

Auberge des Vieux Moulins Banaux

18 route des Moulins Banaux, 89190 Villeneuve l'Archêveque, Yonne

Take a 16th-century mill straddling a vigorous stream, add a quartet of young, international, energetic talent, stir vigorously… and place five minutes from a motorway. You have a recipe for success; these four completed the process in only a few years, and the place is wonderful. They left catering careers in the UK for this little auberge in Burgundy: Nick, English and main chef, serves up great food: a saffron-sauced brochette of scallops with caramelised endives; slender pannacotta strawberry tarte accompanied by a homemade sorbet of roses and strawberries. Bernadette (Dutch) and Sabine (German) alternate between dining room and reception, and Guillaume (Franco-Dutch) pitches in everywhere. There is still carpeting on the corridor walls and, in the bedrooms, a 50s feel, but give them another year or so and the rooms will be as appealing as the food. Join a leisurely feast on the great dining terrace overlooking the large park and river, then try your hand at boules – or walk off lunch on the trail nearby. You are 45 minutes from the Chablis vineyards for wine tastings – the position is perfect.

rooms	15: 13 doubles, 2 triples.
price	€40-€49.
meals	Breakfast €7.50 Lunch & dinner €24-€27. Restaurant closed Monday lunchtimes.
closed	First week November; January-6 February.
directions	A5 exit 19 Villeneuve l'Archevêque. Signed.

	Guillaume Hamel
tel	+33 (0)3 86 86 72 55
fax	+33 (0)3 86 86 78 94
email	contact@bourgognehotels.fr
web	www.bourgognehotels.fr

Map 5 Entry 27

Le Petit Manoir des Bruyères

5 allée de Charbuy aux Bruyères, 89240 Villefargeau, Yonne

A rococo place unlike anything you've ever seen. Behind the creeper-clad façade with only the Burgundian roof as a clue, is eye-boggling glamour: a vast beamed living room, an endless polished dining table, rows of tapestried chairs, many shiny ornaments. Upstairs, stagger out of the loo, once you've found the door in the trompe l'œil walls, to cupids, carvings, gildings, satyrs, velvet walls and clouds on the ceilings. There's a many-mirrored bathroom reflecting multiple magical images of you, marble pillars and gold-cushioned bath; a Louis XIV room with red/gold bathroom with gold/ivory taps; an antique wooden throne with bell-chime flush. Madame de Maintenon has a coronet canopy, a long thin *œil de bœuf* window and a shower that whooshes between basin and loo. The 'biscuit' is taken by the deeply, heavily pink suite with its carved fireplace, painted ceilings and corner columns – wild! But such are the enthusiasm of the owners, the peace of house and garden, the quality of comfort, food and wine, that we feel it's perfect for lovers of French extravaganza.

rooms	5: 3 doubles, 2 suites (1 for 3 + child).
price	€120-€220.
meals	Hosted dinner at communal table or separate tables, €40, book ahead.
closed	Rarely.
directions	From Auxerre D965 to Villefargeau; there, right on C3 to Bruyères.

Pierre & Monique Joullié
tel +33 (0)3 86 41 32 82
fax +33 (0)3 86 41 28 57
email jchambord@aol.com
web www.petit-manoir-bruyeres.com

Map 5 Entry 28

Hôtel de la Beursaudière

5-7 rue Hyacinthe Gautherin, 89310 Nitry, Yonne

Monsieur Lenoble's attention to detail is staggering. Not content with creating a buzzing, cheerful restaurant he has lovingly transformed a priory and farm buildings – stables, dovecotes, stone structures on varied levels, wooden verandas topped with red-patterned burgundian roof tiles – into a very seductive hotel. Each bedroom has a trade for a theme: a typewriter and old books for the 'writer'; antique irons for the 'laundress'; horse and ox collars for the 'ploughman'; vine-decorated wooden panels for the 'wine-grower'. The walls have been lightly skimmed in plaster in natural shades of ochre, pigeon-egg grey or light yellow. Floors are terracotta or flagstone, stone walls are painted, rafters exposed and windows round or cottage square with curtains of vintage linens and lace. Beds are kingsize, mattresses are excellent and TVs are hidden in antique cabinets. Most bathrooms are open plan so as not to detract from the beams and volumes. There is even a sheltered sun lounge on the terrace only overlooked by sparrows. A nice place to sit and sample your chilled choice picked up in Chablis.

rooms	11: 5 twins, 6 doubles.
price	€70–€110.
meals	Breakfast €10.
	Lunch & dinner €17.50–€46.
closed	Rarely.
directions	A6 exit 21 Nitry; right to Nitry for 500m. Left at church toward Vermenton for 200m. Signed.

	M & Mme Lenoble
tel	+33 (0)3 86 33 69 70
fax	+33 (0)3 86 33 69 60
email	message@beursaudiere.com
web	www.beursaudiere.com

Map 5 Entry 29

Château de Villette
58170 Poil, Nièvre

Coen and Catherine – he Dutch, she Belgian – fell in love with this little château a couple of years ago, did it up together, then had their wedding here. They've opened just five rooms to guests, so they can spoil you properly! And get to know you over dinner. (Though, if you prefer a romantic *dîner à deux*, they understand.) Deep in the Parc de Morvan, the chateâu was built in 1782 as a summer retreat. Bedrooms, charmingly decorated by Catherine, are large, light and airy, with warm colours and polished floors. Bathrooms are extravagant – new claw-foot baths carry exquisite antique taps – and views sail out of great shuttered windows to meadows and woodland beyond. Your five-course, candlelit dinner, cooked by the caretaker's wife (a talented chef) is served in the dining room, the vaulted 16th-century kitchen, or outside – you choose. The grounds are perfect for duck and pheasant shoots, or fly-fishing in the crystal clear waters. Families would love it here: there are ping-pong and bikes, and a pool a little further away. Beaune and the vineyards lie temptingly close by. *Cash or cheque only.*

rooms	5: 1 twin, 2 doubles, 2 family rooms for 3. Two rooms can be combined to make suites for 3-5.
price	€120-€210. Family €150-€210. Suites €220-€350.
meals	Dinner €38, book ahead. Call ahead to choose menu.
closed	Rarely.
directions	From N6 exit Beaune for Autun. N81 for Moulins for 18km, right to Poil. Through village, 2nd left. Signed.

	Catherine & Coen Stork
tel	+33 (0)3 86 30 09 13
fax	+33 (0)3 86 30 26 03
email	catherinestork@wanadoo.fr
web	www.stork-chateau.com

Map 11 Entry 30

Le Relais Fleuri/Le Coq Hardi

42 avenue du la Tuilerie, 58150 Pouilly sur Loire, Nièvre

Anyone who loves France and what it stands for will coq-a-doodle-do. This small hotel was built in the 30s to cater to the ever-increasing motor trade — from Paris to the south of France. It experienced its heyday in the late 50s and 60s when the rich and famous would stop over for a night or two to wine and dine before heading down to St Tropez. Unfortunately this all ceased when these people became the 'jet set'. These hotels and restaurants are now seeing a revival; often near motorways yet set away from the speed lanes and traffic jams, they are a reminder of a more civilised era when the pace of life was slower and food a priority. Meals are served on a lime-tree-covered terrace overlooking the Loire. Judging by the smiles of the customers staggering away at 4pm it is worth staying here for the food alone. Some of the hotel's original rooms upstairs have terraces over the garden; the newly decorated rooms are pleasantly done in blue or yellow. Philippe has added a small new bistro where those who are just beginning their vacation and have not yet slowed down may be served a quicker meal.

rooms	11: 10 doubles, 1 suite.
price	€45-€80.
meals	Breakfast €9.50 Restaurant lunch & dinner €25-€55. Bistro meals €15.50. Restaurant closed Tuesdays & Wednesdays October-end April.
closed	Mid-December-mid-January.
directions	From A77, exit 25 & continue through Pouilly sur Loire. Hotel opposite Cave Cooperative.

	Philippe & Dominique Martin
tel	+33 (0)3 86 39 12 99
fax	+33 (0)3 86 39 14 15
email	le-relais-fleuri-sarl@wanadoo.fr
web	www.lerelaisfleuri.fr

Map 5 Entry 31

La Dominotte

Jasoupe le Bas, 71150 Demigny, Saône-et-Loire

At the edge of an old Burgundian village, a farmhouse where grapes were gathered, pressed and stored; you can still see the round traces of the barrels on the breakfast room wall. They are less visible in the evening with low lighting and candles when snacks are served from 4 to 6pm; a blackboard announces the daily specialities, maybe snails or a selection of local cheeses and wine. This simply stylish room leads onto the garden, recently landscaped with bushes to obscure the fence around the pool. Surrounding land is flat fields with mature trees in the distance. The Franssens are courageously launching a second career after teaching (she) and sales (he) in Holland. Multi-lingual and welcoming, they have been here since 1998 so are an excellent source for the plethora of cultural visits and gastronomy nearby. Rooms on the ground floor of the barn are more for sleeping than lounging about in; most have mellow exposed stone, some are beamed, all have kept their original slit windows. The views over the garden and pool are best from the airy, spacious family room upstairs with its extra long beds.

rooms	11: 10 doubles, 1 family room for 4 (with kitchen).
price	€85–€115. Family room €145.
meals	Hosted dinner €22–€25 twice weekly.
closed	22 November–mid-March.
directions	A6 Dijon & Beaune exit 24.1 to Bligny les Beaune onto D113, then to Demigny D18; left at T-junc. after Casino & pharmacy; 3rd on left to end of village; last house on right.

	Madame Franssen
tel	+33 (0)3 85 49 43 56
fax	+33 (0)3 85 49 91 35
email	info@la-dominotte.com
web	www.la-dominotte.com

Map 11 Entry 32

Le Monestier

Le Bourg, 71640 St Denis de Vaux, Saône-et-Loire

We almost got lost here, but the valley is a pretty place to lose yourself. You enter a jewel of a village; then into the grounds through wrought-iron gates, past attractive outbuildings and a swimming pool set in the grass, with huge old trees nearby. It looks a little bit like a Home Counties golf club! But no. Margrit and Peter are Swiss and bought the *maison bourgeoise* in 1999; they occupy the ground floor. Peter can be seen walking round in an apron: he is in charge of the cooking and you can expect some truly excellent meals. Not to say that your host is serious; you will find he has a most un-Swiss sense of humour. The reception rooms are comfortable. One bedroom has its own loo and a bathroom down the corridor, but this is made up for by a private terrace on top of one of the towers. You will be very well looked after here: there is even a *fumoir* for after dinner snifters. Tennis, fishing, riding and golf are close at hand. More importantly for many: you will be in the very centre of the Côte Chalonnaise region and could go on foot to visit the vineyards of Mercurey, Givry and Rully.

rooms	6: 6 twins (1 with separate bath across hall, wc in room).
price	€85–€95. Singles €70.
meals	Hosted dinner €24, book ahead. Restaurants nearby.
closed	Closed occasionaly from mid-November–mid-March.
directions	A6 exit Chalon Nord; right for Châtenoy le Royal D978 for 9km for Autun. Left at r'bout for Givry. After 75m, D48 right for Vallée des Vaux, through Mellecey Bourg. Signed.

	Margrit & Peter Koller
tel	+33 (0)3 85 44 50 68
fax	+33 (0)3 85 44 50 68
email	lemonestier@wanadoo.fr
web	www.lemonestier.com

Map 11 Entry 33

L'Orangerie
Vingelles, 71390 Moroges, Saône-et-Loire

Ring the bell on the gate, then wander up through neat gardens. They are alive with colour. Light spills into the sitting room entrance through vine-clad arched windows, with cream walls and Indian rugs adding to the simple elegance of this gracious *maison de maître*. Antiques and travel are David's passion, his gentle Irish brogue enchanting; it's no surprise to hear he interviews European royalty for a 'prestigious' magazine. The grand staircase in the centre of the house could have come straight off a 1930s luxury cruise liner, interesting paintings and stylish oriental fabrics contribute to a mix of styles that somehow go well together. Bedrooms vary in size with seersucker linen and antique prints they are truly lovely and bathrooms are classically tasteful. Being in the heart of Burgundy vineyard country you are also immersed in silence. Terraced lawns lead down to the swimming pool, the trees and meadows. Sybaritic, but in the best possible taste, in one of the most beautiful areas of France. *Cash or Euro cheque only.*

rooms	5 twins/doubles.
price	€65–€95.
meals	Hosted dinner with wine €40, book ahead.
closed	December–February.
directions	From A6, exit Chalon Sud on N80 for Le Creusot; exit Moroges. Signed from village centre.

David Eades & Niels Lierow

tel	+33 (0)3 85 47 91 94
fax	+33 (0)3 85 47 98 49
email	orangerie.mor@infonie.fr
web	orangerie.mor.chez.tiscali.fr

Map 11 Entry 34

Auberge du Cheval Blanc

71390 St Boil, Saône-et-Loire

A tonic if you are tired of the standardisation of all things. Everything about it – from the formal furniture, the striped wallpaper, the parquet floors, the great curtains gathered at the waist, to the gravelled courtyard with trumpet vines, white wrought-iron garden furniture, shuttered and dormer windows – is what the French do with such aplomb. Yet, having said all that, Jany and Martine make the place. He is a well-built Sancerrois, a fitting descendant of generations of bons viveurs and creator of some spectacular dishes in the restaurant – across the road from the hotel. Martine's generosity and kindness add something very special to the hotel. It is a trifle functional upstairs, perhaps, as is often the case, but very much a *maison de maître* and up the most lovely wooden staircase. On the top floor the beams are exposed, and varnished. The two front rooms up there have charming *oeil de boeuf* windows. Bathrooms are all fine, with nothing outstanding to report. Dine under the lime trees in summer and appreciate the survival of such places, and such people.

rooms	10: 6 doubles, 4 twins.
price	€70-€105.
meals	Breakfast €11. Lunch à la carte. Dinner menus €38. Restaurant closed Wednesdays.
closed	10 February–10 March.
directions	A6 exit Chalon sur Saône Sud on D80 for Le Creusot; D981 Cluny for 10km to St Boil. Hotel on right in village.

M & Mme Jany Cantin

tel	+33 (0)3 85 44 03 16
fax	+33 (0)3 85 44 07 25
email	contact@auberge-cheval-blanc.net
web	www.auberge-cheval-blanc.net

Map 11 Entry 35

Le Clos des Tourelles
Château de la Tour, 71240 Sennecey le Grand, Saône-et-Loire

Stuart owns a restaurant so he knows food and wine; he has a big family so he needs space; he loves France so he found a jewel of a château that feels like a home and came away with a vineyard on the side. He is a happy man. And so will you be after a stay at the Clos. There is space to run around and a guard tower (games room and TV for children) and dungeon to explore, an eye-catching collection of outbuildings from the 13th and 15th centuries and the trees, lawns and a large circular driveway to pull it all together. Indoors Nikki's light and clever hand can be felt; soft colours, good fabrics, comfy sofas, antiques and not a whiff of pretension. Big bedrooms are on the first floor, smaller on the top: yellow and blue for Natacha; a four-poster with airy veils for Victoria; crisp white bedspreads on twin beds for Alexandra; balconies for gazing over the gardens, or fireplaces in the corners. Breakfast is in the conservatory and dinner is on the terrace when it's warm. The setting is perfect, the food excellent, the welcome warm. The Redcliffes have only just arrived but they have settled in nicely; you will too.

rooms	10: 8 doubles, 1 triple, 1 apartment for 4 (without kitchen).
price	€80-€150. Apartment €215.
meals	Breakfast €8. Lunch & dinner menus from €20-€30. Dinner with wine, €30.
closed	November-15 April.
directions	A6 exit Chalon Sud or Tournus. Sennecey le Grand on N6 15km from Chalon sur Saône & 8km from Tournus.

	Stuart & Nikki Redcliffe
tel	+33 (0)3 85 44 83 95
fax	+33 (0)3 85 44 90 18
email	info@closdestourelles.com
web	www.closdestourelles.com

Map 11 Entry 36

Château de Messey
71700 Ozenay, Saône-et-Loire

An impressive bull keeps his eye on his harem and shares the buttercup meadows with this 16th-century château surrounded by duck-filled ponds and working vines. Monsieur is the cellar master, Madame manages the château with charming efficiency. Aperitifs in the cellar are part of the evening ritual and Monsieur may surprise you with an enormous bottle of cognac after a dinner of *poulet de Bresse* or Charolais beef with vegetables from the garden. Some of the guest bedrooms are in the beautifully rustic vine workers' cottages built with exposed stone in a U-shape around a grassed courtyard leafy with weeping willow and wall-creeping shrubs. They are right by the river which has formed a lake on its way through; a lovely place to sit out on the grass under the parasols. The pricier rooms in the château are decorated in period-style, graced with high ceilings and long vineyard views. A superior elegance reigns in the salon, overlooking the vines at the back and peonies and rose bushes at the front. A most welcoming if sometimes busy place.

rooms	Château: 2 family rooms for 3, 1 quadruple. Cottages: 5 cottages sleep up to 20.
price	€77-€155. Cottages €210-€600 per week.
meals	Hosted dinner €30.
closed	January.
directions	From A6 exit Tournus; in centre, right on D14 at 1st set of lights. Château on left of D14 between Ozenay & Martailly, 9km from Tournus.

	Marie-Laurence Fachon
tel	+33 (0)3 85 51 16 11
fax	+33 (0)3 85 51 33 82
email	chateau@demessey.com
web	www.demessey.com

Map 11 Entry 37

Le Clos du Chatelet
01190 Sermoyer, Saône et Loire

Washed in barely-there pink, with soft blue shutters, the house was built as a country retreat towards the end of the 18th century – by a silk merchant who must have had a thing about trees. Overlooking the valley of the Saône, with immaculate sweeping lawns, the garden is full of beautiful old ones: sequoias, cedars, chestnuts and magnolias. To one side of the house, an open outbuilding smothered in flowers is home to a collection of antique bird cages. Bedrooms are welcoming havens in elegant muted colours: Joubert in pink-ochre with twin wrought-iron four-posters draped in toile de Jouy; Lamartine in palest aqua enhanced by grey and lilac hangings. All have polished wooden floors and gently sober bathrooms. There's much comfort here, an open fire in the sitting room, period furniture, prints, deer antlers on the wall and an air of calm. A harp stands in the corner of the elegantly comfortable drawing room: we are not sure if it is played but this is the sort of place where it might be. Dinner is by candlelight in the dining room, atmospheric with its old terracotta floor and fountain in the wall.

rooms	4: 3 doubles; 1 double with separate bath (robes & slippers provided).
price	€99–€106.
meals	Dinner €25, book ahead.
closed	Rarely.
directions	A6 exit Tournus for Bourg en Bresse to Cuisery. Right at Cuisery for Sermoyer & Pont de Vaux. In Sermoyer follow chambres d'hôtes signs.

	Mme Durand Pont
tel	+33 (0)3 85 51 84 37
fax	+33 (0)3 85 51 84 37
email	leclosduchatelet@free.fr
web	www.leclosduchatelet.com

Map 11 Entry 38

Château des Poccards

120 route des Poccards, 71870 Hurigny, Saône-et-Loire

It is all most comforting and welcoming, the Tuscan-style villa built in 1820 to woo a Tuscan beauty living in Burgundy. Now run by a husband and wife team ever on the go, the cream and ochre villa has become an exemplary guesthouse. After a day's sampling the restaurants of Lyon, exploring the wine routes of Beaune or the shops of Geneva, what nicer than to return to a big retro tub in a bathroom that sparkles with uplighters and oozes warm towels? Bedrooms are all generously big and different, with pretty terracotta floors and pale-papered walls, cream beds, elegant furnishings and *tout confort*. Some have windows to all sides so you feel you're in the tree tops – bliss when the sun streams in. In the mature park, a serene pool with wooden loungers and vineyard views. Families would be happy here, as would romancers. Excellent breakfasts are supplied by your hosts at white-clothed tables in a gracious room; a piano in the corner, windows to a terrace, a sumptuous parquet floor. Good value for money.

rooms	6 doubles. Some rooms connect.
price	€90–€125.
meals	Good restaurants 10-minute drive.
closed	January-February.
directions	A6 exit 28 to Sennecé Les Maçon toward Laizé. Left to Laizé & Blagny. At stop, 1st left to Hurigny; 1st right up Rue de la Brasse; Château 100m on left.

	Catherine & Ivan Fizaine
tel	+33 (0)3 85 32 08 27
fax	+33 (0)3 85 32 08 19
email	chateau.des.poccards@wanadoo.fr
web	www.chateau-des-poccards.com

Map 11 Entry 39

Burgundy

Château de Flammerans
21130 Flammerans, Côte-d'Or

All is fresh, luxurious, relaxing – and Guy has the perfect pinch of passion for Burgundian cuisine even though he hails from Cantal. Ask to see the 18th-century kitchen with its original painted ceiling where he teaches the secrets of *jambon persillé* or *fricassée d'escargot*. The billiard room and the library are just off the entrance hall with its superb 19th-century ceramic tiles and a handsome iron bannister leads upstairs. You may breakfast on the large balcony overlooking the park, in the sitting room with its creamy walls, oriental rugs, green and gold upholstered easy chairs, or in the elegant dining room. Bedrooms are big and uncluttered with working fireplaces and mineral water on the side tables. You'll find robes in the gorgeous bathrooms along with weathered marbled floors from the south of France. If you are lucky, you'll catch one of the concerts – maybe baroque or jazz – that Guy and Catherine organise every summer. Sit and dream on a bench in a shady glen, gaze at the magnificent red oaks, discover the glistening ponds (one of which was used to clean the carriage wheels). A pleasing place.

rooms	6: 3 doubles, 1 twin, 2 suites.
price	€88–€200.
meals	Breakfast €6.50. Light lunches available. Hosted dinner with drinks, €35–€55, book ahead.
closed	Rarely.
directions	A6/A39/N5. Auxonne D20 towards Flammerans. Signed in Auxonne.

Guy Barrier
tel	+33 (0)3 80 27 05 70
fax	+33 (0)3 80 31 12 12
email	info@chateaudeflammerans.com
web	www.chateaudeflammerans.com

Map 6 Entry 40

Castel de Très Girard
7 rue Très Girard, 21220 Morey St Denis, Côte-d'Or

Nuits Saint Georges, Gevrey Chambertin, Clos de Vougeot, Vosne Romanée – all tongue-twisters in the best sense of the word and all strewn in your path as you travel down the trunk road from Dijon. Why not stop here and be greeted by Sébastien and his young, friendly team who handle everything in the nicest manner? The warmth not only comes from the embers in the fireplace by the leather club chairs but from the general ambience of this recently renovated wine press and 18th-century Burgundian manor. There are confident touches of burgundy reds (naturally) or sun-yellows in the padded fabrics on the beds and just enough stone and beam have been exposed to give the large bedrooms character; small vestibules ensure ultimate peace. Even the big, gleaming white bathrooms have views over the rooftops or to the Côte de Nuits vineyards. The chef and his assistant *pâtissier* are poets with a magic touch transforming the freshest ingredients into pure delight. Sébastien picks out artists of the moment to be shown on the walls and best bottle of wine for your repast. Not to be missed.

rooms	9: 2 doubles, 5 triples, 2 suites.
price	€90-€122. Triples €140-€178. Suites €160-€180.
meals	Buffet breakfast €12. Lunch €16-€75. Dinner €37-€75.
closed	15 February-15 March.
directions	15km from Dijon. A31 exit Dijon Sud for Nuits St Georges on N74, then right to Morey St Denis. Signed.

	Sébastien Pilat
tel	+33 (0)3 80 34 33 09
fax	+33 (0)3 80 51 81 92
email	info@castel-tres-girard.com

Map 6 Entry 41

Château du Saulon

Route de Seurre, 21910 Saulon la Rue, Côte-d'Or

Don't rush through, stay awhile, and you'll eat very well under the vaulted ceiling in the old stables, charming with fresh flowers and candelabra on the tables. Wine is a speciality here; Guillaume will organise an introduction to the burgundy grape or, if your taste buds are finely tuned, he may suggest a session on the *grands crus*. A *cave à vins* along with a well informed staff is just up the road. The 27-hectare park surrounding this listed 18th-century château may be the only bit of land *not* planted with vines. The bedrooms in the château are classic or contemporary; wooden headboards, sober curtains, all with good bedding and big bathtubs. Feeding off a sweeping central stone staircase they let in light and views to the lawns and trees. Third-floor rooms have lower ceilings and smaller windows. Intimacy and character successfully inhabit the seven rooms in the cleverly converted cook house, now called Le Pavillon. Linger over coffee on the terrace; the swans and ducks floating by on the lazy meandering river set the pace here, so just relax.

rooms	30: Château: 22 doubles; Pavillon: 7 doubles, 1 single.
price	€75–€120. Single €60–€65.
meals	Buffet breakfast €10. Lunch, set menu, from €20 (weekdays). Lunch & dinner €28–€38. Restaurant closed Sun evenings & Mon lunch.
closed	February–6 March.
directions	A31 exit Dijon Sud for Longvic to toll. Exit Terminal Rail Route D996, left at r'bout for Fenay. Right at Chevigny for Seurre. 2km. Signed.

	Guillaume Sevellec
tel	+33 (0)3 80 79 25 25
fax	+33 (0)3 80 79 25 26
email	info@chateau-saulon.com

Map 6 Entry 42

Château d'Ecutigny
21360 Ecutigny, Côte-d'Or

This is a real castle. It was built in the 12th century to station soldiers guarding the Duke of Burgundy's land from marauding French. Bits were added over the years but it was abandoned at the end of the 18th century and fell to ruin, then was rescued by Françoise and Patrick. The château is an historic monument, with the secret passages and Rapunzel towers to prove it, but has been made light, airy and really beautiful inside, without a trace of having been 'done up'. The rooms are in muted colours – not quite pastels – and sparsely furnished with a subtle mix of country pieces and elegant antiques. Bathrooms are large, with cast-iron baths on feet and some with warm terracotta tiles. The floors throughout the château are either mellow terracotta or wood – no walking barefoot on icy stone. Children will love exploring the cellars, stables and farm and Françoise will not be fazed by them: she used to run a crèche! This may be why the place runs so smoothly. Comfortable and relaxed despite the grandeur, your hosts are full of smiles, and the food and wine generously flow. A guest says, "Great food, magical place."

rooms	6: 5 doubles, 1 suite for 4.
price	€100–€130. Suite €200.
meals	Picnic lunch with wine available. Hosted dinner with aperitif & wine, €40. Children's menus €10–€20.
closed	Rarely.
directions	From A6 exit Pouilly en Auxois. Follow signs to Bligny sur Ouche, then Ecutigny. Last turning on right on leaving village.

Françoise & Patrick Rochet
tel	+33 (0)3 80 20 19 14
fax	+33 (0)3 80 20 19 15
email	info@chateaudecutigny.com
web	www.chateaudecutigny.com

Map 11 Entry 43

Hôtel de Vougeot
18 rue du Vieux Château, 21640 Vougeot, Côte-d'Or

Rows of vines sweep down an incline, surround the regal Château de Clos de Vougeot (shown above) in tones of pale yellow stone like a sepia photograph, and come to an abrupt halt at the back doorstep of this this modest converted townhouse, The best rooms here have views of both. For centuries Clos de Vougeot was considered the finest of all burgundies; the Cisterian monks planted some of the vines in the 12th century. Thirty hogsheads were sent to Rome in 1371 to celebrate the election of Pope Gregory XI; the gift-bearing abbot was soon made a cardinal. The cloister, cellar and enormous presses are among the most interesting examples of architecture in Burgundy. You are on your own here with a key to come and go as you like. Everything has been kept simple and clean; the rough outlines of the dark timbers are a nice contrast to the white walls, light coloured bedspreads, new parquet floors and honey-pine furniture. Splash out on one of the huge rooms. A copious buffet breakfast served under the stone arches of the ground floor will be a perfect start to your day.

rooms	12: 8 doubles, 1 triple, 2 quadruples, 1 room for 5.
price	€49-€85.
meals	Buffet breakfast €9. Restaurants in village.
closed	4 January-25 January.
directions	A31 exit Nuits St Georges, D74 towards Vougeot. Hotel in village.

Alain Senterre

tel	+33 (0)3 80 62 01 15
fax	+33 (0)3 80 62 49 09
email	contact@hotel-vougeot.com
web	www.hotel-vougeot.com

Map 11 Entry 44

Château du Créancey
21320 Créancey, Côte-d'Or

Fiona and Bruno fell in love with Créancey on sight – a brave and passionate response to crumbling 17th-century walls and fallen beams. They have lavished a small fortune on a stylish restoration, lacing ancient bricks and mortar with contemporary luxuries: exposed oak beams scrubbed clean, lime-rendered walls to soak up the light, an infusion of antiques that mix with the odd minimalist piece. Sumptuous, uncluttered bedrooms have huge beds, old rugs, fresh flowers, plush armchairs. Bathrooms are equally faultless (imagine the best of everything and you are halfway there). Even the taps burst with water, the rarest of French rarities. An exceptional breakfast with homemade jams is taken in the hall. In the sitting room, the enormous fireplace can burn whole trees (well, almost). There's a snug library, too, a dovecote in the garden and, 300m from the château, a line of trees flank the Canal de Bourgogne. Bring your bike and pedal on the footpath past the Charolais cattle that graze in the surrounding fields. On your doorstep, enough châteaux, cellars and monasteries to keep you busy for a month.

rooms	5 + 1: 2 doubles, 1 twin, 1 family for 3, 1 suite for 4. 1 small house for 4.
price	€160–€230. House €560–€720.
meals	Dinner €50, only for groups occupying whole château.
closed	Rarely.
directions	From A6, exit at Pouilly en Auxois. At 1st r'bout to Créancey; D18 1km into village. Château on left; entrance at rear opposite Mairie.

Fiona de Wulf

tel	+33 (0)3 80 90 57 50
fax	+33 (0)3 80 90 57 51
email	chateau@creancey.com
web	www.creancey.com

Map 6 Entry 45

La Terre D'Or

Rue Izembart La Montagne, 21200 Beaune, Côte-d'Or

Jean-Louis can share his love for Burgundy with you in many ways: he can indulge you in wine tasting and explain how those elegant vintages are produced, he can arrange cooking lessons with a local chef, or show you a vestige of Roman art. All this (and more) by bike, horseback, jeep or hot-air balloon. He and Christine have two houses ready, both surrounded by a large terraced garden and century-old trees. One is contemporary and multi-levelled, the other is stone-walled and traditional – both with sitting rooms and kitchens with everything you need. The large bedrooms – each with a separate entrance – have magnificent views of the vineyards and the Saône Valley; some have private terraces or patios. The Martins have used old beams, polished wine-growers' tables and chairs. You might have one of your wine classes in the grotto under the house where a river used to run; the stalagtites are still there. Jean-Louis can also be persuaded to host a barbecue by the pool. This is the kind of place where you book for two nights and end up staying a week. *Group price for themed holidays: wines, cooking, culture.*

rooms	2 houses for 2-14. Main house: 4 doubles, 1 twin. Cottage: 1 double, 1 family duplex for 4.
price	€130-€195. Cottage €360.
meals	Breakfast €12. Picnic available.
closed	Rarely.
directions	From Beaune, D970 for Auxerre & Bouze Les Beaunes. After 2km right to La Montagne. Well signed.

	Christine & Jean-Louis Martin
tel	+33 (0)3 80 25 90 90
fax	+33 (0)3 80 25 90 99
email	jlmartin@laterredor.com
web	www.laterredor.com

Map 11 Entry 46

Le Clos

Rue Gravières, 21200 Montagny Les Beaune, Côte-d'Or

Breakfast on the terrace overlooking the neat and pretty *jardin de curé*, then choose your suntrap in the garden – full of recesses and hidden corners. Or, under the shade of big trees, wander among the quaint agricultural machinery that sculpturally dots the lawns. The rustic white-shuttered farmhouse has been recently renovated with tender loving care to reveal exposed limestone walls and massive rafters. There's a charming country breakfast room and a light and lofty lounge, whose ancient tiles have been garnished with oriental rugs and sofas. Bedrooms are large, with matching floral bed linen and curtains, new carpets, substantial antiques, double glazing to obscure distant motorway hum and the odd exotic touch. Bathrooms sparkle and there are no half-measures: big bathtubs, walk-in showers, an abundance of towels and robes. No restaurant, but have a drink at the bar and and a chat with Alain – a professional hotelier with a dry sense of humour. The pretty residential village is deep in wine country – and when you've had your fill of burgundies and beaunes, there are mustards to try in a nearby village!

rooms	24: 19 twins/doubles, 5 duplex suites.
price	€65–€105. Suites €130–€200.
meals	Breakfast €9. Restaurant 100m; many others in Beaune, 3km.
closed	December or January.
directions	From Lyon A6 exit 24.1 towards Beaune Centre; 300m r'bout to Montagny Les Beaune on D113. Signed.

	M & Mme Alain Oudot
tel	+33 (0)3 80 25 97 98
fax	+33 (0)3 80 25 94 70
email	hotelleclos@wanadoo.fr
web	www.hotelleclos.com

Map 11 Entry 47

Château de Chassagne-Montrachet

5 rue du Château, 21190 Chassagne-Montrachet, Côte-d'Or

You are in top wine country. The driveway passes through a small vineyard to the businesslike château – winery in the middle, chambres d'hôtes to the right. The stark 19th-century exterior does not prepare you for the modernism within: the sweeping wooden stairway, the slate and pink-marble floor, the stunning leather furniture, the extraordinary billiard room with bamboo decoration and underfloor lighting. The refreshing irreverence continues upstairs; you might spot a Jacobsen 'egg' chair, relish the sumptuousness of purple walls and oak floor or enter a room of zen-like calm. Windows show the vineyards floating away to the hills of the Massif Central or the Saône valley; on a good day you can see the Alps. Bathrooms are amazing; most have tubs surrounded by wooden decking, one has a double sink of rough-cast bronze mounted on rock – half basin, half art. Breakfast at two large steel tables on sculpted chairs by a wonderful fireplace and floor-to-ceiling doors. Château Montrachet is a few hundred metres away and there's excellent walking in the hills. *Wine tasting sessions by previous arrangement.*

rooms	5 doubles.
price	€250.
meals	Lunch €48, with fine wines for tasting. Walking distance to excellent restaurant.
closed	Christmas & New Year's Day.
directions	From Beaune, N74 exit Chassagne-Montrachet; château signed at village entrance.

	Francine Picard
tel	+33 (0)3 80 21 98 57
fax	+33 (0)3 80 21 97 83
email	contact@michelpicard.com
web	www.michelpicard.com

Map 11 Entry 48

Château Andelot

Rue de l'Eglise, 39320 Andelot les Saint Amour, Jura

Winding narrow roads lead higher and higher, through woods and foothills, until you reach the top… and conical towers, a mighty keep and thick-walled ramparts spread along a cliff top, and the wooded valley falling away. Pass through the monumental entrance portal and the adventure begins: the 12th-century castle is as dramatic inside as out. The bedrooms – main château or rampart buildings – are grand but uncluttered spaces of antiques, fine fabrics, cool tiles, rich rugs and lavish bed covers; bathrooms are as luxurious as a starry hotel. All have million-dollar views over plunging valleys to the Jura mountains and the Swiss border; even Mont Blanc on a good day. Why get up? Why, indeed. No need to make breakfast, or dinner; fruits and vegetables are grown on the grounds; the château comes with staff – very helpful, too. Eat in the vaulted dining room below the vast, beamed, tapestry-hung sitting room with plump sofas, soft carpeting and oils. Tennis court, swimming pool, formal garden and terrace; a very special place for celebrations and reunions. *Reservation mandatory, call well in advance.*

rooms	6: 5 doubles, 1 twin.
price	€135-€195. Partial (€3,000 p.w.) or whole château (€6,900 p.w.): min. 4 nights.
meals	Dinner €40, book ahead. Children's menu €20.
closed	Nov-April. Call to reserve out of season.
directions	A39 exit 10 onto D56, then D3 to St Amour & Andelot. 2km after Thoissia, on left, small lane leading to castle gate.

	Harry & Susan Belin
tel	+33 (0)3 84 85 41 49
fax	+33 (0)3 84 85 46 74
email	harry@evermay.org
web	www.chateauandelot.com

Map 11 Entry 49

Château d'Epenoux
70000 Pusy - Epenoux, Haute-Saône

Next to the dear little 18th-century château – once the home of one of Napoleon's generals – stands a tiny baroque chapel tenderly maintained by the mistress of the house. Irene and Fernand have given both the facelift they deserved – windows sparkle and floorboards gleam. Your friendly, unassuming hosts, ex-news people peacefully at home in their new role, have opened up four airy bedrooms on the first floor to guests. All are generously big and different: the suite, prettily papered in blue, its twin beds draped with soft white duvets, its windows overlooking majestic trees, copses and lawns, the large double panelled in French green, elegant with 18th-century bedstead, the fresh, feminine Mona Lisa, all deep pink walls and cream sofa. Sparkling white bathrooms come with lashings of hot waterr, and in the blue-carpeted salon florally upholstered armchairs embrace you along with a welcome pre-dinner aperitif; after which a refined dinner will be delivered by Irene to a grand dining table – your slices of perfectly roasted duck fillet complemented by Fernand's much-loved wines.

rooms	4: 3 doubles, 1 suite.
price	€80.
meals	Dinner with aperitif, wine & coffee, €23.
closed	Rarely.
directions	From Chaumont, N19 to Vesoul, then D10 for approx. 4 km. Château on left at entrance to village of Epenoux.

	M & Madame Klufts
tel	+33 (0)3 84 75 19 60
fax	+33 (0)3 84 76 45 05
email	fernand.klufts@wanadoo.fr
web	www.chateau-epenoux.com

Map 6 Entry 50

Photo © Paris Tourist Office; David Lefranc

paris – île de france

Le Relais du Louvre

19 rue des Prêtres St Germain l'Auxerrois, 75001 Paris

Look down the throats of gargoyles. Soak up the history. The Revolutionaries printed their newsletter in the cellar; the place inspired Puccini's Café Momus in *Bohême* and is utterly delightful, as are the charming young managers who greet you from the antique desk. Everywhere, antiques and oriental rugs complement the modernity of firm beds and perfect bathrooms. Front rooms look onto the church's Gothic flights of fancy and along to the austerely neo-classical Louvre; others give onto a light-filled patio. Top-floor junior suites have twin beds and a non-convertible sofa (no cluttering up), pastel walls, exuberant upholstery and heaps of light from mansard windows. The apartment (pictured) is big and beautiful with fireplace, books, music, old engravings and a superb veranda kitchen. Other, smaller rooms are luminous, fresh and restful – yellow, a favourite colour, brings sunny moods into small spaces. You feel softly secluded and coddled everywhere. The sense of service is highly developed and as there is no breakfast room, breakfast comes to you. *On each floor, two rooms can make a family suite.*

rooms	20 + 1: 14 twins/doubles, 2 suites, 4 singles. 1 apartment for 4.
price	€145–€180. Singles €99. Suites €205–€244. Apartment €380.
meals	Breakfast in bedroom €10. Light meals €5–€15.
closed	Rarely.
directions	Metro: Louvre-Rivoli (1), Pont Neuf (7). RER: Châtelet-Les Halles. Car park: Private car park on request €20. Bus: 67 69 72 74 85.

	Sophie Aulnette
tel	+33 (0)1 40 41 96 42
fax	+33 (0)1 40 41 96 44
email	contact@relaisdulouvre.com
web	www.relaisdulouvre.com

Map 5 Entry 51

Hôtel Saint Merry

78 rue de la Verrerie, 75004 Paris

If you love the old and utterly unusual and are not afraid of a few stairs, this is for you. The hotel huddles against the late-Gothic church of St Merry whose clock tower cornice thrusts its way into the top-floor suite; in the first-floor reception you find an elaborate pew, linen-fold panels, a telephone in a confessional; in another room, a couple of buttresses provide the most original of low-flying bed canopies. From brocante and flea market came the wherewithal to make the old house worthy of its origins, neo-Gothic pieces were reworked to create this astounding environment, atmospheric paintings chosen to enhance it. The sober décor sets off the festival of carving: plain velvet or 'medieval-stripe' fabrics, great cast-iron light fittings, original beams and stonework – and some strangely colourful bathrooms (the new shower rooms are excellent). The big rooms are almost majestic, the cheaper ones are smaller and more basic, the suite a masterpiece of style and adaptation (surely Paris's only Gothic salon). *No lift. Difficult access in pedestrian street.*

rooms	12: 6 doubles, 3 twins, 2 triples, 1 suite for 6.
price	€160–€230. Suite €335–€407.
meals	Breakfast €11.
closed	Rarely.
directions	Metro: Hôtel de Ville (1, 11), Châtelet (1, 4, 7, 11, 14): RER Châtelet-Les Halles. Car park: St Martin. Bus: 38 47 75.

	Pierre Juin
tel	+33 (0)1 42 78 14 15
fax	+33 (0)1 40 29 06 82
email	hotelstmerry@wanadoo.fr
web	www.hotelmarais.com

Map 5 Entry 52

Hôtel de Notre Dame
19 rue Maître Albert, 75005 Paris

Hidden from the tourist tides in a select little area, yet a stone's throw from Notre Dame, the fine old frontage opens onto a superb tapestry, bits of antiquity on oriental rugs and deep armchairs. These people genuinely like people and greet you with smiles and humour. As does the brilliant conservatory-like breakfast room: big window to the street, 'rusted' tables, metal chairs with soft yellow cushions. If the convoluted corridors declare the age of the building (1600s), contemporary style dictates their smart look. Bedrooms also mix old and new. There are beams and exposed stones – some enormous – and cathedral views through smaller windows on higher floors. Fittings and furniture are in custom-made pale curvy wood, spotlights are discreet, new padded upholstery is warm and colourful with mixes of yellow, red and blue and the translucent screen doors to bathrooms are an excellent idea for small layouts (not all baths are full size). The black eunuch officially portrayed as Marie-Antoinette's feathered fan bearer lived here... A welcoming place.

rooms	34: 26 doubles, 8 twins.
price	€139–€150.
meals	Breakfast €7.
closed	Never.
directions	Metro: Maubert Mutualité (10). RER: St Michel-Notre Dame (exit 3). Car park: Rue Lagrange. Bus: 47 63 86 87.

	Jean-Pierre Fouhety
tel	+33 (0)1 43 26 79 00
fax	+33 (0)1 46 33 50 11
email	hotel.denotredame@libertysurf.fr
web	www.hotel-paris-notredame.com

Map 5 Entry 53

Le Notre Dame Hôtel
1 quai St Michel, 75005 Paris

At the very hub of Latin Quarter life – students crowd the pavements, cars crowd the bridge, Notre Dame rises serene behind – you climb the mirrored staircase to a warm red welcome. The hotel is splendid: communal spaces brightly decked in red checks, the salon-breakfast room spreading its windows so your eyes are caught by plunging views of river, cathedral and great 'police palace'. Nearly all rooms have at least two windows onto this ancient picture; only the five cheapest, soberly pretty and quieter, give onto a dull courtyard. They are very attractive, not huge but uncluttered, and full of light from the river. Double-glazing keeps the noise out, air-conditioning keeps the air breathable. Excellent fabrics are all from the house of Pierre Frey; a light cherrywood laminate adorns desktops, bedheads and clever block panelling; there are hand-enamelled bedside lights from northern France and framed prints from England; new dark green marble bathrooms with bright white fittings are extremely smart behind their translucent Japanese-style doors and the top-floor duplex suites are fun and full of character.

rooms	26: 14 doubles, 9 twins, 3 duplex suites.
price	€150–€199. Suite €244.
meals	Breakfast €7.
closed	Rarely.
directions	Metro: St Michel (4). RER: St Michel-Notre Dame. Car Park: Notre Dame. Bus: 24 47 63 86 87.

	Jean-Pierre Fouhety
tel	+33 (0)1 43 54 20 43
fax	+33 (0)1 43 26 61 75
email	hotel.lenotredame@libertysurf.fr
web	www.paris-hotel-notredame.com

Map 5 Entry 54

Grand Hôtel des Balcons
3 rue Casimir Delavigne, 75006 Paris

Les Balcons has the lot: an idea of service which produces tea on winter afternoons, a clothes line over the bath, a practical room where clients can work or children play, a daily feast of a breakfast (sumptuous cooked spread, fresh fruit salad…) that's free on your birthday! Owners and staff appear to work with lightness and pleasure. Having decorated her Art Nouveau hotel by taking inspiration from the floral 1890s staircase windows, Denise Corroyer now teaches *ikebana* and flowers the house – brilliantly – while her son Jeff manages – charmingly. Rooms are simple yet pleasing. The five big family rooms have smart décor and pretty modern lamps, parquet floors and two windows, good bathrooms (two basins, pretty tiles) and loads of space. Other rooms are not big but purpose-made table units use the space judiciously, amusing prints decorate the walls and front rooms have balconies. At the back, you may be woken by the birds. An eagle eye is kept on maintenance, beds are firm, bathrooms good, colours and fabrics simple and bright. Remarkable value, super people.

rooms	50: 25 doubles, 14 twins, 6 singles, 5 family rooms for 4.
price	€90–€210.
meals	Breakfast €12.
closed	Never.
directions	Metro: Odéon (4, 10). RER: Luxembourg. Car Park: École de Médecine. Bus: 24 63 86 87 96.

	Denise & Pierre Corroyer & Jeff André
tel	+33 (0)1 46 34 78 50
fax	+33 (0)1 46 34 06 27
email	resa@balcons.com
web	www.balcons.com

Map 5 Entry 55

Hôtel du Danube
58 rue Jacob, 75006 Paris

Built in the 1870s as a private mansion, this soft civilised hotel rejoices in a dazzling black and red salon and a pale salmon patio where potted palms sit on bright green 'grass', iron tables can be laid for breakfast and elegant façades rise skywards. The quietest rooms look over this or the smaller lightwell with its pretty trompe l'oeil skyscape. Others have more activity – and more noise – under their double-glazed windows (the higher, the quieter). Style and fittings vary widely, twisty corridors change levels, it's a warm, long-lived-in place. Superb 'superior' rooms have two windows, some very desirable antiques, armchairs and smart fabrics, yet they feel intimate and friendly. Their bathrooms are carefully done too. 'Standard' rooms all have blue-laminate bamboo-trim desk units and nice 'wooden-plank' wallpaper with some quaintly old-style bathroom tiling – but all necessities are there. The attic room is the most appealing of these. And you all meet as equals in the charming countrified breakfast room and appreciate the bevy of young helpful staff at reception.

rooms	40: 25 double, 9 twins, 5 family, 1 suite.
price	€125–€180. Family rooms & suite €250.
meals	Breakfast €10.
closed	Never.
directions	Metro: St Germain des Près (4). RER: Musée d'Orsay. Car park: St Germain des Près. Bus: 39 48 63 95 96.

	Séverin Ferrand & Michel Sario
tel	+33 (0)1 42 60 34 70
fax	+33 (0)1 42 60 81 18
email	info@hoteldanube.fr
web	www.hoteldanube.fr

Map 5 Entry 56

Hôtel Lenox Saint Germain
9 rue de l'Université, 75007 Paris

The jazzmen-inlaid Lenox Club bar has real atmosphere. It is used by publishers for drinks after work, by film stars for interviews, by writers for literary wrangles… utterly St Germain des Prés, great fun, and no longer the hotel breakfast room (which is now in the vaulted basement). Hotel entrance and lobby have been transformed into a symphony of pure 1930s style: strict lines straight and curved, plain natural materials, a fascinating frieze motif and a superb framed inlay of a panther. Staff are friendly and immediately make you feel welcome. Upstairs are large rooms and (much) smaller ones, all different. Some have old furniture, some have more modern units, there are hand-painted cupboards and intriguing 1930s pieces. Colour schemes are mostly muted. Rooms on the little rue du Pré aux Clercs are quieter than the others; you may have the added luxury of a balcony. We really liked the corner rooms with two windows and lots of light. Bathrooms are good and extra shelving for pots and paints is provided by little trolleys. An excellent place that makes you feel you belong.

rooms	34: 17 doubles, 12 twins, 5 suites.
price	€120-€205. Suites €260-275.
meals	Breakfast €11-€14.
	Lenox Bar snacks €5-€10.
closed	Never.
directions	Metro: St Germain des Prés (4).
	RER: Musée d'Orsay.
	Car park: Rue des Saints Pères.
	Bus: 48 39 63 68 69 83 94

	Madame Laporte
tel	+33 (0)1 42 96 10 95
fax	+33 (0)1 42 61 52 83
email	lenoxsaintgermain@wanadoo.fr
web	www.lenoxsaintgermain.com

Map 5 Entry 57

Hôtel de Buci
22 rue Buci, 75006 Paris

At the heart of the little shopping streets behind St Germain where galeries, restaurants and clothing stores are encroaching on the well-loved street market, the Buci feels like another antique shop, full of beautifully chosen and utterly desirable pieces: while their charming, energetic son manages the hotel, the owners love looking for old things. In the salon where every picture is worth a good look – the themes are horses and women – every portrait is intriguing – and every chair or lamp has a story. Come evening, the morning's gentle classical music turns to jazz to fit the 1930s atmosphere and in the basement piano bar/breakfast space, you can sit on superbly ornate red sofas. Bedrooms are less unusual but still high class. Done with good repro furniture and remarkable fabrics from top design houses (a different one for each floor), they are sun yellow and red-currant, cornflower blue and cream, checks, stripes and florals in a rich coordination of canopies, pelmets and quilts. The pretty bathrooms are excellent too and you will enjoy the monogrammed linen. A good, reliable and quiet place.

rooms	24: 12 doubles, 8 twins, 4 suites for 3-4.
price	€190-€335. Suites €350-€600.
meals	Breakfast €17-€22. Afternoon tea served.
closed	Never.
directions	Metro: St Germain des Prés (4), Mabillon (10). RER: St Michel-Notre Dame. Car Park: St Germain des Prés. Bus: 58 70.

	Frédéric Lassalle Mayor
tel	+33 (0)1 55 42 74 74
fax	+33 (0)1 55 42 74 44
email	hotelbuci@wanadoo.fr
web	www.hotelbuci.fr

Map 5 Entry 58

Hôtel Opéra Richepanse
14 rue du Chevalier de St George, 75001 Paris

At the centre of a throbbingly busy shopping and business district, the cool 1930s look and courteous welcome of the Richepanse promise rest and quiet in proper four-star fashion. The marquetry, the panelling, the smooth suede furniture and the stylish mouldings of the lobby/salon were all custom-designed for the deep renovations. It feels clean-cut and rich. There's a minor concession to things more ancient in the atmospheric stone vault where the floor is blue, the marble bistro tables shine and the sumptuous breakfast buffet calls. Bedrooms are a good size, some are enormous. They have blue carpets, clean-limbed 1930s-style furniture and excellent thick-textured fabrics for straight-hung curtains and well-fitting bedcovers – no swags, no frills, no fuss. This gives space to appreciate the interesting reproductions that draw the eye and even, in the magnificent great suites, original paintings. Bathrooms are, of course, superb with the latest in basin design, triple mirrors and simple, smart tiling. Modern comforts, old-style attention and service.

rooms	38: 20 doubles, 15 twins, 3 suites.
price	€230–€350. Suites €450–€590.
meals	Breakfast €14–€19.
closed	Never.
directions	Metro: Madeleine (8, 12, 14). Concorde (1, 12). RER: Auber & Roissy bus-Opéra. Car Park: Madeleine. Bus: 42 52 84 94.

	Édith Vidalenc
tel	+33 (0)1 42 60 36 00
fax	+33 (0)1 42 60 13 03
email	hotel@richepanse.com
web	www.richepanse.com

Map 5 Entry 59

Edouard VII

39 avenue de l'Opéra, 75002 Paris

One stylish and notable resident, Edouard VII, must have enjoyed gazing from his terrace onto the wide avenue fronted by the bronze-roofed Opéra Garnier. It was completed in 1875, two years before the hotel. The grand style still lingers with elegant modern touches by the Corbel sisters whose family has owned the hotel for over 50 years. They chose graceful contemporary sculptures, a Murano chandelier and Napoléon III *cabinets de curiosité* to set off the huge circular lobby; a strong red and blue striped English carpet to echo the colours of the original stained-glass windows behind the bar; sober, rich oak panelling and a steamer wardrobe for the sitting spaces. Fresh flowers and orchids flourish in just the right places. It all feels spacious and solid. Up in the good-sized bedrooms thick fabric in soft salmons, pale yellows and warm ochres are mixed with care. Hats off to a light-hearted oval breakfast room which doubles as a plush little restaurant, Angl'Opéra. Chef Gilles Choukroun, house magician, marries flavours and colours to brighten the eye and entrance the palette.

rooms	69: 33 doubles, 27 twins, 4 singles, 5 suites for 2-4.
price	€309-€485. Singles €295. Suites €525-€1,100.
meals	Buffet breakfast €23. Lunch €19. Dinner à la carte €40.
closed	Never.
directions	Metro: Opéra (3, 8, 7), Pyramides (14, 7). RER: Auber. Car Park: Vendome, Marché Saint Honoré. Bus: 95 29 68 27 21 81.

	France Claque
tel	+33 (0)1 42 61 86 02
fax	+33 (0)1 42 61 47 73
email	infos@edouard7hotel.com
web	www.edouard7hotel.com

Map 5 Entry 60

Aviatic

105 rue de Vaugirard, 75006 Paris

Here the Marquise de Maintenon secretly raised the illegitimate children of King Louis XIV and his mistress, Madame de Montespan, away from the prying eyes of the King's court. But the name Aviatic honors more recent residents: the first aviators based in Paris during WWI. Some things have remained intact since then: a stylish glass marquee and its lanterns, the golden letters over the door. Others have been restored to their former glory: a big airy entrance hall, a delightful Empire lounge all bright and cheerful, in keeping with the welcome of the young staff. In the bedrooms there is a clever touch in the choice of gingham patterns, tasteful stripes teamed with flowered fabric, an antique desk or richly carved wooden headboard. And a bow is made to the bohemian, artistic populaces of Montparnasse and St Germain des Près: a collection of vintage posters runs all the way up to the mouldings of the breakfast room. Staff are full of ideas as to where to dine – you are well looked after here. Note that the rooms at the back are quieter. *Ask for a picnic basket for lunching in Luxembourg Gardens.*

rooms	43: 36 twins/doubles, 6 triples, 1 suite. Some connecting rooms.
price	€135–€175. Suite €250–€310.
meals	Breakfast €12.
closed	Never.
directions	Metro: Montparnasse (6, 4, 12, 13). RER: Luxembourg. Car park: Private hotel parking. Bus: 89 91 95 96.

	Monsieur Philippe Bourgeois
tel	+33 (0)1 53 63 25 50
fax	+33 (0)1 53 63 25 55
email	welcome@aviatic.fr
web	www.aviatic.fr

Map 5 Entry 61

Villa Opéra Lamartine
39 rue Lamartine, 75009 Paris

As they say on the movie posters, Monsieur Tamès *is* Villa Opéra Lamartine. He started as master of the ship in the days when the hotel was a bare-bones, no-stars, stairs-only building; the rooms were rented by the month. Today he joyfully stands at the helm (behind a warmly pannelled reception desk) of a spic-and-span, toile de Jouy-ed tribute to the literary and romantic Paris of the 19th century. This area, built in the 1820s and rapidly occupied by the likes of Georges Sand and Chopin, Dumas and Delacroix – and the hotel's namesake, Alphone de Lamartine – was baptised the New Athens. Each room is therefore named after one of the 'stars' of that epoch with engravings or drawings depicting the artist or a scene from the era. Rooms are compact, clean and functional with tasteful quilted bedspreads in subtle plaids, clear colours or a cool beige and white. Some bathrooms have windows, some rooms connect to make suites. Monsieur knows his neighborhood like the back of his hand; ask him to direct you to the Musée de la Vie Romantique with its rose-strewn garden just up the street.

rooms	28: 11 twins, 11 doubles, 6 singles.
price	€145–€160. Singles €110.
meals	Breakfast €12.
closed	Never.
directions	Metro: Notre Dame de Lorette (12), Le Peletier (7). RER: Auber. Car park: Square Montholon. Bus: 20 21 24 26 27 29.

	Monsieur Tamès
tel	+33 (0)1 48 78 78 58
fax	+33 (0)1 48 74 65 15
email	lamartineopera@wanadoo.fr
web	www.hotel-paris-lamartine.com

Map 5 Entry 62

Hôtel Prince de Conti
8 rue Guénégaud, 75006 Paris

The narrow rue Guénégaud, just off the riverside, is one to savour slowly. Thankfully, most of the galleries and one-of-a-kind shops have been there almost as long as La Monnaie, the French Mint, now revamped with interesting exhibitions and gift shop. Even our favourite ethnic jewellery shop feels like a gallery as the owner knows the origin of every bead necklace. The Prince de Conti – the Princess lived here in 1670 – feels as authentic the moment your feet hit the lobby's parquet floor. The choice is eclectic but it works: a comfy sofa fits perfectly in the bay window, a faïence stove sits next to one of the chinoiserie bamboo chairs and a lovely bronze figure in movement watches all from its three-legged pedestal. If you are splurging and want a view, ask for the suite on the top floor with its antique desk, checked armchairs and double-sinked bathroom; another interesting choice would be one of the ground level rooms with French windows that open onto the interior courtyard. If you're on a budget, the smaller rooms on the courtyard will suit; ask for one with two windows.

rooms	26: 21 doubles, 5 twins, 2 duplexes for 3.
price	€155–€280.
meals	Breakfast €13.
closed	Never.
directions	Metro: Saint Germain de Près (4),Odéon (10, 4), Pont Neuf (7). RER: St Michel-Notre Dame. Car park: Rue Mazarine. Buses: 58 70.

	Elaine Touber
tel	+33 (0)1 44 07 30 40
fax	+33 (0)1 44 07 36 34
email	princedeconti@wanadoo.fr
web	www.prince-de-conti.com

Map 5 Entry 63

Hôtel Résidence Monceau
85 rue Rocher, 75008 Paris

Beautifully crafted wooden doors and slatted interior shutters are just two of the warm details added in the recent renovation. There are original touches in the pretty white-tiled bathrooms too: stylish free-floating basins on anthracite shelves, warm teak floors, a delicate frieze of colourful candy-like buttons across a wall, a trompe l'oeil foot-rug under the basin. Especially well-designed are the little vestibules, almost small dressing rooms, with their well-lit cupboards, hidden mini-bars and safes. The larger twin rooms are at the front of the hotel, some with small terraces, others with hanging geraniums. Double rooms are on the back, some with windows opening onto a little courtyard. The reception area with its colonial bamboo furniture and bar is next to be renovated; a mahogany floor and a glassed-in veranda delineates the breakfast area. Not far from the Champs Elysées, the hotel's real attraction is its proximity to the Parc Monceau. Once a tiny village, its gardens were a mad fantasy of the Duc of Chartres – discover pyramids, pagodas, temples, windmills, islands, crooked paths and 'woodlands'.

rooms	51 twins/doubles.
price	€170-€180.
meals	Breakfast €11.
closed	Never.
directions	Metro: Villiers (2), Europe (3). RER: Charles De Gaulle-Etoile. Cark park: Rue de Rome. Bus: 30 94.

Elaine Touber

tel	+33 (0)1 45 22 75 11
fax	+33 (0)1 45 22 30 88
email	info@relais-monceau.com
web	www.relais-monceau.com

Map 5 Entry 64

Hôtel Prince de Condé

39 rue de Seine, 76006 Paris

In one of the smallest hotels in the city on one of the most sauntering streets – named after the great river to which it leads – enormous attention to detail. Paris is full of vaulted cellars transformed into breakfast rooms but it is rare to find one done in such style: a red patterned carpet warms the exposed stone, little round tables invite intimacy and low-riding armchairs clothed in broad stripes and fun patterns are a lesson in comfort and cosiness – with an elegant porcelain service to match. There are canopies over beds, cloth-lined walls, double glazed windows and just the right English chair or Napoleon III desk to personalise a bedroom. The large suite on the top floor under the roof gets a royal bathroom: jacuzzi tub, double basins and swish Italian faucets. It's big enough to wear red and green medallion wall paper, sit a couple of plaid armchairs in a corner and still have room for a moss-green upholstered sofa and cushions trimmed in red cord. Lots of galleries for gazing and people for watching on rue de Seine and the rue Buci nearby.

rooms	12: 11 doubles/twins, 1 suite for 2.
price	€195. Suite €310.
meals	Breakfast €13.
closed	Never.
directions	Metro: Saint Germain des Près (4), Odéon (10, 4), Pont Neuf (7), Mabillon (10). RER: St Michel- Notre Dame. Car park: Rue Mazarine. Bus: 58, 70.

Elaine Touber

tel	+33 (0)1 43 26 71 56
fax	+33 (0)1 46 34 27 95
email	princedeconde@wanadoo.fr
web	www.prince-de-conde.com

Map 5 Entry 65

Hôtel Les Jardins du Luxembourg

5 impasse Royer Collard, 75005 Paris

Freud once trampled this same cul-de-sac when he stayed here in the winter of 1885-86 – and we know that the curtains round his bed were yellow: his disciple Ernest Jones relates that he applied chemical tests to make sure they did not contain arsenic. Now there are curtains at the windows only, some falling nicely to the floor, and original beams are still on view in some rooms, especially those under the eaves. We can imagine Freud sitting in front of the fireplace (still there) in the little salon; Art Deco chairs and brass lights over paintings give it an intimate feel. The reception area, by contrast, is a big open space, and room keys hang over a handsome mahogany desk that doubles as a bar. Facing it is a long wrought-iron park bench with colourful cushions to remind us that Luxembourg Gardens are just across the street. Keep your eye out for the cement patterned tiles here: a delightful ochre and orange checkerboard in the breakfast room and joyful little trompe l'oeil lizards and vine wreaths in the bathrooms, some of which have free standing basins, four-legged bath tubs and mirror speckled walls.

rooms	26: 18 doubles, 7 twins, 1 single.
price	€140-€150.
meals	Breakfast €10.
closed	Never.
directions	Metro & RER: Luxembourg. Car park: Rue Soufflot. Bus: 38 58 82 85 89 84.

Elaine Touber

tel	+33 (0)1 40 46 08 88
fax	+33 (0)1 40 46 02 28
email	jardinslux@wanadoo.fr
web	www.les-jardins-du-luxembourg.com

Map 5 Entry 66

Hôtel Relais Saint Sulpice
3 rue Garancière, 75006 Paris

Almost on the back doorstep of Saint Sulpice, tucked into one of those tiny magic streets untouched by the passage of time, this is the pefect hideaway for sleuthing around for clues for *The Da Vinci Code* or spotting the literati of Saint Germain des Près. You might almost miss the entrance if you are not careful; it's more an entryway into an aristocratic 18th-century home than a door to a hotel. The womb-like salon continues the lived-in feeling with screened mahogany bookcases, back-lit *objets* lining the top shelves, a pair of 1940s armchairs and a couple of large Chinese jars; a big gilt mirror sits in a corner to reflect light from the high windows. No reception desk to speak of here, just a friendly spirit behind a small desk to hand out the keys to your small but cosy room. The attention to detail is impressive – perhaps a fringe-like frieze along the top walls and door or an elegant wrought-iron bed and bistro table – while most bathrooms have little trompe l'oeil 'rugs' of colourful tiles under the basins. A glass roof and a bounty of greenery give a winter garden feel to breakfast.

rooms	26: 19 doubles, 7 twins.
price	€175–€210. Triples €245
meals	Breakfast €12.
closed	Never.
directions	Metro: Saint Sulpice (4), Mabillon (10). RER: Cluny-La Sorbonne. Car park: Place Saint Sulpice. Bus: 58 70 63 86 87.

	Elaine Touber
tel	+33 (0)1 46 33 99 00
fax	+33 (0)1 46 33 00 10
email	relaisstsulpice@wanadoo.fr
web	www.relais-saint-sulpice.com

Map 5 Entry 67

Cazaudehore - La Forestière

1 avenue Kennedy, 78100 St Germain en Laye, Yvelines

The rose-strewn 'English' garden is like an island in the great forest of St Germain and it's hard to believe the buzzing metropolis is just a short train journey away. The first Cazaudehore built the restaurant in 1928, the second built the hotel in 1973, the third generation apply their imaginations to improving both and receiving their guests with elegant French charm. The buildings are camouflaged among the greenery, summer eating is deliciously shaded under rose-red parasols; hotel guests have the elegant, beamed dining room with its veranda to themselves (there are several seminar and reception rooms). Food and wine are the main focus – the wine-tasting dinners are renowned and chef Grégory Balland's seasonal menus are a delight, skilfully mixing tradition and invention: you will eat supremely well here. Bedrooms are much cared for too, they've been renovated in a refined but unostentatious style with good fabrics, original colour schemes – saffron, blue and lightning green, for example – period furniture and prints, and masses of character.

rooms	30: 13 doubles, 12 twins, 5 suites.
price	€190-€205. Suites €250-€270.
meals	Breakfast €16. Lunch & dinner menus with wine, €50-€65. À la carte €85. Children's meals €23.
closed	Rarely.
directions	A13 for Rouen exit 6 for St Germain en Laye on N186. N184 for Pontoise. Hotel on left 2.5km after château.

	M Philippe Cazaudehore
tel	+33 (0)1 39 10 38 38
fax	+33 (0)1 39 73 73 88
email	cazaudehore@relaischateaux.com
web	www.cazaudehore.fr

Map 5 Entry 68

Saint Laurent

2 place Lebreton, 78490 Monfort L'Amaury, Yvelines

Slow-paced medieval Monfort L'Amaury, 45 minutes from Paris, is home to some remarkable Renaissance stained-glass windows in the town church, 16th-century cobblestone paving, a Ravel festival in October and this suberb private home built under Henry IV at the beginning of the 17th century. The renovation is recent and thorough – a lift, excellent soundproofing –   and in good taste: old rafters reign in some bedrooms, the exposed beamed ceiling in the breakfast room is splendid and skilful carpentry is evident in the light oak used in the panelling, headboards and cupboards that warm the pure white walls and simple elegant bedspreads. Ground-floor rooms have private terraces looking out on the lawn where Madame Delabarre puts out fine summer chairs for relaxing under the huge linden trees. Each room bears the name of a tree or plant in the nearby Rambouillet forest, and a framed ode to the fern, beech or rhododendron has been created by an artist. There is a big accent on a full breakfast here which includes ham, eggs and cheese. A nice weekend stop before heading for Paris or the airports.

rooms	12: 8 doubles, 3 twins, 1 suite.
price	€90-€150. Suite €170.
meals	Breakfast €11; €8 on weekends. Restaurants within walking distance.
closed	1-22 August.
directions	From Paris, A13, A12, N12 towards Dreux then Monfort L'Amaury. In Monfort, through gates for car park.

	Madame Christiane Delabarre
tel	+33 (0)1 34 57 06 66
fax	+33 (0)1 34 86 12 27
email	reception@hotelsaint-laurent.com
web	www.hotelsaint-laurent.com

Map 5 Entry 69

Château de Poigny

2 rue de l'Eglise, 78125 Poigny la Forêt, Yvelines

The entrance bodes well: graceful overhanging trees and a tiny hidden door stuck in a sun-spottled vine-covered stone wall, just like in *The Secret Garden*. Ring the bell; if Antoine Meley is not there, Taïb will greet you and walk you through more trees up the path and into a big country mansion set back in its little park with a pond at the rear. When Antoine bought the house for his family in 2005 he continued to receive guests as he was planning to renovate and had not the heart to cancel the reservations. And then, as if by magic, he caught the bug and now loves the whole idea. The little reception area and big oval table in the dining room are just about the only things that haven't changed, the park has been cleared of its overgrowth and is slowly taking form, the walls are fresh with paint, the bedding is new. One room has a low brass table and a Moroccan inlay trunk, another is Chinese red and bronze for an oriental touch. Some bathrooms are a good size, the other smaller ones are next on the list for the Meley touch. It's nice to see a lovely house come into its own.

rooms	5: 4 doubles, 1 family room for 4.
price	€65-€70.
meals	3 restaurants in village.
closed	Rarely.
directions	From N10 north of Rambouillet exit Poigny La Forêt; D937, then D936 & D107 to Poigny 5km. Follow signs for 'église' and 'chambre d'hôtes'. 2 restaurants in village.

	Antoine Meley
tel	+33 (0)1 34 84 73 42
fax	+33 (0)1 34 84 74 38
email	le-chateau-de-poigny@wanadoo.fr

Map 5 Entry 70

Hôtel de Londres

1 place du Général de Gaulle, 77300 Fontainebleau, Seine-et-Marne

Gaze on the Château de Fontainebleau, one of France's loveliest buildings, from your room in this 18th-century hostelry that stands opposite. The hotel has been in the family for three generations; Monsieur Philippe runs it quietly and considerately, while his mother holds reception with charm. The sitting room has an 18th-century classical look; also rich colours, comfy armchairs, plump cushions, fine displays of flowers. The breakfast room has the feel of a small brasserie, and both rooms have views to Fontainebleau. Bedrooms, on the upper floors, are similarly classical in style – smart, spotless, traditional; colours are bold, fabrics floral. A sense of timelessness pervades this peaceful place, and you could hardly be better placed for exploring the Forest of Fontainebleau, the hunting grounds of kings. As for the château, it was built around the keep of a smaller medieval building, was completed in 1550 and has been added to over the years; the gallery of François I is considered one of the finest in Europe. You can visit free on Sundays and it's magnificently floodlit at night.

rooms	12: 4 doubles, 1 single, 2 triples, 5 suites.
price	€110–€160. Suites €150–€180.
meals	Breakfast €10.
closed	23 December-9 January; 12-18 August.
directions	A6 exit Fontainebleau for Château. Hotel opposite Château.

	Philippe Colombier
tel	+33 (0)1 64 22 20 21
fax	+33 (0)1 60 72 39 16
email	hdelondres1850@aol.com
web	www.hoteldelondres.com

Map 5 Entry 71

Photo Corel

normandy

Le Manoir de Savigny
50700 Valognes, Manche

Walk around the grounds and you might catch deer nibbling on acorns or a coypu by the lily-covered lake. At the end of a poplar lined avenue, surrounded by meadows, it's hard to believe this handsome manor house is ten minutes from busy Valognes. Dating from the 16th century, it's part of an attractive group of farm buildings including an old cider press. The Bonnifets have kept original features – floor tiles, beamed ceilings, spiral stone staircase – blending them with strong colours and *objets* from their travels in Indonesia and Morocco. The result is a warm, relaxed, faintly exotic feel. Bedrooms are large and light-filled, with seagrass or rugs on stripped wood floors, pale plaster walls, striking beds – maybe brass or pretty wrought-iron – lacy bedcovers and a carefully chosen antique or two. Bathrooms are richly tiled, strikingly coloured, perhaps with a roll top or corner bath. Breakfast, in the sunny dining room with its vast fireplace, carved chairs and dark beams, is a generous spread. Well-placed for Cotentin's beaches, Bayeux, Cherbourg – or borrow bicycles and pack a picnic.

rooms	5: 4 doubles, 1 suite for 5.
price	€55-€80. Suite €135.
meals	Restaurant 1.5km. Many others within 3km.
closed	Rarely.
directions	From Cherbourg N13 exit Valognes to St Sauveur le Vicomte on D2. Then D24 for Le Gibet. 50m first left towards Savigny. 1km.

	Corrine & Eric Bonnifet
tel	+33 (0)2 33 08 37 75
email	reservation@manoir-de-savigny.com
web	www.manoir-de-savigny.com

Map 3 Entry 72

Hôtel Restaurant Le Mesnilgrand
50260 Négreville, Manche

Deep in the countryside, along tiny lanes which look as though they might peter out at any moment, is this lovely, converted, 18th-century cider farm — restaurant, small hotel, yurt (Mongolian tent) and creative activity centre all rolled into one. The dynamic young English owner, Tina, along with Claire the gardener/ecologist and Stéphane the chef/teacher, provide rare opportunities. You could find yourself wild-mushrooming, joining one of the yoga weekends, nature trailing or, chef by your side, searching out the finest fish, cheese or cider from the local market. You eat in a setting to match his culinary skills: exposed beams, stone walls, good white table cloths, fresh flowers. The energy and creativity of your hosts know few bounds. Le Mesnilgrand is family-friendly; rooms are comfortable, silent and simply decorated, and have good bathrooms. Go horse riding, with or without specialist instruction, paint by the lake or just recline in the English-style bar. And there's a teepee for the children. Everything can be arranged. *Yoga, reiki & cooking weekends. Children under three free.*

rooms	6: 5 doubles, 1 family room.
price	€80. Half-board €130 per room.
meals	Dinner €25-€30.
closed	January-February.
directions	From Cherbourg RN13 exit St Joseph on D146 for Rocheville. Over dual carriageway, on for 5km; signed (outside Négreville).

	Tina Foley
tel	+33 (0)2 33 95 09 54
fax	+33 (0)2 33 95 20 04
email	tina@mesnilgrand.com
web	www.lemesnilgrand.com

Map 3 Entry 73

Château de Saint Blaise

50260 Bricquebec, Manche

You will be staying in the coach house, not the château. Everything will be perfect, right down to the bathroom flowers. When Ernst bought the coach house a few years back nothing remained of the building but the walls. He rescued two staircases, one stone, another spiral, and a balustrade from another place; you would never know the old building had ever lapsed from grace. The sitting room is blue and burgundy, with wooden floors and a marble fireplace. The Grande Suite is an unusual shade of dark blue, with a Napoleon III bed and draped curtains; one window overlooks the courtyard, with its round pond of pink lilies and fish, the other looks onto fields. The Petite Suite is in pink and beige, with the same views and a narrow but elegant bed. You are served breakfast in a small, pretty room, with flowers on the table. It can be as late as you like and the staff will be delighted to light the fire in winter. There is fresh orange juice, coffee or tea and the eggs exactly as you like them. Such luxury – and there's an exquisite pool, too.

rooms	2 suites in coach house.
price	€220-€250.
meals	Restaurant 3km. Other excellent ones 15km-20km.
closed	November-March.
directions	N13 for Valonges exit Bricquebec. D902 for 10km then right on route Les Gromonts. Château entrance 100m on left.

	M Ernst Roost
tel	+33 (0)2 33 87 52 60
fax	+33 (0)2 33 87 52 61
email	info@chateaudesaintblaise.com
web	www.chateaudesaintblaise.com

Map 3 Entry 74

Château de la Roque

50180 Hébécrevon, Manche

As you come up the poplar-lined drive into the circular courtyard at the end of the day, the windows blink like diamonds. The land falls away to a lake on the other side of this 16th- and 17th-century country house. Your host leads you through the entrance passing collections of precious stones, pictures of ancestors on the farm, leather-clad bellows, a majestic grandfather clock framed by two long windows, Norman statues and a mass of potted plants. Continuing up a circular stone staircase, reach the large, light bedrooms furnished with the same care for detail, colour and comfort: oriental rugs, an antique writing desk, good bed linen. The Delisles raise organic chickens, pigs, sheep, cows, turkeys and ducks and make their own bread in a wood-fired oven. Dinner comes after a refreshing glass of their *pommeau* (a Norman speciality of calvados and apple cider). You can ask for a picnic lunch and stroll around their lake or explore the nature reserve nearby; perfect – wildlife and peace. .

rooms	15: 11 twins/doubles, 2 triples, 2 suites for 3-4.
price	€79-€90. Triples €94. Suites €134.
meals	Hosted dinner at communal table €24. Children's meals €13.
closed	2-15 January.
directions	From D974, exit 7 to Périers on D900 toward St Gilles. At r'bout, D77, Château on right.

	Mireille & Raymond Delisle
tel	+33 (0)2 33 57 33 20
fax	+33 (0)2 33 57 51 20
email	mireille.delisle@wanadoo.fr
web	www.chateau-de-la-roque.fr

Map 3 Entry 75

Le Castel
50210 Montpinchon, Manche

The perfect mistress' hideaway – deep in Normandy countryside, large but not palatial, grand but not ornate. The Parisian socialite, who built this 19th-century mansion for his lover, chose well. Tucked in two hectares of park and garden with views of rolling meadows, it's private but not isolated – 15 minutes to Mont Martin, beaches and Coutances, an hour to Mont St Michel and the Bayeux Tapestry. Nick and Jon create a house-party atmosphere which you can join or not as you choose. There's plenty of space: two salons are scattered with French and oriental furniture, while a white baby grand and large Kylie Minogue doll create striking notes! French windows open to the terrace and garden. Eat here or with other guests amongst cut-glass and candlesticks in the dining room. The menu might include roast duck with raspberries, pears in red wine and local cheeses. Bedrooms are classic country house: striped or silk wallpaper, polished French beds, perhaps an escritoire or a marble washstand. Treat as a relaxing stopover near channel ports, or stay and chat to the new pet llama.

rooms	5: 3 doubles, 1 twin, 1 family room for 3-4.
price	€100-€140.
meals	Hosted dinner with wine, €30. Book ahead.
closed	Never.
directions	From Montpinchon, D102 to Le Pavage; right at junction then immed. left onto D252 for 1.6km; on left, look for two white gates; use the 2nd set.

	Nicholas Hobbs & Jon Barnsley
tel	+33 (0)2 33 17 00 45
email	enquiries@le-castel-normandy.com
web	www.le-castel-normandy.com

Map 3 Entry 76

Le Manoir de l'Acherie

Ste Cecile, 50800 Villedieu les Poêles, Manche

A very short way from the motorway this hotel, deep in the Norman countryside, is a lovely, ever-so-French discovery: an old granite house with immaculately tended gardens and an ancient granite cider press sunk into the lawn brimming over with red roses. At one side is a chapel, now bedrooms; on the other is an extension providing a sort of *cour d'honneur* entrance. Some of the furniture is authentically old though most is solid quality repro in the 'rustic' Norman style; rooms are carpeted, bed covers are patterned, curtains are frilly. Mother and daughter Cécile handle the hotel and restaurant service, father and son run the kitchen – they have won several prizes for their culinary efforts. The tables are dressed in prim, cream tablecloths. Dark wooden beams, well worn floor tiles and a giant stone fireplace create a pleasant, cosy feel. The small number of people running this establishment and the quiet unstressed, unhurried but efficient way they do so, is admirable. The only concession one must make is to arrive before 7pm and the last orders in the restaurant are at 8.30pm.

rooms	19: 11 doubles, 6 twins, 2 singles.
price	€45–€110. Singles €38. Half-board €60–€90 p.p.
meals	Breakfast €8. Lunch & dinner €16–€37. Children's meals €9. Restaurant closed Mon September–June; Sun evenings mid-October–week before Easter.
closed	2 weeks Nov; 2 weeks Feb.
directions	A84 exit 38 Brecey-Villedieu for Vire. Over 2nd r'bout for 2km; over main road with Président dairy opp.

	M & Mme Bernard Cahu
tel	+33 (0)2 33 51 13 87
fax	+33 (0)2 33 51 33 69
email	manoir@manoir-acherie.fr
web	www.manoir-acherie.fr

Map 3 Entry 77

Les Hauts de la Baie du Mont Saint Michel

7 avenue de la Libération, 50530 St Jean Le Thomas, Manche

General Eisenhower slept here and took the bed with him! It was returned, however, as you will return to this informal house, with its ornate Art Deco reception rooms and unusual interior design. Everyone is taken with the spot: perched in a beautiful garden above the sea, with exceptional views to Mont Saint Michel. Madame Leroy is warm, bubbly, and as theatrical as her house. The bedrooms range from a canopied four-poster and Art Deco frieze to a delicately pretty pale pink double, with blue-green paintwork, or the new Napoleon suite in fuchsia pinks and purple. Bathrooms have their original 19th-century porcelain fittings. The beach, 100m away, is pebbled but others are just a short drive. Breakfast might keep you going until supper: a buffet of proper French food, it includes charcuterie, cheese, five different breads, 12 different jams and homemade cake. Outside, find a steep terrace exuberant with magnolias, rhododendrons, azaleas, camellias, canna lilies and those misty views. Travel across the bay at low tide – to Mont Saint Michel – by foot, on horseback, or with a guide.

rooms	8: 5 doubles, 2 twins, 1 suite for 4.
price	€75–€180.
meals	Dinner €38 with wine, book ahead. Three excellent restaurants within 5-minute walk.
closed	Rarely.
directions	From Cherbourg, N13 to Valognes; D2 to Coutances; D971 to Granville; D911 (along coast) to Jullouville; on to Carolles & St Jean Le Thomas (6.5km from Jullouville).

André & Suzanne Leroy

tel	+33 (0)2 33 60 10 02
fax	+33 (0)2 33 60 15 40
email	contact@chateau-les-hauts.com
web	www.chateau-les-hauts.com

Map 3 Entry 78

La Ramade

2 rue de la Côte, Marcey les Grèves, 50300 Avranches, Manche

La Ramade, half a century old, was built in golden granite by a livestock merchant who made his fortune. Véronique took it on in 2000 and transformed it from B&B into charming hotel, fulfilling a long-held dream. Her individual interiors are a pleasing mix of modern and *brocante* finds – with Veronique's own Breton cradle sweetly displayed on the second floor. Bedrooms feel feminine and are named after flowers. Blue-carpeted Laurier has white-painted furniture and steps to a bathroom with a sunken bath, Coquelicot has a poppy theme and matching yellow curtains and towels. Pretty Eglantine has a canopied bed and afternoon sun streaming through large windows, Amaryllis – tailor-made for wheelchairs – a superb hydromassage shower. The grounds are filled with mature trees that give privacy from the road, and you are near Mont St Michel and the sea – a great spot for children who will love the guided tour across the great bay at low tide. Véronique now has a licenced bar for samplings of the local *pommeau* as an apéritif or a calvados before tucking into bed.

rooms	11: 4 doubles, 3 twins, 1 suite, 3 family rooms for 3-4.
price	€61-€112.
meals	Breakfast €8.50. Light supper €14 off-season, book ahead. Creperie within walking distance; many restaurants in Avranches.
closed	January-6 February; 20-30 November.
directions	From Avranches D973 for Granville; over river, then left on D911 for Jullouville; immediately on right.

	Véronique Morvan
tel	+33 (0)2 33 58 27 40
fax	+33 (0)2 33 58 29 30
email	hotel@laramade.fr
web	www.laramade.fr

Map 3 Entry 79

Le Gué du Holme

14 rue des Estuaires, Saint Quentin sur le Homme, 50220 Ducey, Manche

A mouthwatering story of Normandy unfolds: the sea, the orchards and the meadows are reduced to their essence in the plump Chausey oysters, the smooth foie gras with its tart apple compliment and the renowned *pré salé*, lamb grazed on sea-flooded grass. Michel, the hugely enthusiastic owner-chef, has a deeply rooted commitment to his Norman food – the more local the better. It is hard to spot the simple elegance of Le Gué du Holme from the outside. It was all the more surprising to find rooms overlooking a small lavender-spiked, rose-trellised garden. Breakfast is served outside on cheerful pink and white porcelain with sweet butter under silver cupolas and a delightful mix of breads. The Lerouxs are sensitive to detail and colour; the rooms feel crisp, an antique trunk lives in the corridor, the warmth and brightness of the welcome is reflected in the dining room with brass light fixtures, wood trim and ochre walls. Always attentive, the Lerouxs have conjured up a new weekday bistro lunch. Well away from the summer crowds, low-key, impeccable. *Minimum stay three nights.*

rooms	10: 9 doubles, 1 suite for 3.
price	€65-€95. Half-board €90-€110 p.p.
meals	Breakfast €10. Lunch & dinner €27-€58. Restaurant closed Saturday lunchtimes, Sunday evening & Mondays October-Easter.
closed	11-18 November; 2 weeks in February.
directions	From Caen, N175 to Avranches. Exit Cromel at War Museum. Left on r'bout D103. Over 2nd r'bout to St Quentin. Hotel opp. church.

	M & Mme Leroux
tel	+33 (0)2 33 60 63 76
fax	+33 (0)2 33 60 06 77
email	gue.holme@wanadoo.fr
web	www.le-gue-du-holme.com

Map 3 Entry 80

Château de Boucéel

50240 Vergoncey, Manche

The embroidered linen sheets enfold you in a smooth embrace that is a metaphor for the Boucéel experience. The Count's family have lived in the listed château since it was built in 1763 but he and the Countess have worked in Paris and Chicago and theirs is an elegant, unstuffy lifestyle which you are welcome to join. He, a quietly simple aristocrat, will recount fascinating details from his family history while she, energetic and communicative, prepares a succulent apple cake for your breakfast. The delightful bedrooms, named and portraited for the uncles and grandmothers who slept there, are beautifully done in just the right dusty yellows and misty greys for the original panelling, and have superb parquet floors, antiques and personal touches. And if you meet the kindly lady ghost, be properly polite to her, she's a *marquise*. Breakfast, on fine china, is in the soft green, round, panelled and mirrored dining room with French windows to the lush park, which comes complete with grazing geese, lake and ancient chapel. It's a treat to stay in this gently grand and gracious château.

rooms	5: 2 doubles, 3 suites.
price	€125–€160.
meals	Restaurant 6km.
closed	Mid-November–March. Call for out of season reservations.
directions	From Avranches for Mont St Michel, exit 34 to N175; exit D40 for Mont St Michel & Antrain. Left for Antrain. After 6km on D40 left for St Senier de Beuvron on D308. Château 800m.

	Comte & Comtesse Régis de Roquefeuil-Cahuzac
tel	+33 (0)2 33 48 34 61
fax	+33 (0)2 33 48 16 26
email	chateaudebouceel@wanadoo.fr
web	www.chateaudebouceel.com

Map 3 Entry 81

Le Château de Sully
Route de Port en Bessin, 14400 Sully, Calvados

From the veranda, the view of giant crescent-shaped flower beds filled with flamboyant mixtures of tangled flowers is stunning. This elegant 18th-century building combines classical architecture with an exquisite setting, every detail inside and out carefully orchestrated. Yellow is the dominant colour for the formal dining room, while russet reds tone in with the bar and sober leather sofas in the main salon. In another lounge, table-games and a billiard board guarantee some fun too. The first-floor bedrooms looking out over neat lawns are beautifully decorated, and the attic rooms one floor up are cosy and inviting. There are more bedrooms, an indoor pool and a fitness centre in the *petit manoir* annexe. There are traces of children's paintings still to be seen in the 16th-century chapel, and lots of outdoor space for your little darlings. Inside, however, they will have to resist the temptation to thunder past delicate objects, as well as promise to sit up straight in the dining room. Good value, remarkably, for this really is a most magnificent place.

rooms	22: 19 doubles, 2 triples, 1 suite.
price	€110–€140. Triples €150–€160. Suite €170–€195.
meals	Breakfast €13. Dinner €42–€70.
closed	December–February.
directions	From Bayeux D6 for Port en Bessin. Château on right approx. 3km after Bayeux.

	M & Mme Brault
tel	+33 (0)2 31 22 29 48
fax	+33 (0)2 31 22 64 77
email	chsully@club-internet.fr
web	www.chateau-de-sully.com

Map 4 Entry 82

Manoir de Mathan
14480 Crépon, Calvados

A perfect size is this elegant manor house, introduced by a lovely crunching sound on the gravelled driveway and a 17th-century baroque arch. Finding this sober elegance in a typical Bessin farm, with its large courtyard and outbuildings, makes you wonder if all the farmers around here weren't aristocrats. Stay awhile and relax in the lounging chairs on the lawned grounds with the branches of mature trees overhead. It's evident that the renovation was done with much loving thought and care; revealed and enhanced are the lovely rafters, exposed stone walls, original fireplaces and spiral staircase. Bedrooms were given proper space and light, bathrooms well integrated – not tacked on as afterthoughts. The beds are big, the furniture regional but light and well-chosen, the windows large with over-the-field views. Suites are timber-strewn, some with canopied beds, and there are two rooms on the ground floor for easy access. Meals are a five-minute stroll to the sister hotel up the road (La Rançonnière). Perfectly placed on the way to Bayeux *and* near the landing beaches: you'll need two or three days to enjoy it all.

rooms	13: 6 doubles, 7 suites.
price	€88–€108. Suites €138–€178.
meals	Breakfast €10. Other meals at Ferme de la Rançonnière: Lunch & dinner €9–€43.
closed	Rarely.
directions	Reservation/check in at Ferme de la Rançonnière: Caen exit 7 to Creully on D22 for 19km. Right at church for Arromanches on D65. 1st on right.

	Vereecke & Sileghem families
tel	+33 (0)2 31 22 21 73
fax	+33 (0)2 31 22 98 39
email	ranconniere@wanadoo.fr
web	www.ranconniere.com

Map 4 Entry 83

Ferme de la Rançonnière

Route d'Arromanches, 14480 Crepón, Calvados

A drive through the narrow crenellated archway into the vast grassy courtyard and history leaps out and grabs you. It was originally a fortified *seigneurie* – the tower dates from the 13th century – to protect against English reprisal sorties after William the Conqueror arrived in England. Inside there are exposed timbers and stone walls everywhere. One amazing duplex has stone steps which lead down into a double bedroom then up a worn spiral staircase into the tower with another bedroom. Rustic is the look here; an antique butter churn in the corridor and a well-worn kneading trough in a large family room remind you that this was a working farm. Off the new restaurant there is a large, vaulted-ceiling, stone-flagged floor sitting area with a wood fire at one end making a perfect spot for after-dinner coffee. The bright breakfast room and terrace face south to catch the morning light. Young, efficient Isabelle Sileghem and her husband, with help from a devoted staff, keep this place humming. Book ahead for the best rooms. A wonderful place.

rooms	45: 35 twins/doubles. Manoir: 10 suites.
price	€45–€128. Suites €138–€158.
meals	Breakfast €10. Lunch & dinner €15–€44. Restaurant closed 3-25 January.
closed	Rarely.
directions	From Caen exit 7 to Creully on D22 for 19km. There, right at church for Arromanches on D65. In Crépon, hotel 1st on right.

	Vereecke & Sileghem families
tel	+33 (0)2 31 22 21 73
fax	+33 (0)2 31 22 98 39
email	ranconniere@wanadoo.fr
web	www.ranconniere.com

Map 4 Entry 84

Hostellerie de Tourgéville

Chemin de l'Orgueil, 14800 Tourgéville Deauville, Calvados

There were real stars in the 70s, when film director Claude Lelouch built his glorified 'Norman quadrangle' as a club for friends; now there are just giant photographs. But his adorable private cinema is still here, as are pool, gym and sauna. Timbers and stones are genuinely old; the all-glass ground floor is thoroughly modern. Open-plan sitting and dining areas are in blond oak, soft cushions and warm colours. The chef has an excellent reputation, by the way. Most rooms are soberly decorated with high-quality fabrics, matt satin curtains, beige carpet, the odd antique and those ubiquitous film stars. Ground-floor rooms and triplexes (effectively up-ended suites with the bathroom on a balcony between salon and bedroom) have small private terraces. Triplexes also have fine double-height fireplaces on their stone-flagged floors, plus two deep sofas. A dream of a mini Tudor manoir hides away in the forest, perfect for a honeymoon couple. A very special place to stay: Lelouch calls it "a hotel for people who don't like hotels". *Minimum stay three nights May-August.*

rooms	26: 6 doubles, 13 duplex & 6 triplex apartments, 1 cottage for 4 (without kitchen).
price	€125-€175. Duplex €190-€240. Triplex €270-€330. Cottage €280-€340.
meals	Breakfast €16. Dinner €39-€56.
closed	12 February-7 March.
directions	A13 exit for Deauville N177; left at r'bout D27; 1st left; 1st left D278.

Wilhelm Stoppacher
tel   +33 (0)2 31 14 48 68
fax   +33 (0)2 31 14 48 69
email   reservation@hostellerie-de-tourgeville.fr
web   www.hostellerie-de-tourgeville.fr

Map 4 Entry 85

Maison de Lucie

44 rue Capucins, 14600 Honfleur, Calvados

Named after Lucie Delarue Mardrus, the romantic novelist and poet who was born here, the 1850 house in the heart of old Honfleur is shielded by a high wall. It's an exciting new project for a charming couple who have put creativity and energy into the renovation. Sunshine illuminates panelled walls and leather settees, the parquet-ed salon has an Edwardian air, and bedrooms, elegantly colour-themed, are on three floors. Furnishings are immaculate and new – plum taffeta curtains, a burgundy velvet settee – beds are big and reading lamps won't ruin your eyes. Bathrooms are awash with potions and lotions, there are fresh orchids and vivid rugs, rolltop baths and antique chests of drawers. And wide views over rooftops and estuary. Our favourite room rests under the eaves, but all are lovely. In the courtyard's Pavillon, the old *guardien*'s house is now three guest rooms furnished in a deliciously decadent 1930s manner. Soak away your cares in the brick-walled jacuzzi and dine on *viennoiseries* at breakfast – either in bed or in the sun.

rooms	7: 5 doubles, 2 suites.
price	€120–€210. Suites €285–€330.
meals	Breakfast €16.
closed	25 November–20 December.
directions	Five minutes from A13, signed from Eglise Sainte Cathérine.

	Nadim Haddad & Muriel Daridon
tel	+33 (0)2 31 14 40 40
fax	+33 (0)2 31 14 40 41
email	info@lamaisondelucie.com
web	www.lamaisondelucie.com

Map 4 Entry 86

Château Les Bruyères
Route du Cadran, 14340 Cambremer, Calvados

Marcel Proust was indulged here when he visited the spa in Cabourg; he'd be pampered still. Through the imposing gates, down the beech and chestnut avenue, past the manicured lawns… expectations rise as you approach and are met on arrival. Monsieur is chef de cuisine, madame keeps thoroughbreds, their daughter spoils you with massages and essential oils and the family has an obvious predeliction for beautiful things. Château les Bruyèrres is a houseful of treasures and chinoiserie. Orchids on the dining table, modern art on the walls, plush red-carpeted corridors and fine repro furniture; it is very civilised. In the salon are big rugs on black and white tiles, a flurry of small armchairs and settees, a large open fire and glazed cabinets full of fine china. Ten tickety-boo bedrooms await in the 19th-century château and a further four in the 18th-century slate-hung manor that adjoins it; all ooze luxury and calm. Outside are several acres of parkland in which hides a turquoise pool. *Gastronomic & pampering weekends.*

rooms	14: 8 doubles, 2 twins, 1 triple, 2 singles, 1 apartment (no kitchen).
price	€105-€195. Singles €75. Apartment €230-€350.
meals	Breakfast €12. Dinner €35-€65. Restaurant closed Mondays & Tuesdays September-June.
closed	Never.
directions	A29 exit 'La haie tondue' towards Falaise & Bonneboscq, then D16 to Cambremer. In front of church, on left 150m.

	Madame Harfaux
tel	+33 (0)2 31 32 22 45
fax	+33 (0)2 31 32 22 58
email	contact@chateaulesbruyeres.com
web	www.chateaulesbruyeres.com

Map 4 Entry 87

Manoir de Courson

Notre Dame de Courson, 14140 Livarot, Calvados

A majestic 17th century manor of small brick and timbered splendour is a vision after leaving a narrow leafy lane charged with trees and wildflowers; spot the the short, round tower which dates from the 11th century. You breakfast here in the handsome beamed dining room by the truly monumental fireplace, and sleep in the guest quarters across the way in the renovated farmhouse. Your charming host has put her heart and talent into the redecoration of these in perfect harmony with the stones and woodwork of the ancient frame: linen curtains, large seagrass carpets on smooth old terracotta tiles, pale grey painted walls and original crooked beams, a pair of Napoléon III chairs, fabulous, walk-in showers in unusual bathrooms. Each unit has its separate entrance, and panoramic eyeful of this lovely old (listed) house. The pool is well hidden behind a hedge surrounded by exotic plants in large pots. When you wake at dawn all is idyllic silence as you gaze upon orchards, woodland and pastures; the cows in the distance seem immobile in their meditative munchings. Nothing jars and this is worth every penny.

rooms	3: 1 double, 2 suites.
price	€120–€180.
meals	Breakfast €10. Good restaurant in village, 1km.
closed	November–March
directions	From A86 towards Alençon & Le Mans, exit Orbec & la Vespière, then towards Livarot. 10km from Orbec, after water tower, 2nd right.

	Diane Marquet de Vasselot
tel	+33 (0)2 31 32 30 69
fax	+33 (0)2 31 32 30 69
email	dianedevass@aol.com
web	www.manoirdecourson.com

Map 4 Entry 88

Château du Mesnil d'O

Le Mesnil d'O, 14270 Vieux Fumé, Calvados

The approach to this 18th-century chateau lifts the spirit. Stone pillars and tall iron gates mark the entrance from the road, a tree-lined avenue set in five hectares of garden and parkland leads to the front door. The four bedrooms, one with listed wallpaper from 1905, are on the first floor up a beautiful staircase in white stone from Caen; the wrought-iron handrail and balustrade are listed. A square landing at the top with a long view over the park is a perfect place to spread your newspaper on a lovely old dining table; bookshelves burst with literature and line the length of one wall. Family portraits abound in the corridor along with the odd antique; fresh flowers are lovingly placed in the bedrooms and on the landings. Breakfast in the dining room is a feast for the eye: blue velvet chairs, chevron parquet floor, panelled walls with painted scenes above the doors and a wonderful Louis XVI buffet displaying its collection of old plates. One might feel overawed by such splendour, but the warm welcome of Monsieur Chanbaneix makes the visitor feel instantly at home. You will be loath to leave.

rooms	4: 3 doubles, 1 suite for 4.
price	€110.
meals	Restaurants within 5km.
closed	Rarely.
directions	From Caen N13 to Paris. In Vimont, right on D47 then D40 towards St Pierre sur Dives 7km; on right.

	Guy de Chanbaneix
tel	(0)2 31 20 01 47
fax	+33 (2) 31 20 32 87
email	+33 lemesnildo@wanadoo.fr
web	www.lemesnildo.com

Map 4 Entry 89

Château La Cour

14220 Culey Le Patry, Calvados

Warm and charming hosts, David and Lesley's attention to detail is impressive; not everyone can take a 13th century château, once part of the estate of the Ducs of Harcourt, and successfully blend such elegance and comfort. Expect bold décor – striped yellow wallpaper with pink and blue curtains – and subdued luxury: Lloyd Loom chairs, marble fireplaces and Egyptian cotton. One room has a curved wooden staircase that leads to a stunning bathroom above. A house for feasting: supper is served in the stone-flagged kitchen in front of the open fire, while English china, damask and candelabra set the table in the formal dining room for dinner. David grows for Lesley to cook, and his organic potager (three varieties of potato, 50 of vegetable) is a delightful diversion. High stone walls shelter it from unkind winds, fruit trees shade the lawn, and long narrow beds make for easy harvesting. Bedrooms face south and overlook the garden. The Cravens are keen conservationists; barn owls nest in the end wall of the house and there is good birdwatching. The Normandy beaches, Bayeux and its tapestry are within easy reach.

rooms	5: 3 doubles, 1 twin, 1 apartment for 2 (without kitchen).
price	€130–€150. Apartment €750 per week.
meals	Hosted supper/dinner with wine €32–€45; book ahead.
closed	Rarely.
directions	D562 south from Thury Harcourt for 5km; right onto D133 for Culey le Patry; left onto D166; 2nd right onto D211. Château on right approaching village.

	David & Lesley Craven
tel	+33 (0)2 31 79 19 37
fax	+33 (0)2 31 79 19 37
email	info@chateaulacour.com
web	www.chateaulacour.com

Map 4 Entry 90

Le Pavillon de Gouffern
61310 Silly en Gouffern, Orne

More mansion than lodge, Gouffern was built 200 years ago by a wealthy gentleman with plenty of fellow hunters to entertain. But the scale of this elegant 'pavilion' is perfect for today's traveller. It stands in an estate of 80 hectares and guests can walk, bicycle or ride in the private forest in total peace and seclusion. Big windows let in lots of soft light to illuminate the newly renovated décor: hunting themes, an Edwardian salon with leather chairs and oak floors, an unfussy elegance that gives a sense of the quiet class of a good country house. Recently renovated bedrooms, some of them in the well-converted outbuildings, are big and eminently comfortable (smaller on the top floor), new bathrooms have all the necessary bits and meals are served in the handsome dining room — the food has been much praised. In the grounds, the delightful Doll's House, built for children of another age, is now an idyllic suite (honeymoon specials arranged)… and you may play billiards by the fire in the bar. A nearby stable delivers horses to the door and, if you are lucky, the chef will cook your freshly caught trout.

rooms	20 + 1: 19 doubles, 1 single. 1 cottage for 4.
price	€80–€200. Cottage €250.
meals	Breakfast €10. Picnic available. Lunch & dinner €25–€50.
closed	24–25 December.
directions	Exit Argentan on N26. Hotel 7km from Argentan in the forest of Silly en Gouffern. Signed.

	Karelle Jouaux & Vincent Thomas
tel	+33 (0)2 33 36 64 26
fax	+33 (0)2 33 36 53 81
email	pavillondegouffern@wanadoo.fr
web	www.pavillondegouffern.com

Map 4 Entry 91

Hôtel Saint Pierre

6 rue de la Liberation, 61150 Rânes, Orne

Legend has it that a fairy left a tiny footprint on the top of the tower in this small town. They say she disappeared in a flash upon a forbidden word whispered by her husband, impatient at her tardiness. Madame Delaunay is the keeper of the tower keys and the owner of this large flint stone house, just across the road. So pocket the keys and explore the castle on your own – the surrounding park makes for a wonderful evening stroll. Monsieur and Madame are justly proud of their Norman heritage and of their region's top class produce. Marc uses these for his local dishes; you can also buy choice pâtés, tripe, calvados and *pommeau*, a light cognac with strong apple-cider overtones. As for the rooms, much care has gone into the coordinated drapes, bedcovers and wallpapers; bathrooms are on the small side. This is a family affair and the Delaunays obviously enjoy the profession and particularly the contact with guests. There is even a baby alarm system and parents can choose to give their children an early dinner and then enjoy a meal on their own, while the little ones join the land of fairies and footprints.

rooms	12: 9 doubles, 3 triples.
price	€48-€65.
meals	Breakfast €8. Picnic available. Lunch & dinner from €15-€38. Restaurant closed Friday evenings; light meal in room available.
closed	Rarely.
directions	From Argentan, D924 for Flers. After Ecouche, left on D916 to Rânes. Hotel just off r'bout in town centre.

	Françoise & Marc Delaunay
tel	+33 (0)2 33 39 75 14
fax	+33 (0)2 33 35 49 23
email	info@hotelsaintpierreranes.com
web	www.hotelsaintpierreranes.com

Map 4 Entry 92

Auberge de la Source
La Peleras, 61600 La Ferté Macé, Orne

Using reclaimed beams and stone, Christine and Serge built the Auberge de la Source – they did a lot of the work themselves – on the site of his parents' 18th-century apple press. Unfortunately that means no more cider, but they serve a superb one made just down the road. Both the restaurants – one smaller and cosier, the other with huge sliding windows – and the bedrooms were designed to make the most of the view down to the lake, which is the hub of a huge sports complex. Apart from windsurfing and a sailing school, there's riding, a climbing wall, archery, fishing and something called 'swing-golf', easy to learn, apparently. Children have a play area, pony rides, mini-golf and pedal boats. If you want real nature the forest is nearby where you will see huge stags without too much searching. The auberge has big rooms catering for families, all cosy with huge beams and chunky antiques mixed in with more modern furniture. The food is simple, centring on steaks cooked over a wood fire, with fresh farm produce to go with them. A great choice for families with small children or sporty teenagers.

rooms	5: 1 double, 4 family rooms.
price	€54–€90.
meals	Picnic €10.
	Lunch & dinner from €13.
closed	Rarely.
directions	From La Ferté Macé, D908 for Domfront Mont St Michel. After 2km right to auberge. Signed.

	Christine & Serge Volclair
tel	+33 (0)2 33 37 28 23
fax	+33 (0)2 33 38 78 83
email	auberge.lasource@wanadoo.fr
web	perso.wanadoo.fr/auberge.lasource

Map 4 Entry 93

Bois Joli

12 avenue Philippe du Rozier, 61140 Bagnoles de L'Orne, Orne

You are bang in the middle of pretty, fashionable Bagnoles de L'Orne, the only spa town in the area and with waters that flow at 24 degrees; boating lake, casino and spa remain. Bois Joli was a pension built in the mid-1800s for those seeking the cure; it sits on the edge of the Fôret d'Andaine in an acre of lawn, shrubs and sequoias. It has always been a smart getaway – Pompidou and Rommel stayed here; Rommel never paid for his room. Décor is traditional, understated, elegant. In the salon: comfortable chairs, books, newspapers, flowers in pewter vases and a piano you may play; in the dining room, fine rush-seated chairs and stiff white napery. The food is good: homemade brioche and orange pressé for breakfast; oysters, *magret de pigeon* and apricot tart for dinner. Slip off your shoes in a carpeted bedroom, immaculate with matching wallpaper and bedcover in toile de Jouy or pale flower. Old country wardrobes add character; staff are discreet. The hotel arranges mushroom-picking weekends in the woods, and there's masses to do in town: golf, cycling, riding, swimming, tennis.

rooms	20 doubles.
price	€66-€142.
meals	Breakfast €10.
	Lunch & dinner €19-€52.
closed	Never.
directions	From Argentan, D916 for Mayenne, follow signs for Bagnoles Lac. Signed.

	Yvette & Daniel Mariette
tel	+33 (0)2 33 37 92 77
fax	+33 (0)2 33 37 07 56
email	boisjoli@wanadoo.fr
web	www.hotelboisjoli.com

Map 4 Entry 94

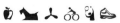

Hôtel de la Cathédrale

12 rue St Romain, 76000 Rouen, Seine-Maritime

In one of the cobbled streets of historic old Rouen with the cathedral looming over it – is this half-timbered hotel in a city of timber-frame houses. There is a large breakfast/tearoom with a non-working but imposing stone fireplace, exposed beams with their joists and comfortable armchairs. Views go straight through to the delightful little cobbled courtyard which is set with garden furniture, potted plants, small shrubs, a riotous creeper and geraniums that tumble from window boxes – a lovely spot for breakfast (an excellent one at that) or afternoon tea. Rooms are spotless and simple; the ones overlooking the street are the biggest, with old-style double windows and elaborately moulded cupboard doors. From some bedroom windows you see two Gothic marvels: the cathedral towers and the magnificent tracery of Saint Maclou – your soul will be safe here. Do remember this is an old building so insulation between the rooms can be thin. Laurent is running a remarkable-value hotel plumb in the middle of a city that cries out to be explored. *Car park: Hôtel de Ville.*

rooms	25 twins/doubles. Rooms can connect for family suites.
price	€62–€72.
meals	Breakfast €7.50. Tea room for snacks. Meals available locally.
closed	Rarely.
directions	In Rouen centre to rue St Romain; 1st street along east side of Cathedral to unload luggage. Pedestrian street so park in 'Parking Hôtel de Ville', a 5-minute walk from hotel.

	Laurent Delaunay
tel	+33 (0)2 35 71 57 95
fax	+33 (0)2 35 70 15 54
email	contact@hotel-de-la-cathedrale.fr
web	www.hotel-de-la-cathedrale.fr

Map 4 Entry 95

Le Relais de la Poste

60 rue Constant Fouché, 27210 Beuzeville, Eure

Generations ago this was an old postal inn; now the Bosquer family have proudly created a small, solid, very provincial town-centre hotel. Entering through blue archways you are warmly met in a friendly reception area. From here you are led up an old-fashioned stairway to carpeted, floral bedrooms with generous double beds. Rooms on the garden side are the quietest, especially on Tuesday, market day. Food is important here, and the bistro-esque restaurant is perfect for the place – fresh flowers on the tables and a majestic bar which spans the room. The regional food is specially well cooked and served; Monsieur has been recently annointed by "Restaurateurs de France". Town square activity can be observed from the small terrace in front; dining extends to the smaller terrace inside the archway. The Bosquers welcome families; their *prix fixe* menus and modest room prices should leave change for future exploration of this rich area. Beuzeville is on the road to Port l'Evêque, 10 minutes' drive from Honfleur, and has some interesting antique shops. Engagingly, unpretentiously 'correct'.

rooms	14: 11 doubles, 3 triples.
price	€47-€64. Half-board €120-€140 per room.
meals	Breakfast €7.80. Lunch & dinner €19.50-€40. Restaurant closed April & Tues noon & Thurs May-mid-November. Sunday dinner served only July & August.
closed	11 November-March.
directions	Paris A13 exit 28, left on N175 for Beuzeville. Between Pont Audemer, Rouen & Pont l'Evêque.

	M & Mme Bosquer
tel	+33 (0)2 32 20 32 32
fax	+33 (0)2 32 42 11 01
email	lerelaisdeposte@wanadoo.fr
web	www.le-relais-de-poste.com

Map 4 Entry 96

Le Moulin de Connelles

40 route d'Amfreville sous-les-Monts, 27430 Connelles, Eure

Bring your boater, hop in a green and red-trimmed flatboat right out of a Monet painting and punt along a quiet arm of the Seine after a morning at Monet's Giverny garden, 20 minutes away. Watery greens, pinks and that scintillating veil of haze that is so particular to this part of Normandy intensify the impressionist mood. Then look up at the vision of an extraordinary half-timbered, chequer-boarded, turreted manor house and you will have to pinch yourself, hard. It's only after a moment that you realise that part of the house is on an island; hidden paths lead through flowering bushes to a private pool. Young Karine keeps up the family tradition of quiet hospitality here while bringing the park and its flowerbeds up to snuff; bedrooms and restaurant are to follow under her magic wand. Step around to the garden and marvel at the rows of copper pots through the kitchen windows, reflections of the lovely meals served in the restaurant. Reserve a room with a balcony overlooking the river or splurge on the suite, with its bathtub in the tower. Bring your paintbrushes. *Boats for hire for trips up-river.*

rooms	13: 7 doubles, 6 suites for 4.
price	€120-€170. Suites €145-€245.
meals	Breakfast €13.
	Lunch & dinner €33-€56.
	Children's meals €12.
closed	Rarely.
directions	From A13 exit 18 Louviers on N15 towards Pont de l'Arche for 4km; right to St Pierre du Vauvray, Andé & Connelles. Signed.

Karine Petiteau

tel	+33 (0)2 32 59 53 33
fax	+33 (0)2 32 59 21 83
email	moulindeconnelles@moulindeconnelles.com
web	www.moulindeconnelles.com

Map 4 Entry 97

Château d'Emalleville

17 rue de l'Église, 27930 Emalleville, Eure

An elegant, listed 18th-century château, Emalleville has it all: perfectly landscaped and formal gardens, vast woodlands for walking (and autumn shooting), a tennis court, an ancient fallen mulberry that has rebuilt itself, a cosy suite in the converted beamed dovecote (a favourite) and fine rooms in the orange brick and limestone coach house and outbuilding. There is perfect toile de Jouy in some of the rooms and most beds are canopied. Contemporary touches here and there work nicely: photos and drawings dedicated to the dancer who took Paris by storm in Josephine, a colourful bullfighting theme in Seville, while Giverny is floral and feminine. All open directly to the lawns. Tucked away behind the precious vegetable garden and orchard is the pool. Breakfast is served in the *salle de chasse*: try the mulberry or wild plum jam. The lady of the manor's exquisite taste has woven a magic web from floor to ceiling, from Jouy print to antique wardrobe: you will feel like prince and princess here. And you're only 30 minutes' drive from Giverny.

rooms	8: 6 doubles, 2 suites for 4-5.
price	€80-€120. Suites €140-€210.
meals	Restaurant 8km.
closed	Never.
directions	From Evreux, D155 for Louviers & Acquigny. Through Boulay Morin, 500m after village, left to Emalleville. Right at war monument; château opposite church; ring bell.

	Frédérique & Arnaud Tourtoulou
tel	+33 (0)2 32 34 01 87
fax	+33 (0)2 32 34 30 27
email	tourtoulou@chateaudemalleville.com
web	www.chateaudemalleville.com

Map 4 Entry 98

Château de la Puisaye
Lieu-dit La Puisaye, 27130 Verneuil sur Avre, Eure

In their own 20-hectare heaven, two cats, two dogs, horses and a fleet of farmyard fowl. You'll like it here, too. A scatter of shuttered windows in a classically pale façade, this house oozes 19th-century country-house elegance. Large and airy, rooms are lightly furnished with antiques, huge mantelpiece mirrors and glass-panelled doors flooding spaces with light. The salon and library have elaborate woodwork while the dining room, with its gleaming table and silver candlesticks, invites a lingering breakfast – a feast of homemade pastries, jams and cooked dishes. On request, Diana – a stylish cook – will make dinner, perhaps some foie gras followed by truffle-stuffed guinea fowl; ingredients come fresh from the potager and 19th-century greenhouse. In the bedrooms, creamy paintwork and old-fashioned French wallpaper, marble fireplaces and snowy bed-linen create an ordered calm. Welcoming and relaxed, Diana, a former English solicitor, and her French husband moved here to indulge her love of horses. With carp in the pond, mushrooms in the forest and croquet in the garden, it's just about perfect.

rooms	5 + 1: 3 doubles, 1 twin, 1 suite for 4. Cottage for 8.
price	€75-€95. Suite €115-€145. Cottage €400-€650.
meals	Dinner €22; menu gourmand €37; Normandy platter with cider, €14.
closed	One week in winter.
directions	From Verneuil sur Avre on D839 towards Chartres, D56 towards Senonches for 1.5km; right onto C19 to château.

	Bruno & Diana Costes
tel	+33 (0)2 32 58 65 35
fax	+33 (0)2 32 58 65 35
email	info@chateaudelapuisaye.com
web	www.chateaudelapuisaye.com

Map 4 Entry 99

Photo Corel

brittany

Hôtel des Trois Fontaines

56740 Locmariaquer, Morbihan

Jean-Pierre is properly proud of his small, architect-designed hotel, set back from the Locmariaquer (Lock-mahry-a-care, a pause and accent on the first syllable) road. Enfolded by greenery and garden, the 10-year-old building has sound-insulated rooms and every other modern comfort. The theme is fittingly nautical. Floors are light wood, furniture is French-modern, the feel is pristine, and you can see the sea from several bedrooms. The rooms are wood-panelled in cabin mode, with floor-length cotton curtains in cheerful colours and matching bedspreads. The twins on the ground floor open to a little piece of private terrace each triple has a high ceiling and bay window. Best if all – if you love old stones – the megalithic site of Locmariaquer is just around the corner. Built between 4,500BC and 3,700BC – and excavated and restored during the last two decades – these superb ancient monuments include a dolmen and a burial mound. The village itself is typically Breton, and pretty; you can catch boats for trips exploring the bay and beyond and there are several little places to eat.

rooms	18: 10 doubles, 5 twins, 3 family rooms for 3.
price	€70-€130. Family rooms €110-€150.
meals	Breakfast €11. Restaurants 250m.
closed	14 November-25 March.
directions	Exit N165-E60 for Locmariaquer. Signed at town entrance.

	M Jean-Pierre Orain
tel	+33 (0)2 97 57 42 70
fax	+33 (0)2 97 57 30 59
email	contact@hotel-troisfontaines.com
web	www.hotel-troisfontaines.com

Map 2 Entry 100

Le Logis de Parc er Gréo

9 rue Mané Guen, Le Gréo, 56610 Arradon, Morbihan

The neat new building is a metaphor for Breton hospitality. The front is a high north wall – it may seem forbidding but once inside you know that it shelters house and garden from the wild elements, that fields, woods, sea and the coastal path are just yards away. Eric prepares itineraries for guests, boating is on the spot, swimming a little further away or in the pool on site. Warm colours, oriental rugs and fine family pieces sit easily on the tiled floors of the many-windowed ground floor, Eric's father's watercolours lend personality to all the rooms, and the unusual candlesticks in the hall and ancestral portraits, including a large Velazquez-style child in a great gilt frame, are most appealing. Salon and dining room open widely onto terrace and garden – wonderful places to relax or play with the children on the big lawn. Rooms, attractive in shades of red, green and salmon, are functionally furnished. Your hosts, their charming young family and their enthusiasm for their project – to stop being clients in boring hotels and do things properly themselves – make this an easy, friendly place to stay.

rooms	15: 7 doubles, 7 twins, 1 suite.
price	€72-€126. Suite €149-€265.
meals	Breakfast €11. Restaurants 3km.
closed	Mid-November–mid-March. Sometimes open Christmas.
directions	From Vannes D101 for Ile aux Moines. Ignore left turns to Arradon. Left to Le Moustoir then on to Le Gréo & follow signs.

	Eric & Sophie Bermond
tel	+33 (0)2 97 44 73 03
fax	+33 (0)2 97 44 80 48
email	contact@parcergreo.com
web	www.parcergreo.com

Map 3 Entry 101

Villa Kerasy Hôtel

20 avenue Favrel et Lincy, 56000 Vannes, Morbihan

Bamboos and cherry trees, koi carp and stone statues – the presence of the East is strong. Influenced by an East India Company trading post nearby (now a small museum), Jean-Jacques and Serg have taken the Spice Route as their theme. The 1914 building, once a bra factory, is attractive enough from the outside; inside it's completely captivating. From the moment you pass the two sentinel stone elephants, you're enveloped in luxury. The bedrooms are all different, with muted, subtle colours, lovely fabrics, intriguing pictures, fresh flowers… Some overlook the street, others the entrancing walled Japanese garden. Thoughtfulness and attention to detail are apparent throughout – even the buddha has a fresh camellia dropped into his capacious lap – but there's no hint of pretentiousness. Jean-Jacques and Serg have much experience in the hotel trade and know exactly how to make you feel cherished without impinging on your space. The day begins with a fabulous breakfast and you're just a five-minute walk from the centre of Vannes, where there are any number of good restaurants for lunch and dinner.

rooms	13: 6 doubles, 6 twins, 1 suite for 2-4.
price	€155-€160. Suite €280-€320.
meals	Breakfast €13. Excellent restaurants in town.
closed	Mid-November-mid December; first 3 weeks in January.
directions	From N165 exit Vannes centre; follow signs to Hôpital or Gare SNCF; then signs to hotel.

	Jean-Jacques Violo
tel	+33 (0)2 97 68 36 83
fax	+33 (0)2 97 68 36 84
email	info@villakerasy.com
web	www.villakerasy.com

Map 3 Entry 102

Château de Talhouët
56220 Rochefort en Terre, Morbihan

Your arrival is straight out of a Wilkie Collins' novel. Up a gloomy, bumpy, muddy lane smelling of moss and fungi, then wow! The imposing 16th-century granite manor house has views that reach all the way to the Aze valley and the cliffs of Rochefort en Terre. Jean-Pol bought the 1562 ruin – originally built by the crusading Talhouët family – 16 years ago, thus fulfilling a long-held dream. He's also restoring the grounds: woodland, terraced fields, wildflower meadow and a series of fascinating walled gardens, English and French. Floors are wonderful: either stone worn to satin or polished wood with Persian rugs. The sitting room manages to be both cosy and vast, with its old rose panelling, antique chairs and soft, deep sofas. There's a giant bookcase for browsing through, and a tempting selection of magazines. Jean-Pol will join you for a drink as you discuss the menu; delicious dinners are cooked by a charming young chef. Then to bed up an impressive stone stair; you will sleep under fancy florals and softly painted beams. Be woken by birdsong and a gentle view.

rooms	8 doubles.
price	€125-€205.
meals	Dinner €45.
closed	15-30 November.
directions	From Redon D775 through Allaire 9km; right D313 through Malansac to Rochefort en Terre; D774 for Malestroit 4km. Left onto small road 2km. Entrance on left; château another 500m.

	M Jean-Pol Soulaine
tel	+33 (0)2 97 43 34 72
fax	+33 (0)2 97 43 35 04
email	chateaudetalhouet@libertysurf.fr
web	www.chateaudetalhouet.com

Map 3 Entry 103

Château du Launay
Launay, 56160 Ploërdut, Morbihan

A dream of a place, another world, another time, beside bird-swept pond and quiet woods. Launay marries austere grandeur with simple luxury, fine old stones with contemporary art, rich minimalism with exotica. In the great white hall, a large decorated Indian marriage chest shares the Persian rug with two bronze stags. The staircase sweeps up, past fascinating art, to big light-filled rooms where beds are white, bathrooms are plainly, beautifully modern, light and colour are handled with consummate skill. The second floor is more exotic, the corridor punctuated with an Indian gate, the rooms slightly smaller but rich in carved colonial bed, polo-player armchairs, Moghul prints. For relaxation, choose the gilt-edged billiard room, the soberly leather-chaired, book-filled library or the stupendous drawing room with a piano (concerts are given), a giant parasol and many sitting corners. A house of a million marvels where you take unexpected journeys and may find yourself on a horse on old Roman roads or pike fishing in the park. Your charming young hosts know how to receive – and food is deliciously varied.

rooms	8: 4 doubles, 2 twins, 2 apartments for 2-4 (without kitchen).
price	€115-€180.
meals	Breakfast €10. Dinner €26, book ahead.
closed	December-March.
directions	From Pontivy, D782 for 21km to Guémené; then D1 for Gourin to Toubahado for 9km. Don't go to Ploërdut. In Toubahado right on C3 for Locuon for 3km. Entrance immediately after Launay sign.

	M & Mme Bogrand
tel	+33 (0)2 97 39 46 32
fax	+33 (0)2 97 39 46 31
email	info@chateaudulaunay.com
web	www.chateaudulaunay.com

Map 2 Entry 104

Château de Kerlarec
29300 Arzano, Finistère

The plain exterior belies the 19th-century festival inside – it's astonishing. Murals of mountain valleys and Joan of Arc in stained glass announce the original Lorraine-born baron ("descended from Joan's brother") and the wallpaper looks great, considering it too was done in 1830. In the gold-brocade-papered salon, Madame Bellin lavishes infinite care on every Chinese vase, gilt statuette and porcelain flower; sit in an ornate black and green chair by the red marble fireplace and soak up the atmosphere. Staircase and bedrooms have more overflowing personality, mixing fantasy with comfort, some fascinating furniture, lovely old embroidered linen on new mattresses and bathrooms of huge character. On the top floor, slip through a 'slot' in the rafters from sitting to sleeping space and discover a gold and white nest. Expect porcelain and silver at breakfast and reserve your crêpes or seafood platter for a candlelit dinner one night. Your enthusiastic hostess lavishes the same attention on her guests as on her house – and the bassets will walk with you in the park.

rooms	6: 1 double, 5 suites.
price	€88–€100.
meals	Lunch & dinner €25–€37. Seafood dinner €50.
closed	Rarely.
directions	From Quimperlé D22 east to Pontivy for 6km; château on left - narrow gate.

	Monique & Michel Bellin
tel	(0)2 98 71 75 06
fax	(0)2 98 71 74 55
email	chateau-de-kerlarec@wanadoo.fr
web	www.chateau-de-kerlarec.com

Map 2 Entry 105

Château-Hôtel Manoir de Kertalg

Route de Riec sur Belon, 29350 Moëlan sur Mer, Finistère

So many contrasts. Driving through thick woods, you expect the old château in its vast estate, but the hotel is actually in the big, blocky stables, built in 1890 for racehorses (who even had running water): it became a hotel in 1990 when the tower was added. The salon is formal and glitzy with its marbled floor, modern coffered ceiling, red plush chairs – and intriguing dreamscapes by Brann. You will be welcomed with polished affability by the charming young owner, and possibly by visitors come for tea and ice cream, a favourite summer outing. Even the 'small' bedrooms are big; château décor is the rule: brocading, plush lace, satin and gilt-framed mirrors. The 'big' rooms are exuberant: one has the full Pompadour treatment in gold, pink and white, another is richly Directoire in curved cane and coffee-coloured velvet. The tower rooms are cosier, old-fashioned posh, but have space for a couple of armchairs. Some bathrooms are to be modernised, yet all are solid good quality and the value is remarkable. Wild woodland walks beckon and, yet, there's a helipad – somehow the two worlds meet and embrace.

rooms	9: 6 doubles, 2 twin, 1 duplex for 4.
price	€95–€190. Duplex for 4 €240.
meals	Breakfast €12. Five restaurants 2–8km.
closed	November–Easter.
directions	From N165 west exit Quimperlé Centre to Moëlan sur Mer. There, right at lights for Riec & follow signs (12km from N165).

	M Le Goamic
tel	+33 (0)2 98 39 77 77
fax	+33 (0)2 98 39 72 07
email	kertalg@free.fr
web	www.manoirdekertalg.com

Map 2 Entry 106

Manoir du Stang

29940 La Forêt Fouesnant, Finistère

There is ancient grandeur in this 'hollow place' (*stang*) between the remarkable dovecote arch and the wild ponds. On the tamed side: a formal French courtyard, a blooming rose garden, lines of trees, some masterly old stonework. But the welcome is utterly natural, the rooms not at all intimidating. The eighth generation of the Huberts like guests to feel at home in their family mansion with a choice antique here, an original curtain fabric there, an invigoratingly pink bathroom to contrast with a gentle Louis Philippe chest — always solid, reliable comfort and enough space. Views are heart-warming, over courtyard, water and woods, the peace is total (bar the odd quack). Communal rooms are of stupendous proportions, as befits the receptions held here. The dining room can seat 60 in grey-panelled, pink-curtained splendour, its glass bays looking across to the gleaming ponds. Masses of things sit on the black and white salon floor — a raft of tables, fleets of high-backed chairs, a couple of sofas, glowing antique cupboards — and you still have space and monumental fireplaces.

rooms	24 twins/doubles.
price	€75-€150.
meals	Breakfast €9. 2 restaurants in village 1km; 2 at 2km.
closed	20 September-mid May; open by arrangement for groups.
directions	From Quimper, N165 exit Concarneau & Fouesnant on D44 then D783 for Quimper. Entrance left on private road. Parking a little away from hotel.

	Hubert family
tel	+33 (0)2 98 56 97 37
fax	+33 (0)2 98 56 97 37
email	manoirdustang@wanadoo.fr
web	www.manoirdustang.com

Map 2 Entry 107

Château de Guilguiffin
Le Guilguiffin, 29710 Landudec, Finistère

The bewitching name of the rough knight who became first Baron in 1010 (the King rewarding him royally for battle services with a title and a swathe of wild, remote Brittany), the splendour of the place, its vast, opulent rooms and magnificent grounds, seduced us utterly: it is a powerful place, grand rather than intimate, unforgettable. Built with stones from the ruined fortress that originally stood here, the present château is a jewel of 18th-century aristocratic architecture. Philippe Davy, the latest descendant, knows and loves old buildings, his ancient family seat in particular, and applies his energy and intelligence to restoring château and park. He repairs, decorates and furnishes in all authenticity; bedrooms are richly, thickly draped and carpeted; reception rooms glow with grandeur and panelling; superb antiques radiate elegance. In the park he has planted thousands of bulbs and bushes and cleared 11km of walks. He likes to convert his visitors to his architectural convictions and is a persuasive preacher. Guilguiffin is deeply, fascinatingly unusual.

rooms	6: 4 doubles, 2 suites.
price	€135-€160. Suites €170-€220.
meals	Good choice of restaurants nearby.
closed	December-February, but open by arrangement.
directions	From Quimper D785 for Pont l'Abbé until airport exit. Then D56 5km to D784 for Audierne. 3km before Landudec look for signs.

	Philippe Davy
tel	+33 (0)2 98 91 52 11
fax	+33 (0)2 98 91 52 52
email	chateau@guilguiffin.com
web	www.guilguiffin.com

Map 2 Entry 108

Hôtel du Centre
Le Port, 29681 Roscoff, Finistère

You can tell that this place has a young owner — there's such a fresh and refreshingly un-pompous atmosphere. It's right on the seafront in the old part of Roscoff, with a lively bar called Chez Janie looking out over the boats. It was here that the onion-sellers used to come to sign their contracts with Janie; her photo, in Breton costume, still hangs on the wall. Black and white stairs take you up to the hotel reception (at ground level on the street side). All is chic, uncluttered and colourful, ranged on the panelled walls are pictures of traditional local costumes and the furniture is blond wood and ultra modern. Also on this floor, overlooking the port, is a stylish, inexpensive and good bistro-style restaurant. More stairs, this time with red and grey bannisters and a red carpet, to whisk you up to bedrooms. These have a naïve charm, and are perfect: reclaimed furniture has been sandblasted and sprayed dove-grey; fabrics are warm red or striped tawny; sheets are white and crisp; bathrooms are simple, modern and very good. All in all, tremendous value and well-nigh irresistible.

rooms	16: 15 doubles, 1 suite for 5.
price	€59–€108.
meals	Breakfast €8. Lunch & dinner from €10.
closed	Mid-November–March.
directions	From Morlaix D58 to Roscoff. Hotel on sea front over bar 'Chez Janie'.

	Jean Marie Chapalain
tel	+33 (0)2 98 61 24 25
fax	+33 (0)2 98 61 15 43
email	conctact@chezjanie.com
web	www.chezjanie.com

Map 2 Entry 109

Le Temps de Vivre
19 place Lacaze Duthiers, 29680 Roscoff, Finistère

You can't help wondering what this 16th-century pirate's house would have looked like in the old days – or, indeed, what its owner would have made of its recent reincarnation. Revamped à la Philippe Starck, the décor is off-white with wooden floors, linen blinds and dark minimalist furniture. Splashes of red upholstery add warmth, as do fresh orchids in every room. The beds are large, the sheets are crisp and bathrooms are polished limestone, some with black marble walk-in showers. Some rooms are in the main granite and slate house overlooking the church and pretty square, and could be noisy in summer; others, in a 19th-century annexe with stunning sea views, are reached via a small walled garden at the back… let the waves lull you to sleep. A shame not to eat in while you're here: Monsieur Crenn's beautifully styled restaurant, of which he is owner and chef, looks out on the Ile de Batz and people come from miles around. So before you catch the ferry back to Plymouth, tarry here awhile and allow yourself some 'temps de vivre'.

rooms	14: 10 twins/doubles, 2 doubles, 2 suites for 2-3.
price	€95–€260. Suites €180–€260.
meals	Breakfast €14. Lunch & dinner €40–€110. Restaurant closed Sunday evenings, Monday & Tuesdays lunchtimes.
closed	Two weeks in October & March; one week in January.
directions	25km from Morlaix, in the centre of Roscoff, Place de l'Eglise. Limited parking in front of hotel.

	Line & Jean-Yves Crenn
tel	+33 (0)2 98 19 33 19
fax	+33 (0)2 98 19 33 00
email	contact@letempsdevivre.net
web	www.letempsdevivre.net

Map 2 Entry 110

Le Brittany
Boulevard Ste Barbe, 29681 Roscoff, Finistère

A very convenient place to stay for those travelling to or from Plymouth or Cork. This is an old Breton manor house with an imposing, rather austere looking façade which overlooks the harbour and is far enough away from the terminal buildings so that views are of the lovely Ile de Batz, only a short boat ride away. We must prepare you for the entrance to the hotel from the car park at the rear – quite a surprise. You come in onto a balcony on the first floor overlooking the reception area and look down onto a huge chandelier, an expanse of marble floors, lovely rugs and curtains which hang down two storeys. Behind the reception is a photograph of Madame shaking hands with Prince Charles: he might just have just had an excellent meal of locally caught fish in the dining room, with its arched windows and magnificent views of the harbour, or just had a brew in the bar sitting in one of the leather chairs. A warm welcome is a priority here and there's attention to detail, too – maybe a jug of fresh flowers in your bedroom or a bowl of strawberries. *Special half-board prices for those having thalassotherapy.*

rooms	25: 13 doubles, 10 twin, 2 suites for 3-4.
price	€108-€158. Suites €178-€258.
meals	Breakfast €11-€13. Dinner €29-€69.
closed	November-21 March.
directions	Exit Morlaix from N12. From ferry terminal right for 300m.

	Patricia Chapalain
tel	+33 (0)2 98 69 70 78
fax	+33 (0)2 98 61 13 29
email	hotel.brittany@wanadoo.fr
web	www.hotel-brittany.com

Map 2 Entry 111

Grand Hôtel des Bains

15 bis rue de l'Eglise, 29241 Locquirec, Finistère

Marine purity on the north Brittany coast: it's like a smart yacht club where you are an old member. The fearless design magician has waved a wand of natural spells – cotton, cane, wood, wool, seagrass: nothing synthetic, nothing pompous. Sober lines and restful colours leave space for the scenery, the sky pours in through walls of glass, the peaceful garden flows into rocks, beach and sea. Moss-green panelling lines the deep-chaired bar where a fire leaps in winter. Pale grey-panelled bedrooms have dark mushroom carpets and thick cottons in stripes and checks of soft red or green or beige or blue. Some have four-posters, some have balconies, others are smaller, nearly all have the ever-changing sea view. Bathrooms are lovely, with bathrobes to wear to the magnificent indoor sea-water pool and spa treatment centre. Staff are smiling and easy, the ivory-panelled dining room with its sand-coloured tablecloths is deeply tempting and children are served early so that adults can enjoy the superb menu. The luxury of space, pure elegant simplicity and personal attention are yours.

rooms	36 twins/doubles.
price	€125-€295.
meals	Lunch & dinner €34-€50. Excellent wine cellar.
closed	Never.
directions	From Rennes-Brest N12 exit Plestin les Grèves, continue to Locquirec. Hotel in centre. Through gate to car park on right.

	Madame Nicol
tel	+33 (0)2 98 67 41 02
fax	+33 (0)2 98 67 44 60
email	hotel.des.bains@wanadoo.fr
web	www.grand-hotel-des-bains.com

Map 2 Entry 112

Ti al Lannec

14 allée de Mézo-Guen, 22560 Trébeurden, Côtes-d'Armor

With dozens of English antiques, it is superbly French — soft and fulsome: an Edwardian seaside residence perched on the cliff, its gardens tumbling down to rocky coves and sandy beaches; only waves and breezes through the pines can be heard (the beach club closes at midnight). Inside, a mellow warmth envelops you in armfuls of drapes, bunches, swags and sprigs. Each room is a different shape, individually decorated as if in a private mansion with a sitting space, a writing table, a good bathroom. Besides the florals, stripes and oriental rugs, there is a sense of space with the use of white fabric and with views onto the sea or ancient cypresses. Some bedrooms are big, with plastic-balconied *loggias*, some are ideal for families with convertible bunk-bed sofas. Salons are cosily arranged with little lamps, mirrors, old prints; the sea-facing restaurant serves excellent food. The Jouanny family are deeply part of their community and care immensely about guests' welfare: they create a smart yet human atmosphere, publish a daily in-house gazette and provide balneotherapy in the basement.

rooms	33: 22 twins/doubles, 3 singles, 8 family rooms for 3-5.
price	€152–€349. Singles €82–€107.
meals	Breakfast €14. Lunch & dinner €23–€74. Children's meals €16.
closed	December–February.
directions	From N12 Rennes-Brest road, exit 3km west of Guingamp for Lannion onto D767. In Lannion, follow signs to Trébeurden. Signed.

	Jouanny family
tel	+33 (0)2 96 15 01 01
fax	+33 (0)2 96 23 62 14
email	resa@tiallannec.com
web	www.tiallannec.com

Map 2 Entry 113

Manoir de Kergrec'h

Kergrec'h, 22820 Plougrescant, Côtes-d'Armor

Come taste the experience of a perfect château in the hands of a perfect couple of *chatelains* whose ancestors bought the place on returning from exile after the French Revolution. Just 200m from the sea, exposed to the wild Breton elements, it was originally a Bishop's seat, built with hunks of local granite and fortified as befitted a lord of the 17th-century church. It is now a vegetable farm, run by the younger Vicomte, with superb grounds and a luxurious interior of marble fireplaces, gilt mirrors, antiques and a classically French salon flooded with ocean light. Guestrooms, big, gracious and richly decorated with thick hangings and old prints, have parquet floors, good rugs and lovely family furniture. The tower room, in an older part of the building, is deliciously different, more 'rustic', with its timbers and mezzanine and the new loo fitted to the original, still functioning 14th-century plumbing! The twin-basined bathrooms are all superb yet respectful of the old frame and breakfast in the more austere dining room is a Breton feast to linger over in good company.

rooms	8: 6 doubles, 1 twin, 1 family room for 3.
price	€110–€170.
meals	Restaurants in Tréguier 6km.
closed	Last 3 weeks January.
directions	From Guingamp, D8 to Tréguier, then north to Plougrescant. There right after church (leaning spire) & right again 200m along, white gates.

	Vicomte & Vicomtesse de Roquefeuil
tel	+33 (0)2 96 92 59 13
fax	+33 (0)2 96 92 51 27
email	kergrec.h@wanadoo.fr

Map 2 Entry 114

Château Hôtel de Brélidy
Brélidy, 22140 Bégard, Côtes-d'Armor

From upstairs you can see across bucolic fieldscapes to Menez-Bré, Armor's highest spot at 302m. The old guest rooms here are cosy, quilty, family-antiqued; a newly refurbished one shows off its blue and while toile de Jouy draped round an iron four-poster bed and a marble surround to sink in the new bathroom. Below are the beamed salon and billiard room, their vast carved fireplaces built above the two great dining-room fireplaces — such strength. The worn stone staircase and an iron man fit well; so will you, enfolded in the personal attention that is Brélidy's keynote. In the west wing, on the site of the original open gallery, guests in the suite can parade before waist-high windows like lords and ladies of yore. More modest rooms lie below, carefully decorated with soft colours, enriched with antiques; four have private entrances with little terraces and there's a huge terrace for all up above. In the gentle garden, the converted bakery is ideal for families and there's an indoor jacuzzi. Beyond are two rivers, two ponds with private fishing, and everywhere is utter peace. You can hire mountain bikes, too.

rooms	14: 7 doubles, 4 twins, 1 suite, 1 suite for 4, 1 cottage for 4.
price	€78-€195. Suites €139-€205. Cottage €113-€183.
meals	Buffet breakfast €12. Dinner €28-€34.
closed	January-March.
directions	From N12 exit Lannion-Tréguier to Tréguier. D712, D8 then D15 to Brélidy; signed.

	Carole & William Langlet
tel	+33 (0)2 96 95 69 38
fax	+33 (0)2 96 95 18 03
email	chateau.brelidy@worldonline.fr
web	www.chateau-brelidy.com

Map 2 Entry 115

Manoir de la Hazaie
22400 Planguenoual, Côtes-d'Armor

Chunks of Breton history – violence, greed and bigotry – happened here where country peace now reigns. The Marivins, she an artist/pharmacist, he a craftsman/lawyer, cherish every minute of its past and have filled it with family treasures: *la maison musée*. The salon combines grandeur and warmth, ancient stones, antiques and a roaring fire. Ancestral portraits hang beside Madame's medieval paint and pottery scenes. Tournemine's red ceiling inspired a powerfully simple colour scheme, plain furniture and a great canopied bed. Airily feminine Tiffaine has wildly gilded, curlicued Polish furniture and a neo-classical bathroom romp: statues, pilasters, a mural of *Girl in Hat*. Baths have sybaritic jacuzzi jets. Rooms in the mill-house, with fine old floor tiles and lovely rugs, open onto the garden – ideal for families. Row on the pond, glide from Hadrian's Villa into the pool, listen to the underwater music and whale sounds, sleep in luxury. Past owners have all left their mark: the admiral's anchors, the priest's colours. *Medieval weekends.*

rooms	6: 5 twins/doubles, 1 suite for 4.
price	€136–€214. Suite €214–€240.
meals	Breakfast €13. 30 restaurants within 8km.
closed	Rarely.
directions	From N12 Rennes-Brest road exit St René on D81; D786 for Pléneuf Val André. Just before Planguenoual, right, following signs, for 2.2km. Entrance opp. La Ferme du Laboureur museum.

	Jean-Yves & Christine Marivin
tel	+33 (0)2 96 32 73 71
fax	+33 (0)2 96 32 79 72
email	manoir.hazaie@wanadoo.fr
web	www.manoir-hazaie.com

Map 3 Entry 116

Manoir du Vaumadeuc
22130 Pleven, Côtes-d'Armor

Paradise. The approach down a long drive through mature trees and grass leads to the impressive granite exterior of this 15th-century manor. As you enter through the old, massive wooden door which leads into the manorial hall the whole place seems untouched by time. This is just as it must have been hundreds of years ago – a huge stone fireplace dominates the far end, there's a high vaulted beamed ceiling, an enormously long banqueting table and hunting trophies on the walls. It is easy to imagine former guests feasting and making merry after the hunt. A magnificent staircase leads to bedrooms on the first floor, decorated and furnished in period style. They are magnificent and comfortable, with no frills, quite masculine, à la hunting and shooting fraternity. All rooms are large and some are enormous; one of them has stairs leading down into a room the size of a tennis court. The bathrooms are smart and spotless. Such a courteous, warm welcome from Monsieur O'Neill; his family has owned this listed house with its superb dovecote, a keep pond for fish, a garden and acres of woods for generations.

rooms	13: 10 twins/doubles, 3 suites.
price	€90–€195. Suites €135–€225.
meals	Breakfast €10. Picnic available. Dinner for a minimum of 10 guests, book ahead.
closed	Occasionally.
directions	From Plancoët D768 towards Lamballe for 2km. Left on D28 for 7km to Pleven. Manoir 100m outside village.

M & Mme O'Neill
tel +33 (0)2 96 84 46 17
fax +33 (0)2 96 84 40 16
email manoir@vaumadeuc.com
web www.vaumadeuc.com

Map 3 Entry 117

Hôtel Manoir de Rigourdaine

Route de Langrolay, 22490 Plouër sur Rance, Côtes-d'Armor

At the end of the lane, firm on its hillside, Rigourdaine breathes space, sky, permanence. The square-yarded manor farm, originally a stronghold with moat and all requisite towers, now looks serenely out over wide estuary and rolling pastures to the ramparts of Saint Malo and offers a sheltering embrace. The reception/bar in the converted barn is a good place to meet the friendly, attentive master of the manor, properly pleased with his excellent conversion. A double-height open fireplace warms a sunken sitting well; the simple breakfast room – black and white floor, solid old beams, plain wooden tables with pretty mats – looks onto courtyard and garden. Rooms are simple too, in unfrilly good taste and comfort: Iranian rugs on plain carpets, coordinated contemporary-chic fabrics in good colours, some good old furniture, pale bathrooms with all essentials. Six ground-floor rooms have private terraces onto the kempt garden – ideal for intimate breakfasts or sundowners. Good clean-cut rooms, atmosphere lent by old timbers and antiques, and always the long limpid view. We like it a lot.

rooms	19: 10 doubles, 4 twins, 3 triples, 2 quadruples.
price	€58–€82.
meals	Breakfast €7. Snacks & wine can be provided. Restaurants in Ploufër sur Rance & Pleslin.
closed	Mid-November–Easter.
directions	From St Malo N137 for Rennes. Right on N176 for Dinan & St Brieuc; over river Rance. Exit for Plouër sur Rance for Langrolay for 500m; lane to Rigourdaine.

	Patrick Van Valenberg
tel	+33 (0)2 96 86 89 96
fax	+33 (0)2 96 86 92 46
email	hotel.rigourdaine@wanadoo.fr
web	www.hotel-rigourdaine.fr

Map 3 Entry 118

Villa Reine Hortense

19 rue de la Malouine, 35800 Dinard, Ille-et-Vilaine

A mysterious Russian prince, poet and aesthete, Nikolas de Vlassov, built this house at the turn of the last century as a tribute to Reine Hortense de Beauharnais, daughter of Empress Joséphine and mother of Napoléon III. It is the only property of its type with direct access to the beach; in fact, it is on the beach with its feet firmly planted on the rocks below. The entrance leads straight into a Versailles parqueted salon with views over the sandy Dinard bay and across to St Malo. A ceiling-height green and white ceramic stove from 1850 is there for beauty only, as is the grand piano. Memorabilia and portraits line the trompe l'oeil marbled staircase topped with a 17th-century Cordoba leather trunk. All bedrooms are named for queens: you can play Reine Hortense and sit in her silvered copper bathtub, then dry off on the balcony overlooking the bay; be yellow and sunny in 'Anne d'Autriche' with access to the veranda; or Elisabeth in blue and white with a canopy and draped bed. The Benoists will take good care of you here – all is charm, all is light.

rooms	8: 6 doubles, 1 twin. 1 suite for 4.
price	€140-€220. Suite €280-€370.
meals	Breakfast €14. Restaurants 5-minute walk across the beach in Dinard centre.
closed	5 October-25 March.
directions	From Rennes, N157 for Dinard, follow signs Centre Ville & Plage. Left around beach. Signed. Parking opposite hotel.

Florence & Marc Benoist

tel	+33 (0)2 99 46 54 31
fax	+33 (0)2 99 88 15 88
email	reine.hortense@wanadoo.fr
web	www.villa-reine-hortense.com

Map 3 Entry 119

Hôtel Alba

17 rue des Dunes, 35400 Saint Malo, Ille-et-Vilaine

The English aristocrat who built Hotel Alba as his seaside mansion in 1850 chose the site well. Only the sweep of the esplanade separates the elegant terrace from the beach; sitting in the bar when the tide's in, you feel you're at sea, gazing on an infinity of water. The hotel was bought by Monsieur Robert two years ago; since then it has been overhauled and redecorated. The results are fresh and inviting. You'll feel glad to be here, from the moment you drive down the narrow quiet street at the back to park beside the vivid flower beds under the palms. The reception area is manned 24 hours a day and Monsieur is warm and outgoing, with a decided sense of humour. The bedrooms are comfortable: soft lighting, restful colours – cream, oatmeal, terracotta – and natural fabrics. Headboards and wardrobes are lime-washed pine. If you're lucky you'll have a room with its own small balcony and wonderful views over the beach. Wander along the sand and you reach the old walled part of St Malo, the Intra Muros, and its maze of shops and restaurants.

rooms	22: 7 doubles, 9 twins/doubles, 4 triples, 2 family rooms for 4.
price	€70–€140. Triples & family rooms €130–€170.
meals	Breakfast €12. Good choice of restaurants nearby.
closed	Never.
directions	N137 for Saint Malo. Follow signs Thermes Marin, Hotels, Gare. Right at beach front on D155. On left, before Thermes Marin.

	M & Mme Robert
tel	+33 (0)2 99 40 37 18
fax	+33 (0)2 99 40 96 40
email	info@hotelalba.com
web	www.hotelalba.com

Map 3 Entry 120

Château de Bonaban

35350 La Gouesnière, Ille-et-Vilaine

The imposing gateway gives you a hint of what's in store long before the avenue of trees ushers you into the presence of this austerely splendid building. History weighs heavy: the first castle here was built in Roman times, the present one was pillaged during the Revolution. Climb the stately flight of steps to the main door and enter a vast hall with a sweeping marble staircase. Chandeliers, elegantly upholstered antique chairs, magnificent curtains and paintings set the tone of grandeur for the rest of the hotel. The 'Prestige' bedrooms are big, high-ceilinged and sumptuous; the 'Romantics' (on the top floor) are fractionally smaller, with sloping ceilings and a cosier, more modern feel. (If you're on a lower budget, there are simpler, cheaper rooms out in the old coach house, now converted into the Pavillon.) The restaurant – either in the full panoply of a state room or in the more intimate surroundings of a circular turret – is excellent. Madame is from Czechoslovakia and a gentle, thoughtful hostess. The grounds, flanked by the river, are wonderfully quiet.

rooms	32: 20 doubles, 3 twins, 8 family rooms for 3, 1 suite for 4.
price	€80-€185. Suite & family rooms €205-€285.
meals	Breakfast €12. Lunch & dinner €23-€45, book ahead. Restaurant closed Wednesdays.
closed	Rarely.
directions	N137 exit Chateauneuf; D76 to Cancale, La Gouesnière. Through village on D4 towards Dol. Hotel on right after leaving village.

	Madame Vlasta Siler
tel	+33 (0)2 99 58 24 50
fax	+33 (0)2 99 58 28 41
email	chateau.bonaban@wanadoo.fr
web	www.hotel-chateau-bonaban.com

Map 3 Entry 121

Le Valmarin

7 rue Jean XXIII, St Servan, 35400 St Malo, Ille-et-Vilaine

So close to the ferry terminal, this hotel has an unexpectedly large rose-filled garden with sunloungers and tables dotted around under mature cedars and a copper beech. The gracefully proportioned *malouinière* was built in the early 18th century by a wealthy ship owner. Most bedrooms overlook the back garden, light rooms with high ceilings, tall windows carefully draped to match the bed covers. Second floor rooms have sloping ceilings and a cosier feel, with exposed beams, white walls and pale blue carpets and paintwork. There are lavender bags in the wardrobes, plenty of books in French and English, and breakfast at the small yellow and blue dining tables with a view on the back garden. Or, have a lie-in and ask for your cafe au lait in bed before exploring the fabulous ramparts of the city. There are equestrian facilities and excellent thalassotherapy spas nearby or take an ocean ride to the islands of Jersey, Guernsey, Sark or Herm. Enquire about leaving your car at the hotel.

rooms	12 doubles.
price	€95-€135.
meals	Breakfast €10.
closed	January-February. Call for out of season reservations.
directions	In St Malo follow signs for St Servan & town centre. Left at r'bout 'Mouchoir Vert' for St Croix Church; right at church; 20m to hotel.

Gérard & Françoise Nicolas

tel	+33 (0)2 99 81 94 76
fax	+33 (0)2 99 81 30 03
email	levalmarin@wanadoo.fr
web	www.levalmarin.com

Map 3 Entry 122

Château du Pin
35370 Iffendic, Ille-et-Vilaine

Watercolourist and photographer, the brave, artistic Ruans have launched with passionate enthusiasm into renovating a small château with a ruined chapel, antique stables and a thrilling atmosphere. Traces of seigneury date from the 15th century; the owners' sense of space and colour will triumph. The original staircase curves up to the 'literary' guest rooms — mauve/silver Proust, ochre/gold Georges Sand, theatrical suite Victor et Juliette — and each shower is behind a great rafter. The vastly magnificent drawing/billiard room wears rich reds, has two large windows back and front plus a small window on a gable wall which sits on top of the mantlepiece; it's brilliant, and great fun. A small cottage with a romantic garden and interior courtyard sits in the nine-hectare park. Your gentle hosts love cooking; breakfast is a treat with crêpes, homemade jams and cakes, fruit and yogurt; they then share dinner and stimulating talk with you. This is a land of legends; the Brocéliande forest, the Emerald coast, the gulf of Morbihan, and Dinard and Saint Malo all nearby for exploration.

rooms	4 + 1: 2 twins, 2 family suites for 4. Cottage for 3-4.
price	€75-90. Suites & cottage €95-€125. Cottage €350- €500 p.w.
meals	Dinner with wine, €23, book ahead.
closed	Rarely.
directions	From Rennes N12 west to Bédée 23km; D72 to Montfort sur Meu; D125 for St Méen le Grand; château 4km on left.

	Catherine & Luc Ruan
tel	+33 (0)2 99 09 34 05
fax	+33 (0)2 99 09 34 05
email	luc.ruan@wanadoo.fr
web	www.chateaudupin-bretagne.com

Map 3 Entry 123

Château de la Foltière

Parc floral du Haute Bretagne, 35133 Le Châtellier, Ille-et-Vilaine

Come for the gardens – and Monsieur! He loves having guests, and the gardens, all 20 hectares, are his pride and joy. They date from 1830 when the château was built, designed to be fashionably informal. The château has the usual sweeping drive and imposing stairway and hall. Rooms are vast. The feel is hushed stately home, yet it's not the least bit precious and children are welcomed, even spoiled, with mazes and bridges, slides and surprises. Bedrooms have tall windows and are big enough to tango in: peachy Degas with its own dressing room, deep-red Renoir (these two interconnect – ideal for families); blue 'Monet' with its original porcelain loo; 'Sisley', a symphony in yellow; 'Pissaro', perfect for wheelchair users. Breakfast on homemade croissants (and, when Madame is around, Breton crêpes) or charcuterie and cheese. Then seek out the grounds – magnificent from March to October. Paths meander round the huge lake and past groves and secret corners bursting with camellias and narcissi, azaleas and rhododendrons, old roses and banks of hydrangea.

rooms	5: 4 doubles, 1 suite.
price	€120-€130. Suite €150.
meals	Breakfast €12.
	Many restaurants nearby.
closed	20-28 December.
directions	From Rennes & Caen A84 exit 30 for Fougères. Signed. Parc Floral par St Germain en Cogles.

	Alain Jouno
tel	+33 (0)2 99 95 48 32
fax	+33 (0)2 99 95 47 74
email	foltiere@parcfloralbretagne.com
web	www.parcfloralbretagne.com

Map 3 Entry 124

Photo Corel

western loire

Hôtel Fleur de Sel

Rue des Saulniers, 85330 Noirmoutier en l'Ile, Vendée

Noirmoutier has a personality all its own: this group of simple white buildings in its mediterranean garden is typical. Built in the 1980s, it sits peacefully between sea and salt marsh, long sandy beach and little yachting harbour. It is perfect for family holidays, with tennis court, golf driving range, big pool and outdoor jacuzzi. Bedrooms are good too, some in classic cosy style with country pine furniture and fabrics, others more bracing with ship-shape yew furniture and yachting motifs; several have little ground-floor terraces. The delightful, caring owners have humour and intelligence; their daughter's paintings are sometimes shown here. The chef has worked with the very best in Paris and meals are served by courteous waiters in the airy, raftered dining room or on the oleander-lined terrace. It is all clean-cut, sun-warmed, impeccable and welcoming. There is a bridge, but try and come by the Passage du Gois causeway, open three hours round low tide: an unforgettable four kilometre drive 'through the sea' where shellfish-diggers cluster. The island is, of course, very popular in summer.

rooms	35: 30 doubles, 5 family rooms.
price	€79–€155. Half board €73–€115 p.p.
meals	Breakfast €11. Lunch €25.50. Dinner €35–€46.
closed	2 November–March.
directions	From Nantes ring road south-west D723, D751, D758 to Beauvoir sur Mer. Road to Noirmoutier via Le Gois only possible at low tide. Otherwise take bridge. Hotel 500m behind church.

	Pierre Wattecamps
tel	+33 (0)2 51 39 09 07
fax	+33 (0)2 51 39 09 76
email	contact@fleurdesel.fr
web	www.fleurdesel.fr

Map 8 Entry 125

Hôtel du Général d'Elbée

Place du Château, 85330 Noirmoutier en l'Ile, Vendée

The general in question came to a sorry end, shot on the square for raising an army of Vendéen royalists against the Revolution, but was allowed, as an officer, to face the firing squad in his armchair. This house is where the rebellion was planned, a solid, powerful building down by the bridge, just below the castle, at the heart of life in Noirmoutier. The sea air makes the colours soft and limpid, the land and seascapes are flat and bewitching (Renoir was very taken with this spot), the inner garden and swimming pool were a haven for the general's privileged guests. Inside, the atmospheric old building is fittingly furnished with excellent country antiques, 18th-century fireplaces and fresh flowers. Bedrooms in the wing over the garden have been recently redecorated and are very pleasant indeed. Some of those in the 18th-century part, which also has a big terrace over the canal, have varied shapes but all bathrooms are excellent. The suites under the rafters on the second floor are ideal for families and a quiet, careful welcome is waiting for all. *Traffic can be heavy at peak hours.*

rooms	27: 23 doubles, 4 suites for 3-4.
price	€80-€150. Suites €160-€280.
meals	Breakfast €14. Dinner available at Hôtel Punta Lara, 2km.
closed	October-March.
directions	From Nantes ring road south-west D723, D751, D758 to Beauvoir sur Mer. Road to Noirmoutier via Le Gois only possible at low tide. Otherwise take bridge.

	Christophe Lamiaud & Olivia Savry
tel	+33 (0)2 51 39 10 29
fax	+33 (0)2 51 39 08 23
email	elbee@leshotelsparticuliers.com
web	www.generaldelbee.com

Map 8 Entry 126

Hôtel du Martinet

Place de la Croix Blanche, 85230 Bouin, Vendée

Madame Huchet describes the Martinet as a country hotel that is by the sea. It's a fair description: sitting by the pool in the garden the atmosphere is bucolic, but by the sea, just down the road, the feel is very different. Halfway down the Vendée coast, Bouin is a working seaside village – the pretty church was built in the 14th and 15th centuries – not somewhere that has sprung up for the tourists. Madame Huchet's son Jean-François runs oyster beds off the village, and busy little fishing ports are clustered along the coast. This is a real family hotel and Emmanuel, an absolute delight, is the chef and kitchen gardener specialising, not surprisingly, in fresh fish and seafood. Meals are either in a cosy blue-panelled dining room or in a more summery room with a veranda giving onto the garden. The rooms are simply but attractively decorated, some in the main house and some alongside the swimming pool. A great place to bring children for a holiday: the hotel is relaxed and informal, there are country walks as well as beaches and Jean-François will be happy to take you to see his oysters.

rooms	30: 23 twins/doubles, 1 triple, 6 duplexes for 4-6.	
price	€55-€74. Duplexes €96. Half-board €55-€76 p.p.	
meals	Breakfast €7-€10. Lunch and dinner from €23.	
closed	Rarely.	
directions	51km south-west of Nantes on D751 past Bouaye, then D758 through Bourgneuf en Retz towards Noirmoutier for 9km.	

	Françoise Huchet
tel	+33 (0)2 51 49 08 94
fax+33	(0)2 51 49 83 08
email	hotel.martinet@free.fr
web	www.lemartinet.com

Map 8 Entry 127

Château de la Cacaudère
Thouarsais-Bouildroux, 85410 La Caillère, Vendée

The 19th-century, golden-stone chateau had been abandoned for 50 years when the Montalts discovered it. She is Parisian, he Spanish; together they have achieved miracles. Madame, a pianist by training, has a fine eye for colour and a lightness of touch; music and château are her passions. (She also produces fine fruit tarts for breakfast.) Much of the furniture has been picked up on postings abroad – a wardrobe from a London auction house, a scroll-top bed from Korea – then put together with French flair. Bedrooms range from smallish to large; one has steps down to a pretty little pink room for a child, another a reading room in a turret. Bathrooms are similarly stylish and pleasing, one with a old curvy tub with Savoy taps, another with a trompe l'oeil ceiling of the sky. Pass the kitchen on your way to breakfast and catch a glimpse of polished copper pans – immaculate, spotless. There's a big, comfy sitting room with long windows looking to the garden; it's large and leafy, filled with copper beeches and pines, walled orchard and pool. Sheep graze peacefully, and there's an old garage for bikes and ping-pong.

rooms	5: 2 doubles, 1 twin, 1 family room for 3, 1 quadruple.
price	€75–€125.
meals	Barbecue available for guest use. Restaurants 5km & 15km away.
closed	September–April.
directions	From Niort, A83 to Fontenay le Comte, D938 for Bressuire. 1km after Place Viète, left on D23 for La Caillère. Before La Caillère, D39 right for Thouarsais-Bouildroux. 1km before village.

	M & Mme Montalt
tel	+33 (0)2 51 51 59 27
fax	+33 (0)2 51 51 30 61
email	chris.montalt@wanadoo.fr

Map 8 Entry 128

Château de la Flocellière

85700 La Flocellière, Vendée

You really need to see La Flocellière from a helicopter: the aerial view is the most striking – the origin of the name is 'Flower of the Sky', so that gives you an idea of how impressive it is. The castle – the part the family live in looks like a château, the rest is definitely a castle, complete with towers and battlements – was built around 1090 and is listed. You stay in the château itself: rooms are vast, gracious and opulent, with huge windows on two sides onto the gardens and park; most have showers camouflaged behind cupboard doors and baths. You can lounge around in the sitting room in the gallery, visit the library or explore the park and the magnificent kitchen garden below the ruined walls. The pool is tucked away nearby but out of sight and you may be given a full tour of the estate and the château. If you want to eat in, dinner is either with the Vicomte and Vicomtesse or on your own if you prefer. Lots to see round about: the historical enactment at Puy du Fou is only seven kilometres away so you can pretend the last few centuries never happened.

rooms	6 + 2: 5 doubles, 1 suite for 4. 2 houses for 8.
price	€120–€170. Suite €145–€220. Houses €1,400–€1,800 per week.
meals	Breakfast €10. Dinner €45–€54, book ahead.
closed	Rarely.
directions	From Paris A11 for Angers, A87 for La Roche sur Y, exit Les Herbiers; D755 for Pouzauges to St Michel Mont Mercure. Left to La Flocellière & to church; left on rue du Château.

	Vicomte & Vicomtesse Patrice Vignial
tel	(0)2 51 57 22 03
fax	+33 +33 (0)2 51 57 75 21
email	flocelliere.chateau@wanadoo.fr
web	www.flocellierecastle.com

Map 8 Entry 129

Hôtel Villa Flornoy

7 avenue Flornoy, 44380 Pornichet, Loire-Atlantique

Villa it is, a large one, in a quiet road just back from the vast sandy beach and protected from the sea-front bustle. Built as a family boarding house in the 1920s, Flornoy still stands in the shade of a quieter age: high old trees, nooked and crannied seaside villas in stone, brick and wood. Inside it is just as peaceful. After being greeted by the delightful new and young owners – enjoy sitting in the salon: garden view, four tempting 'corners', well-chosen prints and the occasional interesting *objet*. Rooms – mostly a good size, a few with balconies – have a pretty, fresh feel, nothing frilly, just plain or Jouy-style wall fabrics, coordinated colours and patterns, good modern/traditional furniture, excellent beds and white bathrooms with fine new fittings. Sylvie has refreshed some rooms in tones of ivory and string adding wood panelling for a more by-the-seaside feel. It is simple, solid, attractive and in the morning you will enjoy a generous breakfast in the light dining room or under the trees in the green and blooming garden. Really good value and a relaxed welcome. *Walking distance to beach.*

rooms	30: 22 twins/doubles, 8 triples.
price	€68–€100.
meals	Breakfast €8. Dinner €20–€22. Restaurant closed October-March.
closed	Mid-November-January.
directions	In Pornichet to Centre Ville, right onto Avenue Général de Gaulle for 300m. Avenue Flornoy on right just after Hôtel de Ville on left.

	Sylvie Laurenson
tel	+33 (0)2 40 11 60 00
fax	+33 (0)2 40 61 86 47
email	hotflornoy@aol.com
web	www.villa-flornoy.com

Map 3 Entry 130

Le Tricot

8 rue du Tricot, 44350 Guerande, Loire-Atlantique

Sunshine pours in past cream shutters and bathes the house in light. In the living room, windows face east and west so dawn and sunset are heavenly; once the last rays ebb away, the marble fireplace, piano and coat of arms come into their own. The dining room is as impressive; doors lead out to the garden, there's a black and white tiled floor and a splendid portrait of the Duke of Anjou – later Philip V of Spain. Bedrooms have exquisite Japanese fabric on the walls, polished boards and old rugs; French antiques are dotted about. Bathrooms are new, with showers or deep tubs and oodles of towels. The pale stone house dates from 1642 and is the largest inside the city ramparts, surrounded by a walled garden of box-trimmed flowerbeds and mature trees. Guerande is a fascinating medieval city and all the sights are within walking distance, the beach just a short drive. The rest of the peninsula could occupy you for weeks; go sea fishing, ride, explore the bustling harbours – and do visit the salt marshes, its fascinating salt museum and waterways of The Grande Brière, a haven for bird life.

rooms	4: 1 doubles, 1 twin, 1 twin/double, 1 family room for 4.
price	€90–€130. Family room €160–€195.
meals	Restaurants in town.
closed	Mid-November–March.
directions	Enter Guerande through Porte Bizienne, 1st right on rue du Tricot; house on right at end of cul de sac.

	Loïc & Andréa de Champsavin
tel	+33 (0)2 40 24 90 72
fax	+33 (0)2 40 24 72 53
email	letricot@aol.com
web	www.pays-blanc.com/chambres-tricot

Map 3 Entry 131

La Mare aux Oiseaux

162 Ile de Fédrun, 44720 St Joachim, Loire-Atlantique

A perfect little inn in a low-lying village deep in the watery wilderness of the Brière Regional Park. People even come for lunch by boat: it has the charm and simplicity of a remote staging post and the exquisite sophistication of an increasingly reputable table. Eric Guérin, an adventurous and attractive young chef, trained with the best in Paris and now applies his lively culinary creativity in his own kitchen. Appropriately in this watery landscape, he delights in mixing earth fruits and water creatures – he calls it "good French traditional with a zest of young Parisian". His pretty, low-ceilinged dining room, with rough rustic walls and smartly-dressed chairs, is the ideal setting for this experience; bedrooms under the thatch – three of them sit on stilts above the water – are for quiet nights after days of marshy discoveries and evenings of gourmet pleasure. Eric's artworld background is evident in his choice of gently contemporary, uncluttered décor and country antiques. The garden is green, the welcome genuine and the food... out of this world.

rooms	11: 9 doubles, 2 twins.
price	€80-€150. Half-board €160-€230 per room.
meals	Breakfast €9-€11. Lunch & dinner €35-€80. Restaurant closed Monday lunchtimes.
closed	9-23 January; 6-27 March.
directions	Nantes for La Baule, exit Montoir de Bretagne for Parc Naturel Brière to St Joachim; left at lights to Fédrun for 2km. Auberge opposite La Maison du Parc.

	Eric Guérin
tel	+33 (0)2 40 88 53 01
fax	+33 (0)2 40 91 67 44
email	courriel@mareauxoiseaux.fr
web	www.mareauxoiseaux.fr

Map 3 Entry 132

Château de Cop-Choux
44850 Mouzeil, Loire-Atlantique

The name refers to the old lime kilns on the estate and comes from *couper la chaux* – so, nothing to do with cabbages. Where to start: the elegant house, the pool, the animals, or Gerdie's works of art? Your friendly hosts are Dutch and a stained-glass window of an owl symbolises their contentment at having traded life in the lowlands for life in the Loire. The park is huge, with chestnut trees lining the approach and a menagerie of peacocks, chickens, goats, pony, cats and two Highland cattle (in no danger of being eaten). The house, built in 1795, is full of light; several rooms have windows on three sides. Gerdie conjures up works of art from nothing: a metal doll in a mosquito-net wedding dress, flower-pot men by the door. Bedrooms are dreamy and named after herbs. Violette has filmy blue fabric floating at tall windows, Romarin has exquisite carved twin beds (and an interconnecting room). Bathrooms are gorgeous. You can have a just-laid egg for breakfast in a pretty panelled room, or on the terrace; then amble across lawns to the pool. Jan makes his own wine, just enough to drink with friends.

rooms	6: 5 double, 1 twin.
price	€89-€104.
meals	Dinner with drinks €32, book ahead. Restaurants in Ancenis, 12km.
closed	Rarely.
directions	A11 exit 20 for Ancenis; N23 for Nantes; D164 towards Nort sur Erdre for 11km, right after Pont Esnault. Signed.

	Jan & Gerdie Liebreks
tel	+33 (0)2 40 97 28 52
fax	+33 (0)2 40 97 28 52
email	jan.liebreks@wanadoo.fr
web	www.cop-choux.com

Map 3 Entry 133

Le Palais Briau

Rue de la Madeleine, 44370 Varades, Loire-Atlantique

A glorious Palladian house perched high on the hillside overlooking the Loire valley. Built in the 1850s by François Briau, an early industrialist who made his fortune building railways, the house is palatial, lovingly restored and saved from commercial modernisation by the present owners. Faithful to the era in which the house was built, they have even held on to Briau's original furniture and fittings (of which he was immensely proud). Madame radiates exuberance and charm; Monsieur is an artist and designer whose impeccable taste has been stamped on every interior. A remarkable colonnaded stair sweeps up to the guests' sitting and dining rooms – pure Napoleon III. Bedrooms are light and large; three are blessed with magnificent views, all have separate dressing-rooms. Exquisite wallpapers, brocade canopies above polished mahogany beds, fine linen, flowers – all elegant and glamorous. Bathrooms are sumptuous and orientally-tiled. The grounds too are fabulous; large areas are completely wild and overgrown and contain the remains of a vast *orangerie*. A breathtaking place.

rooms	4: 3 doubles, 1 suite for 2 with children's bed.
price	€100–€160.
meals	Good restaurants nearby.
closed	Rarely.
directions	From Angers, N23 for Nantes. Château signed left at r'bout on entering Varades.

	Thérèse & François Devouge
tel	+33 (0)2 40 83 45 00
fax	(0)2 40 83 45 00
email	+33 devouge@palais-briau.com
web	www.palais-briau.com

Map 3 Entry 134

Château de Challain
49440 Challain la Potherie, Maine-et-Loire

There's a window for every day of the year, a fireplace for every week, a roof top (peak) for every month and a tower for every season; it's so beautiful in this 19th-century château you'll wish you could sample them all. Enter any one of the bedrooms and you feel you've stepped into an oil painting – each is lavish with old hats, quills and ink pots, pens, books and antiquarian knick-knackery, all perfectly placed. The walls are covered in silk, antique bed frames are topped with supremely comfortable mattresses and the US-imported furniture exactly fits the bill. In the bathrooms, exquisite Italian marble and onyx washbasins are matched by thick, fluffy towels. Breakfast on croissants, breads, fruit juices and jams; dinner may be a delightful meal from the château cook – or you may decide on a short jaunt to one of the excellent gastronomic restaurants nearby. The landscaped gardens are beautiful, with countless varieties of ancient trees and a lake – home to graceful swans and their gangly offspring. Meander the day away here, or venture out; perhaps a river trip at Angers, or a visit to the lovely white sands of La Baule.

rooms	4 suites for 2-4.
price	€200-€480.
meals	Dinner with wine €50, book ahead. Lunch available.
closed	Rarely.
directions	From Nantes A11 exit 18 to Candé, then to Challain la Potherie. Signed in village.

	Cynthia Nicholson
tel	+33 (0)2 41 92 74 26
fax	+33 (0)2 41 61 54 25
email	chateauchallain@aol.com
web	www.chateauchallain.com

Map 3 Entry 135

Château des Briottières

49330 Champigné, Maine-et-Loire

This heavenly *petit château* has been in the same family for 200 years and is now occupied by the relaxed and endearing Monsieur de Valbray, his wife and six children. *La vieille France* is alive and well and your hosts manage to envelop you in elegant living, while providing a family atmosphere. A magnificent library/billiard room leads into a small sitting room; if it's grandness you're after, share your pre-dinner aperitif with Monsieur in the huge, and hugely aristocratic salon, replete with family portraits, tapestries and fine antiques. Sweep up the marble staircase to the bedrooms on the first floor, feel the comfort of the beds (the newest are king-sized), gaze on park views. Several bedrooms have been recently redecorated but traditional furniture and fabrics prevail. Some beds are charmingly canopied, and the sumptuous family suite includes a small governess's room. Some bathrooms are marbled; the more expensive sport extras such as towelling robes. In the grounds is a delightful country-style *orangerie* built in 1850 which can be rented for two nights or more.

rooms	16 + 1: 4 twins/doubles, 3 doubles, 1 single, 1 family room for 3. 1 'cottage' for 12.
price	€90-€320. Single €90. Cottage from €1,800.
meals	Breakfast €12. Candlelit dinner €40, book ahead.
closed	Christmas, 3 days; 2 weeks in Feb.
directions	From A11, exit 11 Durtal to D859 for Châteauneuf sur Sarthe. D770 to Champigné; D768 for Sablé; left at Marigné sign; 4km further.

	François de Valbray
tel	+33 (0)2 41 42 00 02
fax	+33 (0)2 41 42 01 55
email	briottieres@wanadoo.fr
web	www.briottieres.com

Map 4 Entry 136

Château du Plessis Anjou

49220 La Jaille Yvon, Maine-et-Loire

You can sail off from the grounds in a balloon; two of the best *sons et lumières* are within easy reach, and so are the châteaux and wineries of the Loire. Built in the 16th century, Le Plessis has always been in the family and has been taking guests for years. Though large and very elegant, the château, set in 14 hectares of wooded park, is inviting rather than imposing, with curving tiled roofs, white walls and creeper-covered shutters. Dinner, at a long table in a rather ornate dining room with Roman friezes, could include salmon, duck with apricots, cheese and a crisp fruit tart; fruit (masses of raspberries) and vegetables come directly from a walled potager. One bedroom is striking, with a lofty beamed ceiling and beds set in a deep turquoise alcove. Beds are turned down at night: water and chocolates placed on bedside tables. There's a small pond brimming with fish and lilies, Piroutte the pony for rides, and Salsa, the fox terrier.
A guide available for many activities.

rooms	8: 6 doubles, 2 suites.
price	€120–€150. Suites €200.
meals	Breakfast €10. Hosted dinner with wine, €48, book ahead.
closed	Rarely.
directions	From A11 exit Durtal on D859 to Châteauneuf sur Sarthe; D770 for Le Lion d'Angers for 18km. Right on N162 for Château Gontier. After 11km right on D189 for La Jaille Yvon.

	Valérie Benoist
tel	+33 (0)2 41 95 12 75
fax	+33 (0)2 41 95 14 41
email	plessis.anjou@wanadoo.fr
web	www.chateau-du-plessis.com

Map 4 Entry 137

Domaine de l'Oie Rouge

8 rue Nationale, 49350 Les Rosiers sur Loire, Maine-et-Loire

Recline in bed and watch the Loire flow past the garden. The 19th-century townhouse sits in large peaceful gardens; in another, smaller building Christiane runs an art gallery. One of the two bedrooms with a view, Camélia, has an astonishingly ornate 1930's, brown-tiled bathroom with a tub raised right in the middle – Another room, Santal, opens to the garden and its wonderful trees; it has Chinese doors behind twin beds and a large Thai Buddha. Each room is individual, each lavishly French. Christiane's husband, a retired chemical engineer, spent some time working in India. He has swapped chemistry for cookery, buys much of his produce from a local organic farm (which, amazingly, grows 22 varieties of tomato) and serves up excellent local dishes. Christiane likes to host dinner, and this works well when a small number of guests stay; both your hosts will be happy to help you decide what to see and make the most of your stay. The gardens here are lovely – worth exploring if you are green-fingered or simply admire those who are.

rooms	4 family rooms for 3.
price	€65-€83.
meals	Dinner €25, book ahead. Restaurant closed on Mondays.
closed	Rarely.
directions	15km from Saumur D952 for Angers. Domaine on right at village entrance.

	Madame Christiane Batel
tel	+33 (0)2 41 53 65 65
fax	+33 (0)2 41 53 65 66
email	c.batel@wanadoo.fr
web	www.domaine-oie-rouge.com

Map 4 Entry 138

Château de Verrières

53 rue d'Alsace, 49400 Saumur, Maine-et-Loire

The château was built in 1890 by a certain Général Baillou de La Brosse to host the balls and grand soirées that he so enjoyed. The décor remains virtually unchanged. The house is in huge grounds – unusually so since it is right in the old town of Saumur – and aristocratic French cavalry officers used to hone their equestrian skills here. Your hosts speak impeccable English, are very welcoming and love to talk about the château's restoration. Every trace of necessary updating – central heating, rewiring – has been carefully concealed. Big bedrooms have huge windows; some look onto the park, others the elegant Academy of Cavalry, or the Château de Saumur. Bathrooms are as luxurious as you'd expect, with masses of thick white towels. Swim in the heated pool or be whisked off by a horse and carriage for a trot around the town (and don't miss the wonderful market). Yolaine, a refined and accomplished cook, and wouldn't dream of using any but the freshest vegetables – or of serving anything other than homemade jam.

rooms	10: 8 doubles, 1 twin, 1 suite.
price	€120-€280.
meals	Breakfast €12. Dinner €39.
closed	February, but open by request.
directions	A85 exit Saumur for Saumur-Centre, over 2 r'bouts. Left for Château de Saumur at 2nd set of lights. Verrières 100m on right.

	Yolaine de Valbray-Auger
tel	+33 (0)2 41 38 05 15
fax	+33 (0)2 41 38 18 18
email	chateaudeverrieres@wanadoo.fr
web	chateau-verrieres.com

Map 4 Entry 139

Hôtel Anne d'Anjou

32 quai Mayaud, 49400 Saumur, Maine-et-Loire

Any malign inhabitants of the château could have tossed rocks onto the roof of this elegant townhouse. It stands just below, on the banks of the Loire in a picture-book position. The main staircase has a fine wrought-iron balustrade and trompe l'oeil that gives the impression of a dome. The reception area, big and filled with light, has just a discreet desk to welcome you. The bedrooms on the first and second floors look either onto the river and the road, or onto the courtyard and château. Two of the rooms are especially fine: the Salle Empire has terracotta panelling and moulded friezes, and the Salle Epoque a splendid old chequered tiled floor and grey panelling. Another room has a fine parquet floor and a balcony overlooking the river. Top-floor rooms have solid old ceiling beams and views of the château. Some front rooms are plainer, look over the road and the Loire, but are in the listed part of the building, so soundproofed windows cannot be installed. The owners are breathing fresh life into this lovely old building, and doing so with a mixture of dynamic (ex-naval) efficiency and flair.

rooms	45: 41 doubles, 2 family, 2 apartments for 4 (no kitchen).
price	€76–€170.
meals	Buffet breakfast €10. Lunch & dinner €30–€55. Restaurant closed Sundays.
closed	Never.
directions	From Saumur follow signs to Saumur Centre. Along south bank of Loire on Chinon-Fontevraud road. Below château 500m after theatre.

	Jean-René Camus
tel	+33 (0)2 41 67 30 30
fax	+33 (0)2 41 67 51 00
email	anneanjou@saumur.net
web	www.hotel-anneanjou.com

Map 4 Entry 140

Le Domaine de Mestré

49590 Fontevraud l'Abbaye, Maine-et-Loire

History oozes from every corner of Mestré. A Roman road, a cockleshell for the pilgrims who stayed en route to Compostela, part of a 13th-century chapel – and the mill and tithe barn remind us that monks farmed here when Mestré was part of the vast Abbey. Most of the present building is 18th century: the family have farmed here for 200 years and keep alive the traditions of French country hospitality. Monsieur runs the eco-conscious farm, milking by hand. Madame makes fine natural soaps, and cooks; two daughters help out. All take pride in providing wholesome, home-grown food and elegant service. Big, rustic-style rooms are furnished with old family furniture – huge sleigh beds or brass beds with wool-stuffed mattresses and fluffy eiderdowns – and some have great views over to the wooded valley. The sitting room is pure 'Victorian parlour' with its dark panelling, red wallpaper, card table and leather-bound books; the dining room is simply delightful. A sense of timeless welcome and class enfolds the privileged guest. *60% of food is home-produced.*

rooms	12: 8 doubles, 2 singles, 2 suites.
price	€60-€70. Singles €40. Suites €106-€120.
meals	Breakfast €8. Dinner €24 (except Thursdays & Sundays), book ahead.
closed	20 December-March.
directions	From Saumur D947 for Chinon. Right in Montsoreau for Fontevraud l'Abbaye. 1st right 1.5km after Montsoreau; signed.

	Dominique & Rosine Dauge
tel	+33 (0)2 41 51 75 87
fax	+33 (0)2 41 51 71 90
email	domaine-de-mestre@wanadoo.fr
web	www.dauge-fontevraud.com

Map 4 Entry 141

Le Chai de la Paleine
10 place Jules Raimbault, 49260 Le Puy Notre Dame, Maine-et-Loire

Despite doing all the restoration in a 19th-century bourgeois manor house, opening a new hotel in the old wine warehouse *(chai)* and having five children under 15, Caroline and Philippe are unfailingly relaxed and welcoming. Perhaps their secret is that they want everyone to fall in love with La Paleine, as they did. Old buildings are scattered here and there: a hen house with nesting holes in its walls now used as a bike store, an old wash-house in the middle of the lawn with a stone trough and fireplace and hide-outs can be found in semi-secluded corners of the grounds. The brand new rooms are simple, uncluttered, stylish. Children will love having breakfast sitting inside one of two enormous wine casks, or *foudres*, big enough for six. There are two sitting rooms with soft green and beige sofas, bookcases for browsing, a fully equipped kitchen and an honesty bar. On the edge of an interesting village with an auberge just down the road for supper, you will find a great family atmosphere, homemade jam and yogurt for breakfast and a bag of walnuts to take home.

rooms	10: 4 doubles, 1 twin, 5 family rooms for 3-5.
price	€56-€58. Singles €49.
meals	Good auberge 200m; closed Wednesdays.
closed	1-15 February.
directions	From Saumur for Poitiers exit Le Puy. Take 2nd right at Le Puy Notre Dame, signed 'Toutes Directions'.

Philippe Wadoux
tel	+33 (0)2 41 38 28 25
fax	+33 (0)2 41 38 42 38
email	p.wadoux@libertysurf.fr
web	www.relais-du-bien-etre.com

Map 9 Entry 142

Auberge du Port des Roches

Le Port des Roches, 72800 Luché-Pringé, Sarthe

If you can see yourself sitting at the edge of slow green water of an evening, perhaps watching out for the odd fish, this is the place for you. Not grand – this is the Loir not the Loire, an altogether less glamorous river – but we can hear you saying: "Oh, what a pretty spot". Valérie and Thierry have been here about eleven years, are young, very friendly though a touch shy, and full of enthusiasm for their auberge. Their main business is probably the restaurant – they can seat about 50 people in two rooms and the riverside terrace heavy with roses and perfumed plants– but Valérie is justly proud of the effort she has put into the bedrooms and into the way everything positively sparkles. Rooms are not large but done in fresh colours, sky blue, for example, with crisp white bedcovers. At the front you will have a view over the Loir. A small lane does run past the hotel, but windows are double glazed. This is a very quiet, very French place to stay, within easy reach of the châteaux and very good value.

rooms	12: 9 doubles, 2 twins, 1 family room for 3.
price	€45-€60.
meals	Breakfast €7. Picnic available. Lunch & dinner €21-€45. Restaurant closed Sunday evenings, Mondays & Tuesday lunchtimes.
closed	February; 1 week in autumn.
directions	From La Flèche, N23 to Le Mans for 5km; right on D13 to Luché-Pringé. Through village for 2km, right on D214. Signed.

	Valérie & Thierry Lesiourd
tel	+33 (0)2 43 45 44 48
fax	+33 (0)2 43 45 39 61

Map 4 Entry 143

Château de Vaulogé
72430 Fercé-sur-Sarthe, Sarthe

A fairytale place! The Radinis, from Milan, wanted their children to have an international education so moved to Geneva, then found Vaulogé. Marisa and her daughter now run the hotel, and Marisa devotes herself to the garden, her latest project being the horseshoe-shaped potager for fresh dinner produce. The original part of the château was built in the 15th century: this is where the family lives. Later Vaulogé was remodelled in a troubadour style, giving it two circular towers with conical slate roofs; when the shock waves of the Revolution had faded, the aristocracy reclaimed their houses. If it's space you're after, stay in Casanova: a huge round tower room, with terracotta floor and amazing, near-vertical beams – excellent for propping books on. (There are plenty of books: Marisa feels a house is not properly furnished without them.) There are other round rooms – La Petite Tour is smaller, and ravishingly pretty. The whole place is enticing with flowers and little nooks and crannies, often put to good use as wardrobes or cupboards. The grounds are lovely, with lilies on the moat and a delicate stone chapel.

rooms	6: 3 doubles, 1 triple, 2 suites.
price	€200-€250.
meals	Dinner with drinks €50, book ahead.
closed	Rarely.
directions	A11 exit 9 Le Mans Sud. D309 for Noyen via Louplande, Chemiré le Gaudin. 1.5km after Ferc sur Sarthe, right at small chapel.

	Mme Marisa Radini & Micol Tassan Din
tel	+33 (0)2 43 77 32 81
fax	+33 (0)2 43 77 32 81
email	vauloge@mail.com
web	www.vauloge.com

Map 4 Entry 146

Château de la Barre
72120 Conflans sur Anille, Sarthe

Immerse yourself in ancient grandeur. Resplendent in 40 hectares of parkland, the château has been in the family since 1421. The portraits and furniture in the Grand Salon are as they were in 1784; join the Comte and Comtesse for welcome drinks under the vast chandelier. She is English, he French and both are young and enthusiastic hosts. Book in for a candlelit dinner (and special wines) served on fine china; move on to a brandy and a chaise longue in the Salon Rose – or billiards in the medieval *pièce à feu*, under the watchful eye of Kakou the parrot. And sweep up to bed. In one immense wing are five bedrooms, all different. Expect golden fabric walls and grand oils in Chambre Jaune; red and white stripes in the twin-bedded Suite des Fleurs; heaps of toile de Jouy and polished parquet in the serene Chambre Bleue; in the vast Chambre Marin, a canopied suite fit for a king. Some windows have balconies overlooking the grounds, bathrooms have antique tubs or jacuzzis, outside are bicycles from which you may discover the bucolic Perche. *Children over eight welcome.*

rooms	5: 3 doubles; 1 double bedded suite, 1 twin bedded suite, each with adjoining single.
price	€130-€180. Suites €260.
meals	Hosted dinner with wine, €40; by arrangement. Excellent restaurants 3km & 12km.
closed	Rarely.
directions	A11 Le Mans & Rennes, exit La Ferté-Bernard. D1 for St Calais. Château 3km before St Calais, to right directly off D1.

	Comte & Comtesse de Vanssay
tel	+33 (0)2 43 35 00 17
email	info@chateaudelabarre.com
web	www.chateaudelabarre.com

Map 4 Entry 147

Hotel Oasis

La Sourderie, 53700 Villaines La Juhel, Mayenne

Efficient anglophile Monsieur Chedor runs a happy ship. You couldn't fail to feel well cared for: bedrooms are spotless and well-equipped, there are leather settees in the bar and a personal trainer in the gym. The cosy, woody reception sets the tone: all the beams, joists, exposed stones and wafer-brick walls you'd expect from a restored farmhouse with outbuildings. Bedrooms are in the stable wing: some off a raftered corridor upstairs, some at ground-floor level. White walls and old timbers, attractive repro country furniture, comfy armchairs, writing desks and super bathrooms. The bar has an English pubby feel and serves decent food (there's also pizzeria/grill in the courtyard), the lounge is snug with plants, pool and piano and the breakfast room is a treat: red-clothed tables on a flagged floor and a big stone fireplace crackling with logs in winter. A shame to stay just a night, there's so much to see in the area, from the 24-hour race at le Mans to the 14th-century château at Carrouges. And you could squeeze in a round of mini-golf before breakfast. Excellent value.

rooms	13: 10 doubles, 1 twin, 2 family rooms for 3.
price	€40–€66.
meals	Breakfast €6.50. Light meals available.
closed	Never.
directions	From N12 at Javron, D13 to Villaines La Juhel. On right entering village.

	Steve Chedor
tel	+33 (0)2 43 03 28 67
fax	+33 (0)02 43 03 35 30
email	hoteloasis@hotmail.com
web	www.oasis.fr

Map 4 Entry 150

Photo Corel

loire valley

Hôtel Diderot

4 rue Buffon & 7 rue Diderot, 37500 Chinon, Indre-et-Loire

In the large sunny courtyard, contentment radiates from the very walls; climbers romp merrily up pergolas, roses peek around the olive tree, tables and chairs rest in shady corners. You'll want to linger here over breakfast, and the 66 varieties of homemade jam are the perfect excuse. In winter you have a low-beamed and charming dining room with a vast fireplace lit on cool days – a survivor from the original 15th-century house. Bedrooms feel like beautiful rooms in a family home and each is different in style: Napoleon III, Art Deco, contemporary. All have simple, elegant fabrics, pretty pictures, fresh flowers, a good supply of books. Those facing the courtyard are light and airy, those at the back overlook a quiet street, darker but cool and appealing. Further (ground-floor) rooms in the new *Pavillon* are modern with cheerful colours, those in the *Annexe* are more functional. Françoise and brother Laurent are naturally, delightfully hospitable, and having lived in this town all their lives they know its history well. Castle, churches, restaurants and river lie just beyond the door.

rooms	27: 17 doubles, 10 twins.
price	€51–€73.
meals	Breakfast €7. Great choice of restaurants within 10 minutes.
closed	Last 3 weeks of January.
directions	From Paris, A10 exit 24 after Tours. D751 to Chinon. Signed.

	Françoise & Laurent Dutheil
tel	+33 (0)2 47 93 18 87
fax	+33 (0)2 47 93 37 10
email	hoteldiderot@hoteldiderot.com
web	www.hoteldiderot.com

Map 4 Entry 151

Domaine du Château de Hommes

37340 Hommes, Indre-et-Loire

A tit had just made its nest in the post box and Madame was hoping that the guests wouldn't disturb it. No hunting, no shooting on this 178-hectare estate; lots of deer and birdsong here. The courtyard setting is certainly splendid: the moat and the ruins of the old castle, with one little tower still standing, make a thoroughly romantic setting for this great house, originally the tithe barn built just outside the castle wall. Inside, a vast baronial hall and fireplace welcome you and the atmosphere becomes more formal with a huge dining table, a pair of candelabra at either end. In the big bedrooms, antique furniture (beautifully Italian in one case) goes hand-in-hand with lavish bathrooms. Two rooms give onto the fine courtyard bounded by outbuildings; two look out to open fields and woods. In contrast, the stone walls and terracotta tiles of the Tower Room, which overlooks the moat, give a more rustic feel – its bathroom down a narrow spiral staircase. A paved terrace leads onto a large lawned area starring a huge walnut tree, actually two trunks twined round each other, then fields, then woods. Very peaceful.

rooms	5: 2 twins, 3 doubles.
price	€87–€115.
meals	Hosted dinner with aperitif, wine & coffee, €28.
closed	Rarely.
directions	From Tours N152 for Saumur. In Langeais D57 to Hommes. There, D64 for Giseux. Château on right on leaving village.

	Hardy Family
tel	+33 (0)2 47 24 95 13
fax	+33 (0)2 47 24 68 67
email	levieuxchateaudehommes@wanadoo.fr
web	www.le-vieux-chateau-de-hommes.com

Map 4 Entry 152

Château de la Bourdaisière

25 rue de la Bourdaisière, 37270 Montlouis sur Loire, Indre-et-Loire

A superlative, princely experience: a history-laden estate with formal gardens and native woods, a Renaissance château on the foundations of a medieval fortress, vaulted meeting rooms and a little boudoir for intimacy as well as a bright, floral breakfast room onto the garden. Guest rooms? François I has a bathroom the size of a bedroom, rich dark green beams and quantities of old books in his magnificent terrace suite; Gabrielle d'Estrées is gorgeously feminine as befits a mistress of Henri IV, who wears rich, regal red; Jeanne D'Arc has amazing beams and a loo in a tower (smaller rooms are less grand). The drawing room is the princes' own – they drop by, their books lie around, their family antiques and paintings furnish it. Authenticity and good taste are rife, the place is genuinely special yet very human and your hosts are charmingly friendly. The brothers de Broglie grow 200 aromatics and 500 types of tomato. Celebrate the real thing at lunch with a glass of Château Bourdaisière.

rooms	20: 8 doubles, 3 twins, 1 family room for 3, 2 apartments for 3-5 (without kitchen). Pavilion: 6 doubles.
price	€120-€220. Apartments €230.
meals	Breakfast €12. Dinner for groups only €41, book ahead.
closed	Mid-December-mid-February.
directions	From A10, exit Tours Centre for Amboise, then D751 to Montlouis sur Loire. Signed.

	Prince P.M. de Broglie
tel	+33 (0)2 47 45 16 31
fax	+33 (0)2 47 45 09 11
email	contact@chateaulabourdaisiere.com
web	www.chateaulabourdaisiere.com

Map 4 Entry 153

Domaine de l'Hérissaudière

37230 Pernay, Indre-et-Loire

Wander through wild cyclamen under giant sequoias, take a dip in the elegant pool, enjoy an aperitif on the flower-scented terrace. You could get used to country house living here, French-style. Madame – a charming, cultured woman – welcomes you as family to her home. The classic manor house, built in creamy tufa stone, wrapped in 18 acres of parkland, is all light, elegance and fresh flowers. Walls are hung with gilded mirrors and bold paintings, tables covered with interesting *objets*. Relax in the sunny salon or the clubby library with its books and games table. Bedrooms, overlooking the park, are large, gracious and subtly themed, perhaps with rich Louis XV furnishings or a blue and yellow Empire style. The Chinon suite, tucked away, is good for children; the former hunting room is wheelchair-friendly; bathrooms are grand with original tiling and marble floors. Breakfast is a gourmet feast. Madame offers light suppers, weekend summer buffets or will recommend local restaurants. Loire châteaux, Tours, golf and cycling trails (bikes to hire) are nearby; tennis, pétanque, croquet are in the grounds.

rooms	5: 1 double, 1 twin, 3 suites for 3-5.
price	€100-€150. Suites €115-€170.
meals	Breakfast €10. Occasional light supper €25, book ahead.
closed	Rarely.
directions	D959 toward Angers-Laval. 7km after La Membrolle sur Choisille left on D48 to Pernay-Langeais. After 2km, left on private road. Signed.

	Madame Claudine Detilleux
tel	+33 (0)2 47 55 95 28
fax	+33 (0)2 47 55 95 28
email	info@herissaudiere.com
web	www.herissaudiere.com

Map 4 Entry 154

Château de l'Aubrière

Route de Fondettes, 37390 La Membrolle sur Choisille, Indre-et-Loire

Even before the Comtesse greets you, the fairytale turrets and sweeping lawns drop polite hints that you are among the aristocracy. Yet the 1864 château has a family feel, its ornate towers good-humouredly at odds with the kids' bikes by the back door – evidence of the Lussacs' five children. Rest assured, it is sumptuous inside. The bedrooms are magnificent, each named after a Loire château — caress the beautiful old elm wardrobe in Langeais, sink into the deep blue and red comfort of enormous Chenonceau, compose your postcards at the Napoleon III writing desk of Villandry. One bathroom is faux-black marble with red carpets while others have jacuzzi baths; all sparkle with gilt-framed mirrors and light fittings. Downstairs you dine at individual tables surrounded by some magnificent portraits. Scallop salad, duck confit, vegetables from the garden and lavender ice cream may tempt you – but save room for bacon and green-tomato jam at breakfast. There's plenty to do here: swim in the heated pool, admire the formal gardens or explore the 15 hectares of grounds with views. Tours is nearby.

rooms	13: 8 doubles, 1 single, 3 suites, 1 suite for 4.
price	€95–€140. Single €70. Suites €160–€190.
meals	Breakfast €10. Dinner from €40. Restaurant closed Wednesdays.
closed	October-end April.
directions	A10 exit 19 to Tours Nord & Le Mans. Follow signs for Le Mans on N138; exit La Membrolle & Choisille. Signed.

	Comte & Comtesse Régis de Lussac
tel	+33 (0)2 47 51 50 35
fax	+33 (0)2 47 51 34 69
email	aubriere@wanadoo.fr
web	www.aubriere.fr

Map 4 Entry 155

Hostellerie de la Mère Hamard

37360 Semblançay, Indre-et-Loire

Watch the world from your window, the locals clutching their baguettes on their way home from the boulangerie. You are in the middle of a little village and it's peaceful here – yet Tours is no more than a 10-minute drive. Other bedroom windows look onto the garden, full of flowers and birds. The old *hostellerie* sits opposite the church and was built as a presbytery in the 18th century; now Monique and Patrick are doing it all up in a light, modern way. The four largest rooms – two are above the restaurant, in a big old house over the way – have a sofa that can double as a bed. The smaller rooms on the first and second floors are to have pale walls, light, bright fabrics and furniture hand-painted by the Pegués' daughter. Another reason to stay is the food – traditional but with original touches: leek flan with mussels; scallops with passion fruit sauce, roasted pigeon with stewed onions, a stuffed saddle of rabbit with crayfish. Local artists often hang their pictures in the restaurant- perhaps you will be tempted to buy. In summer you may eat outside, in the enclosed little garden to the front.

rooms	11: 7 twins, 4 suites.
price	€63-€86.
meals	Breakfast €8.50.
	Lunch & dinner €18-€46.
	Restaurant closed Sun eve & Mon.
	Traditional restaurant 5km.
closed	15 February-15 March.
directions	From Tours, N138 for Le Mans, then left for Semblançay. Hotel in centre of village, opposite church.

	M & Mme Pegué
tel	+33 (0)2 47 56 62 04
fax	+33 (0)2 47 56 53 61
email	reservation@lamerehamard.com
web	www.lamerehamard.com

Map 4 Entry 156

Le Fleuray Hôtel
37530 Cangey, Indre-et-Loire

Perfect if, like most of our readers, you have a helicopter — or a hot-air balloon. Pretty perfect, too, for ordinary mortals, for Peter and Hazel have created a haven of peace. The raw material was ideal: a solid, handsome old manor house with duck pond and barns, mature trees and bushes: all that was needed to persuade them to settle. The rooms in the barn are just right for families; slightly cut off from the rest, their French windows open onto the garden. The Newingtons are unstuffy and easy-going, genuinely enjoying the company of visitors. Truly a family affair; Jordan and Cassie, the older children, are a big part of the picture and are rapidly becoming professionals. They have created a slightly English mood, with lightly floral sofas into which you can sink, bookcases, flowers and prints — and a plain carpet in the sitting room. The bedrooms are big and fresh, many with white cane furniture and floral covers on the huge bed. It must be fun to dine outside on the patio under parasols, on pink tablecloths and green chairs. It's fun in the winter, too, with an open fire and Hazel's superb cooking.

rooms	15: 9 twins/doubles, 6 family rooms with terrace.
price	€78-€115.
meals	Breakfast €10. Dinner €28-€38. Children's meals €15.50.
closed	One week in November; one week in January. Open Christmas.
directions	From A10 exit 18 Amboise & Château Renault. D31 to Autrèche. Left on D55 to Dame Marie Les Bois. Right on D74 for Cangey. 8km from exit.

	Newington Family
tel	+33 (0)2 47 56 09 25
fax	+33 (0)2 47 56 93 97
email	lefleurayhotel@wanadoo.fr
web	www.lefleurayhotel.com

Map 4 Entry 157

Domaine des Bidaudières

Rue du Peu Morier, 37210 Vouvray, Indre-et-Loire

Sylvie and Pascal Suzanne have made their mark on this classic, creamy-stoned ex-wine-grower's property. Unstuffy and outgoing, this young couple lend a stylish sophistication to the place and produce a small quantity of their own wine, having planted new vineyards to the terraced rear. Cypress trees stand on the hillside behind and give an Italianate feel. Bedrooms are fresh and contemporary, each immaculate and carpeted and decorated in Designers Guild fabrics. All are light, south-facing and have valley views. The sitting room, where the kitchen used to be, was actually built into the rock – a hugely attractive, stone-floored room with a low rocky ceiling and an open fire at one end. Guests can idle away the afternoon in the elegant swimming pool on the lower terrace which lies alongside the carefully restored *orangerie*. There is even a direct access to the pool via the lift in the main house. Families are welcome to stay in the more rustic 'troglodyte' apartment nearby. *Cash or Euro cheque only.*

rooms	6 + 1: 4 doubles, 1 twin, 1 suite for 3, 1 cottage for 3 (without kitchen). 1 apartment for 5.
price	€110. Suite €130. Cottage €95. Apartment €140.
meals	Meals available locally.
closed	Rarely.
directions	From Paris, A10 exit 20 Vouvray onto N152 for Amboise. In Vouvray D46 for Vernou sur Brenne; 2nd street on left after r'bout.

	M & Mme Pascal Suzanne
tel	+33 (0)2 47 52 66 85
fax	+33 (0)2 47 52 62 17
email	contact@bidaudieres.com
web	www.bidaudieres.com

Map 4 Entry 158

Château de Perreux

36 rue Pocé, 37530 Nazelles, Indre-et-Loire

General de Gaulle's sister lived here during the war and took in refugees. Now Eric and Rudolph receive guests – in style. There are two salons with antiques and old paintings, one rich red, with a remarkable fireplace, the other yellow velvet; corridors are Persian-rugged, bath towels are embossed with the château's name. Eric was in the diplomatic service and has picked up treasures on his travels, Rudolphe is a designer and has re-upholstered most of those treasures himself. Both are charming, full of stories about this restoration and their new life. Bedrooms are period pieces: one suite is dove-grey and pale blue, another blue and gold with paintings of Baghdad; two big rooms are in a tower, two smaller have a Japanese feel. All are bright and sunny with park or valley views. These seven hectares, with pool, are reached via two tunnels under the road; there are some amazing trees, a small island and river (you may fish) and a listed, 19th-century aquarium-grotto. Ungrand people in the grandest of settings – and two sweet dogs, one named Sarah, the other William.

rooms	7+ 1: 5 suites, 2 singles. 1 small house for 3-4.
price	Suites €150. Singles €120. House €210.
meals	Dinner €30-€40, book ahead.
closed	Rarely.
directions	From Paris, A10 exit 18 Amboise; towards Rocade for 10km. Right at 1st r'bout for Pocé, then towards Nazelles on D1.

	Eric Nicolas & Rudolphe Beduchaud
tel	+33 (0)2 47 57 41 50
fax	+33 (0)2 47 57 58 57
email	chateaudeperreux@wanadoo.fr
web	www.chateau-de-perreux.com

Map 4 Entry 159

Le Vieux Manoir

13 rue Rabelais, 37400 Amboise, Indre-et-Loire

Just imagine visiting Amboise, doing a whistle-stop tour of the magnificent château, a spot of lunch, and then staying in a beautiful manoir from whose wine cellars runs a secret tunnel to the château's very grounds. Gloria ran a wonderful B&B in Boston before resettling in France with her husband to fulfil a dream of restoring a 17th-century jewel and its Maison de Gardien. The litte two-storey house is a dream of a two-bedroom cottage with a sitting room and a kitchen only Americans know how to do – perfect for families with children over five. In the main house, rooms are filled with fascinating French brocante and family antiques. Bedrooms bow to the ladies: Colette is beamed and bright in a red and white theme, Madame de Lafayette's hand basin sits in an antique dresser, bevelled mirrors and hand-made tiles sparkle in the bathrooms. There's a salon, a snooze-friendly library and a convivial conservatory for fine breakfasting which opens onto a cheery French-formal town garden. With 30 restaurants nearby, your only problem will be in choosing where to step out for dinner.

rooms	7: 5 doubles, 1 triple, 1 apartment for 4 (without kitchen).
price	€125-€170. Apartment €170-€245.
meals	Restaurants in town.
closed	November-February. Call for out of season reservations.
directions	In downtown Amboise, from Quai Général de Gaulle, turn onto Ave des Martyrs at post office. Rue Rabelais on left after 150m, one way, narrow.

	Gloria & Bob Belknap
tel	+33 (0)2 47 30 41 27
fax	+33 (0)2 47 30 41 27
email	info@le-vieux-manoir.com
web	www.le-vieux-manoir.com

Map 4 Entry 160

Le Manoir Les Minimes

34 quai Charles Guinot, 37400 Amboise, Indre-et-Loire

Every detail has been thought out with tender care, lovingly chosen antiques and *objets* placed to create a light sophistication. A far cry from the Minimes order who had a convent here until it was destroyed in the French Revolution; then this noble townhouse took the site. Between majestic Loire and historic castle, the manor has 18th-century grace and generous windows that look onto its big courtyard, the castle and the lustrous river. Before opening Les Minimes in 1998, the charmingly young and enthusiastic Eric Deforges was a fashion designer, hence his faultless eye for fabric, colour and detail. Exquisitely decorated rooms are big – slightly smaller on the top floor, with beams and river views from their dormers – and have luxurious bathrooms. The masterpiece is the suite where the toile de Jouy wall fabric seems to be one single piece. The elegant chequered hall leads to a series of interconnecting salons. There's a smaller, more intimate television room and a breakfast room in soft yellow and grey. With fresh flowers everywhere, this feels more like a smart home than a formal hotel.

rooms	15: 13 twins/doubles, 2 suites.
price	€95–€160. Suites €195–€230.
meals	Breakfast €11.50. Will provide menus & make reservations in local restaurants within walking distance.
closed	2006: Mid-Nov–mid-December. 2007: Mid-January–mid-February.
directions	From A10 for Amboise. Over Loire, then right on D751 for town centre. Hotel on left approaching town centre.

	Eric Deforges & Patrice Longet
tel	+33 (0)2 47 30 40 40
fax	+33 (0)2 47 30 40 77
email	manoir-les-minimes@wanadoo.fr
web	www.manoirlesminimes.com

Map 4 Entry 161

Château des Ormeaux

Route de Noizay, D1-Nazelles, 37530 Amboise, Indre-et-Loire

The view's the thing   from the turreted 19th-century château built around a
15th-century tower, take in the glories of 27 hestares. Corner rooms on two
floors – original panelling on the first floor, sloping ceilings on the second – have
tiny little *boudoirs* off the main room in the turret. A decent size, with elaborate
bedcovers and drapes and massive bathrooms, the bathrooms are grand in a turn-
of-the-century way. One room, blue and gold, has a marble fireplace and an
armoire à glace, a wall of mirrors hidden behind an apparently ordinary cupboard;
another, decorated in ochre and maroon, a crystal chandelier and plushly canopied
bed. Two new rooms have been carefully restored in the 18th-century *logis*, the
former home of the château 'manager', with visible beams and lime rendering.
Everyone dines at a long table in the elegant dining room, where meals are served
by one or more of your hosts – there are three in total – and enhanced by
background Bach and candlelight. Best of all, from wherever you stand (or swim)
those valley views are superb.

rooms	8: 5 doubles, 3 twins.
price	€112–€150.
meals	Dinner at communal table, €41, book ahead.
closed	Rarely.
directions	From Paris A10 exit 18 Amboise, D31 towards Amboise. Right at Autrèche to D55 to Montreuil en Touraine; D5 to Nazelle; right on D1 towards Noizay; Chateau end of village after La Bardouillère.

Emmanuel Guenot & Eric Fontbonnat

tel	+33 (0)2 47 23 26 51
fax	+33 (0)2 47 23 19 31
email	contact@chateaudesormeaux.fr
web	www.chateaudesormeaux.fr

Map 4 Entry 162

Hôtel du Bon Laboureur et du Château

6 rue du Docteur Bretonneau, 37150 Chenonceaux, Indre-et-Loire

This little hotel, in the village of Chenonceaux, a mere stroll from the château, started life as a coaching inn in the 18th century. Now in the hands of the fourth generation, it has expanded into an adjoining building, the old village school, and into a somewhat grander building with a rather pretentious tower known tongue-in-cheek as 'The Manor'. The bedrooms are light and airy with plenty of space and are kept in tiptop condition. One is in psychedelic green and yellow, another is more traditional in pink and another, smaller, in fresh blue and white. The heart of the hotel is in the original building, with its elegant 18th-century style dining room and a simpler, more relaxed one next to it. In summer, tables with starched white cloths, candles and flowers are set on the terrace under the trees. A good spot for seeing the châteaux with children as there are family rooms and the garden has a pool. Amboise, Chaumont, Chambord and other châteaux are within easy reach so you can make your visits and return with time for a swim and a cocktail before dinner. A large potager behind the hotel supplies vegetables.

rooms	27: 24 doubles, 3 apartments for 4 (without kitchen).
price	€80–€130. Apartments €145–€180.
meals	Breakfast €9. Picnic €9. Dinner €29–€65. Restaurant closed low season Wednesday lunch & Thursdays.
closed	Mid–November–mid–December; January.
directions	From Blois, cross Loire onto D751 then D764 to Montrichard. Follow signs to Chenonceaux; on right.

	Isabelle & Antoine Jeudi
tel	+33 (0)2 47 23 90 02
fax	+33 (0)2 47 23 82 01
email	laboureur@wanadoo.fr
web	www.bonlaboureur.com

Map 4 Entry 163

Le Cheval Blanc
5 place de l'Eglise, 371501 Bléré, Indre-et-Loire

Set in the flowered, cobbled and car-free church square of old Bléré, the White Horse Inn has been known for years as one of the best tables in the highly gastronomic Royal Valley and Michel Blériot is keeping that reputation very much alive. He calls his cuisine "lightened classical" and plans his creations around fresh seasonal ingredients. Eating is either in the traditional French atmosphere of original beams, high, rich-draped windows, pale Louis XVI chairs, tall-stemmed glasses and fresh flowers on snow-white cloths, where a certain formality reigns in honour of the fine food or, in warm weather, outside in the delightful creeper-clad courtyard. The professional yet delightful staff give really good service. Sleeping is done upstairs in rooms that are all fairly similar in their beamed ceilings, quilted floral prints and little lamps. Swimming is at the bottom of the pretty ornamental garden – a rare treat for an urban hotel. The atmosphere is altogether light, fresh and attractive and Bléré is a perfect base for château-crawling – but come above all for the food.

rooms	12: 10 twins/doubles, 2 triples.
price	€57-€85.
meals	Breakfast €8. Weekday lunch €17. Dinner €39-€56. Restaurant closed Sunday evenings & Mondays out of season.
closed	January-mid-February.
directions	From Tours towards Chenonceaux D140; 4km before Chenonceaux left on D3 to Bléré.

	Michel & Micheline Blériot
tel	+33 (0)2 47 30 30 14
fax	+33 (0)2 47 23 52 80
email	le.cheval.blanc.blere@wanadoo.fr
web	www.lechevalblancblere.com

Map 4 Entry 164

Château de Reignac

19 rue Louis de Barberin, 37310 Reignac sur Indre, Indre-et-Loire

A remarkably balanced restoration is this four-star hotel, full of elegance and charm, where the 'old' is underplayed and the 'new' is discreet. So many personalities stayed or were connected with this château that Erick decided to theme the rooms adding a portrait or special object – and a biography. 'Lafayette', who inherited the château and visited until 1792, is a small suite with two bathrooms all in subtle greens and yellows with an attractive writing desk for your historical novel and a private terrace for a balmy evenings. Alex Fersen, a Swedish nobleman who swooned for Marie Antoinette, is in pale blues and yellows with a statue of his beloved and a claw-foot bath. Lime and mauve work wonders in the *grand salon* – enormous sparkling mirrors and flower-dressed chimney – while the exotic smoking room/bar – Zanzi-bar – is in dark browns with cane furniture. Books can be borrowed from the properly sober library where an Egyptian theme runs through the art on the walls. The guests-only restaurant serves a daily changing menu, full of spicy, original touches. We think you will like it here.

rooms	11: 6 doubles, 1 twin, 3 suites for 3, 1 apartment for 4 (without kitchen).
price	€150–€180. Suites €220. Apartment €280.
meals	Breakfast €14. Dinner with wine from €44.
closed	Rarely.
directions	A10 towards Bordeaux, exit 23 Tours Sud; N143 toward Loches for 22km; Reignac on left; château next to church.

	Erick Charrier
tel	+33 (0)2 47 94 14 10
fax	+33 (0)2 47 94 12 67
email	contact@lechateaudereignac.com
web	www.lechateaudereignac.com

Map 4 Entry 165

Domaine de la Tortinière

Les Gués de Veigné, 37250 Montbazon, Indre-et-Loire

It seems unreal, this pepperpot-towered château on a hill above the Indre, the bird-filled woods where wild cyclamen lay a carpet in autumn and daffodils radiate their light in spring. Then there's the view across to the stony keep of Montbazon, so this is an exceptional spot with tennis, a heated pool, fishing or rowing on the river, too. Bedrooms are perfect, decorated with flair and imagination, be they in the château or in a converted outbuilding. One of these, an adorable Renaissance doll's house, has two smaller rooms and a split-level suite; the orchard cottage, for playing shepherdesses, is big and beautifully furnished – the desk invites great writings. Bathrooms are luxurious, some smaller than others. Guests enjoy taking the underground passage to the orangery to dine in simple elegance, inside or on the terrace. Soft lighting, panelled reception rooms, deep comfort and discreet friendliness here in this real family-run hotel: the warm, humorous owners are genuinely attentive, their sole aim is to make your stay peaceful and harmonious.

rooms	30: 23 doubles, 7 suites.
price	€140-€300. Suites from €280.
meals	Breakfast €15. Picnic €15. Dinner €39. Restaurant closed Sunday evenings November-March.
closed	20 December-February.
directions	2km north of Montbazon. From Tours N10 south for Poitiers for 10km. In Les Gués, right at 2nd set of lights. Signed.

	Xavier & Anne Olivereau
tel	+33 (0)2 47 34 35 00
fax	+33 (0)2 47 65 95 70
email	domaine.tortiniere@wanadoo.fr
web	www.tortiniere.com

Map 4 Entry 166

Château du Vau

37510 Ballan Miré, Indre-et-Loire

Philosopher Bruno and Titian-haired Nancy, an intelligent and engaging couple with four young children, have turned his family château into a delightful, harmonious refuge for the world-weary traveller. The demands of children to be taken to dancing lessons and guests needing intellectual and physical sustenance are met with quiet composure and good humour and the cosy, book-lined, deep-chaired sitting room is a place where you find yourself irresistibly drawn into long conversations about music, yoga, art... The sunny breakfast room is charming with its stone-coloured floor tiles and pretty fabrics. Generations of sliding children have polished the bannisters on the stairs leading to the large, light bedrooms that are beautifully but unfussily decorated – splendid brass bedsteads, Turkish rugs on parquet floors, old family furniture, pictures and memorabilia – the spirit of zen can be felt in the search for pure authenticity. On fine summer evenings you can take a supper tray *à la* Glyndebourne in a favourite corner of the vast grounds.

rooms	5: 3 doubles, 1 twin/double, 1 suite for 3-4.
price	€105–€110.
meals	Buffet dinner €26 June-August. Hosted dinner with wine €41, September-May.
closed	Rarely.
directions	From Tours D7 towards Savonnières & Villandry. Left at Renault garage 2km before Savonnières. On for 2km to crucifix. Right, château 500m.

	Bruno & Nancy Clement
tel	+33 (0)2 47 67 84 04
fax	+33 (0)2 47 67 55 77
email	chateauduvau@chez.com
web	www.chez.com/chateauduvau

Map 4 Entry 167

Manoir de la Rémonière

37190 Azay-le-Rideau, Indre-et-Loire

Come for the remarkably authentic 15th-century château: behind the mullioned windows there are regal rooms, genuine antiques, four-posters and thick rich drapes in Henri IV, Agnès Sorel and Diane de Poitiers. Balzac and Rabelais have more modest quarters under the roof. Rémonière stands on 2,000 years of history: the stable block overlooks the fourth-century Gallo-Roman remains so its guest spaces have mosaics, ochre-sponged walls, very effective murals of Roman scenes, roof windows to the archeology. The main house is enchanting, so perfectly restored and furnished. Here, breakfast is at a long, candlelit table by a huge carved fireplace; the corridor has royal red carpet and old portraits; the levels change with the centuries and the atmosphere enters your blood. Through a clearing the view to Azay le Rideau is unsurpassed, the quiet is broken only by birds singing in the great trees, the owl wheezing behind the children's turret. There are ducks and hens galore and a family of donkeys in the pasture. You may be roped in to chase one of the escaped dwarf goats who cavort in the field.

rooms	9: 6 twins/doubles, 1 suite for 4. Orangerie: 2 duplexes for 4.
price	€90–€180.
meals	Good restaurants in Azay (1km) & Saché (4km).
closed	Rarely.
directions	A10 exit 24 Joué les Tours, D751 for Chinon. Through Azay past château to La Chapelle St Blaise. Left on D17; entrance 800m on left. Signed.

Chantal Pecas

tel	+33 (0)2 47 45 24 88
fax	+33 (0)2 47 45 45 69
email	info@manoirdelaremoniere.com
web	www.manoirdelaremoniere.com

Map 4 Entry 168

Château de Brou

37800 Noyant de Touraine, Indre-et-Loire

Swing through wrought-iron gates into an enchanted world. Wild boar – deer, if you're lucky – accompany you through a thickly wooded valley which opens to reveal an elegant Renaissance château, all towers, turrets and soft tufa-stone. This is unashamed luxury. The grand salon converts from deep sofa and roaring fire sitting room to glittering dining room, candlelight flickering off antiques, gold leaf and vast portraits. A tiny gothic-arched chapel offers more intimate dining. Menus can be fancy with foie gras or simple regional fare, much from the kitchen garden. Bedrooms, spread over three floors, are large, opulent and distinctly different – rich fabrics, canopied beds, grand paintings. Charles VII has stone walls, beams and a mezzanine bedroom; Rabelais, tucked under the eaves, has a silk bed head; Gabrielle is prettily romantic. Several have bathrooms in round towers. Tours or Chinon vineyards are nearby; you might prefer walks through your 100 hectares of woodland or quiet moments of watery contemplation by the pond or on the terrace. A place to self-indulgently recharge the batteries.

rooms	12: 6 doubles, 3 twins/doubles, 2 suites for 4, 1 family room for 4.
price	€115-€165. Suites & family rooms €200-€280.
meals	Breakfast €15. Lunch & dinner €35. Picnic hampers available. Restaurant closed Tues Oct-April; Mon Sept-June.
closed	2 January-3 March.
directions	A10 exit 26 Sainte Maure; D760 to Chinon; right in Noyant de Touraine 100m after 2nd set of lights.

	M & Mme Moreau
tel	+33 (0)2 47 65 80 80
fax	+33 (0)2 47 65 82 92
email	info@chateau-de-brou.fr
web	www.chateau-de-brou.fr

Map 9 Entry 169

Hôtel Château des Tertres

Route de Monteaux, 41150 Onzain, Loir-et-Cher

Artist in residence. A classic mid-19th century nobleman's house surrounded by mature wooded parkland in the Loire valley — but not all is traditional inside. The young, energetic Monsieur Valois is an inventive soul, and his sense of fun pervades this lovely place. Many of the rooms *are* period pieces, including the sitting rooms and the largest of the bedrooms, and some are remarkably ornate. The smallest rooms, though, are minimalist — symphonies of creamy yellow and white with suspended glass basins. That a creative spirit is at work is evident, too, in the gardener's lodge whose four guest rooms have been furnished with panache: one with a massive Italian four-poster, another with a perspex bedhead and a row of medieval steel helmets lined up on the wall! The stero systems are cleverly disguised. Your host is extremely hospitable and will let you in on the secrets of the château if you ask: before it was restored to its original elegance it had an amazingly chequered career, having been a German military headquarters, a school for metal workers and a chicken farm in three of its former lives.

rooms	18: 10 doubles, 5 twins/doubles in château; 2 family rooms for 3-4, 1 suite for 4 in gardener's lodge.
price	€75-€112.
meals	Breakfast buffet €10. Restaurant 2km; excellent choice within 5km.
closed	Mid-October-Easter.
directions	From A10 exit Blois. N152 for Amboise & Tours. Right to Onzain opp. bridge to Chaumont. Left in village for Monteaux. Château 1.5km on right.

	Bernard Valois
tel	+33 (0)2 54 20 83 88
fax	+33 (0)2 54 20 89 21
email	chateau.des.tertres@wanadoo.fr
web	www.chateau-tertres.com

Map 4 Entry 170

Château de Frileuse

41120 Les Montils, Loir-et-Cher

Once upon a time, there was a brilliant perfumer who lived in Paris and created amazing scents for the great and the good. One day, he bought himself a château in the Loire, not far from the big famous one nearby, and set up home with his charming Brazilian wife Elza. Together they restored the house, repairing and adding to the attractive but neglected 19th-century pile until it became fit for all the lucky guests who passed that way. As his grandmother had been an artist in the south of France, Nicolas displayed her colourful, abstract paintings all around, thus enhancing the beauty of the antique wallpapers and their flitting birds of paradise. Nicolas did not forget the art of perfumery and built a distillery for a thousand and one carefully labelled bottles with an individual scent in each. He also began work on a perfume garden and embellished guests' bathrooms with 'his' and 'her' colognes. Then added a delightful salon, billiards and books. You are five minutes from the International Garden Festival at Chaumont, and all paths (cycle and foot) lead to the Loire. *Ask about perfumery workshops.*

rooms	4 + 1: 2 doubles, 1 suite for 2, 1 family room for 3. 1 apartment for 4.
price	€120-€180. Apartment €180-€260.
meals	Restaurants 1km.
closed	November-March.
directions	From Blois, D751 to Chaumont sur Loire; entrance 1km before Candé sur Beuvron, on left.

	Elza Dejean & Nicolas de Barry
tel	+33 (0)2 54 44 19 59
fax	+33 (0)2 54 44 98 33
email	info@chateau-de-frileuse.com
web	www.chateau-de-frileuse.com

Map 4 Entry 171

La Petite Fadette
Place du Château, 36400 Nohant, Indre

Just off the main road, this tiny unspoilt village takes you back two centuries to Georges Sand's quiet country childhood, whence she proceeded to make her name, rather noisily, as an early advocate of feminism and free love (with Chopin, Musset, et al). Opposite her elegant château with perfect strolling gardens, this pretty country inn amongst a cluster of village houses of age and character fits the scene perfectly. Arched doors open into the simple tea room where pink-clothed tables lead to the grand piano and the old oak stairs up to the bedrooms. Under the stairs is a luxurious loo for diners and beyond is a sophisticated restaurant whose vaulted wooden ceiling and magnificent fireplace frame elegantly laid tables, ready for the chef's tempting dishes. The staff is attentive and friendly, the wine list extensive. Bedrooms are all different, done in traditional style with antiques, good fabrics and up-to-date bathrooms. As breakfast is only served till 9am, you may want to take it in the village. An inn, a château and a town of exceptional atmosphere — evocative and memorable.

rooms	9: 6 doubles, 2 twins, 1 suite.
price	€65-€140.
meals	Breakfast €12.
	Lunch & dinner €19-€50.
closed	Rarely.
directions	From Chateauroux, D943 for La Châtre. 5km before La Châtre, left into Nohant. Hotel in village centre opposite church.

	M Bernard Gabriel Chapleau
tel	+33 (0)2 54 31 01 48
fax	+33 (0)2 54 31 10 19
web	www.aubergepetitefadette.com

Map 10 Entry 172

Le Manoir des Remparts
14 rue des Remparts, 36800 St Gaultier, Indre

Behind imposing gates and high walls – the house is built on the outside of the old city ramparts – lies this charming 18th-century manor. The place is a gem: a gravelled courtyard and wisteria-clad barn at the front, a large, tree-filled walled garden with summer house at the back. Your hospitable and punctilious Dutch hosts have renovated the house with sympathy and style – Ren is an interior designer – preserving the beautiful fireplaces, the parquet floors and the marvellous oak staircase. Bedrooms are really comfortable. The style is essentially Provençal, with Souleiado and toile de Jouy wallpapers, country antiques, old paintings, pillows decked in antique linen. One room has a metal-framed four-poster with red check curtains. Bathrooms are sumptuous, traditional fittings offset by seagrass floor covering and elegant drapes; a chintzy armchair sits by a claw-footed bath. Generous breakfasts are taken in the blue coach house. There's a sitting room to retire to, warm and inviting with a large fireplace. A nostalgic vision of some perfect time – it's a treat to stay here. *Children over 14 welcome.*

rooms	4 suites with possible adjacent rooms for families.
price	€135.
meals	Picnic available. Excellent restaurant nearby.
closed	15 December–5 January.
directions	A20 for Limoges, N151 Le Blanc & Poitiers. Entering St Gaultier stay on Le Blanc road; over 2 sets of lights; right, then immed. left across Le Blanc road. Pass supermarket to Thenay, on for 500m; on right.

	Ren Rijpstra
tel	+33 (0)2 54 47 94 87
fax	+33 (0)2 54 47 94 87
email	manoirdesremparts@wanadoo.fr
web	www.manoir-saintgaultier.com

Map 9 Entry 173

Château de Boisrenault

36500 Buzançais, Indre

Built by a 19th-century aristocrat as a wedding present for his daughter – well overdue, she'd had two sons by the time it was finished – this is a turreted, customised, Renaissance château. Noble and imposing on the outside, it's very much a family home within. Furniture, objects, pictures, all have a tale to tell and there's no shortage of hunting trophies and stags' heads on the walls. Reception rooms are lofty, with huge fireplaces. One sitting room has a baby grand; another, smaller and cosier, is lined with books. Each bedroom is an adventure in itself. Named after the family's children and grandchildren, the rooms feature a hotchpotch of pieces from different periods, including some excellent antiques. A couple of stuffed pheasants make unusual lampshades in Hadrien's room and offset the yellow walls. Meals are taken at a vast table in the dining room; be sure to book if you'd like dinner. A delicious pool is discreetly tucked away behind trees in the grounds; table tennis and table football are a godsend on rainy days. A good place for a family stay in summer.

rooms	7 + 2: 2 doubles, 1 twin, 4 family rooms. 2 apartments for 4-5.
price	€71-€98. Family rooms €95-€125. Apartments €292-€427 per week.
meals	Dinner €19, book ahead.
closed	Rarely.
directions	From A20 exit 11 on D8 to Levroux; D926 for Buzançais. Château on left 3km before town.

	Florence du Manoir
tel	+33 (0)2 54 84 03 01
fax	+33 (0)2 54 84 10 57
email	boisrenault@wanadoo.fr
web	www.chateau-du-boisrenault.com

Map 9 Entry 174

Château de la Verrerie

Oizon, 18700 Aubigny sur Nère, Cher

Live the life of a gentle aristocrat, or his mistress if you prefer. Tucked deep in a forest, this 15th-century château was once the home of Charles 11's lover, the Duchess of Portsmouth. The current Count — whose family have been owners for 150 years — is a charming, cultured, amiable aristocrat who enjoys sharing his good fortune. It has everything a good château should have: courtyard, gothic chapel, Italian loggia, music room (for concerts), grazing horses, lawns sweeping to a lake and fleets of grand but comfortably furnished rooms. As well as a gracious salon, there are intimate sitting areas between the bedrooms — heaped with sofas, books and games. Guest rooms, overlooking the park or lake, are outrageously stunning — rich fabrics, soft carpets, vast windows, family antiques. Some have four-posters, others painted ceilings, one has a veranda, another two claw-foot baths. Yes, two. There's canoeing and horse riding nearby or woodland walks on your estate. Dine gastronomically on local produce in the Hansel & Gretel style cottage restaurant. Service is impeccable, warm and friendly.

rooms	12: 5 twins, 4 doubles, 2 suites.
price	€155-265. Suites €360.
meals	Breakfast €14-€18.
	Lunch & dinner €25-€40.
	Restaurant closed Tuesdays.
closed	20 December-January.
directions	From Paris A6 & A77 exit Vierzon & Bourges. D940 to Aubigny sur Nère. Signposted.

	Comte Béraud de Vogüé
tel	+33 (0)2 48 81 51 60
fax	+33 (0)2 48 58 21 25
email	info@chateaudelaverrerie.com

Map 5 Entry 175

Château d'Ivoy
18380 Ivoy le Pré, Cher

Every antique bed is appropriately canopied (Kipling: frothy mosquito net on carved Anglo-Indian bed; Lord Drummond: the olde English feel), every superb bathroom a study in modern fittings on period washstands. Ivoy is home to an interior designer who has achieved miracles since buying it from a famous entomologist who had planted a near tropical rainforest in one stateroom, now the fine-furnished, Spode dining room. It was built for Mary Stuart's purser: the Stuarts were allowed to create a Scottish duchy here that lasted 200 years and it became the Drummond family seat after the battle of Culloden. The front is stern, the back opens wide onto sweeping lawns, park and hills – all bedrooms face this way. The house radiates refinement and your hostess's infectious delight. She will welcome you in her grey-green hall with its lovely sandstone floor and ceramic stove, invite you to use the library (home to a huge spider... imprisoned in a glass paperweight) or the salon, and will then retire discreetly. A very special place to stay. *Children over 12 welcome.*

rooms	6: 5 doubles, 1 twin.
price	€145-€195.
meals	Good choice of local restaurants.
closed	Rarely.
directions	From A10 exit Salbris D944 for Bourges to Neuvy sur Barangeon; left on D926 to La Chapelle d'Angillon; D12 to Ivoy. Château on right 300m after church, entrance through L'Etang Communal.

	Marie France Gouëffon-de Vaivre
tel	+33 (0)2 48 58 85 01
fax	+33 (0)2 48 58 85 02
email	chateau.divoy@wanadoo.fr
web	www.chateaudivoy.com

Map 5 Entry 176

Château de Beaujeu
18300 Sens Beaujeu, Cher

Sweep up the tree-lined avenue, pass the stables and the dovecotes in the yard, step back in time: your turreted 16th-century château has been in the family since the Revolution. Downstairs rooms are filled with generations of possessions, including magnificent Aubusson tapestries on the walls. Every item tells a story: the stags' heads on the wall were shot by a grandmother a century ago. It is a rare pleasure to spend a night under the roof of a château so untouched by modernity. No carefully renovated 'features' here, everything is as it was: the wallpapers may be a bit faded, but the colours are original and unsynthetic. The trompe l'oeil is all of a piece, in spite of the cracks. Bedrooms are comfortable, with gracious windows overlooking the park and the bathrooms have all been done up beautifully. The suites in the tower are lovely, with splendid mouldings, windows and doorways in curved glass. Try the splendid yellow room with its canopied bed. Dinner is a classic affair: aperitif, a fish starter, roast chicken, apple tart. Authentic, out of the ordinary and so close to the Sancerre vinyards.

rooms	6: 4 doubles, 1 twin, 1 suite for 4.
price	€90–€160. Suite €185.
meals	Hosted dinner €45, book ahead.
closed	November–Easter.
directions	From Sancerre D955 for Bourges. Right on D923 for Aubigny sur Nère. Left on D7 to Sens Beaujeu. There, left at fountain, D74 for Neuilly en Sancerre. Down hill, château at end of drive.

	Mme Monique de Pommereau
tel	+33 (0)2 48 79 07 95
fax	+33 (0)2 48 79 05 07
email	info@chateau-de-beaujeu.com
web	www.chateau-de-beaujeu.com

Map 5 Entry 177

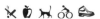

Hôtel Restaurant Le Lion D'Or

10 rue de la Judelle, 18240 Léré, Cher

The pretty village of Léré hugs the Canal de Briare, inviting you to wander its lanes and market. In one quiet side street you'll find the inn, content in its old age: endearing young owners have filled the horse troughs with exuberant flowers and the place with new life. The bedrooms are unpretentious spaces: clean, tidy and comfortable; those on the second floor have old rafters, all have large bathrooms and views over the rooftops. The restaurant has been spruced up too; potted palms peek out from corners, bright gauze curtains flutter at windows, pictures and simple lime-washed furniture keep everything cheerful. Samuel cooks fresh local food with creativity and spirit: a hint of his Vietnamese grandmother revealed in the odd spice here, an unexpected flavour there. Take breakfast in the restaurant or the sheltered courtyard lulled by the chiming church clock (atmospheric by day, perhaps a touch intrusive by night), then head off to explore the villages and the spectacular bridge downstream where the canal crosses the Loire. A true auberge: simple and delightful.

rooms	8: 4 doubles, 1 twin, 2 triples, 1 family duplex for 4.
price	€48–€53. Half-board rates in week.
meals	Breakfast €7.50 Lunch €25–€48 (Tues-Fri menu from €22). Dinner €32–€48. Restaurant closed Monday.
closed	Rarely.
directions	A77 exit 23 Cosne Cours sur Loire; D955A for 2km. At r'bout, 3rd exit on rue Alphonse Boudin for 2km. Right after port.

	Samuel & Séverine Tingaud
tel	+33 (0)2 48 72 60 12
fax	+33 (0)2 48 72 56 18
email	contact@le-lion-dor.com
web	www.le-lion-dor.com

Map 5 Entry 178

Prieuré d'Orsan
18170 Maisonnais, Cher

Art as nature or nature as art? Go ahead, pinch yourself, your feet are still on the ground even though your spirit has been miraculously lifted by the harmony and elegance of this priory and its gardens. Patrice, an architect and landsape designer, saved the house from abandonment 15 years ago; originally built in 1107 as a convent, it stands in rural France at its most unspoilt. The oldest remaining buildings, probably the refectory and dormitory, are from the 16th century and form three sides of a square, enclosing beautifully restored gardens, open to visitors. There is no 'hotel' feel to the place at all, and the visitors to the gardens don't make it feel busy either. The reception rooms on the first floor are an interconnecting series of sitting rooms integrating the professional kitchen at one end; contemporary unfussy chic. You will dine on homemade bread and home-grown produce under a leafy pergola when it's warm. Bedrooms have pine-panelled walls with shutters, windows and doors painted in a soft grey-green. You will look out onto the wonderful garden; serenity and contemplation are yours.

rooms	6: 3 doubles, 3 triples.
price	€180-€280.
meals	Breakfast €18. Lunch €38. Dinner €48.
closed	November-April.
directions	From Paris exit 8 from A71 to St Amand Montrond; D925 towards Lignières; D65 towards Le Chatelet. Orsan half-way between Lignières & Le Chatelet.

	Patrice Taravella
tel	+33 (0)2 48 56 27 50
fax	+33 (0)2 48 56 39 64
email	prieuredorsan@wanadoo.fr
web	www.prieuredorsan.com

Map 10 Entry 179

Photo Domaine des Etangs entry 184

poitou – charentes

Château de Saint Loup sur Thouet

79600 St Loup Lamairé, Deux Sèvres

This château inspired Perrault to write *Puss in Boots*! It has an ancient and fascinating history. The Black Prince incarcerated John the Good here after the Battle of Poitiers in 1356 and it was rebuilt in the 17th century by the Marquis of Carabas, whose magnificence so impressed the fairy-tale writer. Charles-Henri de Bartillat visited the château on Christmas Eve 1990, fell in love with it and 10 days later had bought it. Saint Loup is a *monument historique*, open to the public for a short time each Sunday afternoon. The count, charming and passionate about his home, is painstakingly restoring the house and the grounds (using 18th-century plans drawn up by Jacques Boyer de la Boissière). Rooms are lofty and light in the château, medieval in the keep: the Black Prince room in the old kitchens has two vast fireplaces and thick red-stained beams; the Bishop's room in the château has a splendid canopied bed between two big windows overlooking the garden. Aperitifs are taken in the *orangerie* on the other side of the moat – Charles-Henri makes sure guests get to meet each other before dinner. A stunning place.

rooms	15: 13 doubles, 2 singles. Entire château, or keep (6 bedrooms, dining and sitting rooms), can be rented.
price	€150–€190. Singles €115.
meals	Breakfast €15. Dinner with wine, €65, book ahead.
closed	Rarely.
directions	From Airvault D46 to St Loup Lamairé. Château visible on entering village.

	Comte Charles-Henri de Bartillat
tel	+33 (0)5 49 64 81 73
fax	+33 (0)5 49 64 82 06
email	st-loup@wanadoo.fr
web	www.chateaudesaint-loup.com

Map 9 Entry 180

Le Logis Saint Martin

Chemin de Pissot, 79400 Saint Maixent-l'Ecole, Deux Sèvres

Run with efficiency by Bertrand and Ingrid Heintz, this 17th-century *gentilhommerie* offers that most attractive combination for travellers – solidly comfortable rooms and an excellent restaurant. It is set conveniently on the outskirts of town in a little wooded valley with a small stream running just outside. The bedrooms are smallish, beamed, elegantly furnished and very comfortable; the bigger rooms, with lovely old rafters, are on the top floor. The tower has been converted into a charming apartment: a sitting area downstairs; a smallish stone-walled bedroom up steepish stairs. As you would expect in France, the menu is local and seasonal and it is served in an elegant restaurant or in the pleasantly shaded and tranquil garden. Bertrand Heintz earned his stars at one of the top hotels in Paris and there is a classic feel to the food and the place; basic skills are sometimes hard to come by but the waiters here know how to carve and fillet at your table. Add an attentive, helpful staff, an excellent wine list, homemade ice creams and breads and you will be glad you came.

rooms	11: 7 doubles, 2 singles, 1 triple, 1 apartment for 2 (no kitchen).
price	€110–€172.
meals	Breakfast €16. Lunch €35–€48. Dinner €48–€75. Restaurant closed Mon; Sat & Tues lunchtimes.
closed	January.
directions	From Poitier exit 32; N11 until St Maixent l'Ecole; follow signs for Niort, left at 4th set of lights, left onto the river quays. 400m from lights.

	Ingrid & Bertrand Heintz
tel	+33 (0)5 49 05 58 68
fax	+33 (0)5 49 76 19 93
email	contact@logis-saint-martin.com
web	www.logis-saint-martin.com

Map 9 Entry 181

Le Pigeonnier du Perron

Le Perron, 86530 Availles en Chatellerault, Ter-de-Belfort

René Descartes once owned this *petit seigneurie*; its deeds go back to the 15th century. The Thiollet family has only been here for 150 years. Father and son are fully occupied in their wine laboratory in Cahors, Emilie, in her early twenties, fresh from hotel school, now prepares the meals – fish is her speciality – and runs the place smoothly with help from Fridda. Family connections guarantee an excellent selection of wines from Cahors – of course – but also from Poitou and the Val de Loire. Sun-ripe tomatoes, green and red peppers, cucumber and courgettes are home-grown along with essential herbs for the kitchen; a stone-flagged terrace with good outdoor furniture makes an inviting spot for alfresco dining. Farm buildings are grouped around a sunny courtyard and hollyhocks push up from every imaginable nook and cranny. Bedrooms are smallish but simply and pleasantly decorated with the odd splash of colour; floors are pale pine, walls soft-sponged or of pale exposed stone. One in the dovecote has a little balcony, many look over the fields and valley. Good value.

rooms	15: 11 doubles, 4 twins. 1 room with separate wc.
price	€60.
meals	Breakfast €7. Dinner €16-€18.
closed	Rarely.
directions	A10 exit 27 for Chatellerault. At 2nd roundabout for Cenon; through Cenon for Availles; 1st right after village sign. Signed on right after approx. 1km.

Emilie Thiollet

tel	+33 (0)5 49 19 76 08
fax	+33 (0)5 49 19 12 82
email	accueil@lepigeonnierduperron.com
web	www.lepigeonnierduperron.com

Map 9 Entry 182

Hôtel Les Orangeries

12 avenue du Docteur Dupont, 86320 Lussac les Châteaux, Vienne

Even before you step inside, the pool beneath the mature trees of the landscaped garden at the back will convince you that these people have the finest sense of how to treat an old house and garden: the harmony of the deep wooden deck, raw stone walls, giant baskets and orange trees (*naturellement*) draws you in. The young owners fell in love with the place and applied all their talent – he's an architect – to giving it an authentic 18th-century elegance in contemporary mood. Indoors, stripped oak doors, exposed stone walls, warm wood or cool stone floors are radiant with loving care, like valued old friends. Olivia has given each bedroom it's own sense of uncluttered harmony with new-stained old furniture and a super bathroom; the split-level suites are a delight. The Gautiers' passions include the old-fashioned games they have resuscitated for you: croquet and skittles outside, two kinds of billiards, backgammon and mahjong in the vast games room inside. Their delightful enthusiasm for this generous house is catching; it makes you feel that maybe the world isn't such a bad place after all. Book early.

rooms	11: 7 doubles, 4 apartments for 4-5 (without kitchen).
price	€65-€115. Apartments €95-€170.
meals	Breakfast €12. Lunch snacks. Dinner €28.
closed	Mid-December-mid-January.
directions	Exit Poitiers for Limoges on N147 to Lussac les Châteaux (35km from Poitiers). Ask for route via Châtellerault if arriving from north.

	Olivia & Jean-Philippe Gautier
tel	+33 (0)5 49 84 07 07
fax	+33 (0)5 49 84 98 82
email	orangeries@wanadoo.fr
web	www.lesorangeries.fr

Map 9 Entry 183

Domaine des Etangs

Le Bourg, 16310 Massignac, Charente

Eight hundred beautiful hectares of woodland and lakes. At its heart, the fabulous château – to gaze upon. Then rooms in hamlets scattered through the grounds – to spend a night in. And in what style! Old beams and stones and gleaming wooden floors, copper baths, bright checks and wicker, a glass floor panel revealing an ancient fireplace downstairs – the old farm buildings have been revived to create a mixture of rustic and refined, each room decorated to bring out its quirks. Pure, simple luxury peeps from every corner; you can book a room or a house, even an entire hamlet for a wedding. From some, the restaurant may be three kilometres away, but there are bikes and buggies for nipping about (though you can drive). The domaine's restaurant is in a converted long barn, its stone floor dotted with smart green chairs, its white tablecloths with dainty dishes. Masses to do away from the tennis court and pool: make walnut oil in the working mill, go night deer stalking, hire a boat, listen to live jazz. In spite of its size, the place has the charm of a small hotel, thanks to Stéphanie and Marc. Paradise!

rooms	21 + 7: 15 twins/doubles, 4 suites for 2-3, 2 family rooms for 4-6. Houses for 2-10.
price	€125-€175. Suites & family rooms €200-€350. Houses €275-€1,050.
meals	Breakfast €15. Lunch & dinner €26-€34.
closed	January-Mid-March.
directions	From Angoulême N141 to La Rochefoucauld, then D13 to Massignac. Domaine on right before village.

	Stéphanie & Marc Aupiais
tel	+33 (0)5 45 61 85 00
fax	+33 (0)5 45 61 85 01
email	info@domainedesetangs.fr
web	www.domainedesetangs.com

Map 9 Entry 184

Château de Nieuil
16270 Nieuil, Charente

François I built the château as a hunting lodge in the 16th century, but swapped Nieuil for a bigger plot when he opted for the grander Chambord on the Loire. A gambling Count sold it to grandparents of the Bodinauds. Its hunting days are now over and Luce and her husband have instead created a hommage to our feathered friends: a magical birdwatching walk round the outside of the moat, a tree skeleton painted white and dotted with nesting boxes and feed trays; each room named after a bird and if you are not awoken by real ones, an alarm will sing 'your' song. The château is grand and beautifully decorated: one room has a small children's room up a spiral stair, another a tiny reading room in a turret; most look onto the formal garden at the back. The food is wonderful; Luce has been Michelin-starred but now chooses to run a more relaxed restaurant in a converted barn. And there's more: an art gallery with excellent works by contemporary artists and an antique shop in the old kitchens. Open-hearted, open-armed – these people love what they do, and it shows.

rooms	27: 11 doubles, 6 singles, 7 triples, 3 suites.
price	€110-€240. Singles €99-€190. Triples €160-€260. Suites €210-€360.
meals	Breakfast €15. Lunch €25-€50. Dinner €36-€50. Rest. closed Sun eve, Mon/Tues lunch Sept-June.
closed	2 November-6 April.
directions	N141 to La Rochefoucauld then Chasseneuil. 6.5km after Chasseneuil, left on D739 to Nieuil. Signed.

	M & Mme Bodinaud
tel	+33 (0)5 45 71 36 38
fax	+33 (0)5 45 71 46 45
email	chateaunieuilhotel@wanadoo.fr
web	www.chateaunieuilhotel.com

Map 9 Entry 185

Hostellerie du Maine Brun

Asnières sur Nouère, 16290 Hiersac, Charente

The only sounds to wake you in your bedroom come from the birds and the water gushing beneath the hotel – a 16th-century mill, sympathetically remodeled in the 1930s. You may even forget you are in a hotel at all. The rooms have a mix of French 18th- and 19th-century furniture and heavily draped curtains loaded with gold and cream. The flowers look as if they have been freshly picked from the garden. Raymond and Sophie have managed the trick of making the place feel traditional but not stuffy. The only modern touches are in the bathrooms, designed for wallowing rather than a mere splash. Children are welcome, but unless yours are period items – better seen than heard – they may not blend in. There is a big pool, however, with plenty of sunshades and chairs. You can breakfast in the sunny dining room or on the terrace, and if you are planning to explore, Cognac is nearby. Raymond will proudly show off his own distillery, explain the intricacies of the process and let you sample his home brew. A man in the know with an excellent wine cellar.

rooms	20: 10 doubles, 8 twins, 2 suites.
price	€110-€120. Suites €165.
meals	Breakfast €12. Lunch & dinner €30-€40. Closed Mon & Tues lunchtimes 24 April-24 Sept. Closed Sun evenings to Tues lunchtimes low season.
closed	November–January.
directions	From Angoulême N141 for Cognac for approx. 8km. C2 right for Asnières sur Nouère. Hostellerie just along on left.

	Sophie Menager
tel	+33 (0)5 45 90 83 00
fax	+33 (0)5 45 96 91 14
email	hostellerie-du-maine-brun@wanadoo.fr
web	www.hotel-mainebrun.com

Map 9 Entry 186

Château de l'Yeuse

65 ruc de Bellevue , Châteaubernard, 16100 Cognac, Charente

A delightful conceit: a miniature folly of a Charente château, dazzlingly striped in brick and creamy stone, with a modern extension in flamboyant style. It is just five minutes from Cognac yet is wrapped in parkland with views to the Charente river – utterly charming. Bedrooms are in the newer part – with fun, trompe l'oeil-flourished corridors – large and light in bold country-house style and with ultra-modern bathrooms. Book a room overlooking the river. By contrast, the 'old' château is all classical proportions, elegant furnishings and traditional comfort. Wallow in the cigar salon with its deep armchairs and glass-fronted cabinets, work your way through the 100-year-old cognacs. It's posh frocks for dinner in the chandelier-hung dining room, all stiff white napery and black jacketed waiters. The excitement over chef Pascal Nebout's cuisine is palpable. Céline, the young manageress, energetic yet ever-calm, will advise on visiting distilleries and music festivals. Discover the secret garden, relax around the pool, find a shady terrace or treat yourself to a massage in the hamman. Sophisticated living.

rooms	24: 21 doubles, 3 suites.
price	€95-€162. Suites €205-€314.
meals	Breakfast €14. Lunch €27-€67. Dinner €42-€67. Restaurant closed Saturday lunchtimes; also Sunday evenings off-season.
closed	2-12 January.
directions	From Paris A10 exit 34. Follow signs St Jean d'Angély & Cognac then for Angoulème; D15 to St Brice & Quartier de l'Echassier.

Céline Desmazières & Pascal Nebout

tel	+33 (0)5 45 36 82 60
fax	+33 (0)5 45 35 06 32
email	reservations.yeuse@wanadoo.fr
web	www.yeuse.fr

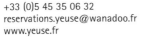

Map 9 Entry 187

Logis du Fresne
16130 Juillac le Coq, Charente

The Butler family came to France 100 years ago to make cognac and Tone's husband Christophe has been in the business all his life. She is from Norway, and had a children's clothing label there; they are the loveliest hosts. They bought the old, elegant Logis five years ago and opened in 2003, fulfilling their vision of a refined place to stay with a chambres d'hôtes feel. The façade is wonderful and inside just as good. The whole feel is light and fresh and the style turn-of-the-century Norwegian: old terracotta tiles on the ground floor, pale painted beams, a cosy library, an elegant salon. Bedrooms are as serene. Those on the first floor have uncluttered chic: a gilded mirror hangs above an open fire, an oriental rug graces a limed floor… those above are more modern. The two-room suite has its own stairs; bathrooms are well-lit and beautifully modern. Breakfast outdoors, at tables forged by the village blacksmith, on delicious pastries, hire a classic car and spin off with a picnic and a bottle of champagne. The grounds, with hidden pool and 15th-century tower, are worth a visit in themselves.

rooms	11: 10 twins/doubles, 1 suite.
price	€90–€115. Suite €165. Half-board option.
meals	Breakfast €10. Picnic baskets available. Dinner €32. Restaurants in Cognac & Segonzac.
closed	November–February. Call for out of season group reservations.
directions	From Cognac, D24 for Segonzac then D736 for Juillac le Coq. 500m after village on right.

	Tone Butler
tel	+33 (0)5 45 32 28 74
fax	+33 (0)5 45 32 29 53
email	logisdufresne@wanadoo.fr
web	www.logisdufresne.com

Map 9 Entry 188

Hôtel Le Chat Botté

2 place de l'Eglise, 17590 St Clément des Baleines (Ile de Ré), Charente-Maritime

Are you de-mineralised? Need some coddling? A pine-panelled, pale-chaired house decorated with pastels and peace, this is part of a family circle: one sister is your hotel hostess, another has her beauty salon right here where you can be wrapped in seaweed and reflexologised, a third has a B&B nearby and two brothers have a restaurant each, one of them next door. You can choose to have your *énergétique* breakfast on the sweet little patio in the garden, with three types of flowering jasmine to stimulate your morning senses, or in the grey-blue dining room… before shiatsu and a bicycle tour of the island. The garden provides fresh flowers for the house, the sea and sky that limpid light that filters into the simple, country-furnished, quilted bedrooms which give onto the church square, the garden or the patio; we preferred the patio aspect but all are havens from the heat of the summer beaches. Bathrooms and linen are of excellent quality. The island has salt marshes, one of Europe's biggest bird sanctuaries, and the Baleines lighthouse for stupendous views. A charming, peaceful place. *26 km from the bridge.*

rooms	23: 20 twins/doubles, 3 suites.
price	€66–€155. Suites €195–€245.
meals	Breakfast €9.50–€13. Family-owned restaurant next door.
closed	Last week of November–15 December; 5 January–12 February.
directions	From La Rochelle over bridge to Ile de Ré; head towards Le Phare des Baleines. Opposite church in St Clément. 30km from bridge.

	Mmes Massé-Chantreau
tel	+33 (0)5 46 29 21 93
fax	+33 (0)5 46 29 29 97
email	hotelchatbotte@wanadoo.fr
web	www.hotelchatbotte.com

Map 8 Entry 189

Hôtel de l'Océan

172 rue St Martin, 17580 Le Bois Plage en Ré, Charente-Maritime

Seasoned travellers, Martine and Noël tried to find a hotel that felt like a home. Although they had worked in antiques and interior design, they realised after a spell running a restaurant that this was what they should be doing – but where? They knew it had to be on an island and after toying with Corsica and the Ile de Ré, they stumbled upon a rather sad old hotel, the Océan, and knew they had found 'their' hotel. Set back from the dunes in a garden pungent with rosemary and lavender, the hotel has 24 bedrooms: some around an inner courtyard, others like tiny cottages among the hollyhocks. They are all different. Children will love the curtained cabin bed set in a buttercup yellow alcove. Floors are covered in sisal matting and Martine and Noël's ships, lighthouses and shells are dotted around against cool, soothing colours. After your *pastis* on the decked terrace, your supper will involve a lot of fresh fish and herbs. The dining room is another success, with cream boards on walls and ceiling and palest greeny-grey carved chairs. It's fresh without being cold and clean without being clinical.

rooms	29: 21 doubles, 4 twins, 3 triples, 1 quadruple.
price	€61-€150.
meals	Breakfast €10. Lunch & dinner €22-€32. Restaurant closed Wednesdays except during school holidays.
closed	2 January-2 February.
directions	A10 exit 33 for La Rochelle. N248 then N11 Rocade round La Rochelle for Pont de l'Ile de Ré. At Le Bois Plage hotel in town centre.

	Martine & Noël Bourdet
tel	+33 (0)5 46 09 23 07
fax	+33 (0)5 46 09 05 40
email	info@re-hotel-ocean.com
web	www.re-hotel-ocean.com

Map 8 Entry 190

Hôtel de Toiras

1 quai Job Foran, 17410 Saint Martin de Ré, Charente-Maritime

It is one year old and already studded with stars. Exquisite is the first word, refined is the second, then you stop thinking and let the senses rule. Revel in the soul of this quayside hotel, inspired by the illustrious figure of Jean de Caylar de Saint Bonnet de Toiras, no less, who protected the island from the English in 1627. So the arts of navigation and hunting set the tone and imbue the rooms with memories of 17th-century ship owners' houses. Linking the old part with the new is a cool and fragrant garden with three palm trees. Then a reception room that feels like a study, black and white tiles in an elegant living room/library, open fires, a small bar, soothing music, happy young staff. Each gracious, immaculate bedroom – some are large, some are small – carries reminders of courtesans, writers, botanists or sailors; the detail in fabrics, paintings, *objets* and books is both rich and meticulous. All this, and an island of big skies and beaches - and bicycles: 60 miles of cycle paths crisscross its vineyards and pine forests. Bliss.

rooms	17: 8 doubles, 2 twins, 7 suites.
price	€110-€260. Suites €250-€480.
meals	Breakfast €18-€20.
closed	Never.
directions	From La Rochelle, over bridge to Ile de Ré; on quay. In summer season, call for code.

	Olivia Mathé
tel	+33 (0)5 46 35 40 32
fax	+33 (0)5 46 35 64 59
email	contact@hotel-de-toiras.com
web	www.hotel-de-toiras.com

Map 8 Entry 191

Château des Salles
17240 St Fort sur Gironde, Charente-Maritime

A pretty little château with great personality, Salles was built in 1454 and scarcely touched again until 1860, when it was 'adapted to the fashion' (profoundly). One hundred years later, the enterprising Couillaud family brought the estate guest house, its vineyard and stud farm into the 20th century. Behind its fine old exterior it exudes light, harmony, colour and elegant informality with spiral stone stairs, boldly-painted beams and warm, well-furnished bedrooms bathed in soft colours and gentle wallpapers. Salles is a friendly family affair: sister at guest house reception, brother at vines and horses, mother at her easel — her watercolours hang in the public rooms, her flowers decorate bedroom doors — and in the kitchen. At dinner, refined food made with local and home-grown produce is served with estate wines. Sylvie Couillaud will help you plan your stay — she knows it all and is almost a mini tourist office. It's a congenial, welcoming house: people come back again and again and one guest said: "She welcomed us like family and sent us home with goodies from her vineyard".

rooms	5: 4 doubles, 1 triple.
price	€76–€130.
meals	Breakfast €9. Dinner €35.
closed	November–March.
directions	A10 exit 37 Mirambeau. Château between Lorignac & Brie sous Mortagne at junction of D730 & D125.

	Sylvie Couillaud
tel	+33 (0)5 46 49 95 10
fax	+33 (0)5 46 49 02 81
email	chateaudessalles@wanadoo.fr
web	www.chateaudessalles.com

Map 8 Entry 198

Photo Château Les Merles entry 211

aquitaine

Château Le Lout

Avenue de la Dame Blanche, 33320 Le Taillan Médoc, Gironde

If the dusky pink walls, first-floor loggia and green windows give Le Lout the look of a somewhat patrician Italian villa rather than a French château, this is because its original owner chose an architect from Siena to build his country retreat. When Colette and Olivier bought it, the house had been empty for 18 years and was in need of a lot of attention. Colette not only brought a feel for period detail but plenty of elbow grease: she did much of the work herself. A flight of stone steps leads into a white stone hall, sparsely decorated with tapestries and the odd old chest. One side leads to the kitchen and office, the other to a dining/breakfast room with fine chinoiserie wallpaper framed by soft green panelling. A stone staircase leads to the bedrooms which are a treat. All have wooden floors; you may find rich orange walls with contrasting cool bedding, or soft cream walls set off by fresh green-patterned cotton, enhanced by lace and rugs. Children will be happy with the pool and huge grounds. You can now have a great meal at their new restaurant in Le Taillan, only 2km away.

rooms	8: 4 twins/doubles, 1 twins, 3 suites for 3-4.
price	€115-€155. Suites €155-€255.
meals	Breakfast €13. Hosted dinner with wine, €45, book ahead.
closed	Rarely.
directions	Rocade for Bordeaux & Merignac (airport). Exit 7 N215 to Lesparre & Lacanau. After 1km on D2 for Pauillac. After 2.5km, left at lights to N33 for Le Taillan; 1km. Signed.

	Colette & Olivier Salmon
tel	+33 (0)5 56 35 46 47
fax	+33 (0)5 56 35 48 75
email	chateau.le.lout@wanadoo.fr
web	www.chateaulelout.com

Map 8 Entry 199

Villa Prémayac

13 rue Prémayac, 33390 Blaye, Gironde

The house is down a quiet back street of Blaye, a bustling little town with a pretty hilltop citadel. There's not a huge amount to do here – apart from quaff some famous wines – but the place is perfect for golfers. There are six courses within a putt of the villa *and* Roger, your host, was a player of repute. He now edits a golfing magazine. This is a new enterprise for him and Léa who have furbished five bedrooms for guests in the oldest part of the house. It's a bit of a rabbit warren, albeit a well-renovated one. Big bedrooms, named after Greek gods, are plushly carpeted. Ceres is golden with a flowery canopied bed, Aphrodite spring-green with rose-strewn drapes; they overlook small enclosed terraces. Bathrooms are tiled, with shiny fittings, and are vast, big enough to swing a club in. There are two small gardens, one Roman and one zen, with bonsai trees. The south-facing hills of Blaye, on the banks of the Gironde, have been lined with vines since the Romans came. Set off for the wine villages and châteaux of Pauillac and Medoc – a 45-minute drive – or catch the ferry from Blaye. Cognac is even nearer.

rooms	5 doubles.
price	€85.
meals	4-5 restaurants within walking distance.
closed	Rarely.
directions	In Blaye, follow Centre Ville signs.

	Léa Golias
tel	+33 (0)5 57 42 27 39
fax	+33 (0)5 57 42 69 09
email	premayac@wanadoo.fr
web	www.villa-premayac.com

Map 8 Entry 200

Château Saint Aignan

Avenue Saint Aignan, 33450 Saint Loubès, Gironde

Enter a charming small 18th-century château based on a design by the architect of the Bordeaux Opera House. And the opera gets into full swing once inside: note the first reception room, its ceiling upholstered into a thousand pleats, its grand displays of china, its central sparkling chandelier. More reception rooms follow, the largest seating 200 for dinner: the château's raison d'être is its parties and weddings (check when you book that you won't bump into one). At other times peace reigns... and outside is a mature park of ancient magnolias, clipped hedges and a fabulous pool. The Saint Aignan estate has been in Madame's family for three generations; she is sad the vines have gone but she puts her energies into her guests now and is full of plans for Rolls Royce vineyard tours and courses in table decoration. Drapes soar, walls are papered and patterned, parquet gleams; there's an unbelievably long shag-pile rug in the honeymoon suite and nymphs dance over a circular beige bathtub under the eaves. Exuberantly, unashamedly French – with a hostess attractively hands-on.

rooms	3: 2 doubles, 1 suite.
price	€95-€170.
meals	Breakfast €12. Light meals €25.
closed	Christmas-2 January.
directions	A10 Bordeaux/Paris exit 42, follow signs to Saint Loubès. Avenue on right facing church; château 300m on left.

	Cloé Viralès
tel	+33 (0)5 57 97 16 70
fax	+33 (0)5 57 97 16 71
email	virales@aol.com
web	www.chateau-saint-aignan.com

Map 8 Entry 203

Château Lamothe Prince Noir

33450 Saint Sulpice et Cameyrac, Gironde

Turn off a suburban road into the pages of a fairy tale. A creeper-clad, stone château framed by two towers sits serenely in the middle of a moat. Knights on white chargers, at the very least Rapunzel, should soon appear. Or possibly Edward, the Black Prince, who used it as a medieval hunting lodge. Slip between the trees, over the bridge and be welcomed by the Bastide family. Warm and charismatic, they have given the château a stylish opulence without detracting from its character. Large bedrooms have canopied beds, strong colours, antique bed linen and a rich but comfortable assortment of furniture. One suite has a Mexican theme, another, overlooking the moat, has murals of the seasons. Bathrooms are grand with gold taps, Venetian glass and most have windows. Breakfast on the rose-covered terrace or in the elegant, chandelier-hung salon. Light suppers or, for groups of guests, slap-up dinners with family silver and lacy napery can be arranged. Visit Bordeaux, beaches, play golf, fish in the moat. The Bastides can arrange riding, wine tastings, even a local masseuse. You will be treated as family guests.

rooms	8: 2 doubles, 1 single, 3 suites for 2, 1 suite for 3, 1 family room for 3-5.
price	€150-€230. Singles €75. Family room €245-€290.
meals	Light supper with wine €35-€45, book ahead. Restaurant 5-min drive.
closed	Rarely.
directions	From Bordeaux N89 exit 5; D13 to St Sulpice. There, 2nd right across from bakery towards stadium. Gate 800m on left. Signed.

	Jacques & Luce Bastide
tel	+33 (0)5 56 30 82 16
fax	+33 (0)5 56 30 88 33
email	chat.lamothe@wanadoo.fr
web	www.chateaulamothe.fr

Map 9 Entry 204

Château Le Mas de Montet

Petit Bersac, 24600 Ribérac, Dordogne

A nose for fine living brought John and Richard to this serene place. At the end of an avenue guarded by plane trees – gloriously French – is the château, slate-topped and turretted in Renaissance style. Once frequented by Mitterrand and his labradors – one suite is named in his honour – it has been extravagantly restored. Reception rooms lined with eau de nil brocade are sated with auction house finds, richness and softness bring instant seduction and bedrooms, named after French writers – Corneille, Voltaire, Madame de Lafayette – have all you'd hope for the price, British electrical sockets included! Beds are big and supremely comfortable, four-posters canopied and draped, bathrooms Deco-white… the one in the tower has its own chandelier. Copious breakfasts are served at tables in the Orangery where later you dine on Perigordian delicacies; doors open in summer to a big terrace. 50 hectares of parkland, wildlife and pool sweep down to the fish-rich Dronne. Grand yet easy, this is the perfect place for stressed city souls to unwind.

rooms	11: 4 doubles, 1 twin, 5 suites, 1 apartment for 2 (without kitchen).
price	€132–€189. Suites €158–€310.
meals	Breakfast €14. Lunch €20. Dinner €36–€45.
closed	November-March.
directions	A10 then N10 to Angoulême, south to Libourne, then Montmoreau, then Aubeterre. Signed on D2/D20 between Aubeterre & Ribérac.

	John Ridley & Richard Stimson
tel	+33 (0)5 53 90 08 71
fax	+33 (0)5 53 90 66 92
email	reception@lemasdemontet.com
web	www.lemasdemontet.com

Map 9 Entry 209

Château Les Farcies Du Pech'

Les Farcies, 24100 Bergerac, Dordogne

The neat and tidy winery a mile from Bergerac makes a leafy out-of-town stay. The tone is set by the impeccable cream and French-grey façade: here is a chambre d'hôtes that is both elegant and homely. The Dubards, who took over 10 years ago, live in a separate wing, work hard at their enterprise and are developing a shop to promote the wine. (Do not go home empty-handed from one of the oldest vineyards in the world: this predates Bordeaux.) Inside, whitewashed walls rub shoulders with polished timbers, all is immaculate and not a thing out of place. Big, nicely proportioned bedrooms have high ceilings and gleaming floors, pale sponged walls, striped curtains, traditional lamps and the odd choice antique; windowless bath and shower rooms are halygon-lit. White cotton duvet covers trimmed with beige linen have matching pillows, but nothing is busy or overdone. Windows overlook gentle parkland and grazing deer, all feels settled, there's no one to rush you at breakfast and Madame Vidalencq, your courteous hostess, helps you plan your day.

rooms	5 doubles.
price	€110.
meals	Restaurants in town.
closed	Rarely.
directions	From Bergerac N21 towards Périgueux; right after Centre Leclerc. Signposted 'Les Farcies'.

	Serge Dubard
tel	+33 (0)5 53 82 48 31
fax	+33 (0)5 53 82 47 64
email	vignobles-dubard@wanadoo.fr
web	www.chambre-hote-bergerac.com

Map 9 Entry 210

Château Les Merles

Tuilières, 24520 Mouleydier, Dordogne

The 19th-century French façade conceals an interior of Dutch minimalism suffused with light. Old and stylish new march hand in hand and a Dutch chef heads the kitchen bringing skill and finesse to the cooking: great spit roasts, Bergerac wines, vegetables from the organic garden. A rustic-chic bistro (Philippe Starck chairs on charming old flags), a restaurant in the stables, two light-streamed sitting rooms, a bucolic nine-hole golf course to one side… A golfers' haven it is, but who wouldn't be happy here? The family-run hotel – two sisters in charge – brims with generosity and professionalism. A black and white theme runs throughout – matt-black beds, white bedspreads, black frames, white lamp shades, black towels, white roses – the austerity offset by a rich gilt-framed mirror or a fuchsia fauteuil. Outside is a vast gravelled courtyard with striking white dining chairs and black parasols, a terrace looks south to the shimmering pool and the hills are braided with vines. Civilised, classy, welcoming. *Children's daycare available on request.*

rooms	15: 11 doubles, 1 single, 2 suites, 1 apt for 4 (no kitchen).
price	€120-€160. Single €100-€120. Suites €165-€185. Apt €225-€250.
meals	Breakfast €12.50. Lunch & dinner €18.50-€50. Restaurant closed Tuesday.
closed	Never.
directions	From Bergerac D660 for Sarlat. At Tuilières, left onto D36 for Pressignac. Château 200m.

	Judith Wagemakers & Karlyn van Grinsven
tel	+33 (0)5 53 63 13 42
fax	+33 (0)5 53 63 13 45
email	info@lesmerles.com
web	www.lesmerles.com

Map 9 Entry 211

La Métairie
24150 Mauzac, Dordogne

If you love horses you'll be in your element: you can relax on the terrace and watch them in the next field. You can also ride close by. La Métairie was built as a farm at the turn of the last century and converted into a hotel some 40 years ago, a U-shaped building smothered in wisteria and Virginia creeper. There's no road in sight and you really do feel 'away from it all' – yet the Dordogne and its cliff top villages are just minutes away. Borrow bikes if you're feeling energetic! Bedrooms are large and cheerful, full of sunshiney yellows; beds are huge. They have room for a couple of comfy chairs, too. Bathrooms match – large and cheerful – and three ground-floor rooms have French doors and a semi-private patio. The pool is big enough for a proper swim and when you come out you can read under the trees – there are plenty right by the pool. In summer you can eat out here, or on the flowery terrace. The dining room has black and white floors, washed stone walls and well-spaced tables. Go ahead, indulge, order the four-course Périgourdine menu. You can swim it off later.

rooms	10: 9 doubles, 1 suite.
price	€105–€140. Suite €170–€230. Half-board mandatory in high season €110–€163 p.p.
meals	Breakfast €15. Lunch €18–€25. Dinner €38; Périgourdine menu €45.
closed	November–March.
directions	From Lalinde, D703 for Le Bugue. At Sauveboeuf, D31 through Mauzac. Signed.

	M Heinz Johner
tel	+33 (0)5 53 22 50 47
fax	+33 (0)5 53 22 52 93
email	metairie.la@wanadoo.fr
web	www.la-metairie.com

Map 9 Entry 212

Domaine de la Barde

Route de Périgueux, 24260 Le Bugue sur Vézère, Dordogne

A sensational place. Once a weekend cottage for the 13th-century nobility who owned it, the Domaine has now become a luxurious but immensely friendly and easy-going hotel. The owner, unlike most restorers of ancient buildings, began with the grounds which they arranged as a perfect *jardin à la française* saving several centuries-old trees in the process, before they tackled the mill, the forge and the manor house. There is an informal 'family' feel about the place which in no way detracts from the professionalism of the management: the priority is your comfort, and it shows in their staff and in the immaculate, lavish but personal decoration and furnishing of the bedrooms. They also have a flair for the dramatic visual touch – witness the glass floor under which flows the millstream in the old mill, the *oeil de boeuf* window in the forge and the 'menacing Eros' who surveys you as you stroll through the gardens. There's plenty to do; the swimming pool has a jet-stream massage, there's table tennis and, in the *orangerie*, a sauna.

rooms	18: 15 twins/doubles, 3 suites for 2-3.
price	€88-€169. Suites €170-€217.
meals	Breakfast €14. Lunch & dinner €36-€55.
closed	3 January-March.
directions	From Périgueux N89, exit 16; D710 to Le Bugue. 1km before Le Bugue, Domaine signed on right.

	M Patrick Dubourg
tel	+33 (0)5 53 07 16 54
fax	+33 (0)5 53 54 76 19
email	hotel@domainedelabarde.com
web	www.domainedelabarde.com

Map 9 Entry 213

Hôtel Les Glycines

4 avenue de Laugerie, 24620 Les Eyzies de Tayac, Dordogne

Potential for name-dropping here: Prince Charles stayed for several days in the 60s with his Cambridge tutor. Les Glycines has been lodging people since 1862, when it was a *relais de poste*. It has been enlarged over the years, with the stables being turned into more rooms once they were no longer needed for horses. The gardens are fabulous: they were planted by the son of a head gardener at Versailles. You meander down to the pool under arches laden with roses and honeysuckle and there is even a vegetable garden too. Just past the lobby you enter the dining room which runs the breadth of the building and overlooks the garden. The Lombards took over seven years ago, threw themselves into decoration and have even added another terrace last year. Pascal leads the orchestra in the kitchen; do try his roast veal with choice local ham and truffled polenta. Don't be put off by the busy road and the station nearby: once in the garden you could be in the country, though you might ask for a room at the back or in the annexe. Families can have interconnecting rooms, which sleep five comfortably.

rooms	27: 23 doubles, 4 family rooms for 3.
price	€78-€220.
meals	Breakfast €12. Picnic lunch €12-24. Lunch €22-€47. Dinner €34-€75. Restaurant closed Monday noon.
closed	November-Easter.
directions	From Périgueux, D47 to Sarlat. Over river, on left immediately before Les Eyzies station.

	Pascal Lombard
tel	+33 (0)5 53 06 97 07
fax	+33 (0)5 53 06 92 19
email	glycines.dordogne@wanadoo.fr
web	les-glycines-dordogne.com

Map 9 Entry 214

Hôtel du Manoir de Bellerive

Route de Siorac, 24480 Le Buisson de Cadouin, Dordogne

The manoir was built by Napoleon III for one of his *belles*, and used as a stopover on the route to Biarritz. The entrance hall is huge with a double staircase leading to a gallery; in a niche behind reception is a saintly statue, one of several that came with the house. Off the hall is a bar panelled head to toe in black marble, scattered with glass tables atop huge oriental ginger jars; such is the sumptuousness of the place. The owners, she Parisien, he Alsatian, are charming and omni-present, overseeing an ever-helpful staff. Bedrooms come in three categories – Traditional, Privileged and Exclusive – and are deliciously decorated. Swags and padded walls are the order of the day, floors wear Turkish rugs, bathrooms are sizeable and full of mirrors, the newest, in the Orangery, fashionably tiled in earthy shades. The gourmet cuisine has been bestowed with stars, plates and crowns; in summer you dine under a green and white striped awning. Breakfast out here, overlooking the river, makes a perfect beginning to each day: chocolate croissants, hot rich coffee. Grand, intimate, brilliantly placed.

rooms	22: 3 doubles, 15 twins/doubles, 4 apts (without kitchen) for 3-4.
price	€152-€195. Apartments €225-€235.
meals	Breakfast €18. Lunch & dinner €29-€65. Restaurant closed Mon-Wed.
closed	January-February.
directions	From Toulouse A10 exit 55 for Souillac, then Bergerac. In Périgueux head for Le Bugue & Sarlat on D710, D703, D31e.

	M & Mme Clevenot
tel	+33 (0)5 53 22 16 16
fax	+33 (0)5 53 22 09 05
email	manoir.bellerive@wanadoo.fr
web	www.bellerivehotel.com

Map 9 Entry 215

Café de la Rivière
Le Bourg, 24220 Beynac et Cazanac, Dordogne

In honey-stoned Beynac, overlooking four châteaux and the gentle river, a restaurant with rooms. It is run by an honest and hard-working couple – both corporate escapees – and enhanced by a talented chef. On south-facing terraces hewn out of the rock you are served food that goes beyond the usual *magret de canard*: even fruit crumbles feature here. There's something different every day according to the freshest and best of what the market provides and always a vegetarian option; great value. Rooms, too, are well-priced. You get one at the back (very quiet) or a charming apartment on the top floor. Expect space and simplicity in rooms that are more for sleeping than spending time in: white walls, comfy beds, rugs on waxed wooden floors, voile drapes, double-glazing at the front, air-conditioning for summer. The apartment has a sweet sitting room with a river view and a good little kitchenette. Beautiful, bustling Beynac, whose château was stormed and captured by Richard the Lionheart, is a historic treat, best in May, June and September. *Min. two nights.*

rooms	1 + 2: 1 double. 1 apartment for 4, 1 apartment for 2.
price	€46. Minimum stay 2 nights. Apartments €69; from €295 per wk.
meals	Breakfast €6. Lunch & dinner from €20. Out of season: Friday eves & weekends only. Restaurant closed December-February.
closed	Apartments available all year.
directions	A20 From Brive to Souillac, then D704 to Sarlat. D57 to Beynac.

	Hamish & Xanthe Eadie
tel	+33 (0)5 53 28 35 49
fax	+33 (0)5 53 28 35 49
email	cafe-de-la-riviere@wanadoo.fr

Map 9 Entry 216

Le Relais du Touron

Le Touron, 24200 Carsac Aillac, Dordogne

Such an attractive approach up the drive lined with neatly-clipped box hedges and spiræa – it is all very elegant-looking, surrounded by broad lawns and handsome, mature trees. Reception is in the main entrance hall, by the high open fireplace, but only the big triple bedroom is actually in the main house: all the other rooms and the dining room are in the modern converted barn and stable block with the pool just below. The new dining room has one all-glass wall overlooking the pool and garden beyond and is flooded with light. Madame, with 14 years' experience in Arcachon, is building a reputation for good, interesting food. Bedrooms are above the dining area and have the same decoration in straightforward style: plain carpets and walls, bright bedcovers and curtains and decent lighting. The nearby road is well screened by thick trees and shrubs. Indeed, the three-hectare garden, which also contains a small pond, is a great asset with lots of private corners to be explored and exploited. A delightful bicycle and foot path of six kilometres will take you right into Sarlat.

rooms	18: 13 doubles, 4 twins, 1 family room for 4.
price	€50–€61. Family room €87–€98.
meals	Breakfast €7. Lunch & dinner €15–€34.
closed	15 November–March.
directions	From Sarlat, D704 to Gourdon. Hotel signed on right before Carsac.

	Viala Family
tel	+33 (0)5 53 28 16 70
fax	+33 (0)5 53 28 52 51
email	contact@lerelaisdutouron.com
web	www.lerelaisdutouron.com

Map 9 Entry 217

La Roseraie

11 Place d'Armes, 24290 Montignac Lascaux, Dordogne

Built as the country residence for a Parisian family, it is now a sparkling hotel. Experienced, enthusiastic hoteliers, the Nourrissons have brought their good chef with them. Pretty dining rooms dotted with yellow-clothed tables and posies set the scene for celery and truffle millefeuille and braised guinea fowl with pumpkin and chestnuts; such is their devotion to food there is an 'Initiation à la Gourmandise' menu for children. In summer you spill onto a terrace edged with clipped box… which leads to a garden of mature trees, roses and 19th-century formality, and a delicious palm-fringed pool. The gardens edge the river, prone to flood in winter (one good reason why La Roseraie closes in November). Bedrooms, comfortably pattern-carpeted with traditional furniture soon to be updated, have sweet river and garden views, while two apartments sit privately across the square revealing an unusual mix of the rustic and the frou-frou: fine old beams, stone walls, rococo-style chairs and a fancy four-poster. Medieval Montignac has it all – including the caves at Lascaux.

rooms	14 + 2: 7 doubles, 3 twins, 4 family rooms for 4. 2 apartments for 4.
price	€70-€110. Family rooms €120-€140. Apartments €160. Half-board only, July-August.
meals	Breakfast €11. Lunch from €19. Dinner €21-€41. Half-board only July-August. €80-€125 p.p.
closed	November-Easter.
directions	A20 to Brive; N89 to Périgueux; left to Lardin St Lazare, Montignac centre.

	Vincent & Isabelle Nourrisson
tel	+33 (0)5 53 50 53 92
fax	+33 (0)5 53 51 02 23
email	laroseraie@fr.st
web	www.laroseraie.fr.st

Map 9 Entry 218

Auberge de Castel Merle
24290 Sergeac, Dordogne

This hidden paradise has been in Anita's family for five generations. Her grandfather archeologist added stones from his own digs; Eyzies, the capitol of prehistory, is nearby. Husband Christopher is British and also devoted to this atmospheric place. They have renovated the old buildings with consummate care, keeping the traditional look, using wood from their own land to restore walnut bedheads and doors. Christopher is an enthusiastic truffle hunter and head chef; there's a vast cast-iron cauldron in the banquet room in which he once conjured up a cassoulet for the entire village. This is wild boar country and cooking the beast is one of his specialities. Flowery curtains, pelmets and hand-painted flowers on the walls prettify the dining room; bedrooms have a straightforward country look, with Provençal prints and stone walls. Some rooms overlook the courtyard, others the woods. And the views: the glory of the place is its position, high above the valley of the Vézère, with river, forests and castles beyond – best admired from one of the check-clothed tables on the large, leafy terrace. *Minimum stay two nights.*

rooms	7: 6 doubles, 1 twin.
price	€48–€56. Half-board €45–€48 p.p.
meals	Breakfast €8. Dinner €18–€25. Restaurant closed Sunday lunchtimes.
closed	Mid-October–March.
directions	From Brive A20 or Périgueux A89 to Montignac, then D706 for Les Eyzies. At Thonac left over bridge then right to Sergeac. Signed.

	Anita Castanet & Christopher Millinship
tel	+33 (0)5 53 50 70 08
fax	+33 (0)5 53 50 76 25

Map 9 Entry 219

La Commanderie
245 Condat sur Vezère, Dordogne

Off the medieval street, through the stone archway and the gently-treed gardens, into the steep-roofed *commanderie*. The Commanders of the Order of Malta put up here 700 years ago en route to Santiago de Compostella and a low curved toll passage still forms part of the house, its black slate slabs gloriously intact. This is not so much a hotel as a houseful of guests overseen by diminutive madame, a correct but considerate hostess. An uncontrived collection of antiques warms the friendly bedrooms, each with its own personality – convent-white walls are set off by touches of dark blue, ceilings soar, floors of varying ages and patterns are softened by Indian rugs, maybe there's a crucifix or a pink glass chandelier. Downstairs, guests gather at round tables set with antique cane chairs, floral curtains hang at tall windows and you get two choices per gastronomic course – just right for this unassuming, atmospheric place. There's a pool in the shade of the cedars and the Lascaux Caves are a mile down the road.

rooms	7: 5 doubles, 2 twins.
price	€53-€68.
meals	Breakfast €10. Lunch €20-€25. Dinner €32-€40.
closed	August.
directions	N89 between Brive & Péigueux. At crossroads at Lardin, towards Condat, right to La Commanderie, 50m after church.

	Mme Annick Roux
tel	+33 (0)5 53 51 26 49
fax	+33 (0)5 53 51 39 38
email	hotellacommanderie@wanadoo.fr
web	www.best-of-perigord.tm.fr

Map 9 Entry 220

Manoir d'Hautegente

24120 Coly, Dordogne

The ancient manor, first a smithy, later a mill, has been in the family for 300 years but is paradoxically just 50 years old: burned down in the Second World War, it was rebuilt. The millstream has become a fabulous waterfall feeding a pond that shimmers beneath the bedroom windows and the thoroughly kempt garden is a riot of colour. Hautegente is rich inside too, like a private house, with two sumptuous dining rooms clothed in silk and hung with well-chosen paintings and prints. There's a cosy drawing room where a large fireplace and a vast array of cognacs summon the sybarite. Lavishly decorated bedrooms have fine thick curtains, antiques and pretty lamps; some are small, some enormous and the soft, expensive feel of padded wall fabrics contrasts with the lovely old staircase leading up from the hall. The rooms in the converted miller's house are more modern; four have mezzanines and the ground-floor room is vast. Bathrooms are all beautifully tiled and properly equipped. A splendid and peaceful place.

rooms	17: 12 doubles, 5 triples.
price	€83-€215. Half-board possible June-mid-September €90-€165 p.p.
meals	Buffet breakfast €13.50. Dinner €46-€65. Picnics available.
closed	November-Easter.
directions	From Brive N89 for Périgueux through Terrasson. Left at Le Lardin on D704 for Sarlat, then left at Condat on D62 to Coly.

	Patrick & Marie Josée Hamelin
tel	+33 (0)5 53 51 68 03
fax	+33 (0)5 53 50 38 52
email	hotel@manoir-hautegente.com
web	www.manoir-hautegente.com

Map 9 Entry 221

Domaine du Moulin de Labique
Saint Vivien, 47210 Villereal, Lot-et-Garonne

Ponies in the field, ducks on the pond, goats in the greenhouse and food *à la grande-mère* on the plate – the Domaine du Moulin de Labique glows with warmth and humour. Shutters are painted with *bleu de pastel* from the Gers and the 13th-century interiors have lost none of their aged charm. Your hosts used to run a restaurant, now they do chambres d'hôtes and dinner (seasonal, local, delicious) for guests. Bedrooms are a match for the rest of the place and are divided between those in the main building above a vaulted *salle d'armes*, those in the barn, reached via a grand stone stair, and an apartment in the old bread and prune-drying ovens. There are chunky roof beams, seagrass mats on ancient tiles, lovely old iron bedsteads, antique mirrors and papers flower-sprigged in positive colours (framboise, jade, green). The suite in the barn has its own terrace, some bathrooms have Portuguese tiles: so much to captivate and delight. Outside, old French roses and young alleys of trees, a bamboo-fringed stream, a restaurant in the stables and an exquisite pool.

rooms	8 + 1: 3 doubles, 3 twins, 1 suite for 4. 1 apartment for 4.
price	€90. Suite & apartment €140.
meals	Breakfast €8. Dinner €30.
closed	Rarely.
directions	At Cancon on N21 take D124 towards Mouflanquin; then D153 at Beauregard to St Vivien; on right 1km after St Vivien.

	Hélène Boulet & François Passebon
tel	+33 (0)5 53 01 63 90
fax	+33 (0)5 53 01 73 17
email	moulin-de-labique@wanadoo.fr
web	www.moulin-de-labique.fr

Map 9 Entry 222

Château de Méracq
64410 Méracq Arzacq, Pyrénées-Atlantiques

Madame will give you a warm welcome in excellent English and is always happy to help or just to chat. She is very proud of her château, her dog, her hens and her husband's cooking. He has established a menu that combines the south-west's predilection for foie gras and duck with exotic sprinklings of spices and rose petals. If you take the half-board option, you can juggle your meals around as you like: even by eating more the next day if you miss one. The pretty château is at the end of a long and inviting driveway through large grounds with chairs under shady trees. One oak, just as you reach the château, is 200 years old, perhaps planted by proud new owners. The eight bedrooms are an unusual mix: some in fresh stripes or flowers, others with bold turquoise or rose walls, with contemporary patterns on the beds. The first-floor rooms are grander, with bath and shower, while those on the second floor are simpler but all have their own shower. Rooms have lace-trimmed sheets, bowls of fruit and flowers and even bathrooms have plants. There are no numbers on the doors. As Madame says: "It wouldn't feel like home".

rooms	8: 5 doubles, 1 twin, 2 suites for 4.
price	€90-€180. Suites €250.
meals	Breakfast €8-€11. Lunch & dinner menus from €40, book ahead.
closed	Mid-December-mid-January.
directions	N34 for 12km towards Aire & Mont de Marsan, left on D944 through Thèze. Château on edge of Méracq.

	M & Mme Guerin-Recoussine
tel	+33 (0)5 59 04 53 01
fax	+33 (0)5 59 04 55 50
email	chateau-meracq@wanadoo.fr
web	www.chateau-meracq.com

Map 13 Entry 223

Domaine de l'Aragon

Route de Pau, 64680 Herrère, Pyrénées-Atlantiques

Winged cherubs, buxom wenches, handsome lovers greet you at breakfast — and flicker provocatively in the candlelight over dinner. The wall panels of the *salle à manger* of this 19th-century hunting lodge charm with their friskiness. Helmut and Eva, the young, friendly Austrian owners (perfect English), have retained the mini-château style of the house and lost the pretension — here is grand living in laid-back fashion. Heaps of chandeliers, gilded mirrors, oil paintings, wooden panelling, and no-one to mind if you curl up in front of the fire. Bedrooms are comfortably and traditionally furnished, with boldly coloured walls and floating curtains. First-floor rooms have grand windows, top-floor rooms sit prettily under the eaves. Helmut cooks dinner — he runs an e-commerce business *and* is a trained chef — delivered to an intimate dining room; summer meals are served on a prettily tiled veranda beneath a stripy awning. Pop into Pau, borrow bicycles and explore Béarn, take a day trip to Biarritz. Or relax among the garden's venerable trees and raise a glass to the snow-topped Pyrénées.

rooms	9: 7 doubles, 2 twin.
price	€60–€90.
meals	Breakfast €8. Dinner €20, book ahead.
closed	Rarely.
directions	From Pau N134 to Oloron Ste Marie & Saragosse for 27km; hotel on left entering Herrère.

Eva Kratky & Helmut Fritz

tel	−33 (0)5 59 39 24 63
fax	−33 (0)5 59 39 24 84
email	info@domaine-aragon.com
web	www.domaine-aragon.com

Map 13 Entry 224

Château d'Agnos
64400 Agnos, Pyrénées-Atlantiques

Originally an aristocratic hunting lodge, Agnos was a convent for 30 years until this exceptional couple converted it into a fabulous guest house. Heather, warmly communicative, and Desmond, a talented retired architect, both widely travelled and with a great sense of fun, have done wonders with cells and refectory – and still do all the cooking. The black and white bathroom with the antique cast-iron bath and vaulted ceiling used to be the château's treasure room – it is now attached to the gilt-furnished Henri IV suite. The whole house left us agape: high ceilings framing remarkable mirrors, original paintings set into panelling, a cunning mixture of period and modern furniture and a panelled dining room with a superb floor of ancient yellow and stone-coloured tiles and a black marble fountain. Look out for the medieval kitchen, the old prison. Your hosts would be grateful if you could find the secret passage which King François I is said to have used (he stayed here and he had regular amorous escapades). A place of great style, much history and refined food. *Children over 12 welcome.*

rooms	5: 2 twins, 2 suites for 3, 1 suite for 4.
price	€75–€140.
meals	Hosted dinner €22, book ahead.
closed	Occasionally.
directions	From Pau N134 to Oloron Ste Marie; through town. South on N134 for Saragosse for 1km. In Bidos, right for Agnos.

	Heather & Desmond Nears-Crouch
tel	+33 (0)5 59 36 12 52
fax	+33 (0)5 59 36 13 69
email	chateaudagnos@wanadoo.fr

Map 13 Entry 225

La Tour de Molotov
Biarritz, Pyrérées-Atlantiques

Ah – Biarritz! A word that sets brains throbbing with nostalgia for headier days. But there remains much that can still excite the well-heeled idler. This splendid hotel, high above the town in an unspoiled – indeed, abandoned – landscape, has been kept in the very state in which it was left after the last wild party thrown there by the young bloods of Paris. Here it was, within these walls, that they invented the famous ''Biarritz cocktail'': a lethal concoction of brandy, calvados, cointreau, pure alcohol, a 'mystery' ingredient and a lighted cigar. The cigar was an interesting Molotovian touch, but on this occasion things went wrong and the result was the spectacular demolition of most of the building. Nobody was hurt, but the incident led to the rapid demise of that particular cocktail. Today's young bloods are encouraged to steep themselves in the mood of the place before coming; the owners are entirely forgiving, so it's wise to turn up in a merry condition and equipped with all you need to be able to ignore discomforts. A night under the stars beside those dignified old stones is not to be missed.

rooms	1: Bring your own chaise longue.
price	Worth paying.
meals	Lunch: liquid. Dinner: flaming grills a specilaity.
closed	Never to the open-minded or lovers of incendiary conversation.
directions	Once on the straight and narrow, veer off sharply.

tel	+33 (0)241 241 241
fax	+33 (0)241 241 241
web	www.latourmolatov.bo.mb

Map 55 Entry 226

Maison Garnier

29 rue Gambetta, 64200 Biarritz, Pyrénées-Atlantiques

In glamorous Biarritz, playground of royalty and stars, a jewel of sophisticated simplicity. Pristine-white bathrooms have huge showerheads, bedrooms are done in subtle white, eggshell, dark chocolate and soft coffee with the occasional splash of brilliant colour. The bright breakfast room has Basque floorboards setting off pale walls, red and white striped curtains; white linen is a perfect foil for lovely regional tableware in a red and green stripe and light pours in from great windows. Guests are enchanted by hotel and owners: both have real charm and warmth. In 1999, this old boarding house was turned into a smart and friendly little hotel. So, no hall counter, just a gorgeous wrought-iron stair rail, a 1930s-feel salon with a deep sofa, an old fireplace and a magnificent oriental carpet – the tone is set the moment you arrive. And you will soon be at ease with your delightful, engaging hosts. On a side street, five minutes' walk from that fabulous surfing beach it is just far enough from the center to be out of the hub-bub but close enough to do everything by foot. Remarkable value, book early.

rooms	7: 5 doubles, 2 twins.
price	€90-€130.
meals	Breakfast €9. Lunch & dinner available locally.
closed	Rarely.
directions	From A63 exit Biarritz & La Négresse for Centre Ville & Place Clémenceau. Straight ahead for large, white bank building with clock; left onto Rue Gambetta. Free parking on side street.

	Anne & Yves Gelot
tel	+33 (0)5 59 01 60 70
fax	+33 (0)5 59 01 60 80
email	maison-garnier@hotel-biarritz.com
web	www.hotel-biarritz.com

Map 13 Entry 227

Hôtel Laminak

Route de St Pée, 64210 Arbonne, Pyrénées-Atlantiques

Relaxed, smiling and friendly, Philippe and Chantal are enchanted with their new project. They had just taken over when we visited so the style is still country cottage, but with less emphasis on floral designs. The setting is gorgeous, with all the lush greenery of the Basque countryside at your feet and views up to the mountains. The hotel is on a quiet road outside the village of Arbonne, with a few discreetly screened neighbours and a big, handsome garden filled with mature shrubs and trees. In summer it is a delight to eat breakfast on the terrace. Rooms are neat and attractive, carpeted, wallpapered and with antique pine furniture. You will sleep well here, and be looked after with a quiet and warm efficiency by the owners for whom this place has been a long-cherished dream. You can, too, settle round the open fire in the evenings, warmed by the easy comfort of the place and the satisfying sag of the leather furniture. It is an easy hop to the coast and the throbbing vitality of Biarritz. Those mountains are worth a week's effort in themselves; just below them, the fish await your line.

rooms	12 twins/doubles.
price	€69–€98. Children under 5 free.
meals	Breakfast €10. Light dinner €11–€17, book ahead.
closed	Mid-November–5 December.
directions	A63 exit 4 La Négresse & follow signs to Arbonne; signed.

	Philippe & Chantal Basin
tel	+33 (0)5 59 41 95 40
fax	+33 (0)5 59 41 87 65
email	info@hotel-laminak.com
web	www.hotel-laminak.com

Map 13 Entry 228

Les Almadies

58 rue Gambetta, 64500 Saint Jean de Luz, Pyrénées-Atlantiques

In the heart of busy Basque Saint Jean de Luz, this cool little find. From the discreet street entrance off the tree- and flower-filled square to the understatedly modern furnishings, everything is calm, relaxing and quietly stylish. Jean Jacques and Patricia, a young, gentle, friendly couple, have a clear eye for clean lines and harmony. The wooden floor and Philippe Starck-style chairs in the breakfast room create a lovely bright space in which to start the day; take your fill of fresh fruits, compotes, yoghurts, cheeses and pastries. If it's sunny, eat outside on the balcony overlooking a charming little town *place*. Bedrooms, with French windows and balconies onto quaint side street or square, have an easy-going simplicity – soft colours, embroidered bed covers, white-painted furniture. Bathrooms are a glistening contemporary mixture of wood and white tiles. Spend the day at the beach, hop over to the glorious Guggenheim in Spanish Bilbao, or stay put and explore this border town. No dinners but plenty of restaurants close by. A simple, restful spot – made for lingering.

rooms	7: 4 doubles, 1 single, 2 triples.
price	€75–€120.
meals	Breakfast €10. Restaurants in town.
closed	3 weeks in November.
directions	In Saint Jean de Luz follow signs for Centre Ville & La Poste; with La Poste on your left, 2nd right on Rue d'Esslissagaraiy which becomes Rue du Midi. Here parking is behind hotel.

	Jean Jacques Hargous
tel	+33 (0)5 59 85 34 48
fax	+33 (0)5 59 26 12 42
email	hotel.lesalmadies@wanadoo.fr
web	www.hotel-les-almadies.com

Map 13 Entry 229

Château d'Urtubie

Urrugne, 64122 St Jean de Luz, Pyrénées-Atlantiques

The Chateau d'Urtubie was built in 1341 with permission from Edward III. The keep is still intact, except for the roof which was changed in 1654 to resemble Versailles, using the expertise of local boat builders. Your host, Laurent, is a direct descendant of the builder of the castle, Martin de Tartas, and opened Urtubie as a hotel in 1996 to make sure he can keep it alive. The castle is classified and also operates as a museum: *The Antiques Roadshow* could run an entire series here. You can have a 'prestige' bedroom on the first floor, very grand and imposing: not 'light and airy' which we often praise, but a touch sombre and totally in keeping with the age and style. On the second floor, you have the 'charm' bedrooms, which are slightly smaller. Bathrooms are a mix of ancient and modern, with stylish touches such as airy mosquito nets draped over old-fashioned baths. On the outskirts of a pretty little Basque town, only five minutes' drive from the beach, Urtubie is also set in beautiful gardens. Don't be worried it might be stuffy: Laurent couldn't be more friendly and families are most welcome.

rooms	10: 8 twins/doubles, 1 double, 1 single.
price	€65–€145.
meals	Breakfast €10. Good restaurants in town.
closed	Mid-November–mid-March.
directions	A63 Bayonne & St Sebastien, exit St Jean de Luz Sud onto N10 for Urrugne. Right just before roundabout entering Urrugne. 3km from St. Jean de Luz.

	Laurent de Coral
tel	+33 (0)5 59 54 31 15
fax	+33 (0)5 59 54 62 51
email	chateaudurtubie@wanadoo.fr
web	www.chateaudurtubie.fr

Map 13 Entry 230

Lehen Tokia

Chemin Achotarreta, 64500 Ciboure, Pyrénées-Atlantiques

The extraordinary name of this house means 'The First Place' in Basque, and the place is as extraordinary as its name implies. Built in the 1920s by the Basque architect Hiriart, for a British gentleman and his Mexican-Basque wife, it is a monument to Art Deco. Indeed, Hiriart himself invented the expression to describe the style the house epitomises. With stained glass by Gruber, marble and parquet floors, furnishings, carpets and pictures custom-made, it feels, the owner suggests, as if it has been preserved *dans son jus*, like confit of goose. And here it is now for us to enjoy. The bedrooms, like the rest of the house, make you feel as if you are in a luxurious private home: the panelling, furnishings and fabulous bathrooms have tremendous style. Perfect little jewels, they are themed, decorated and named after precious stones – Diamant, Lapiz-Lazuli, Rubis, Améthyste, Ivoire. As if the architecture isn't enough, the house has the most stunning views over the bay of St Jean de Luz, a rose garden and sumptuous breakfasts. Perfect for those who appreciate Art Deco style.

rooms	7: 6 doubles, 1 suite for 3-4.
price	€80-€150. Suite €180-€215.
meals	Breakfast €10. Excellent restaurants 1km.
closed	13 November-January.
directions	From A63 exit St Jean de Luz Sud to Ciboure. After sign to Kechiloa, left; signed.

Yan Personnaz

tel	+33 (0)5 59 47 18 16
fax	+33 (0)5 59 47 38 04
email	info@lehen-tokia.com
web	www.lehen-tokia.com

Map 13 Entry 231

Hôtel de Charme les Hortensias du Lac

1578 avenue du Tour du Lac, 40150 Hossegor, Landes

Monsieur Hubert has a distinctive touch – he has renovated this jewel of a 30s building in 'Basco-Landais' style with an eye to feng shui. In the paintwork and fabric, soft yellows and pale blues, beiges, whites and off-whites, chocolates and caramels set the tone – and there are lamps, mirrors, archways, curves, candles and bunches of those long yin yang sticks said to direct energy. The rugs and lamps are his inspirations, created by talented artisans. All this and the proximity of the lake create a peaceful, harmonious atmosphere. The basic double rooms are not big but impeccable; the suites and duplexes have either a private terrace or balcony, some with a view of the lake. Real laps can be swum in the long pool alongside a sun deck flanked by molded loungers; strolls can be had on the six kilometres of paths around the lake – but be back for tea and coffee served at 4.30pm. Breakfast is served until noon: eggs, Serrano ham, a multiple choice of cheese, fresh and stewed fruit, French gingerbread, cakes and *viennoiseries*, toast, yogurt, fresh orange juice and…champagne. A week would be perfect.

rooms	24: 11 doubles, 13 suites & duplexes for 2-6.
price	€115-€185. Suites & duplexes €115-€375.
meals	Champagne breakfast €18.
closed	November-March.
directions	A63, exit 8 Bennesse Marenne & Cap Breton follow signs for Hossegor. In centre for beach; 1st right after bridge over canal.

	M Frédéric Hubert
tel	+33 (0)5 58 43 99 00
fax	+33 (0)5 58 43 42 81
email	reception@hortensias-du-lac.com
web	www.hortensias-du-lac.com

Map 13 Entry 232

Photo Corel

auvergne
limousin

Château Ribagnac
87400 Saint Martin Terressus, Haute-Vienne

The door opens onto a family château in a naturally relaxed mood — families and honeymooners would feel at peace here. Patrick and Colette, and their two young girls, chose to swap a London city setting for a small, elegant, 17th-century Limousin château replete with musket holes and surrounded by woods. Later it was renovated by porcelain manufacturers keen to outdo their rivals... hence the glorious flights of fancy in carved oak and stone. Your friendly, multi-lingual hosts usher you up a curving deep oak stair to large, luminous bedrooms; a shapely white bed or floors strewn with light from stained-glass windows, a gilt-framed mirror on a lavender wall, a balcony with an enchanting view, a chic bathroom with creamy mosaics. Breakfast is served overlooking the lake in summer, as are delicious five-course dinners (mushrooms from the woods, Limousin beef from the surrounding fields); an excellent wine list is at hand. There are two salons to retire to — one with black sofas and elaborate fireplace, or wander among the grounds. The château has a small chapel and library as well as a tearoom.

rooms	6: 1 double, 5 suites for 4-5.
price	€100-€175.
meals	Hosted dinner with wine & coffee, €40-€45, except Tuesdays & Wednesdays.
closed	Mid-December-mid-February.
directions	From Ambazac follow signs for 'gare'. Under bridge for D56 to St Martin Terressus. Château on right after 3km.

	Patrick & Colette Bergot
tel	+33 (0)5 55 39 77 91
email	reservations@chateauribagnac.com
web	www.chateauribagnac.com

Map 9 Entry 233

Domaine des Mouillères
23250 St Georges la Pouge, Creuse

A small backwater of a village, a big clearing in the Limousin forest – here is a walker's paradise. On a south-facing slope with only distantly rolling hillsides, fine trees and a couple of donkeys to disturb the eye, the long stone hotel was built in 1870 as a farmhouse for Madame's great-great-grandfather and feels as solid as her lineage. Inside, you get that sense of long-gone days of endless country peace: leather-bound tomes, gilt-framed sepia photographs of Grandmamma or great-aunt Gladys as a baby, palely gentle floral designs on wallpapers and bedcovers. But the warm carpeting, the neat little bathrooms, the stripily plush modern furniture in the lounge betray a thoroughly contemporary care for comfort. And there's a lovely terrace outside. The delightfully friendly owners and their children, the geese and their goslings, the donkeys and their foals (summer population, of course) welcome you and your family into their rural world and Madame will serve you dinners of high authenticity: old family recipes made with fresh local produce. After which, peace will descend.

rooms	6: 4 twins/doubles; 1 double with shower & separate wc; 1 single with separate bath.
price	€58-€84. Single €28.
meals	Breakfast €8.50. Picnic available. Dinner €15-€30. Two restaurants 3km & 7km away.
closed	October-March.
directions	70km from Limoges towards Bourganeuf & Aubusson N141. Left at Charbonnier to St Georges la Pouge.

	Madame Elizabeth Blanquart-Thill
tel	+33 (0)5 55 66 60 64
fax	+33 (0)5 55 66 68 80
email	mouilleres@aol.com

Map 10 Entry 234

La Maison des Chanoines
Route de l'Eglise, 19500 Turenne, Corrèze

Originally built to house the cannons (*les chanoines*) of Turenne, this ancient restaurant-hotel has been in Monsieur Cheyroux's family for 300 years! No wonder the family held on to it – this 16th-century, mellow-stoned house is one of the loveliest we have seen in a village full of steep-pitched slate roofs. Madame, young, charming, elegant, is a fan of fine English fabrics and has used them lavishly for curtains and cushions. Bedrooms are divided between this house and another (equally ancient) opposite, approached via a little bridge from the garden. These well-lit rooms have plain carpets and white walls; bathrooms are luxurious with fluffy towels. The breakfast room is stone-flagged with wickerwork chairs padded in duck-egg blue. The dining room is in the old cannon cellar: small and cosy, with white-clothed tables and vaulted ceiling. You can dine under a fairy-light-strewn pergola in the garden covered with honeysuckle and roses. And the food is a delight; monsieur is chef and will use only the freshest, most local ingredients, including vegetables and herbs from the garden. An enchanting place.

rooms	6: 2 doubles, 2 twins, 1 triple, 1 family.
price	€65–€90.
meals	Breakfast €9. Lunch & dinner menu €30–€40. Open for lunch Sun & holidays. Closed Wed in June.
closed	15 October–week before Easter.
directions	From Brive, D38 to Monplaisir, then D8 for 8km to Turenne. Left uphill following château sign. Hotel on left before church.

	Chantal & Claude Cheyroux
tel	+33 (0)5 55 85 93 43
fax	+33 (0)5 55 85 93 43
email	maisondeschanoines@wanadoo.fr
web	www.maison-des-chanoines.com

Map 9 Entry 235

Au Rendez-Vous des Pêcheurs

Pont du Chambon, 19320 St Merd de Lapleau, Corrèze

The proof of the fishing… is in the 15-kilo pike hanging in the bar of this delectable place – it isn't called Fishermen's Lodge for nothing. The house and its exquisite lakeside setting are intimately linked. Fifty years ago, the Fabrys built a house on the banks of the Dordogne; at the same time a dam was started just downstream. Madame opened a kitchen for the site workers – and the house became an inn, which she now runs with her daughter-in-law. This being Perigord, food looms as large as that great fish. The restaurant, a fine room full of light and plants and Limoges china, overlooks the view reaching off to the distant wooded hills of the gorge; menus are brilliantly short and to the point. Bedrooms are differently decorated in simple, pleasing country style with coordinated bathrooms. The terrace is generous, the garden pretty, the view to treasure. Remarkable value in one of France's gentlest, loveliest pieces of country. Take a trip down the river in a traditional long boat; dismantled in Bordeaux, they were 'walked' back to the region to ship out yet more oak for the wine barrels.

rooms	8 twins/doubles.
price	€40-€48. Half-board mandatory in summer, €43 p.p.
meals	Breakfast €6. Picnic available. Lunch & dinner €16-€45. Restaurant closed Sunday evenings & Mondays, September-June.
closed	12 November-mid February.
directions	42km east of Tulle: D978 to St Merd de Lapleau via Marcillac la Croisille, then D13 to lieu-dit Pont du Chambon.

	Madame Fabry
tel	+33 (0)5 55 27 88 39
fax	+33 (0)5 55 27 83 19
email	contact@rest-fabry.com
web	www.rest-fabry.com

Map 10 Entry 236

Auberge de Concasty

15600 Boisset, Cantal

Half a mile high stands the river-ploughed plateau, the air is strong, the country wild, the space immense. Here, a good square family mansion, built 300 years ago and proud beneath its curvy shingle roof. Over the last 40 years, the Causse family have restored it, bringing everything thoroughly up to date: jacuzzi, Turkish bath and organic or local-grown produce to keep you blooming (lots of veg from the sister's farm next door). The dining room, dominated by a great inglenook fireplace where a fine plant collection lives in summer, and the covered patio overlooking the pool and the valley beyond, are the stage for great shows of foie gras and asparagus, scallops and confits, where the supporting cast is an impressive choice of estate wines; a fine breakfast spread, too. Guest rooms, some in the main house, some in a restored barn, are stylishly rustic with space, good floral fabrics, new mattresses and an evocative name each – no standardisation here, except for the great view – and . You will love the smiling, attentive staff and the warm family atmosphere they generate. *Some rooms with balcony or terrace.*

rooms	13 twins/doubles.
price	€63-€96.
meals	Breakfast €16. Picnic available. Dinner €32-€42.
closed	December-mid-March.
directions	From Aurillac, N122 for Figeac, left to Manhès on D64. From Figeac, N122 then D17 after Maurs.

	Martine & Omar Causse-Adllal
tel	+33 (0)4 71 62 21 16
fax	+33 (0)4 71 62 22 22
email	info@auberge-concasty.com
web	www.auberge-concasty.com

Map 10 Entry 237

Hostellerie de la Maronne
Le Theil, 15140 St Martin Valmeroux, Cantal

Silence and rolling green space! In glorious country where the little Maronne hurtles towards its gorge and brown cows echo the russet of autumn, this 1800s manor looks out to wooded hills and dark mountains. You will meet its charming, subtly humorous owner and be well fed by his wife in a dining room with soft quiet colours and pretty rugs. The lovely double drawing room has deep sofas, two fireplaces, more rugs, some intriguing Madagascan furniture. Bedrooms, all with excellent bedding, vary in size and are on different levels in a small warren of buildings, past flowering terraces and an indoor flower bed. Nearly all have the sweeping valley view (two rooms at the back are up against the hillside); the best are the terrace rooms. Sober décor is enlivened by exotic pieces — framed textiles from India, a solitaire table from Madagascar — and bathrooms are a good size. The pool is ideal for landscape-gazing, there's fabulous walking — give yourself an hour to tour the property — and you will be made to feel very welcome in this house of silence: no seminars, no piped music and headphones for telly — bliss.

rooms	21: 18 twins/doubles, 3 suites.
price	€85-€125. Suites €130-€152.
meals	Breakfast €11.
	Lunch & dinner €25-€70.
closed	November-Easter.
directions	From Aurillac, D922 north for 33km to St Martin Valmeroux, then D37 towards Fontanges.

	M & Mme Decock
tel	+33 (0)4 71 69 20 33
fax	+33 (0)4 71 69 28 22
email	maronne@maronne.com
web	www.maronne.com

Map 10 Entry 238

Hôtel de la Poste

Le Bourg, 15190 Marcenat, Cantal

For a touch of France at its most profound, try this inauspicious little hotel and bistro at the head of a spectacular valley — at 1,200m, smack between two volcanos. This is not a fancy area — although Marie-José and her mother serve up some prize-winning fare on their gingham-topped tables along with an interesting selection of little known wines from the area; things are down-to-earth and the folk are friendly. We arrived on market day and there was a splendid gathering of locals sitting out on the terrace in front of the hotel, nursing their aperitif before lunch. There are unexpected surprises however: just over the hill a Russian Orthodox monastery where the art of icon painting by the resident nuns can be watched once a week; and it is here you will find the only thunder and lightning museum in France. The mystery and beauty of the storm is captured in photos, films, special effects and a spectacular collection of struck-by-lightening objects. Oout of season, it can be opened upon request. Good value, a humble hub for all the beauty that surrounds, and Marie-José speaks perfect English.

rooms	8: 3 doubles, 2 triples, 1 family room; 2 doubles sharing shower.
price	€28–€62.
meals	Breakfast €5.50 Lunch €12. Dinner from €25.
closed	Christmas & New Year for 2 weeks.
directions	A75 exit 23; N122 for Aurillac; right on D679 for Allanche & Condat. Marcenat lies between them on main road.

	Mme Marie-José Andraud
tel	+33 (0)4 71 78 84 78
fax	+33 (0)4 71 78 80 70
web	www.cantal-hotels.com/marcenat/hoteldelaposte

Map 10 Entry 239

Château de Collanges
Le Bourg, 63340 Collanges, Puy-de-Dôme

Wander down from the Chambre Verte (your medieval-styled bedroom) for aperitifs in the salon: it is very French, with formal antiques, high wooden ceilings and dark striped silk wallpaper. Pascale and Denis will join you before he pops into the kitchen to put the finishing touches to dinner. A talented cook, Denis is also a doctor (three days a week at a local surgery) and a dab hand at DIY: he is currently restoring a music pavilion in the garden. You dine in a stone-vaulted room with red walls, on the best local produce and vegetables from Pascale's potager. Most bedrooms look onto parkland and are named after colours; beds, all a good size, are draped, canopied or four-postered, dressed in lovely embroidered antique sheets and pillowcases. Ivoire has steps up to a bath in a curtained alcove: over the top for some, maybe, but certainly dramatic. There's billiards indoors, and, in a quiet corner of the lovely English garden – Pascale's domain – a swimming pool beckons.

rooms	5: 3 doubles, 1 triple, 1 suite for 4.
price	€79-€139. Suite €150-€180.
meals	Dinner €38, by arrangement except Mondays & Thursdays. Restaurants 10 minutes' drive.
closed	18 November-18 December; 5 January-5 February.
directions	A75 exit 17 for Ardes sur Couze dans St Germain Lembron; 3km further to Collanges.

	Pascale, Denis & Félus
tel	+33 (0)4 73 96 47 30
fax	+33 (0)4 73 96 58 72
email	contact@chateaucollanges.com
web	www.chateaudecollanges.com

Map 10 Entry 240

Château de Maulmont

St Priest Bramefart, 63310 Randan, Puy-de-Dôme

This extraordinary place, built in 1830 by Louis Philippe for his sister Adélaïde, has long views and architecture: medieval crenellations, 16th-century brick patterning, Loire-Valley slate roofs, neo-gothic windows, even real Templar ruins – a cornucopia of character. The owners provide activities on 23 hectares of parkland – a golf driving range, riding nearby, fishing, swimming – and cultivate a certain 'formal informality'. They have preserved original features – carved inside shutters, the orginal spit in the kitchen, the astounding banqueting hall with its stained-glass portraits of Adélaïde in various moods – and collected some stunning furniture. Bedrooms go from small to very big, from plain honest comfortable with simple shower room to draped and four-postered château-romantic in the tower (the *luxury* rooms are worth the difference). And do visit the King's Room, a round blue and white (original paint!) 'tent' in a tower, for a brilliant whisper-to-shout effect. Stephane Roesch, the star-studded chef makes dining more than tempting and staff are alert and eager.

rooms	19 + 3: 12 doubles, 6 twins, 1 family suite for 3-4. 3 apts for 4-6.
price	€80-€180. Suite €195-€220. Apartments €200-€275.
meals	Breakfast €12-€14. Lunch & dinner €34-€60; with wine €65-€80. La Taverne weekday menu €20.
closed	January-5 February.
directions	N209 for Vichy; D131 for Hauterive; there, right to St Priest Bramefant; D55, right at r'bout on D59 to Randan.

Mary & Théo Bosman

tel	+33 (0)4 70 59 03 45
fax	+33 (0)4 70 59 11 88
email	info@chateau-maulmont.com
web	www.chateau-maulmont.com

Map 10 Entry 241

Photo Corel

midi – pyrénées

La Domaine de la Borie Grande

Saint Marcel Campes, 81170 Cordes sur Ciel, Tarn

The 18th-century house in two hectares of parkland combines understatedly elegant luxury with a country B&B mood – wholly delightful. It is a beautifully-kept home where you will find artistic flair and a love of cooking (vegetables from the neighbour, a stock of local wines and produce). A place of friendly proportions and lovingly collected antiques, where soft yellow cushions and gilt-edged fauteuils add sparkle to a palette of taupe, cream and soft grey. Enter a square hall off which lead three reception rooms: a cosy one for contemplation, a tranquil drawing room for tea and a grand salon for aperitifs and conversation. A stunning carved armoire – from the owner's geat grandmother – takes pride of place, the deep cream sofa could seat a dozen, a big pale rug warms a terracotta floor and Cordes is perched high on the hill: magical. You will be guided up a sweeping stair to large and luminous bedrooms where antique rugs strew polished parquet, crisp linen enfolds new beds and white bathrooms come with big mirrors and oodles of towels. And the garden has tennis and a pool. *Cash or cheque only.*

rooms	3: 1 double, 1 twin, 1 suite.
price	€80.
meals	Hosted dinner €30 with aperitif, wine & coffee; book ahead.
closed	Rarely.
directions	In Cordes sur Ciel follow signs toward Laguépie. Right at bend on bottom of hill leaving Cordes; straight on 1km to church in Campes; left to St Amans. On left, 500m from church.

	Marian Clark
tel	+33 (0)5 63 56 58 24
fax	+33 (0)5 63 56 58 24
email	laboriegrande@wanadoo.fr
web	www.laboriegrande.com

Map 15 Entry 242

Hôtel Cuq en Terrasses

Cuq le Château, 81470 Cuq Toulza, Tarn

Even the name is appealing. Come to the Pays de Cocagne, their brochure says. Where is that exactly, you may wonder, have I drunk that wine? It is in fact an imaginary land of pleasure, from the old French 'land of cakes'. Brochures often stretch the truth, but this place is magical. Philippe and Andonis gave up good jobs in Paris to buy this 18th-century presbytery after coming here on holiday. Perched in a beautiful garden on the side of a hill, between Toulouse and Castres, the tall, mellow stone house with white shutters looks so inviting. All the rooms, including a two-floor suite by the saltwater pool, are full of character, all different, with old terracotta floors, hand-finished plaster, exposed beams and some antique beds. But it is worth staying here just for the bathrooms – all different, in wood and white or terracotta and with hand-painted tiles. Breakfast on a long narrow terrace which blends into the garden. If you manage to drag yourself away to do some sightseeing, come back for fantastic Mediterranean food, bought earlier at the local market. It doesn't get much better.

rooms	7: 3 doubles, 3 twins/doubles, 1 suite.
price	€90–€135. Suite €150. Half-board available with min. 4-night stay.
meals	Breakfast €12. Snacks available. Hosted dinner €33; book ahead.
closed	November-Easter.
directions	N126 to Cuq Toulza. Then D45 towards Revel. After 2km on left at top of hill in old village.

M Philippe Gallice & M Andonis Vassalos

tel	+33 (0)5 63 82 54 00
fax	+33 (0)5 63 82 54 11
email	cuq-en-terrasses@wanadoo.fr
web	www.cuqenterrasses.com

Map 15 Entry 243

Château de Gandels

81700 Garrevaques, Tarn

Roles are clearly divided here: Philippe devotes his time to the magnificent grounds while Martine, who is as friendly as she is elegant, spent five years doing up the château and now, their five children grown and gone, looks after her guests. An accomplished horsewoman, she is happy to take competent guests out for a ride, but her first love is cooking and she devises the evening menu in the local farmers' market each day. Martine enjoys entertaining guests, but if you fancy something more romantic, she is happy to lay a candlelit dinner for two in a quiet room. Antique dealers in Paris before settling here, Philippe and Martine still dabble in the trade as they love it and their eye has really come into its own in the château. The bedrooms are all huge, all look onto the gardens and are all different. Floors are polished wood or tiled with rugs, but while Baldaquin has *toile de Jouy* and an ornate four-poster, another is painted in soft blue with simple though unusual wooden beds and blue and white covers. *20m-long pool.*

rooms	8: 3 doubles, 2 twins, 3 suites for 4.
price	€115-€130. Suites €210-€230.
meals	Snacks available. Dinner with wine, €40. Book ahead.
closed	Rarely.
directions	From D622 Revel & Castres road 2km outside of Revel take D45 to Garrevaques. After 2.5km château signed on right.

	Martine & Philippe Dupressoir
tel	+33 (0)5 63 70 27 67
fax	+33 (0)5 63 75 22 27
email	dupressoir@chateau-de-gandels.com
web	www.chateau-de-gandels.com

Map 15 Entry 244

Château de Garrevaques
81700 Garrevaques, Tarn

The walls were breached under fire of bombards and culverins... Then came the Revolution, then the German occupation; but the family is adept at rising from the ashes and the 17th generation of Ginestes is now in charge. Marie-Christine has all the charm and passion to make a go of such a splendid place – slightly faded in parts, full of interest. There are huge reception rooms, magnificent antiques, some original 18th-century wallpaper by Zuber, wood-block floors, a dining room with wood-panelled ceiling. Up the spiral stone stairs is a games room, with billiards, cards, easy chairs and antiques pieces. The Blue Room next door is vast, stunning. All the bedrooms are charming and colourful, some with matching wallpaper and bed coverings. In the new *Pavillon*: 15 luxury bedrooms, a sparkling new relaxation centre, a second (outdoor) pool and two restaurants, one *gastronomique*, one regional. The garden is studded with old trees as grand as the château. Marie-Christine is unstoppable: cookery courses, itineraries to nearby places of interest, flying lessons next door... you are in good hands.

rooms	23: 2 doubles, 3 twins, 2 triples, 1 suite for 4-5 in château; 12 twins/doubles, 2 triples, 1 duplex for 3-4 in Pavillon.
price	€80-€200. Suite & duplex €280. Half-board €110-€130 p.p.
meals	Buffet breakfast €12. Hosted dinner in château €35, book ahead.
closed	Never.
directions	D1 for Caraman. Opp. Gendarmerie in Revel, D79F to Garrevaques for 5km. At end of village on right.

	Marie-Christine & Claude Combes
tel	+33 (0)5 63 75 04 54
fax	+33 (0)5 63 70 26 44
email	m.c.combes@wanadoo.fr
web	www.garrevaques.com

Map 15 Entry 245

Hôtellerie de l'Abbaye-Ecole de Sorèze

Le Pavillon des Hôtes-Le Logis des Pères, Rue Lacordaire, 81540 Sorèze, Tarn

Now this is good value; no pretence, clean comfortable rooms within a listed compound of buildings, and huge grounds with mature trees. The abbey was founded by Pepin le Bref in 754, became a school under the Benedictines in 1682 and the Royal Military College under Louis XVI. Take advantage of the setting and book at the small Le Pavillon, previously the girl's dormitory. Breakfast on the lovely sheltered terrace of the restaurant or have a drink at the bar and even with a large conference buzzing on across the huge courtyard at the Logis des Pères one is far enough away to not be bothered. With just 17 rooms up a solid wooden staircase (no elevator), all is spartan and spotless. The uppermost rooms have real character with raftered beam. Floors range from terracotta-tiled to carpeted, bathrooms are compact with showers (a few rooms have baths, too), walls are white and incredibly thick, desks and chairs are functional. The more luxy Logis des Pères across the courtyard, once the home of the Dominican fathers, has an elevator and is in another class (shown above).

rooms	52 large doubles in Le Logis des Pères. 17 doubles in Le Pavillon des Hôtes. No elevator or baggage service in Pavillon.
price	Logis des Pères €90-€145. Pavillon des Hôtes €52-€60.
meals	Breakfast €11. Lunch & dinner €20-€35. Restaurant closed Tues.
closed	Rarely.
directions	From Toulouse, A61 exit Castelnaudary, then towards Revel & Sorèze.

	M Jean-Patrice Bertrand
tel	+33 (0)5 63 74 44 80
fax	+33 (0)5 63 74 44 89
email	reception@hotelfp-soreze.com
web	www.hotelfp-soreze.com

Map 15 Entry 246

Domaine de Rasigous
81290 St Affrique les Montagnes, Tarn

The drawing room is the magnet of this exceptional house: gentle colours, fabulous furnishings and, in winter, log fire in marble fireplace. The soft yellow and white dining room is full of modern art collected in Fons and Ben's native Holland. Never twee, the tables are beautifully decorated for good-looking, varied food and local wines (especially the delicious Gaillac). Natural light, bare floorboards with fine rugs or luxurious plain carpets give that country-house feel to the large, heavenly bedrooms, sensitively decorated with rich colours and interesting furniture. The three suites are elegantly unfrilly. Luxurious bathrooms have been ingeniously fitted into odd spaces – the free-standing bath is most handsome. Even the single room, with its sleigh beds, lovely linen and bathroom in a walk-in cupboard, is on the 'noble' floor, not under the eaves. The courtyard is ideal for summer breakfast; gaze at the water-lilies in Ben's water garden, eight different types of frogs will sing and jump for you. The owners' artistic flair and hospitality make this a wonderful place to stay – try to give it at least three nights

rooms	8: 4 twins/doubles, 1 single, 3 suites.
price	€78- 95. Single€50–€75. Suites €120–€125.
meals	Breakfast €11. Dinner €27.50. Restaurant closed Wednesdays. Good restaurant nearby.
closed	Mid–November–15 March.
directions	From Mazamet D621 for Soual for 16km; left on D85 to St Affrique les Montagnes. 2km further on D85. Green sign on left.

	Fons Pessers & Ben Wilke
tel	+33 (0)5 63 73 30 50
fax	+33 (0)5 63 73 30 51
email	info@domainederasigous.com
web	www.domainederasigous.com

Map 15 Entry 247

La Guiraude

31290 Beauteville, Haute-Garonne

The peaceful old farmhouse is surrounded by a warren-like garden of secret nooks and hidden terraces, mature trees and country views — and there's a swimming pool tucked away. Inside all is tranquil. French doors at both ends of the sitting room open, hacienda-like, to terraces, and the room has an Italian feel: Tuscany siennas and ochres, ironwork and terracotta. Bedrooms are large, cool and decorated in classic colours — cream and burgundy, grey and navy, royal blue and gold; two have private terraces looking to the hills. Comfortable beds look inviting in their crisp white linen; swish bathrooms have baskets of extras and an abundance of towels. When you're peckish, Janine brings you a delicious afternoon tea – and it's worth staying for dinner at the long sociable table. Cooking is Alistair's passion and he conjures up a small-choice, three-course menu every night (foie gras with fig compôte, chicken with tarragon cream, *tarte au citron*. Nearby, a Friday market full of farm produce and colour; beyond, forests, gorges and caves. *Minimum stay two nights.*

rooms	5: 2 doubles, 2 twin, 1 family room for 4.
price	€90–€110.
meals	Breakfast €7.50. Dinner €26–€38.
closed	Rarely.
directions	From Carcassonne A61 exit 20 to Vilefranche de Lauragais; right at r'bout; right at T-junc. to Auterive; left on D625; after 4.5km right on small road to La Guiraude.

	Janine & Alistair Smith
tel	+33 (0)5 61 81 42 05
fax	+33 (0)5 61 81 42 05
email	guiraude@wanadoo.fr
web	www.guiraude.com

Map 14 Entry 248

Hôtel Restaurant Relais Royal

8 rue Maréchal Clauzel, 09500 Mirepoix, Ariège

Arrive on a summer afternoon and you'll pass the courtyard tables set for tea. Then through the Renaissance-style gate and into the lobby where terracotta gleams, the grandfather clock ticks away the hours and pretty arched doors lead to a second courtyard and pool. The lofty dining room has a touch of gilt here and there and is a suitable setting for some serious food: guinea fowl with eight spices, roasted tuna with peperade and coriander. Dine in winter in front of a fire in the old kitchen, its walls lined with copper pans; retire with a cigarello to the clubby haze of the Blue Room. Then up the grand ironwork staircase to bedrooms with a modern décor that allows the original features to shine: glorious 18th-century windows, high ceilings and beams (these painted a fashionable white). Fabrics are coordinated, bathrooms are large and luxurious. Gerwin and Roger, cultured and charming – as are their staff – will help you explore. You are in the heart of Mirepoix so the cathedral is a must; there's hiking and biking in the Pyréenées, and Carcassonne is worth at least a day.

rooms	8: 5 twins/doubles, 3 suites for 2-4.
price	€150-€180. Suites €200-€300.
meals	Breakfast €16. Lunch €22-€82. Dinner €29-€82, except Monday. Children's menu €18.
closed	January-7 February.
directions	From Toulouse A66 for Foix. Exit Pamiers, Mirepoix & Carcassonne. D20 to Mirepoix & Bram.

	Mr Gerwin Rutten & Mr Rogier Van Den Biggelaar
tel	+33 (0)5 61 60 19 19
fax	+33 (0)5 61 60 14 15
email	info@relaisroyal.com
web	www.relaisroyal.com

Map 15 Entry 249

Chateau de Beauregard

L'Auberge d'Antan, Avenue de la Résistance, 09200 Saint Girons, Ariège

Paul and Angela have created something memorable here. Paul is French, a chef by training and brimful of energy – an entrepreneur – but it is Angela's intuition and imagination that have wrought the magic inside this little hotel. The château, grafted onto a 17th-century dairy farm in 1820, was in a woeful condition when they bought it. Everyone thought them quite mad but they've saved it triumphantly from decay, using lots of reclaimed materials and even finding some massive old radiators; the new central heating looks perfectly at home. The rooms are full of appeal and interest, the old furniture and fabrics that Angela has tracked down have just enough shabby chic to look as though they've been here forever. Each bedroom is named after a French writer, with a corresponding shelf of their work. Breakfast is served in the pretty winter-garden or, in warm weather, out under the wisteria (the grounds are lovely). Dining at L'Auberge d'Antan is a treat: Paul has turned the stables into a rustic restaurant and you can watch the (very good) Gascon-style food being cooked over a wood fire.

rooms	8: 4 twins/doubles, 1 family room for 3, 2 suites, 1 apartment (without kitchen).
price	€55-€80. Apartment €460-€900 per week.
meals	Breakfast €10. Dinner €30.
closed	November-March.
directions	From Toulouse to Tarbes, A20 exit 20 to Salies du Salat; D117 to Saint Girons, Massat.

	Angela & Paul Fontvieille
tel	+33 (0)5 34 14 07 93
fax	+33 (0)8 75 35 34 55
email	contact@domainedebeauregard.com
web	www.domainedebeauregard.com

Map 14 Entry 250

La Terrasse

42 route de Luchon, 09800 Argein, Ariège

This is it – the sort of simple place you hope to find in rural France but so rarely do. And we found it almost by chance. Jean-Pierre is larger than life, has bales of enthusiasm, loves his local produce, is proud of his cooking and is everywhere at once – his previous life as chef on Le Train Bleu running between Paris and Nice might have something to do with it. There's no sitting room, just a traditional reception in dark wood and a sprinkling of artificial flowers where Jean-Pierre's mother may greet you. Individual tables reach out to an enclosed patio; as you are in the village, views are of the street or houses with the Pyrénées beyond. Pleasant rooms come in clean colours: as expected, bedcovers and curtains are floral, mattresses are new and everything is fresh, simple, spotless – very French. One room is blue and white with a small sitting room and its own terrace for private breakfasts. You are on the pilgrim's route, so it's a good stop-off point for cyclists and hikers (who stay in extra dorms). They say that Winston Churchill slept here too, when he took the waters at Luchon.

rooms	3: 2 suites, 1 family room for 3.
price	€60–€70.
meals	Dinner €20.
closed	November–Easter.
directions	A64 exit 20, D117 to St Girons, then D618. Argein signed left after Audressein.

	Jean-Pierre Cramparet
tel	+33 (0)5 61 96 70 11

Map 14 Entry 251

La Grande Combe

12480 Saint Izaire, Aveyron

An energetic, lovable couple live in this astonishing old place, built on a hillside before a heart-stopping view. You go from level to delightful level: the ancient timber frame holds brilliantly restored rooms done in a simple, contemporary style that makes the old stones glow with pride. The emphasis is on communal living and Nelleke is a passionate and skilful lady in the kitchen. Professional presentation and inventive menus converge in the warmly atmospheric dining room; start, perhaps, with duck terrine, move on to salmon on a bed of sauerkraut with chorizo sausage, then finish with a platter of local cheeses and a lemon tart. Hans prides himself on picking the perfect wine to accompany the meal. Sitting rooms have original paving and bedrooms have ingenious bathrooms, walk-in showers and incredible views – all including the singles, which are small yet fresh. Care is given to a huge organic garden and there are little terraces and a library for quiet times. Don't pay much attention to the bumpy road up; once here you will unwind. No frilly bits, no clutter, an exceptional place.

rooms	9 + 1: 4 doubles, 2 twins, 1 triple, 2 singles. Studio for 2-3.
price	€70. Singles €35. Studio €294-€322 per week.
meals	Hosted dinner with wine €22, book ahead.
closed	Rarely.
directions	From Millau D992 & D999 for Albi; at St Pierre D902 right for Réquista; 4.5km after Faveyrolles, left before bridge, signed.

	Hans & Nelleke Versteegen
tel	+33 (0)5 65 99 45 01
fax	+33 (0)5 65 99 48 41
email	grande.combe@wanadoo.fr
web	www.la-grande-combe.nl

Map 15 Entry 252

Le Mûrier de Viels

12700 Loupiac, Aveyron

You won't meet a soul on the drive to get here – but you may meet a wild deer. This small, intimate hotel, a sprinkling of 18th-century Quercy buildings on many lush levels, hides amongst the oak woods and gazes down upon the river. Come for a smiling South African welcome and an atmosphere of relaxed indulgence: in two years Sue and Mike have worked wonders. The layout of the place is charming, with reception, restaurant and guest rooms scattered among terraces, entwined by secret corners. The pool area has a great view – *everywhere* has a great view; there's space and there's tranquillity. In the bedrooms, exposed stone walls rub shoulders with white plaster, there is stylish modern French furniture and soothing colours, big walk-in showers and fluffy white towels, excellent reading lamps and luxurious pillows. One suite has a fitted wardrobe with antique doors, another a mirrored wall. Every room is pristine. Make the most of 'international cuisine' in a dining room bright with yellow leather chairs – Sue combines her love of interior design with cooking. Then work it all off in the gym.

rooms	7 + 1: 3 doubles, 1 twin, 2 family rooms for 3, 1 duplex suite for 3. Cottage for 5.
price	€58–€75. Family rooms €63–€85. Suite €85–€125. Cottage €500–€700 per week.
meals	Breakfast €8.50. Dinner €21–€25. Picnic available.
closed	November–mid-March.
directions	From Figeac to V. de Rouergue, cross river then immed. right onto D86 for Cajac. 2km, follow signs.

	Mike & Sue Douglas
tel	+33 (0)5 65 80 89 82
fax	+33 (0)5 65 80 12 20
email	info@le-murier.com
web	www.le-murier.com

Map 10 Entry 253

Villa Ric

Route de Leyme, 46400 St Céré, Lot

Jean-Pierre built his house some 20 years ago, high on a steep hill covered in "proper" trees (not conifers). The view from the terrace, where you eat when it's warm, is of rolling hills as far as the eye can see. Food is an important part of your stay here: Jean-Pierre discusses the menu each evening with guests, most of whom choose half-board. Others do drop by to dine, but the emphasis is very much on a restaurant for residents, and food is fresh and inventive. Bedrooms are Laura-Ashley-pretty, perhaps with broad striped wallpaper and fresh white wicker chairs; many have exposed beams. Bathrooms gleam; each matches its flower-themed bedroom. The hotel is at a crossroads, ideal as a stopover for the Auvergne, Dordogne or the journey down to Spain. But why not linger a little longer? In July and August the old timbered market town hosts a well-established music festival: opera, music in the streets, processions and art exhibitions. Elisabeth is a passionate collector of the ceramics of Jean Lurçat, who settled here in 1945 and whose work is shown at a special workroom-museum in town.

rooms	5 twins/doubles.
price	€75–€105. Half-board €75–€105 p.p.
meals	Breakfast €10. Dinner €35–€55.
closed	November-Easter.
directions	From Paris, A20 exit 52 for St Céré, then Leyme. From Toulouse exit 56. Hotel 2km from St Céré.

	Elisabeth & Jean-Pierre Ric
tel	+33 (0)5 65 38 04 08
fax	+33 (0)5 65 38 00 14
email	hotel.jpric@libertysurf.fr
web	www.jpric.com

Map 10 Entry 254

Hôtel Relais Sainte Anne

Rue du Pourtanel, 46600 Martel, Lot

If conversation should flounder, the saying goes, *un ange passe* — an angel is passing overhead. Perhaps there is one in the tiny chapel of Sainte Anne, at the centre of this beautiful cluster of ancient buildings, a reminder of another, quieter time when the hotel was a girls' convent. The chapel is intact and is used occasionally for small concerts and art exhibitions and the whole ensemble has been lovingly and sensitively restored with no jarring architectural mishaps. The large pool is discreetly tucked away and the walled garden, a cunning combination of formal French structure and English informality, manages to retain a strong feeling of the past — young charges playing hide-and-seek in the shubbery, or gathering in the little courtyards or around the fish pond. Inside is equally evocatively atmospheric; warm old stone, fine wallpapers, opulent curtains, heavy rugs and proper attention to lighting. Most of the perfect ground-floor bedrooms have their own terraces, too. Sophisticated surroundings without any self-consciousness — a rare treat.

rooms	16: 7 doubles, 4 twins, 1 single, 4 suites.
price	€70–€160. Suites €135–€245.
meals	Breakfast €12–€15. Hotel will offer lunch & dinner in 2006, €28–€70. Great restaurants within walking distance.
closed	Mid-November–mid-March.
directions	From Brive A20 for Cahors exit 54 for Martel; rue du Pourtanel; hotel on right at town entrance.

	Pierre Bettler & Roland Kurt
tel	+33 (0)5 65 37 40 56
fax	+33 (0)5 65 37 42 82
email	relais.sainteanne@wanadoo.fr
web	www.relais-sainte-anne.com

Map 9 Entry 255

La Terrasse
46200 Meyronne, Lot

A child might build a castle like this: tall and straight, with a mix of round towers, square towers, fat towers and thin towers. It's actually more fortress than château and has stood guard over the Dordogne since the 11th century, though with the scars of much violence. Gilles and Françoise have turned it into an inviting country retreat. Entered from the back through magnificent doors off a pretty courtyard, the entrance lobby has an amazing polished flagstone floor. The more interesting bedrooms are in the oldest part of the building. Most overlook either the river or the pool – set high into the walls with a fantastic view, this is a rare swimming pool with atmosphere. The main dining room is a touch 'interior-designed' but you will love the vaulted 'winter' dining room, or eating on the terrace under the vines. Food is real south-west: wonderful concoctions with truffles and top-quality ingredients. Save it for dinner or you'll miss seeing Rocamadour, the Lascaux caves or canoeing on the river.

rooms	15: 9 twins/doubles, 1 triple, 2 suites for 3, 3 suites for 4.
price	€60–€92. Triple & suites €125–€230.
meals	Buffet breakfast €10. Lunch & dinner €25–€50. Restaurant closed Tuesday lunch.
closed	November–February.
directions	From Limoges A20 exit 55. At r'bout first right to D703 for Gramat Martel. At Le Pigeon D15 to Rocamadour; over bridge to Sozy.

	Gilles & Françoise Liébus
tel	+33 (0)5 65 32 21 60
fax	+33 (0)5 65 32 26 93
email	terrasse.liebus@wanadoo.fr
web	www.hotel-la-terrasse.com

Map 9 Entry 256

Hôtel Beau Site

46500 Rocamadour, Lot

The perfect way to see Rocamadour: stay in this old hostelry, enjoy the stupendous cliff-hanging view from the restaurant and terrace, visit the historic village in the early morning and leave for the day when it fills with trippers. Rocamadour cracks at the seams between 11am and 7pm so return for dinner and a peaceful evening's stroll along the, by-then, walkable streets. The Beau Site is seriously old with a fairly wild history – stones and timbers could tell many a tale. It has belonged to charming Monsieur Menot's family for five generations and the reception area dazzles with medieval antiquities and shiny brasses on old flagstones worn by endless pilgrims' feet. The salon and games room are in the old vaulted kitchens and pantries, but we found fake leather and spindly legs disappointing. Bedrooms vary in size; recently-renovated rooms have pleasant wooden furniture, rich fabrics and good bathrooms. A friendly, welcoming place in an exceptional position. Hotel guests may drive right to the hotel and park in its private car park.

rooms	40: 34 twins/doubles, 3 singles, 1 suite, 2 apartments for 4 (without kitchen).
price	€68–€99. Singles €66–€87. Suite €100–€133. Apartment €92–€123.
meals	Buffet breakfast €10.50. Picnic €7.50. Lunch from €16. Dinner €23–€52.
closed	15 November–6 February.
directions	In Rocamadour take road to Cité. Through medieval gates into village & park in front of hotel.

	Martial Menot
tel	+33 (0)5 65 33 63 08
fax	+33 (0)5 65 33 65 23
email	hotel@bw-beausite.com
web	www.bw-beausite.com

Map 9 Entry 257

Mas Audhuy

Aux Dodus d'Audhuy, 46700 Duravel, Lot

'Dodus' means 'short, plump, contented person', a description Mimie will chuckle over. She and husband Olivier run their unpretentious home with ineffable charm and no fuss. The 150-year old farmhouse and its mature garden snooze in the valley, while inside its stone walls are antiques plucked from the family hoard and big leather armchairs. Two large bedrooms in the converted barn are light and bright with lots of windows; choose between views of fields and horses on one side, or the courtyard and a spot of people-watching on the other. The old pigeonnier decked out in rambling roses hides the double bedroom and its ancient red and cream tiles. Breakfast on the patio; dine in either the courtyard or the restaurant – a bohemian den of assorted wooden tables and cheerful paintings. Mimie's cooking is a homely triumph, thanks to her grandmother's tuition and stacks of fresh vegetables from the potager. Her kitchen opens onto the restaurant, and she will merrily dole out no-nonsense chat alongside her no-nonsense fare. Even a short stay will leave you feeling 'dodus'-like.

rooms	3: 1 double, 2 family rooms for 3.
price	€80–€120.
meals	Dinner €27. Restaurant closed Sunday–Wednesday April–June.
closed	30 November–mid March.
directions	30km west of Cahors, D911 to Villeneuve sur Lot. 2km after Puy l'Evêque, signed on right. Mas 1km before Duravel.

	Mimie & Olivier de Lestrade
tel	+33 (0)5 65 36 44 12
fax	+33 (0)5 65 36 44 12
email	auxdodus@free.fr
web	auxdodus.free.fr

Map 9 Entry 258

Hostellerie La Source Bleue

Moulin de Leygues, 46700 Touzac, Lot

If you like the unexpected, here you have it: a three-acre bamboo forest deep in *la France profonde*. It isn't just any old bamboo, but ranges from dwarf varieties to the 15-foot-high *Phyllostachis violaescens*; Jean Pierre planted most of the exotic ones himself. Meandering walkways lead to a lake full of koi carp and water-lilies: discover discreet little sitting areas, wrap your soul in the silence, this is truly a magical place. The hotel itself is a fascinating ensemble of three mills – one built in the 11th, one in the 12th and one in the 17th century – beside a spring that sparkles true blue, on any but the cloudiest day. With cars parked near but out of sight, the effect is peaceful and inviting, the rushing water soothing you to sleep and providing a cheerful, cooling background. Bedrooms are spread through three buildings and vary. Those in the tower are 60s-style but are due to be done up, others are big and traditional, and one has a private terrace. Despite its size, this is very much a family hotel and would be great for children – though perhaps not the smallest sort.

rooms	15: 12 doubles, 3 suites for 2-5.
price	€69-€79. Suites €125-€135.
meals	Breakfast €7. Picnic €8. Lunch & dinner €15-€36.
closed	15 November-March.
directions	From Villeneuve sur Lot D911 for Fumel & Cahors. By-pass Fumel; after Soturac right for Touzac & follow signs.

	M Jean-Pierre Bouyou
tel	+33 (0)5 65 36 52 01
fax	+33 (0)5 65 24 65 69
email	sourcebleue@wanadoo.fr
web	www.sourcebleue.com

Map 9 Entry 259

Hôtel Restaurant Le Vert

Le Vert, 46700 Mauroux, Lot

The alchemy of family tradition – three generations and 25 years for this young couple – has rubbed off onto the very stones of this unpretentious, authentic country inn where Bernard's skills shine from the kitchen. All is simplicity with fresh flowers, glowing silverware and old flagstones leading you from the small lobby to the dining room. Glance at the blackboard for the day's special to get your appetite going and if the weather is as it should be, head for a table on the terrace under the eaves. The local food cognoscenti are greeted as friends here, always an auspicious sign. You might chose a warm goat cheese, golden roasted with a lavender honey, then a prune-stuffed quail followed by a cherry-studded tiramisu. This is Cahors-wine territory; Eva will advise. The rooms in the garden annexe are big, cool and elegant with beamed ceilings, stone walls and antique furniture lightened by simple white curtains and delicate bedspreads. The pool is hidden on the far side of the garden. In a country where politicians are authors and cooks are philosophers, Bernard's ivory tower is in the kitchen.

rooms	7: 6 doubles, 1 single.
price	€55–€110.
meals	Breakfast €9. Dinner €42. Restaurant closed Thursdays.
closed	November–March.
directions	From Villeneuve sur Lot D911 for Fumel; south of Fumel D139 for Montayral. On past Mauroux towards Puy l'Evêque for approx. 500m. Hotel on right.

Bernard & Eva Philippe

tel	+33 (0)5 65 36 51 36
fax	+33 (0)5 65 36 56 84
email	info@hotellevert.com
web	www.hotellevert.com

Map 9 Entry 260

Domaine de Saint Géry
46800 Lascabanes, Lot

The beauty of the old farm buildings, were enough to inspire this remarkable young couple to purchase a very run-down property in 1986. Now the grassed and paved areas between the buildings are decorated with loads of large-scale exotica – lemon trees, bays, oleanders, olives… and a fountain. A truffle-rich oak and hazelnut forest spreads out behind the buildings. The Dulers also seem to ably manage two small children, a 60-acre cereal farm, an organic vegetable garden and a restaurant – in addition to making and marketing their own sausages, hams, *confits*, and truffle-enhanced foie gras. You can sample all of these delectables and more, as Patrick performs superbly in the kitchen and Pascale handles the divine desserts. Bedrooms are traditionally furnished with solid old wooden bedframes, generous curtains, no frilly bits or clutter – and all come with their own terrace or sitting out space. The delightful pleasures of the table and genuine hospitality are united here in such an intimate and peaceful setting that you may find it difficult to leave. *12km of walking paths*.

rooms	5: 4 doubles, 1 duplex suite for 3.
price	€190–€290. Suite €411.
meals	Breakfast €19. Dinner €79.
closed	5 October–mid-May.
directions	From Cahors, N20 for Toulouse; right for Montcuq & Agen D653 for approx. 500m. D7 left for Labastide Marnhac & on to Lascabanes. Signed.

	Pascale & Patrick Duler
tel	+33 (0)5 65 31 82 51
fax	+33 (0)5 65 22 92 89
email	duler@saint-gery.com
web	www.saint-gery.com

Map 14 Entry 261

Domaine de Cantecor

La Madeleine, 82270 Montpezat de Quercy, Tarn-et-Garonne

Whether you are in the main house or one of the three outbuildings with their garden-level patios, all the colour-coordinated rooms are bright, unfussy and cheerful. The property has masses of character and the owners make it clear that they want you to feel at home. On summer nights the floodlit pool is enchanting and during the day you may well be unable to resist a game of boules on the lawn or the delights of a village fête. Comfortable sofas around an open fireplace, bookshelves stacked with paperbacks, a billiard table in the oak-timbered gallery, a country kitchen (the central meeting place) and samples of wine bought from local growers complete this charming picture. This is a good base for exploring the subterranean caves or sampling the full-bodied wines from this area. Mountain bikes are on hand for those so inclined. Lydi and René keep a good supply of information on all the activities in the area and, between them, can hold their own in English, German, Spanish and Dutch, of course. *Cash or cheque only.*

rooms	5: 4 twins, 1 family room for 4.
price	€55–€70.
meals	Restaurants 600m–2km.
closed	October–March.
directions	A20 exit 58 N20 towards Montauban for 7km; left on D250 for Madeleine; left after 600m. Signed.

	Lydi & René Toebak
tel	+33 (0)5 65 21 87 44
email	info@cantecor.com
web	www.cantecor.com

Map 14 Entry 262

Château de Goudourville
82400 Goudourville, Tarn-et-Garonne

Medieval splendour without the draughts and with hot showers, lashings of atmosphere and romance: Hughes de Gasques established a stronghold here in the 11th century, Simon de Monfort laid siege to Goudourville – in vain – and it was here, after the battle of Coutras, that Henri IV laid 22 flags at the feet of the Countess of Gramont, 'la belle Corisande'. Bedrooms are vast and dramatic with massive four-posters – Clement V, done up in red silk, Charles IX, all stone walls and cream hangings; d'Andouins, with subtle blue-and-cream wallpaper and a pretty, painted four-poster, Gasques, lovely and light in white and cream with a rosy terracotta floor. Baths are deep and bathrooms laden with towels. Muriel gives you the history while Bernard prepares dinner. This is served at small tables in a stone-vaulted dining room with a huge fireplace and you can choose from a selection of medieval dishes or local specialities. There's a tree-filled terrace overlooking the Garonne, a large swimming pool and masses to do and see nearby. Start with the château's beautifully preserved, 11th-century chapel.

rooms	6: 3 doubles, 1 twin, 2 suites.
price	€80–€130.
meals	Dinner €23–€38.
closed	January–February.
directions	From Valence, D953 towards Lauzerte. Signed.

	Muriel & Bernard Marchegay
tel	+33 (0)5 63 29 09 06
fax	+33 (0)5 63 39 75 22
email	goudourville@wanadoo.fr
web	www.goudourville.com

Map 14 Entry 263

Hostellerie du Manoir de Saint Jean

Saint Jean de Cornac, 82400 Saint-Paul d'Espis, Tarn-et-Garonne

Hats off to Anne-Marie, who, after only one year, has impressed the locals (we asked around) with her renovations and her cuisine. This might have not have been so difficult for another native from the town, but she is a transplant from Nice and an ex-antique dealer to boot. The dining room is, of course, outstanding; soft yellow and cream, full of enormous gilt framed mirrors and beautiful drapes framing huge windows. The terrace is particularly lovely and overlooks the formal garden – gradually establishing itself – and the side of the pool. There is a 'menu of the day' based on seasonal produce with the addition of two choices for each course. Anne-Marie hand-picks her wine suppliers and makes sure that they are among those who are producing the most 'natural' product possible; the same philosophy governs the chef's choice for his local produce. Space and more space – from the entrance hall to the corridors to the bedrooms where well-chosen antiques rest in just the right places adding warmth and colour. Bathrooms are bright and airy. A fine beginning, the patina will come: this is a place to watch.

rooms	10: 1 double, 9 suites for 2-4.
price	€100-€116. Suites €150-€170.
meals	Breakfast €13.
	Lunch & dinner €35-€50.
	Restaurant closed Sunday evenings & Mondays.
closed	Rarely.
directions	A62 exit 9; in Moissac, D7 to Bourg de Visa. 9km; well signed.

	Anne-Marie Morgadès
tel	+33 (0)5 63 05 02 34
fax	+33 (0)5 63 05 07 50
email	info@manoirsaintjean.com
web	www.manoirsaintjean.com

Map 14 Entry 264

L'Arbre d'Or

16 rue Despeyrous, 82500 Beaumont de Lomagne, Tarn-et-Garonne

The 'Golden Tree' is Chinese and turn-of-the-century (the previous one); it's a ginkgo biloba and probably the finest in France. David will tell you its story and will explain why he believes Beaumont de Lomagne to be the finest example of a bastide town in south-west France; it's certainly very handsome and the Saturday market is not to be missed. He and Ann, new arrivals, obviously love the place, are doing it up little by little and take great care of their guests; they've given thought to disabled access and are happy to look after cyclists and walkers. Ann's a keen cook and has adopted traditional, regional recipes – adding the occasional English crumble – which you can eat outside in the shaded, pretty garden or in the dining room with its exposed beams. A comfortable, old-fashioned atmosphere reigns in the bedrooms too, with their marble fireplaces, interesting old furniture and pretty decorative touches. Two of the bedrooms have walk-in showers; windows are (mostly) large: some overlook the garden, some the street. A 17th-century gentleman's residence-turned-hotel with plenty of character.

rooms	5: 4 doubles, 1 twin.
price	€55–€65.
meals	Hosted dinner with aperitif, wine & coffee, €20; book ahead.
closed	Rarely.
directions	From A62 exit Castel Sarrasin. From A20 exit Montauban. D928 towards Auch. L'Arbre d'Or opposite Beaumont post office.

	Ann & David Leek
tel	+33 (0)5 63 65 32 34
fax	+33 (0)5 63 65 29 85
email	info@larbredor-hotel.com
web	www.larbredor-hotel.com

Map 14 Entry 265

Maison Monclar / Les Vincens

Route de Puycelci, 82230 Monclar de Quercy, Tarn-et-Garonne

The moment Annie and Barry found their splendid Duercy farmhouse they set about creating a place of repose and stress-free living. Rooms are filled with natural light, peppered with family antiques and dotted with stylish sofas. Annie has imbued each bedroom with its own character: dove-grey furniture and washed aqua walls, toile de Jouy curtains and rattan chairs. Three have their own little terrace. She visits the market each morning, chooses what's freshest and best and plans the evening meal accordingly. In winter you may expect her French country dishes and good wines to be served in front of a log fire; in summer, there's a dining room with magnificent views – and you may eat outside. Annie encourages a house-party feel, but there's no lack of space for those who seek privacy. Outside, 30 hectares of rambling grounds teeming with wildlife; the land, protected from hunters, is a retreat for both man and beast. And there's a lake, big enough to drift away in a boat on and fish. Annie will rustle you up a picnic and deliver it to your chosen lakeside spot. *Minimum stay three nights*.

rooms	5: 3 doubles, 1 twin, 1 family suite for 4.
price	€45–€100.
meals	Picnic lunch €7.50. Dinner with wine & coffee, €22.50.
closed	Rarely.
directions	After Monclar de Quercy, continue on D8. House well signposted.

Annie & Barry Proud
tel   +33 (0)5 63 67 41 31
fax   +33 (0)5 63 67 41 31
email   annie@maisonmonclar.com
web   www.maisonmonclar.com

Map 14 Entry 266

Castelnau des Fieumarcon

32700 Lagarde Fimarcon, Gers

Getting there is almost an initiation. Pass through a large Renaissance portal and spot a music stand and a welcome sign; then ring the gong. If all you hear is birdcall, you are in the right place. Built in the 13th century by local feudal lords – who for a time during the Hundred Year War pledged allegiance to the English crown – this stronghold was left to crumble until 25 years ago when the owners moved in. They restored the ramparts, renovated the houses, creating gardens for each one and left much of the creeper-clad old stone untouched. The houses are not 'interior decorated', but simple, clever touches lend sophistication: framed dried herbs on the painted walls; fairy-light baldaquins; terracotta tiles; a massive Louis XV armoire; antique Gascony treasures. Many have their own kitchens. Castelnau is on high ground so the views from every window – and the pool – are astounding, giving off a timeless hazy glow from the low-lying hills and surrounding fields. Stendhal called it the French Tuscany. He would be at home here: no cars, no TVs, no telephones. A rare pearl.

rooms	12 small houses for 2-9.
price	€90-€250. Whole house: €150-€350; €690-€2,100 per week.
meals	Breakfast €15. Picnic available. Hosted dinner €38-€70, book ahead.
closed	Rarely.
directions	A61 exit for Auch on N2. From Lectoure D7 for Condom 6km; right on D166 to Nerac. Lagarde signed on left after 4km; village 3km on. Look for large gate; ring gong.

	Yves & Nicole Everaert
tel	+33 (0)5 62 68 99 30
fax	+33 (0)5 62 68 99 48
email	office@lagarde.org
web	www.lagarde.org

Map 14 Entry 267

Château de Fourcès
32250 Fourcès, Gers

The château's towers oversee the murmur of activity from the village below much as they always have; their solid stone walls smack of permanence. Sweet Maria's welcome puts you at ease, in spite of the imposing 15th-century setting. Follow the timeworn steps of a glorious spiral staircase to your rooms; they're a good size, and decorated in neutral tones. Renaissance windows are set into creamy exposed stone, and you'll note arrow slits in even older walls. The family suite has a dreamy double view: the Gers hills rolling away like folds of whipped cream, the tiled roofs of the village resting below. Breakfast is served in a tower room, a door leading temptingly to the garden; dinner is in the smallish, pretty restaurant, with its ancient stone well and its terrace for summer; try the acclaimed *pigeonneau* and armagnac soufflé. The village is deceptively sleepy, with visitors flooding in for the glorious spring flower market, the monthly brocante and the annual book fair. You're only 12km from Larresingle, once a stronghold of the Abbots and recently restored to glory. Be immersed in history.

rooms	18: 12 doubles, 6 suites.
price	€135–€155. Suites €210–€230.
meals	Lunch & dinner €28–€45.
closed	Mid-November-28 February.
directions	From Condom, D114 to Larroque, then Fourcès for 12.5km.

	Oliver Lesaffre & Maria Gago
tel	+33 (0)5 62 29 49 53
fax	+33 (0)5 62 29 50 59
email	contact@chateau-fources.com
web	www.chateau-fources.com

Map 14 Entry 268

Hôtel Les Fleurs de Lees

24 avenue Henri IV, 32150 Barbotan les Thermes, Gers

Barbotan has the only baths in France where you can be treated for arthritis, rheumatism and varicose veins – all at the same time. But if you need a holiday, not an overhaul, come to this beautifully-run hotel. Michael is half English, half Chinese and he and Jean have spent their married life working in five-star places in Dubai, Iran, London, Paris, picking up a few tips along the way. Now they have their own clutch of rooms, a lovely pool lined with loungers and a restaurant in which Michael can put into practice his French and international cooking. Interesting bits and pieces brought back from travels dot the décor; bedrooms are rag-rolled and named after flowers. Double rooms are on the first floor, all but one with a large covered terrace, table and chairs; the suites are on the lower ground floor and open to a terrace that leads to the pool. These are themed – African, Oriental, Indian… the honeymoon suite, with drapes over the bed, is a semi-circular symphony in white. If you still need a spin at the spa, now offering anti-stress treatments, Jean will point you in the right direction.

rooms	16: 11 doubles, 5 suites.
price	€65-€85. Suites €115. Full-board option November-March.
meals	Lunch & dinner €19-€31.
closed	November-March. Call for out of season reservations.
directions	From A62 towards Toulouse, exit 3 Langon for Mont de Marsan; D932 Capitieux; left for Gabarret via D124E, D379, D303 through Maillas & Losse on D24.

	Michael & Jean Lee
tel	+33 (0)5 62 08 36 36
fax	+33 (0)5 62 08 36 37
email	contact@fleursdelees.com
web	www.fleursdelees.com

Map 14 Entry 269

Château de Lartigolle

32550 Pessan, Gers

The tree-lined approach, round towers and shuttered windows of this 17th-century château give little away. Yet, inside, cool colours, designer furnishings and texture – a chic complement to gracious windows, polished floors and glorious stone fireplaces. The four young English owners – whose London/New York design backgrounds are in abundant evidence – create a fun and stylish house-party mood. So many rooms to choose from – a club room with deep sofas, a light-flooded library, a TV room for kids, a billiard room. Dining in the central hall, the candlelight flickering off chandeliers, is a grand excuse for dressing up. Nick and Emma's fusion food tastes as good as it looks, and, on warm days, is brought to the courtyard under chestnut trees or the grassy terrace with views over the stunning Gers countryside. Bedrooms are uncluttered spaces of natural colour, pretty wallpapers, modish furniture and brocante finds. Showers – two in round tower rooms – are big and drenching. There's a pool, tennis court, wood and parkland. Fabulous for friends' reunions.

rooms	6 + 1: 5 doubles, 1 twin/double. Dormitory for lots of kids. South wing for rent if extra rooms needed.
price	Mid-September–June from €200. From €9,425 for fully catered weekly rent in summer.
meals	Breakfast €14. Dinner €38.
closed	Rarely
directions	From Auch, D626 to Pessan; 4km after village, right through château gate.

	Austin & Newton Families
tel	+33 (0)5 62 63 26 27
fax	+33 (0)5 62 05 32 13
email	info@lartigolle.com
web	www.lartigolle.com

Map 14 Entry 270

Just 2 Suites

13 chemin de Campuzan, 65220 Puydarrieux, Hautes-Pyrénées

Come for the largest, loveliest bathrooms in the book. Turn-of-the-century double basins and tubs, a grey-painted armoire, a rattan recliner, vintage taps (but lashings of hot water), cherubs and candles. The spreading suites in the solid old farmhouse are a gorgeous example of Dutch sobriety: Janneke's style is "minimalist abundance". Your hosts live in the converted stables; in the house are the suites, one up, one down – plus a library of 1,000 books and DVDs. Imagine white walls and a huge bed, four elegant spears, a framed nude propped on an antique *chiffonnier*; then a room with a sofa, a country table, logs in a vast hearth. Skies are big here and views long, to fields and blue mountains. You eat in the open-sided barn at a long table – the neighbours call it the party room *salle de fête* – and the pool is flanked by loungers from an East German spa… There are many surprises, all of them good. It's peaceful, and beautiful. Spain and Toulouse are an hour, skiing closer, local restaurants offer four-course lunches for 10, dinner is a half-hour drive. But please dine in at least once!

rooms	2: 1 suite for 2-4, 1 suite, both with dining/sitting rooms.
price	€135–€150.
meals	Lunch €25. Dinner €35, book ahead.
closed	Rarely.
directions	A64 exit for Lannemezan, D393 to Galan. Call owners who will meet you at the Mairie *(town hall)*.

Janneke and Peter Schoenmaker
tel +33 (0)5 62 33 68 03
email info@just2suites.com
web www.just2suites.com

Map 14 Entry 271

Le Relais de Saux

Route de Tarbes, Le Hameau de Saux, 65100 Lourdes, Hautes-Pyrénées

A dream of a place. Three to five hundred years old, high on a hill facing Lourdes and some dazzling Pyrenean peaks, the house still has a few unregenerate arrow slits from sterner days. You come in through the leafy multi-coloured garden that spreads across lawns and terraces with corners for reading or painting, a splendid first impression, and enter a house where you feel instantly at home. Bernard Hères inherited Saux from his parents and, with the help of his wife's flair and energy has opened it to guests. They are an enthusiastic and interesting couple who can guide you to fabulous walks, climbs or visits before welcoming you back to deep armchairs in the dark old-timbered salon with its peaceful garden view, or a refined meal in the elegant dining room. Bedrooms are in the same traditional, elegant mood with draped bedheads and darkish carpeted or flock-papered walls. One has no fewer than four tall windows, another has a gorgeous old fireplace, the two second-floor rooms are big yet cosy with their lower ceilings. And carpeted, well-fitted bathrooms for all.

rooms	6 doubles.
price	€90–€96. Half-board €82 p.p.
meals	Breakfast €10. Picnic available. Lunch €28–€56.
closed	Occasionally.
directions	Left 3km north of Lourdes. Signed but difficult to spot. 1st property 100m from main road.

Bernard & Madelaine Hères

tel	+33 (0)5 62 94 29 61
fax	+33 (0)5 62 42 12 64
email	contacts@lourdes-relais.com
web	www.lourdes-relais.com

Map 14 Entry 272

Grand Hôtel Vignemale

Chemin du Cirque, 65120 Gavarnie, Hautes-Pyrénées

The site is outstanding, smack bang in the middle of the glacial Cirque de Gavarnie. It is the Mont Blanc of the Pyrénées, surrounded by horse pastures, granite, snow and ice; not even a souvenir shop to spoil the view. Danielle and Christian chanced upon the place a decade ago, when the building was on its last legs – an eccentric edifice built by an Anglo-Irish count in 1903. For the local pair it was love at first sight: not only were they overwhelmed by the surroundings, they loved all the place has to offer: horses, wild animals, hiking. The residence, in spite of its grand name, has not quite recovered its former glory: more Vegas motel than four-star hotel. But rooms are perfectly adequate and the bedrooms carpeted and comfortable, with modern floral bedcovers, drapes and beige-flocked walls. A few have balconies. Your hosts are relaxed and easy, forever running after horses and resident dogs and cats. It's a great spot for a young family. Lots of horseback riding round the Cirque on the famous Meres horses – a species that thrives at high altitude – and truly wonderful walks.

rooms	24: 8 doubles, 14 twin, 2 family rooms for 4.
price	€130–€300.
meals	Breakfast €12. Picnic on request. Dinner €25, book ahead. Many restaurants within walking distance.
closed	Mid-October–mid May.
directions	From A64 exit Soumoulou or Tarbes Ouest for Lourdes; N21 for Argelès Gazost; D921 for Luz. 49km from Lourdes.

	Danielle & Christian
tel	+33 (0)5 62 92 40 00
fax	+33 (0)5 62 92 40 08
email	hotel.vignemale@wanadoo.fr
web	hotel-vignemale.com

Map 14 Entry 273

Photo La Castellas, entry 282

languedoc – roussillon

Relais des Monts

Les Monts, Route de la Canourgue, 48210 La Malène, Lozère

Monsieur had an unusual start, for a hotelier; a hunting guide in central Africa, he established a reserve for monkeys, lions and giraffes. All a far cry from this old stone hamlet, settled among the woods and fields like a sleepy head on a feather pillow. It is blissfully private. All three bedrooms are impeccable, only one betraying the owner's exotic past: 'Victoria' is decorated in colonial style, has a wall light fashioned from a spearhead and rich yellow walls and sisal floors to evoke hot sand. In contrast, 'Estelle' is pretty with red and white gingham curtains, white furniture and a lovely bow window that fills the room with light. The toile de Jouy suite has frou-frou lamps and curtains and big views. Two rooms have private terraces, one its own entrance, bathrooms are marble. Downstairs, the vaulted breakfast room is embracing and light; your continental breakfast is served on pretty porcelain and the big glass door gives tempting glimpses of the countryside. The Lozère air is pure, the nights silent, there's a good restaurant a mile away and hiking from the door.

rooms	3: 1 double, 1 twin, 1 suite.
price	€160-€200.
meals	Breakfast €15. Restaurants 3km.
closed	November-mid-March.
directions	A75 exit 40 La Canourgue-Gorges du Tarn, La Malène. 3km before La Malène, left for Les Monts.

	M & Mme Laboureur
tel	+33 (0)4 66 48 54 34
fax	+33 (0)4 66 48 59 25
email	relaisdesmonts@aol.com
web	www.relaisdesmonts.fr

Map 15 Entry 274

La Lozerette

Cocurès, 48400 Florac, Lozère

In September 1878, Robert Louis Stevenson set off from Le Monastier with his donkey, Modestine, to walk the 220km to St Jean du Gard. Towards the end of his journey he stopped off at the Cevennes village of Cocurès, on the river Tarn, just above the National Park. Here Pierrette runs the country inn started by her grandmother and passed on to her by her parents. Her father still advises on the best walks. Staff are especially warm and friendly and cope smilingly with all-comers to this busy hotel. Pierrette is very much hands-on, running the reception, taking orders in the restaurant and managing the wine cellar: she is a trained sommelier and will pick you out just the right bottle. Bedrooms are fairly large, with wooden floors and headboards and are done in stripes, checks or flowers: colour co-ordinated but not twee. All have balconies with flower boxes. The whole hotel is spotless without looking clinical. Play boules in the garden, walk in the National Park or follow Stevenson's trail, either on foot, donkey or horseback. The chestnut in all its forms is a speciality here.

rooms	21 twins/doubles.
price	€50–€85. Half-board €50–€68 p.p.
meals	Breakfast €7.80. Lunch €22–€25. Dinner €27–€40. Restaurant closed Tuesday & Wednesday lunchtimes out of season.
closed	November-Easter.
directions	From Florac, N106 for Mende. Right on D998 for Le Pont de Montvert. After 4km hotel on left, signed.

	Pierrette Agulhon
tel	+33 (0)4 66 45 06 04
fax	+33 (0)4 66 45 12 93
email	lalozerette@wanadoo.fr

Map 16 Entry 275

Mas de l'Hospitalet
30140 Bagard, Gard

Perhaps a stopping place for pilgrims, the 900-year-old mellow stone mas is a former commanderie of the Knights Templar, built by order of the King of France. Imagine large and leafy grounds, a saltwater pool, a long sheltered sun terrace… and two courtyards, one for summer breakfasts in the shade of ancient figs, the other vast and bliss for weddings. Bedrooms and apartments border the main courtyard, the cottage is near the pool and every space exudes a luxurious rusticity. Eva has spent four years bringing the mas back to life and has put the final touches to the décor: fine old bedheads and wardrobes, crisp white sofas and linen, garnet-red drapes. A new enterprise so floors are gleaming oak and bath and shower rooms unpolished marble – but large exposed beams show their elegant bones. A Bali baldaquin bed lives in one of the apartments; white china gleams as perfect foil for the night-blue tiles in the kitchens. In the cottage are old tiles and a pretty terrace. A family of quince-coloured Anduze vases dots the courtyard;   the new vaulted restaurant is stunning. *Min. two nights.*

rooms	7 + 3: 6 doubles, 1 twin. 2 apartments for 2, 1 cottage for 2.
price	€65–€135. Apartments & cottage €85–€155.
meals	Breakfast €7. Lunch €10–€15. Dinner €18–€32.
closed	Rarely.
directions	From Alès on N110 south, right at St Christol La Pyramide. 500m on left, long stone wall & tower.

	Eva Strom
tel	+33 (0)4 66 60 61 23
email	evastrom@wanadoo.fr
web	www.masdehospitalet.com

Map 16 Entry 276

Hôtel de l'Estelou

30250 Sommières, Gard

This reconverted train station is excellent value, with charming staff, in the olive and grape rich Cévennes countryside and only a three minute walk to the village. The last train clattered through some 30 years ago, but this clever conversion stops just the right distance short of swamping its origins. As you walk in, the feel is stylishly uncluttered: plain tiled floors, a modern sofa, an understated reception desk. The breakfast room, is a conservatory under the old glass-and-iron-girdered awning of the platform waiting room and has smart, pale-cushioned, wrought-iron chairs; it overlooks the tracks, now filled with a burgeoning rosemary garden. Opposite are six French-windowed rooms. Bedrooms in the main building are smallish but comfortable (some interconnect for families) and simply dressed – rattan chairs, strong earthy colours; bathrooms are freshly tiled. Second-floor rooms are less minimalist with parquet flooring, toile de Jouy fabrics and long views through prettily arched windows across the plains to the Pic Saint-Loup. *Perfect for first or last stop for Nîmes or Montpellier airports.*

rooms	26 doubles.
price	€35-€60.
meals	Breakfast €7. Many restaurants within walking distance.
closed	Rarely.
directions	A9 exit Lunel for Sommières. At r'bout follow signs for Centre Historique; right after bridge for Abais; 100m after house Les Violettes on left; left up hill to hotel.

	Philippe de Frémont
tel	+33 (0)4 66 77 71 08
fax	+33 (0)4 66 77 08 88
email	hoteldelestelou@free.fr
web	hoteldelestelou.free.fr

Map 16 Entry 277

Chez Burckel de Tell

48 Grand Rue, 30420 Calvisson, Gard

There's a secret to this old townhouse in the little market town: from the narrow street it looks nothing special, but enter the private courtyard and it's another world. The courtyard, a wonderful source of light and greenery, is used for art exhibitions and Régis gives lessons: drawing, oil, water colour and pastel. The art studio is at the back of the house. There's a biggish living area for guests and a vaulted dining room for candlelit dinners in a womb-like atmosphere of warm colours and stone walls. Summer breakfast is in the courtyard. Up a spiral staircase, the tempting rooms fan off at different levels – there's a lovely smell of wax-polished stone floors; most are beautifully restored with old doors and good windows that seem to frame pictures. It is all in honest good taste, with simple, solid antique furniture that's genuinely part of the house, and your charming young hostess is eager to help her guests. Nîmes, Montpellier and the Camargue are close by and in summer the house is blessedly cool after the scorching sun. *Minimum stay two nights July & August. Weekend & weekly painting courses.*

rooms	6: 3 doubles, 1 twin, 2 suites for 2-3 (1 with small terrace).
price	€55-€70.
meals	Hosted dinner €18 with wine, (except Saturday), book ahead.
closed	December-January, except during holidays (by arrangement only).
directions	A9 exit Gallargues. N113 for Nîmes. Just after bas Rhône canal, D1 to Calvisson. In village, along main street, two doors from Town Hall.

	Régis & Corinne Burckel de Tell
tel	+33 (0)4 66 01 23 91
fax	+33 (0)4 66 01 42 19
email	burckeldetell@hotmail.fr
web	www.bed-and-art.com

Map 16 Entry 278

Mas de Puech Long

30420 Calvisson, Gard

There is something for everyone here. Miniature ponies to stroke, horses and
ponies to ride, slides in the playground, two courts for boules, bikes and trails,
hungry fish in a pond, a serve-yourself organic garden – even a telescope for star-
gazing. Pottery, silk-painting or mosaics are taught by a resident artist; a chef
prepares a meal and delivers to your door – or lets you in on the fine art of
preparing a truffle or two. Sunday night is barbecue night and everyone is invited.
Friendships are made, children find playmates, travel tips are exchanged. The
rooms are in the fine, stone-built, 18th-century *mas*; a new dining area is in the
inner courtyard. Liesa knows all the local antique markets – you can tell from the
vintage linen and the rolltop bathtubs – and, depending on your hunt list, will
help you decide where to go. She is a mine of information on the prettiest villages
– Sommières and Calvisson are close by – and the best restaurants. After a day's
wandering, slip into in the Moroccan-tiled jacuzzi room before drinks and dinner.
Parquet floors, red ochre walls… nice enough to stay awhile.

rooms	4 + 5: 4 doubles.
	5 apartments for 3-8.
price	€55-€110.
meals	Breakfast €8. Lunch €10-€18.
	Hosted dinner €20-€30, book ahead.
closed	Never.
directions	From Calvisson head for St Etienne
	d'Escates. Once past Mas d'Escates,
	1st left. Signed.

	Liesa Blond
tel	+33 (0)4 66 63 89 54
fax	+33 (0)4 66 63 89 44
email	liesa@liesablond.com
web	www.masdepuechlong.com

Map 16 Entry 279

Jardins Secrets

3 rue Gaston Maruejols, 30000 Nimes, Gard

The 18th-century *relais de poste* hides in a walled garden brimming with mimosa, bougainvillea and roses – yet nothing prepares you for the sensuous, flowing interiors. Annabelle's exquisite taste has weaved its magic from chic-upholstered Louis XVI fauteuil to baldaquin bath lit with candle sconces: an atmosphere of relaxed indulgence reigns. She is the smiling, elegant hostess, he is the inspired cook, bringing you *grillades* and salads to the summer pool. For breakfast you feast on homemade pains aux raisins outside, or at a big farmhouse table beneath a bejewelled chandelier. Tranquillity prevails yet this is in the town centre, so make the most of the bikes and discover the Roman treasures of Nimes. Later return to one of three salons, comfortable with travel books, whisky or brandy as Debussy wafts into that dreamy garden. Then up the fine stone stair with iron balustrade to extravagant bedrooms with huge beds and billowing pillows, hot-water bottles tucked between crisp sheets and your own winter fire. Seductive and special.

rooms	4 doubles.
price	€180–€250.
meals	Breakfast €17.50. Poolside lunches. Dinner €50–€80.
closed	Never.
directions	5 minutes from railway station. Take Avenue Carnot, then 1st small street on right.

	Mme Annabelle Valentin
tel	+33 (0)4 66 84 82 64
fax	+33 (0)4 66 84 27 47
email	contact@jardinssecrets.net
web	www.jardinssecrets.net

Map 16 Entry 280

L'Enclos des Lauriers Roses
71 rue du 14 Juillet, 30210 Cabrières, Gard

The tiny reception gives no clue as to what lies beyond; a secret village within a village. Step across a sunny dining room, through French windows – and blink. Scattered around three swimming pools is a cluster of cottage rooms. Built in stone (from rescued village houses) with pantiled roofs, most have a private terrace or garden. Large, airy, with tiled floors, low beamed ceilings and pretty painted Provençal furniture, each has a different character – perhaps bright saffron or cool Mediterranean colours, a bed tucked under a stone arch or family-friendly extra beds on a mezzanine level. Bathrooms are large, modern and marbled while a fridge keeps picnic food – and wine – chilled. This is a family affair: Madame Bargeton runs the restaurant, Monsieur does the wine – 500 bottles in the cellar – and the sons take care of the buildings and garden. Eat on the terrace or in the dining room, popular with locals and visitors for its good Provençal cooking. Nimes, Avignon and beaches are less than an hour, swim in the Gorges du Gardon or walk amongst the pines and vineyards nearby.

rooms	15: 9 twins/doubles, 2 triples, 3 family for 4, 1 family room for 6.
price	Half-board for 2: €122-€180. €85-€110. Triples €105-€130. Family rooms €135- €250.
meals	Breakfast €11. Lunch & dinner €20-€42.
closed	10 November-10 March; open mid-December-3 January.
directions	A9 ext 24 for N86 to Remoulins. After 3.5km left to St Gervasy for Cabrières. In village centre, signed.

	Bargeton Family
tel	+33 (0)4 66 75 25 42
fax	+33 (0)4 66 75 25 21
email	hotel-lauriersroses@wanadoo.fr
web	www.hotel-lauriersroses.com

Map 16 Entry 281

Hostellerie Le Castellas
Grand Rue, 30210 Collias, Gard

Oodles of style at this fabulously restored country house in the centre of a
Provençal village. The main house, sturdy, green-shuttered, stone-built, acts as
centrepiece to other ancient stone buildings, all of which are linked by gardens,
arbours and an outdoor pool. Every bedroom is different – one Egyptian in
flavour, another Art Deco, a third Provençal – but share terracotta floors,
whitewashed walls and pale, polished beams. Luxury without clutter. The place is
full of surprises: one bathroom, painted pale ochre, has a floor made entirely of
pebbles, a local artist's fantasy; one bedroom has a terrace on its roof. Bathrooms
have fluffy towels and impressive toiletries. The illuminated terrace is a delight at
night, and the treats continue at table, where meals are taken in a beautifully
simple, stone-vaulted dining room. Our inspector loved the delicate flavours
(yet decided to forego the foie gras and champagne at breakfast!). Staff are
solicitous and discreet, and Madame is gracious and charming, a perfectionist in
everything she does.

rooms	17: 12 doubles, 3 singles, 2 suites.
price	€60–€155. Suites €105–€210.
meals	Breakfast €16. Lunch €20–€89. Dinner €47–€89.
closed	January–6 February.
directions	A9 exit Remoulins & Pont du Gard for Uzès on D981; left on D12 to Collias. Signed in village.

	Chantal Aparis
tel	+33 (0)4 66 22 88 88
fax	+33 (0)4 66 22 84 28
email	info@lecastellas.fr
web	www.lecastellas.com

Map 16 Entry 282

La Maison

Place de l'Eglise, 30700 Blauzac, Gard

No noise, just the hoot of an owl and a flutter of doves around the roof tops. An 18th-century mellow-yellow stone house sits in the heart of the village. Church, tower and château stand guard over it, and beyond, vines, fields and woodlands. The views are magical. Old vaulted ceilings, shuttered windows and terracotta floors are a stunning foil for contemporary décor; this is a grand old house infused with an informal spirit. Bedrooms are mostly large: the red room has a small private terrace that looks onto the château walls, the suite has a roof terrace with 360° views. Expect warm sandy walls, Indonesian wall hangings, ethnic fabrics, a fireplace or two. Breakfast is taken leisurely in the walled garden where an ancient tree casts generous shade, or at a long table in the library with other guests. There's a piano in the salon and a swimming pool in the garden. It's no distance at all to restaurants downhill and you can strike out further and visit Nîmes, Avignon, Arles or medieval Uzès. A most welcoming place.

rooms	5: 4 doubles, 1 suite.
price	€95–€180. Singles from €80.
meals	2 bistros in village & others in Uzès, 10 minutes away.
closed	Never.
directions	From Nimes, D979 for Blauzac & Uzès 16km; after Pont Nicolas, left for Blauzac, enter village, house behind church.

Christian Vaurie

tel	+33 (0)4 66 81 25 15
fax	+33 (0)4 66 81 25 15
email	lamaisondeblauzac@wanadoo.fr
web	www.chambres-provence.com

Map 16 Entry 283

Hôtel du General d'Entraigues

Place de l'Evêché, 30700 Uzès, Gard

When you sit on the wide terrace or swim in the mosaic-lined pool you feel some glorious monument might fall into your lap: Uzès is a perfect little Provençal town and Entraigues, in the shadow of Bishop's and Duke's Palaces, is at the heart of it. The hotel is in fact five cleverly connected 15th- and 17th-century houses: an old building with a fascinating history and lots of stairs and corridors leading off the very French lobby where chairs invite you to rest and breathe in the old soul of stones and antiques. In the original part of hotel all bedrooms are accessible by lift, others are over the bridge and up the staircases. Each is an individual discovery: here a private terrace, there an eminently paintable rooftop view, and wonderful furniture with personality and interest. The décor is exposed stone and white render, good fabrics and no clutter. We thought the family rooms were terrific, there's outdoor space and a simple buffet/family restaurant as well as the splendid Jardins de Castille for meals under a floodlit cathedral. Stunning. *Book ahead for limited parking places.*

rooms	36 doubles.
price	€52–€152.
meals	Breakfast €10.50.
	Lunch & dinner €22–€49.
closed	Rarely.
directions	A9 exit Pont du Gard on D981 to Uzès. Follow one-way system round towards Cathedral. Park in car park in front of Cathedral. Hotel opposite.

	Benjamin Savry
tel	+33 (0)4 66 22 32 68
fax	+33 (0)4 66 22 57 01
email	hotels.entraigues.agoult@wanadoo.fr
web	www.lcm.fr/savry

Map 16 Entry 284

Château d'Arpaillargues

Rue du Château, 30700 Arpaillargues, Gard

This noble house, its 15th-century sternness transformed with gracious 18th-century windows, balconies and décor, is a hotel that pampers but does not intimidate. Thick stone walls keep summer scorch at bay, balmy evenings are spent at table in the tree-studded courtyard; refined salons, vaulted dining rooms and a superb staircase are reminders of a more elegant age. History, aristocratic and literary, hangs in the air: Marie de Flavigny, Countess of Agoult lived here, she was Liszt's mistress, mother of Cosima Wagner, and left her husband here for the composer and Paris (an Agoult was also the heroine of *Les Liaisons Dangeureuses*). Rooms are big (slightly smaller in the annexe), very comfortable, with fascinating antiques and features (double doors, fireplaces and mouldings), interesting smallish but mosaic-decorated bathrooms and occasional private terraces. Back through those great iron gates and across the little road are the secluded garden and swimming pool. This is a deeply serene place of ancient atmosphere and modern, not over-luxurious comfort where the welcome is relaxed yet efficient.

rooms	29: 27 twins/doubles, 2 suites.
price	€80–€110. Suites €170–€280.
meals	Breakfast €11. Lunch from €26. Dinner from €42.
closed	October–March.
directions	Uzès D982 to Arpaillargues, 4km. Château on left at village entrance. Well signposted.

	Benjamin Savry
tel	+33 (0)4 66 22 14 48
fax	+33 (0)4 66 22 56 10
email	arpaillargues@wanadoo.fr
web	www.chateaudarpaillargues.com

Map 16 Entry 285

Le Château de Saint Maximin

Rue du Château, 30700 St Maximin, Gard

The light of centuries shines from the simple classical façade and the 12th-century tower, the arches and statue-dotted gallery, the vaulted staircase and great fireplace of this noble house. Currents of European civilisation flow through its several levels – white-stoned Italian pool and delightful French fountain, great Anduze jars on the terrace and silver olive trees in the garden, old tapestries and modern art skilfully placed to catch your attention. Jean-Marc Perry collects glass and has a sure eye for interior design, blending aesthetic refinement and creature comfort to perfection. The great classical tragedian Racine stayed and wrote here: generous bedrooms (the suites are vast), subtly elegant in their châteauesque garments and luxurious bathrooms, are called Phèdre, Bérénice… in his honour. One drawing room has a piano, the other, the only (big) television set in the place; tea is served in Sèvres cups, mouthwatering Provençal specialities finish the day. And from the second floor you look straight from exquisite civilisation out to the wild Cevennes landscape. Stunning.

rooms	6: 4 doubles, 2 suites.
price	€145–€230. Suites €250–€320.
meals	Dinner €45. Restaurant closed November–March.
closed	February.
directions	A9 exit Remoulins & Pont du Gard then D981 for Uzès. Right to St Maximin 4km before Uzès. Château in village centre.

Jean-Marc Perry

tel	+33 (0)4 66 03 44 16
fax	+33 (0)4 66 03 42 98
email	info@chateaustmaximin.com
web	www.chateaustmaximin.com

Map 16 Entry 286

Hôtel Le Saint Laurent

1 place de l'Arbre, 30126 Saint Laurent des Arbres, Gard

A sparkle of château-living sweeps through this quiet hotel, tucked down one of the town's medieval streets. Not surprising; Thierry and Christophe worked in grand establishments before injecting the 14th-century farmhouse-turned-hotel with a sense of élan. From the sun-trapped courtyard, steps lead to a covered veranda, invitingly spread with deep sofas. Inside, stone-flagged spaces show off their statues, gilded mirrors and heavy candlesticks. Bedrooms are intimate – some a slight squeeze – and lavish with antiques, cushions and pretty *objets*. Some have padded bedheads, others romantic canopies, one has a terrace, another is startling in black and white. All very boudoir, and delicious chocolates to welcome you. Large, white bathrooms want for nothing. You will be spoilt by the owners and bubbly staff; breakfast late (great pancakes!) in the vaulted dining room or the Moroccan-tabled courtyard. A beauty salon is planned. Avignon, Uzès and vineyards are close; enjoy the town's music concerts. No evening meals but plenty of local restaurants. *Private locked parking nearby.*

rooms	10: 5 doubles, 2 singles, 3 suites (1 with terrace).
price	€90–€130. Singles €65–€85. Suites €130–€195.
meals	Breakfast €12. Restaurant 20m from hotel.
closed	Never.
directions	A9 exit 22 Roquemanne. Left on N58 to Bagnols sur Cèze; 4km left for St Laurent des Arbres. Hotel in old town centre, signed.

Thierry Lelong & Christophe Bricaud

tel	+33 (0)4 66 50 14 14
fax	+33 (0)4 66 50 46 30
email	info@lesaintlaurent.biz
web	www.lesaintlaurent.biz

Map 16 Entry 287

Domaine du Moulin

Chemin de la Bégude, 30126 St Laurent des Arbres, Gard

The little luxuries of a good hotel and the personality of a B&B in Antoinette's renovated 12th-century mill. She and Otto, both Dutch, have been respectful of age and style: old parquet floors and doors have been revived, a wooden stair polished to glow. Big modern flower paintings and a Belgian tapestry look good on white walls. The river Nizon flows beneath the house and criss-crosses the grounds, several hectares of them – a mill pond flanked by cherry trees (spectacular in spring), an alley of poplars, a lavender field, a pool. And there are swings and slides for the grandchildren, for yours to share. Breakfast is a Dutch feast of hams, cheeses and cherry jams, served at the big table under the tented pergola, or in the all-white dining room with chandelier. Antoinette is lovely and fills the place with flowers. Bedrooms, named after her daughters, have piles of pillows and fine English florals; bathrooms are swish with big showers or two basins; some are air-conditioned, one has a sun terrace of its own. There's a cosy library full of books, and you and the chef choose the menu for dinner.

rooms	4 + 1: 4 twins/doubles. 1 apartment for 7.
price	€69–€168. Apartment €800–€2,200 per week (summer only).
meals	Breakfast €12.50. Dinner by arrangement. Restaurants nearby.
closed	Rarely.
directions	A9 exit 22 Roquemaure for Bagnols sur Cèze. After 4km go beyond left turn for St Laurent les Arbres. Left at Rubis, follow road.

	J A Keulen
tel	+33 (0)4 66 50 22 67
fax	+33 (0)4 66 50 22 67
email	laurentdesarbres@aol.com
web	www.domaine-du-moulin.com

Map 16 Entry 288

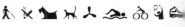

Château Beaupré Deleuze

Chemin de la Bégude, 30126 Saint Laurent des Arbres, Gard

The massive wooden door (so satisfying to knock on!) opens into a secret cobbled courtyard. It's cool here, and delightful among the arches and massive urns. Carla (erudite, blonde, full of laughter) and Pia (an archaeologist) love China, and the rooms of their 18th-century château are dotted with stunning antiques picked up on travels: oriental rugs, lacquered wardrobes, pottery jars, calligraphy. Karl, the chef, cooks Provençal dishes and brilliantly presides over the dining room, beautifully stone-flagged and vaulted, with a long table, leather-seated chairs and a big fire for chilly nights. The bedrooms, all simplicity and light, have fine parquet or glowing tiles, white walls and deliciously crisp bed linen; one has a grey-painted mezzanine for two extra beds, another a fantastic anthracite bath. The sweetest place for breakfast is up on the ballustraded terrace: intimate, peaceful, overlooking the garden's rustling trees and the rooftops of St Laurent. The house is close enough to town to stroll in for dinner, a summer concert or a trip to the Saturday flea market. Well-nigh perfect. *Minimum stay three nights.*

rooms	4: 1 double, 1 duplex for 4, 2 apartments for 2-4 (no kitchen).
price	€100–€120. Apartments €1,000–€1,600 per week.
meals	Dinner €25, book ahead.
closed	Rarely.
directions	A9 exit 22 Roquemaure, left on N580; left for St Laurent 200m; left on Chemin de la Bégude. Château on right.

	Pia Pierre & Carla Copini
tel	+33 (0)4 66 50 31 21
fax	+33 (0)4 66 50 28 78
email	chateau.beaupre@free.fr
web	www.chateau-beaupre.com

Map 16 Entry 289

L'Auberge du Cèdre

Domaine de Cazeneuve, 34270 Lauret, Hérault

No wonder guests return to this big, bustling house. The lively, charming Françoise and her multi-lingual husband Lutz welcome walkers, climbers, cyclists and families. Workshop groups are welcome too: there's a special space for them, separate from the big and comfy sitting room. This is a mellow-stoned auberge, adorned with green shutters, iron balustrades and *orangerie* windows at the rear. Bedrooms are plain, beamy, white, with the odd splash of ethnic colour and terracotta floors that gleam. Except for the new suite, bathrooms are shared; this is not the place for those looking for luxury. Sharing keeps the prices down and there have been no complaints. On the contrary, the atmosphere is one of good humour and laughter. Meals, are chosen from a blackboard menu. A great place for a family to stay: a swimming pool, lots of space to run around in, and *boules* under the chestnut trees before you turn in for the night. The auberge sits in the middle of the Pic Saint Loup, one of the best vineyards in the Languedoc and Lutz's wine cellar makes it a very special place for wine lovers.

rooms	20: 7 twins, 9 triples, 3 quadruples, all sharing 8 bathrooms & 7 wcs; 1 suite with private bath & wc.
price	€40–€110 p.p. Half-board €31–€66 p.p.
meals	Light lunch €8. Full choice menu €25–€35 on weekends.
closed	Mid-November–mid-March.
directions	D17 from Montpellier for Quissac. 6km north of St Mathieu de Tréviers, left to Lauret, 1km. Through village follow signs.

	Françoise Antonin & Lutz Engelmann
tel	+33 (0)4 67 59 02 02
fax	+33 (0)4 67 59 03 44
email	welcome@auberge-du-cedre.com
web	www.auberge-du-cedre.com

Map 16 Entry 290

Château de Jonquières

34725 Jonquières, Hérault

Isabelle met Francois harvesting the family grapes; now the estate is theirs, and is nurtured with passion. The château, remodelled in the 17th century, sits peacefully in the village: all you hear are church bells and the baker's horn. Isabelle has restored the guest wing with enthusiasm but without decorative excess. Up two staircases are four colour-themed bedrooms where sober beds are dressed in best family linen and new towels match bathroom tiles. A rich red carpet in the tower room, restored wallpapers in the Rose, Yellow and Blue rooms, and framed engravings raided from the attic. There's masses to do in the area, with vineyards and fine restaurants to visit and Lac Salagou close by, but why not stay put? There's an ornamental pond in the courtyard, a marble fireplace in the salon, billiards in the summer salon and cards in the playroom tower or you may lounge on the lawns in the shade of the giant bamboo groves. Or take a glass of estate wine to the delightful covered balcony above the Renaissance stairway and gaze over ancient rooftops.

rooms	4: 3 doubles, 1 twin.
price	€85–€90.
meals	Excellent choice of restaurants 2–5km.
closed	Mid-November–mid-March.
directions	From Montpellier to Millau & Lodève on N109. At St André de Sangonis (34km) D130 to Jonquières.

Francois and Isabelle de Cabissole

tel	+33 (0)4 67 96 62 58
fax	+33 (0)4 67 88 61 92
email	contact@chateau-jonquieres.com
web	www.chateau-jonquieres.com

Map 15 Entry 291

Le Sanglier

Domaine de Cambourras, 34700 St Jean de la Blaquière, Hérault

Madame, a Maître Rotisseur, cares for her menus, while Monsieur cares for his very good wine cellar in their deeply renovated sheepfold; just one stone wall survives from before. In the setting of vineyards and evergreen-clad hills, white outcrops, bright red earth and dense Mediterranean vegetation – strongly beautiful, even starkly wild – the Sanglier's rambling garden is welcoming with its terraces and masses of shade for eating and sitting outside. You can follow a good breakfast of fresh cheese, cake and olive breads with a delicious summer lunch and finish with dinner centred on Madame's wild boar speciality, steak grilled on vine stems or local fish. And there's lots to do here: exhibitions in Lodève, medieval St Guilhem, watery delights on Lake Salagou. Bedrooms are comfortable, decorated with mottled beige carpets and pastel bathroom suites. There are some lovely black and white photographs of local people, but come not for décor – the scenery is sublime and food is king. One of France's secret places.

rooms	10: 4 doubles, 5 twins, 1 triple.
price	€67–€87.
meals	Breakfast €9. Picnic from €6. Lunch & dinner €18–€38. Restaurant closed Wednesday lunchtimes out of season.
closed	November–March.
directions	From Montpellier, N109 through St Félix de Lodez for Rabieux, D144 for St Jean de la Blaquière. 2.5 km south of village, 0.5 km off main road.

	Monique Lormier
tel	+33 (0)4 67 44 70 51
fax	+33 (0)4 67 44 72 33
email	hotreslesanglier@aol.com
web	www.logassist.fr/sanglier

Map 15 Entry 292

Domaine du Canalet

Avenue Joseph Vallot, 34700 Lodève, Hérault

An elegant mansion, an enchanted wood and an art gallery for a bedroom. Set in dreamy parkland, this fin-de-siècle house gives nothing away – until you step inside. It is a showcase of contemporary art: sculptures, collages, light installations and paintings are set against the classical proportions of the high-ceilinged, light-filled rooms. Muriel ran a gallery in Paris and champions new artists. Three salons, scattered with artworks, sofas and glossy books, lead into one another. Then up the sweeping staircase to bedrooms that have an assured designer touch. Colours are neutral, paintings bold, furnishings minimalist but luxurious. Bathrooms are sculptural spaces of glass, chrome and wood. Yves looks after the grounds, a magical discovery of canals, secret paths, ancient trees, stone steps and shady ponds... plenty of spots to nourish the soul. And a hidden pool and terrace by the orangerie, perfect for breakfasts and candlelit suppers. Play tennis, cycle (bikes to borrow) or hike in the Cevennes, visit Lodève and the Larzac. Or enjoy a cultural evening with visiting artists and winegrowers.

rooms	4: 2 doubles, 1 twin, 1 suite for 2 + child.
price	€185-€250. Suites €265-€350.
meals	Brunch €15. Dinner from €45, book ahead.
closed	Never.
directions	At Lodève, signs to Bedarieux. At r'bout (Pizza di Maïori) take Ave Joseph Vallot. On left, after small red house next to football field.

	Muriel Lagneau & Yves Berliet
tel	+33 (0)4 67 44 29 33
fax	+33 (0)4 67 44 29 33
email	muriel@domaineducanalet.com
web	www.domaineducanalet.com

Map 15 Entry 293

La Calade
Place de l'Eglise, 34800 Octon, Hérault

Octon is an unspoilt little village, typical of the flavour and architecture so informed by the Languedoc sun. Right under the old church, the owners have created a colourful atmosphere within the white stone walls of the former presbytery. Don't expect great luxury – the setting is simple, the rooms and bathrooms adequate – but there is a freshness about the place when it's hot, and the beds are comfortable. The terrace, shaded by acacia trees and an awning, is very appealing both at breakfast time and in the evenings – it also serves as the sitting area. The overall feel is bright and clean and the new owners couldn't be more friendly and helpful. They particularly enjoy welcoming families with children. The restaurant is becoming very popular with the locals – always a good sign – so book ahead. There are plenty of places to visit, good paths for hikers, excellent local wines and the fabulous Lake Salagou for swimming and sailing. In short, a great base for daily excursions, where the warm welcome and the authentic atmosphere easily make up for somewhat basic comforts.

rooms	7: 3 doubles, 4 family rooms.
price	€41. Family rooms €57–€73.
meals	Breakfast €6. Lunch & dinner €13–€31. Restaurant closed Tues & Wed out of season.
closed	20 December–February.
directions	A75 exit 54 or 55 (Lake Salagou) for Octon on D148. Hotel in village centre next to church; stone steps lead up to entrance.

	Evelyne & Frank Giraud
tel	+33 (0)4 67 96 19 21
fax	+33 (0)4 67 88 61 25
email	lacalade-octon@wanadoo.fr
web	www.hotel-lacalade.com

Map 15 Entry 294

Hôtel de Vigniamont

5 rue Massillon, 34120 Pézenas, Hérault

The townhouse of the Comte de Vigniamont has been revived. Big grey shutters, a brass plaque on a sandy wall, blue wooden flower tubs to keep the cars at bay. Enter a cool flagged entrance, ascend a lovely stone-turned stair – the town is known for them – and step into an elegant, uncluttered, terracotta-tiled salon where stuffed sofas beg to be sunk into and floor-to-ceiling windows overlook 400 years of history. Large, refined bedrooms have pastel colours and pretty fauteuils, an antique wardrobe here, a touch of toile de Jouy there, perhaps French windows opening to a central courtyard. The English McVeighs have worked so hard to restore this place; outgoing and generous, they ran a tea shop, and later a pub, in California. Now they serve generous breakfasts on the sun-washed roof terrace, and, as the sun goes down, it's "raid the pantry" time: aperitifs and delectable tapas. Once weekly a mouthwatering meal is produced. A treat to be in the town of Pézenas, embraced by antiques and artisans, buildings, balconies, restaurants and bars – and with such nice people.

rooms	5: 2 doubles, 1 twin/double, 2 suites.
price	€90–€130.
meals	Hosted dinner with wine, €40; Mondays only.
closed	Rarely.
directions	A9 exit 34 D13 to Pézenas centre. Left at lights, right at T-junc., left on Rue Lous Blanc, right on Joseph Cambon, left into Rue Massillon.

	Robert & Tracy McVeigh
tel	+33 (0)4 67 35 14 88
fax	+33 (0)4 67 55 18 96
email	info@hoteldevigniamont.com
web	www.hoteldevigniamont.com

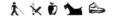

Map 15 Entry 295

La Chamberte
Rue de la Source, 34420 Villeneuve les Béziers, Hérault

When Bruno and Irwin set about converting this old wine storehouse, the last thing they wanted was to create a 'home from home' for guests. This is different, and special. The communal spaces are huge, ceilings high, colours Mediterranean, floors pigmented and polished cement. Bedrooms are simpler than you might expect, but with huge beds, often with a step up to them, and dressed in coloured cottons; bathrooms are shower-only, in ochres and muted pinks, some with pebbles set in the cement floor. The cooking is Bruno's domain: "not my profession but my passion". He may whisk you off to the hills early one morning, stopping on the way home for a loaf of bread and a slab of paté to go with the aperitif. In summer eat on the interior patio, a vast airy space that reaches up to the original barn roof; in winter retreat to a dining room with an open fire. Guests – eight at most – gather for a glass of carefully chosen wine and nibbles but dine at separate tables – stylishly decked with flowers and candles. Bruno feels dinner is an important moment of the day, to be savoured.

rooms	5 doubles.
price	€84–€98. Half-board option, €850 per week per room.
meals	Lunch €25. Dinner with wine, €35.
closed	Rarely.
directions	A9 exit 35 (Béziers Est) for Villeneuve les Béziers; over canal to town centre; 2nd left after Hotel Cigale; look for green gate on right.

	Bruno Saurel & Irwin Scott-Davidson
tel	+33 (0)4 67 39 84 83
email	contact@la-chamberte.com
web	www.lachamberte.com

Map 15 Entry 296

Les Bergeries de Ponderach

Route de Narbonne, 34220 St Pons de Thomières, Hérault

Monsieur Lentin remembers this *bergerie* when it was full of sheep; he now fills it with contented guests. The whole place is an expression of his cultivated tastes in music, painting (he has a permanent art gallery on the premises), food and wine. You enter your room through its own little lobby, from the freize-painted corridor. Notice the attention to detail in the choice of fabrics and furnishings, take in the luxury of the bathroom, make your way to your own private balcony and take a deep breath; you've arrived in a sort of earthly paradise. Les Bergeries is in a truly unspoiled part of the Languedoc. Monsieur Lentin offers the most intriguing and carefully chosen regional cooking with a good selection of organic wines. Sculpting your own perfect holiday here is not difficult, given all that's here for you – maybe one third exercise in the Parc Regional with its wonderful walks, one third culture visiting the cathedral and its pink marble choir and one third gastro-hedonism with your feet under the auberge's beautifully laden table.

rooms	7: 6 doubles, 1 suite.
price	€65–€100. Half-board €70–€90 p.p.
meals	Breakfast €11. Picnic available. Dinner €33.
closed	2 November–15 March.
directions	From Béziers, N112 to St Pons de Thomières, then left for Narbonne on D907. Hotel 1km further, just after swimming pool on left.

	Gilles Lentin
tel	+33 (0)4 67 97 02 57
fax	+33 (0)4 67 97 29 75
email	bergeries.ponderach@wanadoo.fr
web	bergeries-ponderach.com

Map 15 Entry 297

La Bastide Cabezac

Hameau de Cabezac, 11120 Bize en Minervois, Aude

The hotel and, above all, the restaurant are becoming as popular as the Minervois wines that come from the next door Château de Cabezac. Hervé, having directed two restaurants in Paris has now established himself here, built himself a magnificent kitchen and has put in a kitchen garden next to the pool. How can you miss with exquisite food, young enthusiastic staff, and smiley Sabine on top of things? The exterior of this old coaching inn – sunflower yellow walls with ocean blue trim – is intense like the sun that beats down on this land that produces its deep purple powerful wines. There are good-sized bedrooms, each in different pastel shades with plenty of air and natural light, king-size beds and minimalist accessories. The public areas and the interior *cour* on the first floor are warm yellow and, as is proper in hot lands, terracotta tiles are ubiquitous. The restaurant is named l'Olivier in homage to the working olive orchard nearby; they also transplanted a 300-year-old tree as a symbol of their new endeavor and to add a bit of gravitas. A terrific conference room.

rooms	12: 7 doubles, 1 twin, 1 family room for 3, 3 suites for 4.
price	€75-€110. Family room €125-€145. Suites €180-€200. Half-board €35 extra p.p.
meals	Breakfast €10. Lunch & dinner €16-€70. Rest closed Mon & Tues lunch; Sat & Sun lunch off season.
closed	Rarely.
directions	From Narbonne D607. Right at r'bout onto D5 just before crossing bridge; on left.

	Sabine & Hervé dos Santos
tel	+33 (0)4 68 46 66 10
fax	+33 (0)4 68 46 66 29
email	contact@labastidecabezac.com
web	www.labastidecabezac.com

Map 15 Entry 298

Château de Floure

1 allée Gaston Bonheur, 11800 Floure, Aude

Floure started life as a Roman villa, the Villa Flora, on the Via Aquitania between Narbonne and Toulouse: a peaceful refuge from the military post just a couple of leagues away. In the Middle Ages it became a monastery, until in the reign of Henri IV, a local official made it his country retreat. Hidden away behind the austere stone walls, an ivy-draped 18th-century château stands in the centre of matching mellow-tiled cottages and outbuildings, in interesting grounds where you can wander from a formal French garden, through a tree-shaded meadow to the vineyard or the swimming pool. The vaulted bar, complete with grand piano, is in the 12th-century keep. Bedrooms are vast, with beds to match, antique desks and deep comfortable chairs. Some rooms are in the château itself, others gathered around the courtyard. Bathrooms are for luxuriating, with deep tubs and attractive tiles. After dinner settle in the Bergère drawing room, where one wall was painted by the Vicomte de Laguepie in 1762. Carcassonne is only ten minutes' drive away, but it may be hard to leave these peaceful gardens.

rooms	21: 17 doubles, 4 suites for 3-4.
price	€120-€190. Suites €230.
meals	Buffet breakfast €16. Dinner €39-€59.
closed	4 January-mid-March.
directions	A61 exit 24 then N113 towards Narbonne. Pass Trèbes then follow sign to Floure. Hotel in village. Signed.

Madame Dominique Assous

tel	+33 (0)4 68 79 11 29
fax	+33 (0)4 68 79 04 61
email	contact@chateau-de-floure.com
web	www.chateau-de-floure.com

Map 15 Entry 299

Château de Cavanac
11570 Cavanac, Aude

A quiet place, with birdsong to serenade you. The château has been in the family for six generations and dates back to 1612; Louis, *chef et patron*, has a small vineyard, so you can drink of the vines that surround you. A convivial place, with a big rustic restaurant in the old stables, where hops hang from ancient beams and there's an open fire on which they cook the grills. There are several lovely terraced areas, too. Louis and Anne are justly proud of what they are doing – the hotel is quiet and friendly, with much comfort and an easy feel. Big bedrooms are fairly lavish, with four-posters, dramatic canopies, plush fabrics in soft colours. Chinese rugs cover terracotta tiles, while those rooms most recently redecorated have parquet floors and a colonial feel. Outside you stumble upon (not into, we hope) a delightful swimming pool with underwater lighting for midnight dips. There's a very pretty, sun-trapping terrace with plenty of sunloungers. Beyond the smart wrought-iron gates, Languedoc waits to beguile you; horse riding and golf can be arranged, there are cellars to visit, and medieval Carcassonne is close by.

rooms	28: 19 doubles, 2 singles, 3 triples, 4 suites.
price	€80–€155. Singles €65–€70.
meals	Breakfast €10. Dinner from €38. Restaurant closed Mondays. Other restaurants 2-3km.
closed	9 January-6 March; 1-15 November.
directions	From Toulouse, exit Carsassonne Ouest for Centre Hospitalier, then take Route de St Hilaire. Signed. Park in restaurant car park.

	Anne & Louis Gobin
tel	+33 (0)4 68 79 61 04
fax	+33 (0)4 68 79 79 67
email	infos@chateau-de-cavanac.fr
web	www.chateau-de-cavanac.fr

Map 15 Entry 300

La Fargo

11220 Saint Pierre des Champs, Aude

Pluck a handful of cherries on the way to breakfast; gather up the scents of rosemary and thyme. This centuries-old converted forge blends effortlessly with the unspoilt Corbières countryside. Christophe and Dominique, a gentle couple with a hippyish streak, lived the good life rearing goats, before rescuing the building five years ago. Their passion for food, nature and Indonesia – where they winter – is evident. Large, light bedrooms have a charming and simple colonial style – white or stone walls, tiled floors, dark teak, bright ikat bedcovers. Huge bathrooms glitter with mosaic tiles, the showers like tropical rainstorms. Breakfast on the terrace – homemade jams and brioches – under the shade of kiwi trees. Dine here or in the restaurant where clean, modern lines blend well with rustic stonework and food is an adventurous mix of Mediterranean and Asian. Corbières is a natural de-stresser: come for birdwatching, walking, fishing, vineyards, Cathar castles and medieval abbeys. Or wander around la Fargo's potager and orchard, pluck some fruit and lie back in one of dozens of wooden loungers.

rooms	6: 5 doubles, 1 family room for 4.
price	€59–€80.
meals	Breakfast €6. Lunch & dinner €23–€35. Restaurant closed Mon.
closed	15 November–March.
directions	A61 exit Lézignan-Corbières, D611 toward Fabrezan, then D212 to Lagrasse, then St Pierre des Champs. Fargo on right exiting village.

Christophe & Dominique Morellet

tel	+33 (0)4 68 43 12 78
fax	+33 (0)4 68 43 29 20
email	lafargo@club-internet.fr
web	www.lafargo.fr

Map 15 Entry 301

Le Mas Trilles
Le Pont de Reynès, 66400 Céret, Pyrénées-Orientales

There's a disarmingly haphazard feel to the layout of this rambling, honey-coloured farm. Many of the bedrooms are in converted barns, reached by unexpected ups and downs. All but one has its own private terrace; all have cool terracotta floors, painted furniture and a feeling of airy charm. The huge room without a terrace has magnificent views of the Canigou to compensate. The farmhouse dates from 1631: Laszlo and Marie-France bought it as a ruin nearly 20 years ago and spent five years renovating it. Everywhere is bright, pristine and relaxed. Laszlo is Hungarian, Marie-France French, and they are thoroughly likeable hosts. As the lush, gorgeous grounds testify, they are also talented gardeners. Close to the house, all is impeccable and beautifully maintained – a study in flowers, foliage and old, worn stone. Down by the river, on the other hand, things are allowed to become more riotous and wild. You're enveloped in the glorious sound of birdsong and rushing water; there are fine views of the mountains and an intoxicating feeling of space.

rooms	10: 3 doubles, 5 triples, 2 suites.
price	€104–€218. Triples & suites €188–€260.
meals	Light meals on request.
closed	8 October-28 April.
directions	Exit 43 Boulou towards Céret on D115 but do not enter town. Le Mas 2km after Céret towards Amélie les Bains.

Marie-France & Laszlo Bukk

tel	+33 (0)4 68 87 38 37
fax	+33 (0)4 68 87 42 62
email	mastrilles@free.fr
web	www.le-mas-trilles.com

Map 15 Entry 302

Auberge l'Atalaya
66800 Llo, Pyrénées-Orientales

A place of majestic beauty and wild poetry; a timeless Catalan farmhouse clinging to a rocky hillside; an owner of rare taste and talent – poet, philosopher, musician and lover of beauty. Such is l'Atalaya: a house that captures the imagination and promises riches earthly and spiritual. Family antiques are in all rooms, fine fabrics dress lovely old beds, stained-glass windows illuminate corridors, fresh figs may fill bowls in the intimate little breakfast room and in the big, light-filled dining room, mouthwatering meals are served before that boggling view, while the grand piano awaits its pianist. Your hostess has put her heart into renovating the house she bought long ago as a ruin and it has a quiet, cosy, hideaway atmosphere that is also very elegant: the architecture and décor are in harmony and people of sensitive taste feel utterly at home here. The wonderful little village has hot springs, the river gorges are home to rare butterflies, the hills have sheep and Romanesque churches. What a place!

rooms	13: 9 doubles, 3 twins, 1 suite for 2-4.
price	€90-€140.
meals	Breakfast €11. Lunch (weekends only) & dinner €28-€41. Restaurant closed December-March.
closed	3 November-20 December; 20 January-Easter.
directions	From Perpignan N116 west through Prades to Saillagouse. Left for Llo; left for Eyne. Hotel 1km on right.

	Ghilaine Toussaint
tel	+33 (0)4 68 04 70 04
fax	+33 (0)4 68 04 01 29
email	atalaya66@aol.com
web	www.atalaya66.com

Map 15 Entry 303

Auberge du Roua

Chemin du Roua, 66700 Argelès sur Mer, Pyrénées-Orientales

Hard to tell from the spic and span interior that this small hotel was once an 18th-century mill. But this is the south, where life is lived outdoors which here is so special: you could happily spend all day dozing or reading on the quiet garden terrace by the stone-paved pool surrounded by tropical plants. There is ample opportunity to escape the sun's dazzle under the trees, and the views of the Albères are splendid. Bedrooms have been refreshed, are comfortable and a bright modern décor has been used in the newest addition; bathrooms are a good size. This is a family-run hotel; don't be surprised to see a couple of young children about. The dining room, with its white nappery and crystal, is formal and rightly highlights the vaulted ceiling of the old mill – an appropriate setting for the chef's superb *cuisine raffiné*. The terrace by the pool is perfect for al fresco dining. Unusual to find a hotel hidden away in the middle of the countryside where, in these parts, the whole world is at the beach – it's a five-kilometre hop to the ocean and a 20-minute stroll to the centre of bustling Argelès.

rooms	17: 8 doubles, 4 twins, 3 suites, 2 family rooms for 3.
price	€60–€112. Suites & family rooms €109–€149.
meals	Breakfast €10. Dinner €43–€75. Restaurant closed Mon & Wed eve Oct–May. Sun, lunch only, Sept–June.
closed	November–mid-February.
directions	N114, exit 10 for Argelès sur Mer. In town, right at lights, straight on after the underpass; follow signs.

	Magalie Tonjum
tel	+33 (0)4 68 95 85 85
fax	+33 (0)4 68 95 83 50
email	magalie@aubergeduroua.com
web	www.aubergeduroua.com

Map 15 Entry 304

Photo Corel

rhône valley – alps

Au Coin du Feu-Chilly Powder

BP 116, 74110 Morzine, Haute-Savoie

The homeward piste takes you to the door; the cable car, opposite, sweeps you to the peaks. The chalet is named after its magnificent central fireplace… on one side gleaming leather sofas, on the other, red dining chairs at a long table. Everything feels generous here: great beams span the chalet's length, windows look up to the cliffs of the Hauts Forts, high ceilings give a sense of space. There's a reading room on the mezzanine above the living area with books, internet, antique globe and worn leather armchairs, and a small bar made of English oak by a carpenter friend. Bedrooms are alpine-swish and themed: there's the Toy Room for families, the English Room that sports a bowler hat. The carpets are sisal, one room's four-poster is veiled in muslin and the bathrooms have soaps from New Zealand and shower heads as big as plates. The chef produces the best of country cooking, and Paul and Francesca can organise everything, including torchlight descents. There's massage, a sauna, a hot tub outdoors, DVDs to cheer wet days – even an in-house nanny.

rooms	17: 6 doubles, 3 twins, 1 triple, 7 family rooms for 2-5.
price	€60. Half-board mandatory in winter, €457-€845 p.p. per week.
meals	Picnic lunch €5. Dinner €30.
closed	Never.
directions	From Morzine, signs to Avoriaz, then Les Prodains; 2.8 km; on right, just before cable car.

	Paul & Francesca Eyre
tel	+33 (0)4 50 74 75 21
fax	+33 (0)4 50 79 01 48
email	paul@chillypowder.com
web	www.chillypowder.com

Map 12 Entry 305

The Farmhouse

Le Mas de la Coutettaz, 74110 Morzine, Haute-Savoie

This 1771 farmhouse is the oldest in the valley, sitting at the foot of the slopes of bustling Morzine. Come for summer walks, bike rides and mountain air, or snowbound adventure. It's a perfect staging post for the Avoriaz and Portes du Soleil ski arena, and there's a 'ski host' at the hotel who introduces you to the runs free. Comfortably rustic bedrooms are reached via stone stairs; the doubles are big and the triples huge, with dark polished beams, massive radiators and old pine doors with original mouldings. Ask for a room with mountain views. In the garden is a little chalet for two, nicknamed the Love Nest. Your day starts with a huge – not exclusively French – breakfast: croissants warm from the oven, porridge, perhaps kedgeree. After a hard day on the slopes, it's home to cakes and tea. Smiling, ever-busy Dorrien ensures the evening meal, too, is a sociable affair. After drinks in the bar before a log fire, retire to the old cattle shed – now a magnificent dining room, where long, leisurely candlelit dinners are savoured at the big table.

rooms	8: 3 doubles, 1 single, 3 triples, 1 suite for 6.
price	€75-€175. Single €45-€135. Triples €105-€255. Half-board December-May: €95-€190 p.p.
meals	Dinner with wine & coffee, €30-€40. Many restaurants nearby.
closed	One month sometime between May-June.
directions	In Morzine, follow signs for Avoriaz. On Ave Joux Plan, left after Nicholas Sport, then right. On left.

	Dorrien Ricardo
tel	+33 (0)4 50 79 08 26
fax	+33 (0)4 50 79 18 53
email	info@thefarmhouse.co.uk
web	www.thefarmhouse.co.uk

Map 12 Entry 306

Le Moulin de Bathieu

Verclad, 74340 Samoëns, Haute-Savoie

Ski in winter; in summer, explore the mountains – on foot or by bike – or go fishing with Charles. The setting is pure 'Heidi', the views are glorious. In winter snow laps to the door, in summer the terraces tumble with flowers. The Moulin is very much a family affair: she cooks – beautifully – Charles does the rest. The chalet is pale-pine-panelled, warm and homely and with all mod cons, including a heated garage for your boots and skis. The light, airy dining room has big picture windows that pull in the views, and you can eat on one of a number of terraces – they keep creating new ones! – when it's warm. Three times a week the food is regional, and you can order picnics when you like. Wood-panelled bedrooms are big enough to fit sofas or little sitting areas, and a mezzanine level for the children's beds; all bar one have a balcony with a view. The Moulin is just outside the little town of Samoëns, set well back from the road. It's a brilliant place for an active family holiday – fresh air, good food, lovely people… you could happily spend a week here, or more.

rooms	7: 3 doubles, 1 twin, 2 duplexes for 3-4, 1 suite for 2-4.
price	€61-€110. Suite €120-€140.
meals	Breakfast €8.50-€12. Dinner €25-€38.
closed	June-10 July; 6 November-18 December.
directions	A40 exit 18, D4 for Samoëns. Before entry into Samoëns right on D254 for Samoëns. After 1km, hotel on left.

Charles Pontet

tel	+33 (0)4 50 34 48 07
fax	+33 (0)4 50 34 43 25
email	moulin.du.bathieu@wanadoo.fr
web	www.bathieu.com

Map 12 Entry 307

Chalet Odysseus

210 route de Lachat, 74300 Les Carroz d'Arâches, Haute-Savoie

Chalet Odysseus has the lot: comfort (soft sofas, bright rugs, open fire), swishness (satellite TV, sauna, small gym), a French chef who waves his gourmet wand over the dining table once a week, and English hosts who spoil you rotten. Kate and Barry lived in the village for seven years, then built their own house. They have the ground floor of this beautifully solid, purpose-built, new chalet, you live above, and it's the sort of place you'd be happy in whatever the weather. Cheerfully pretty bedrooms come with the requisite pine garb, beds are covered in quilts handmade by Kate, two rooms have balconies that catch the sun, and the tiniest comes with bunk beds for kids. The shower rooms and bathroom are airy and light. As for Les Carroz, most skiers pass it by on their way to high-rise Flaine – a shame, for the village has heaps of character and several fine places to eat. Your own 4x4 gets you to the lifts in minutes, tying you in with the whole of the Grand Massif. Dinners are four-course and there's a *grole* night to boot. Great for a family break, whatever the season. *Ask about catered chalet option.*

rooms	5: 3 doubles, 2 twins.
price	€90.
	Catered: €495-€600 p.p. per week.
meals	Dinner with wine, €40.
closed	May-June; November.
directions	After Cluses N205, left onto D106. 1km before Les Carroz, red & white shuttered chalet on left; next left, signed.

	Kate & Barry Joyce
tel	+33 (0)4 50 90 66 00
fax	+33 (0)4 50 90 66 01
email	chaletodysseus@wanadoo.fr
web	www.chaletodysseuslachat.com

Map 12 Entry 308

Hôtel Le Cottage Fernand Bise

Au Bord du Lac, 74290 Talloires, Haute-Savoie

Not many cottages have 35 bedrooms; not many have this fabulous setting, either – you might be in a Wagner opera as you gaze from the terrace at the sun setting over the Roc de Chère across the Lac d'Annecy. The three buildings which make up the hotel look, unsurprisingly, like Alpine chalets and are set in pretty, well-planted gardens in which you can wander on your way to meet one of the local millionaires or perhaps Wotan himself. Monsieur and Madame Bise run this welcoming, relaxed establishment with a quiet Savoyard efficiency, which, at its heart, has a proper concern for the comfort of guests. *Douillette* – that lovely word which is the French equivalent of 'cosy' – perfectly describes the atmosphere in the bedrooms, with their floral chintz fabrics and comfortable furniture. Well away from the bustle of Annecy itself, but close enough to dabble if you wish; there are multifarious activities for the sporty and inspiration for the arty who wish to follow in the footsteps of Cézanne or Lamartine. Comfort *and* culture – what more could you want?

rooms	35: 17 doubles, 15 twins, 3 suites. Family rooms on request.
price	€100–€320.
meals	Breakfast €16. Lunch €26–€40. Dinner €40–€60. Many restaurants within walking distance.
closed	10 October–25 April.
directions	In Annecy follow signs Bord du Lac for Thônes D909. At Veyrier du Lac follow D909A to Talloires. Well signed in Talloires.

	Jean-Claude & Christine Bise
tel	+33 (0)4 50 60 71 10
fax	+33 (0)4 50 60 77 51
email	cottagebise@wanadoo.fr
web	www.cottagebise.com

Map 12 Entry 309

Hôtel Le Calgary
73620 Les Saises, Savoie

From the outside it looks like two old gasthofs linked in the middle — yet it's new. Le Calgary was built by Les Saises's most famous son, Franck Picard, and named after the resort in which he gained his Olympic gold medal. It's a glorious sight in the spring and summer: petunias, geraniums and mysotis take over the window boxes in their fuchias, periwinkle blues, magentas and mauves. Panelled ceilings span the open-plan sitting area and bar, dark antique furniture sits alongside modern coffee tables, there are big lamps, fresh flowers and an open fire. Patterned red rugs are strewn across the green carpeting throughout the ground floor. Upstairs bedrooms have carved doors, each with an original hand-painted design, the furniture is simple pine, there are built-in cupboards and big windows with balconies and mountain views, and masses of light and space. If you want character, choose a room under the eaves. Jeannette and Jean-Jacques love having children to stay and give families a crèche, an indoor pool and supervised hours in the billiard room. And you're brilliantly positioned for shops and piste.

rooms	35: 6 doubles, 13 twins, 8 triples, 5 quadruples, 3 family rooms for 5.
price	€75. Half-board mandatory in winter, €91–€129 p.p.
meals	Picnic lunch €8. Dinner €23.
closed	May-mid June; September-mid-December.
directions	From Albertville, D925 to La Pierre; left on D218b for Les Saises. On right, at end of village.

	Family Berthod
tel	+33 (0)4 79 38 98 38
fax	+33 (0)4 79 38 98 00
email	contact@hotelcalgary.com
web	www.hotelcalgary.com

Map 12 Entry 310

Le Mas Bleu
07260 Rosières, Ardèche

You might first spot your neighbours through the mists of the steam bath or the bubbles of the jacuzzi. Le Mas Bleu, with its seven blue-shuttered, wisteria-clad cottages, may not be a typical Sawday choice, but it is special. The 18th-century stone farmstead is superbly decorated and supremely peaceful, despite the presence of up to 30 other residents. It is unquestionably alternative – a 'writer's café' in the grounds, Ayurveda and aqua treatments, yoga. Children will love the sandpit, ping-pong, outdoor games and bikes to borrow. It's all run by an energetic and welcoming German couple: Anna, mother of two, and her partner Holger. They have restored the buildings with taste and sensitivity, keeping the exteriors and the original beams intact wherever possible. Estourel is the largest apartment, sleeping seven, with two storeys and a large covered terrace with magnificent views of vineyards and mountains in (almost) every direction. The highlight inside is a vast antique dining table, once used to cut lengths of silk, for which the area is famous. *Minimum stay two nights. Sophisticated spa programme.*

rooms	7 cottages for 2-8.
price	€100. Singles €80. €500–€1,200 per cottage per week. Out of season: €100–€170 per cottage per night.
meals	Breakfast €10. Restaurants within 2km.
closed	Never.
directions	From Nimes to Alès N106; D904 to St Ambroix; D104 to Rosières.

	Anna Niedeggen & Dr. Holger Stephen
tel	+33 (0)6 80 66 12 46
fax	+33 (0)4 75 39 92 79
email	info@thebluehouse.net
web	www.thebluehouse.net

Map 11 Entry 311

Hôtel de Digoine

5 quai Madier ce Montjau, 07700 Bourg Saint Andéol, Ardèche

Silk and its mythical route between China and the south of France is the theme here – and what a sensuous treat this is. Olivier, full of southeast Asian travels, has envisaged each room as a staging post: a Venetian room with a floor in parquet and silks in greys and blues; Chinese reds and yellows for Tibet; blues and reds and a bed on the mezzanine for a séjour in Samarkand; for Mongolia, smooth fabrics and rough bark and wood. It is an exotic décor and quite fitting as this lovely house was once owned by a silk merchant who produced his own cocoons. Downstairs one is enthralled by a series of interlocking reception rooms. In the grand salon, its views over a tributory of the river, the afternoon sun turns the dusty-pink walls golden; even more special is the terracotta-hued breakfast room, reached through a concealed door in the panelling. Food is simple but of high quality – freshly grilled meat or fish, fine cheeses. Breakfast is served at one table in the kitchen, more formally in the dining room, or in the courtyard in the summer. Olivier will happily concoct a picnic hamper if a hike is in the air.

rooms	7 + 1: 4 doubles, 1 twin, 1 family for 3, 1 apartment for 5. 1 house for 19 (no kitchen but can be catered).
price	€85–€90. Family room €110–€115. Apartment €130–€140. Whole house €900; €4,000 per week.
meals	Breakfast €9. Hosted dinner €22.
closed	Never.
directions	Autoroute A7, exit Montelimar Sud to Viviers; N86 to Bourg St Andéol. Quai Madier de Montjau is on the river next to Mairie.

	Olivier Dutreil
tel	+33 (0)4 75 54 61 07
fax	+33 (0)4 75 54 61 07
email	digoine@cegetel.net
web	www.digoine.com

Map 16 Entry 312

Villa Augusta Hôtel Restaurant

14 rue du Serre Blanc, 26130 Saint Paul Trois Châteaux , Drôme

Breakfast in the garden, under the palms and ancient cedar tree, the air heady with jasmine and roses… you may linger all day. This is an unexpected find, an early 19th-century *maison de maître* where old has been subtly blended with new, and given a lavish touch. In the entrance, glowingly restored frescoes mix with modern floor-to-ceiling windows drawing you to that wonderful garden. There's a pool beyond, too. A stone staircase leads to coolly elegant corridors and a flush of glamorous bedrooms. Large beds, large windows, gorgeous fabrics – velvets, silks, voiles – each room is a different colour – cherry red, aubergine, gold. A few simple but exotic antiques add to the rich but restful feel. You may want to dress up for dinner; this is top-notch Provençal dining – raviole de langoustine, foie gras de canard pôelé – served in chic surroundings. A glass terrace adds softness and light. Staff are smiling and professional; Marie runs the place with calm, friendly efficiency. Avignon, Uzès, the Ardêche are easy from here or explore this medieval village. Stay on a Thursday for the hotel's live concerts.

rooms	24: 12 doubles, 10 twins, 1 single, 1 suite.
price	€95-€230. Suite €350-€400.
meals	Breakfast €15-€20. Lunch & dinner €42-€85. Restaurant closed Mondays; Tuesday lunchtimes & Sunday evenings (except August).
closed	Never.
directions	Exit Montelimar Sud; at r'bout head towards St Paul Trois Châteaux, straight ahead. Signposted.

	Maria Dos Santos
tel	+33 (0)4 75 97 29 29
fax	+33 (0)4 75 04 79 03
email	info@villaaugusta-hotel.com
web	www.villaaugusta-hotel.com

Map 16 Entry 313

Le Clair de la Plume

Place de Mail, 26230 Grignan, Drôme

Famous for more than 300 species of old-fashioned and English roses spilling into winding streets, Grignan is a paradise for rose-lovers. Yet pushing open the wrought-iron gates of this pink-façaded guest house, abutting a unique columned fountain once a wash house, brings you into something new. Jean-Luc Valadeau has created such a feeling of warmth and hospitality; as he puts it, "a home with all the comforts of a hotel". His bustling staff are equally attentive, leading you through elegant, cosy rooms, antique pieces catching your eye on the way. The small terraced garden adds to the feeling of privacy and light floods in over the original staircase. The bedrooms are quiet, beautifully decorated – Louis Philippe wardrobes in some, country-style wicker chairs in others – and all have luxurious bathrooms. Stencilled or ragged walls, original floor tiles or shining oak planks – a great combination of good taste and authenticity. After a generous breakfast, the Salon de Thé is open from 10am to 10pm for exotic selections of tea, sandwiches, mouthwatering patisseries and locally-made traditional ice cream.

rooms	10 twins/doubles.
price	€90–€170.
meals	Good choice lof local restaurants.
closed	Rarely.
directions	From Lyon A7 exit 18 Montélimar Sud towards Nyons; D133 then D541 to Grignan. Signed.

	Jean-Luc Valadeau
tel	+33 (0)4 75 91 81 30
fax	+33 (0)4 75 91 81 31
email	plume2@wanadoo.fr
web	www.clairplume.com

Map 16 Entry 314

Michel Chabran

29 avenue du 45 Parallèle, 26600 Pont de l'Isère, Drôme

A tiny jewel, whose main attraction is not the rooms or the setting but the food. Michel Chabran is a prince among restaurateurs, and his sophisticated little hotel, 50 miles south of Lyon, lies in France's gastronomic heart. Served on Limoges china dusted with gold: potato purée with Sevruga caviar, *poularde de Bresse*, hot soufflé of Grand Marnier – subtle, original food that has won Michel many accolades. The à la carte menu stretches to four pages, the set menu two, there are 400 wines and the service is exemplary. It all started in 1943 when Michel's grandfather supplied sandwiches to workers heading south on the first paid holidays to the sun – the rest is history. Bedrooms are modest, cosy, flowery and soundproofed, some face the main road, others the garden. Come for a truffle weekend from November to March: Michel tells you all about the 'black diamonds', then sits you down to a six-course treat, before a blazing fire. Work it all off the next day in the Vercors National Park – or visit Chave, producer of the Hermitage wines that will have seduced you the night before.

rooms	12 doubles.
price	€77–€120. Half-board on request.
meals	Breakfast €18. Lunch €34. Dinner €48–€155.
closed	October–March: Sunday evenings, Wednesday & Thursday lunchtimes.
directions	A7 south of Lyon exit Tain l'Hermitage or Valence North to N7 for Pont de l'Isère. Restaurant & hotel on main street opp. church.

M & Mme Chabran

tel	+33 (0)4 75 84 60 09
fax	+33 (0)4 75 84 59 65
email	chabran@michelchabran.fr
web	www.michelchabran.fr

Map 11 Entry 315

Château de la Commanderie

17 avenue d'Echirolles, 38230 Eybens, Isère

Grand it appears, and some of the makers of that grandeur – Knights Templar and Maltese, princes and prime ministers, presidents and financiers – look down upon you as you eat in the magnificent dining room, a favourite restaurant for the discerning palates of Grenoble. But the atmosphere is of an intimate family-run hotel. The whole place is awash with family antiques and heirlooms, good taste prevails in every room and flowers add that touch of life and genuine attention. Bedrooms are divided among four separate buildings, adding to the sense of intimacy. Rooms in château and chalet are the more traditional with carved wooden beds and gilt-framed mirrors, though some of them give onto a small road. The orangerie's rooms, as you'll discover once you have negotiated the rather plain corridors, look out over fine parkland, and are deliciously peaceful. The least expensive rooms are in the Petit Pavillon, on the road side. But whichever you choose, you will feel thoroughly pampered, and it's excellent value for families. *Signs for 'La Commanderie' indicate an area of town, not the Château.*

rooms	25 twins/doubles.
price	€80–€150.
meals	Breakfast buffet €15. Lunch & dinner €25–€65. Restaurant closed Mondays, Saturday lunchtimes & Sundays.
closed	20 December–3 January.
directions	From Grenoble exit 5 Rocade Sud for Eybens, immediately right at 1st lights for Le Bourg; right after Esso garage. Entrance to hotel 300m on left at turning in road.

	Monsieur de Beaumont
tel	+33 (0)4 76 25 34 58
fax	+33 (0)4 76 24 07 31
email	resa@commanderie.fr
web	www.commanderie.fr

Map 11 Entry 316

Cour des Loges

6 rue du Boeuf, 69005 Lyon, Rhône

Once upon a time, when Lyon was a rumbling, prosperous trade centre, there were four Renaissance houses built for bankers, printers and spice merchants. Even the king came with his court for lengthy visits and decreed Lyon's trade fairs be tax-free. He and the rest of the nobility were entranced by all things Italian. Cour des Loges *is* those four houses, encapsulated under a 20th-century glass roof linking galleries, porticoes, arches and corkscrew staircases; you are inside but feel as if you were in a huge piazza. Jocelyne Sibuet, the owner and decorator, has enhanced that feeling by adding large terracotta pots of sculpted bushes and elegant benches. The bedroom are sensuous with carefully chosen textiles (still a Lyon speciality): red velvets, grey taffetas, mauve linens and silks; each with an eye-catching Renaissance or baroque antique cupboard or trunk. Then there are the hanging gardens overlooking the brick-red roofs – a magical spot for breakfast or a long drink. The chef already has a reputation for one of the best tables in Lyon, no mean achievement. *Valet parking and porter service.*

rooms	62: 52 twins/doubles, 6 suites for 2-3, 4 apts for 3-4 (no kitchen).
price	€230-€350. Suites & apts €460-€590.
meals	Breakfast €22. Lunch menu weekdays €18; à la carte €50- €80.
closed	Never.
directions	From A42/43 for town centre & Place Bellecour. Over Rhône & Saône; right into Quai Romain Rolland; left into Rue Louis Carrand; left into Rue du Boeuf. .

	Véronique Pellicier
tel	+33 (0)4 72 77 44 44
fax	+33 (0)4 72 40 93 61
email	contact@courdesloges.com
web	www.courdesloges.com

Map 11 Entry 317

Château de Longsard
69400 Arnas, Rhône

Orange trees in the *orangerie*, an obelisk amid the topiary chessmen, alleys of 200-year-old lime trees... the formal French garden is just one delight here. An English garden surrounds the formal French one and a kitchen garden and orchard add to the charm. In the entrance courtyard are two spectacular Lebanon cedars (one tricentenial) with huge drooping branches that sweep the ground. Your hosts, much-travelled, sophisticated and informal, enjoy sharing their enthusiasm for the area and its wines and will organise tastings, including their own. Bedrooms, pure château, from pastel to bold with hints of Art Deco, some with fine carved door frames and 17th-century beams to guard your sleep, are eclectically furnished (Olivier's brother is an antique dealer). There are panelled rooms and plainer ones all with polished parquet floors, fine rugs, pictures and engravings. Dinner is certainly worth booking – a typical menu might be stuffed red peppers, chicken in cream and morel mushroom sauce, local cheeses and salad, peaches poached in ...Beaujolais, of course.

rooms	5: 3 doubles, 2 suites for 2-3.
price	€100-€125.
meals	Dinner with wine, €35, book ahead.
closed	Rarely.
directions	From north A6 exit Belleville (or Arnas mid-2006); N6 for Lyon 10km; right D43 to Arnas. Through village; château on right after 1.5km.

	Alexandra & Olivier du Mesnil
tel	+33 (0)4 74 65 55 12
fax	+33 (0)4 74 65 03 17
email	longsard@wanadoo.fr
web	www.longsard.com

Map 11 Entry 318

Château de Pramenoux
69870 Lamure sur Azergues, Rhône

Climb up into the Mont du Beaujolais hills above Lyon. Rivers pulse down on either side and great Douglas pine trees clean the air. As you round a curve, a pair of gothic pepperpot turrets surprisinly pop into view. The château sits in a natural clearing and views from the terrace and bedrooms sweep splendidly down the valley; a small pond in front anchors the eye. Emmanuel, a charming young escapee from the corporate world, will point out the bits that date from the 10th century up to the Renaissance; he has lovingly patched and painted a great deal of it himself. Rooms are big, hugely comfortable and have simply elegant bathrooms. Choose the cherrywood panelled room: a gold and white striped bed and Louis XVI chairs dressed in eau-de-nil. Or be King and Queen and slumber under a canopied bed in a room lined with royal blue and golden fleur-de-lys, a textile re-created by Emmanuel himself with the weavers of Lyon. Passionate opera lovers organize concerts in the summer in the vast reception hall. A wonderfully peaceful place, run by the warmest people. *Cash or cheque only.*

rooms	4 doubles.
price	€120–€140.
meals	Hosted dinner with aperitif and wine, €39, book ahead.
closed	Rarely.
directions	A6 exit Belleville; D37 Beaujeu, at St Vincent left for Quincié en Beaujolais & Marchampt D9 for Lamure. Almost through Lamure, take lane marked Pramenoux facing soccer field & climb.

Emmanuel Baudoin
& Jean-Luc Plasse

tel	+33 (0)4 74 03 16 43
fax	+33 (0)4 74 03 16 28
email	pramenoux@aol.com
web	www.chateau-de-pramenoux.com

Map 11 Entry 319

Château Lambert

69840 Chénas, Rhône

Marty's passion for textiles and his eye for detail make this small 17th-century château a heavenly place to be. It sits smack in the middle of beaujolais country on a hill overlooking the village; vines and more vines stretch over the Soâne plain to the snow-topped Alps just visible in the distance. In front is a trellised terrace, below which a vegetable garden blooms with summer salads : a wonderful setting for a lazy breakfast or an evening aperitif (try their own Moulin à Vent). A fine library takes up an entire wall of the apartment on the ground floor, where neutral walls set off the red plaid chairs on either side of the fireplace and a pair of old rose antique armchairs render a curvy touch of elegance. All is light green and pale prune with touches of a darker red in the upstairs suite. A magnificent canopied bed in the alcove has matching toile de Jouy drapes and bedspread. The high ceilings, good light and muted tones give all the rooms a feeling of airiness and space, like a Vermeer. Marty is young and enthusiastic – a fine host who will make you feel very much at home.

rooms	6: 3 doubles, 1 twin, 2 suites.
price	€98. Suites €129.
meals	Picnic hampers. Hosted dinner €26.50, book ahead.
closed	Rarely.
directions	A6 exit Macon Sud or A40 exit Replonges. N6 towards Lyon. After 12km at La Chapelle de Guinchay, right towards Chénas. At church, take street going up on right. Signed.

	Marty Freriksen
tel	+33 (0)4 74 06 77 74
fax	+33 (0)4 74 04 48 01
email	contact@chateau-lambert.com
web	www.chateau-lambert.com

Map 11 Entry 320

Photo Corel

provence – alps – riviera

Le Mas de la Fouque

Route du Petit Rhône, 13460 Saintes Maries de la Mer, Bouches-du-Rhône

Cowboy boots and weather-beaten faces are as much part of the Camargue as the flamingos and white horses gracing the ponds and grasslands around this hotel. Some of the structures hover above the water on piles, others connect by boardwalks; all are architectually integrated. Bedrooms and suites face south; their own terraces overlook either the pool or the estuary – shared with egrets, herons and frogs, the sole inhabitants to break the silence of your siesta. Stroll along lavender-fringed paths, motor to a private beach or hop on a slow boat for day trip through the nature reserve where lunch is served on a floating cabin. There's water skiing and horses to ride among the flamingos; and, if your equestrian skills are well-honed, you may join the cowboys when they separate the bulls. This is no budget break but Le Mas is unique in its mix of luxury and unspoilt nature. And if you can bear to leave this peace, the quaint seaside town of Les Saintes Maries de la Mer is a few minutes' drive; gypsies gather there for a spectacular festival at the end of May.

rooms	21 + 1: 10 doubles, 4 twins/doubles, 3 suites for 4, 4 suites for 2-3. 1 apartment for 4.
price	€180-€290. Suites €310-€420. Apartment €420-€530.
meals	Breakfast €19. Lunch €39. Dinner €49. Restaurant closed mid-November-mid-December.
closed	Mid-November-mid-March.
directions	From Arles D570 to St Maries de la Mer; right after bird sanctuary on D38. On left 4km before village.

	Viviane Régis
tel	+33 (0)4 90 97 81 02
fax	+33 (0)4 90 97 96 84
email	info@masdelafouque.com
web	www.masdelafouque.com

Map 16 Entry 321

Grand Hôtel Nord Pinus

Place du Forum, 13200 Arles, Bouches-du-Rhône

An Arlesian legend, where Spain meets France, ancient Rome meets the 21st century. Built in 1865 on Roman vaults, it came to fame in the 1950s when a clown and a cabaret singer owned it: famous bullfighters dressed here before entering the arena and the arty crowd flocked (Cocteau, Picasso, Hemingway…). Anne Igou keeps the drama alive today with her strong personality and cinema, fashion and photography folk – and bullfighters still have 'their' superb Spanish Rococo room. The style is vibrant and alive at this show of Art Deco furniture and fittings, great *corrida* posters and toreador costumes, North African carpets and artefacts, fabulous Provençal colours and ironwork. Colour and light are deftly used to create a soft, nostalgic atmosphere where you feel both warm and cool, smart and artistic. Each room is differently interesting, some larger – and lighter – than others. And breakfast is a festival of real French tastes – more magic, more nostalgia. As Cocteau said: "An hotel with a soul".

rooms	26: 19 twins/doubles, 6 suites for 2-4, 1 apartment for 4 (no kitchen).
price	€145-€190. Suites €285. Apartment €450.
meals	Breakfast €14-€20. Lunch & dinner from €30.
closed	Never.
directions	From A54 exit Arles Centre for Centre Ancien. Take Boulevard des Lices at main post office; left on Rue Jean Jaurès; right on Rue Cloître, right to Place du Forum.

	Anne Igou
tel	+33 (0)4 90 93 44 44
fax	+33 (0)4 90 93 34 00
email	info@nord-pinus.com
web	www.nord-pinus.com

Map 16 Entry 322

Le Mas de Peint
Le Sambuc, 13200 Arles, Bouches-du-Rhône

Lucille and Jacques are warm, kind and proud of their beautiful farm. Their 500 bulls, 15 horses and swathes of arable land keep Jacques busy; Lucille tends to the rest. She has introduced an elegant but sober French country-farmhouse feel – no flounces nor flummery, just impeccable style. Bedrooms are deep green or old rose; generous curtains are checked dove-grey; floors come tiled or carpeted in wool. Eye-catching quirkery everywhere – a collection of fine pencil sketches, an antique commode – and some rooms with wonderful mezzanine bathrooms under old rafters. Breakfast royally in the big family kitchen or outside on the wisteria-draped terrace, then discover the secluded pool, encircled by teak loungers, scented with jasmine. The demi-pension option is a must. Dine outside on summer evenings, sheltered by a muslin canopy at tables aglow with Moroccan lamps – a fairytale spot in which to linger over elegant, garden-fresh food. Drift inside for a cognac in the clubby cigar room, take a peek at the black and white photos of bullfighting in the seductive salon. Heavenly.

rooms	11: 2 doubles, 6 twins/doubles, 1 suite, 1 suite for 3, 1 family suite for 3-4.
price	€205-€265. Suites €335-€381. Half-board €61 p.p.; min. stay 3 nights.
meals	Breakfast €20. Lunch à la carte. Dinner €50. Restaurant closed Wed.
closed	10 Jan-11 Mar; 14 Nov-20 Dec.
directions	Arles to St Marie de la Mer D570; 2km after 2nd r'bout, D36 for Le Sambuc.

	Jacques & Lucille Bon
tel	+33 (0)4 90 97 20 62
fax	+33 (0)4 90 97 22 20
email	hotel@masdepeint.net
web	www.masdepeint.com

Map 16 Entry 323

La Riboto de Taven

Le Val d'Enfer, 13520 Les Baux de Provence, Bouches-du-Rhône

A most magical place. Ever slept in a cave? In a canopied bed with ornate cover and hangings, with a luxurious bathroom next door? Here you can if you book far enough ahead. The Novi-Thème family – Christine, Philippe and Jean-Pierre – have farmed here for four generations and still produce their own olive oil. Their 18th century *mas* facing the garden is full of beautiful furniture handed down the generations. The property faces the spectacular cliff-top village of Les Baux de Provence- some say the most beautiful in all of France – the light changing on the cliffs as the day moves on. Walk up stone steps from the garden to a terrace, where the view is even more amazing than from the rest of the house. It is literally built onto the limestone cliff and the overhang of the rock face form the ceilings of the two 'troglodyte' rooms. In this supremely peaceful oasis of light, stone and history, excellent is the food, warm is the welcome. You will wish that you had booked for a week. *Children over 10 welcome.*

rooms	6: 3 doubles, 2 troglodyte suites, 1 apartment for 4 (without kitchen).
price	€160–€280.
meals	Breakfast €16. Poolside lunch €23. Dinner €48. Restaurant closed on Wednesdays.
closed	Early January–early March.
directions	From St Rémy de Provence D5 to Maussane & Les Baux. Past entrance to village & head towards Fontvieille. Hotel on 1st road to right, signed.

	Novi-Thème Family
tel	+33 (0)4 90 54 34 23
fax	+33 (0)4 90 54 38 88
email	contact@riboto-de-taven.fr
web	www.riboto-de-taven.fr

Map 16 Entry 324

Mas de l'Oulivié

Les Arcoules, 13520 Les Baux de Provence, Bouches-du-Rhône

How refreshing to find a hotel that brings together old and new so harmoniously and with such impeccable taste. Having fallen in love with the olive groves, lavender fields and chalky white hillsides of Les Baux de Provence, the family built the hotel of their dreams 15 or so years ago: a creamy-fronted, almond-green-shuttered, Provence-style structure, roofed with reclaimed terracotta tiles, landscaped with cypress and oleander. Every last detail has been carefully crafted, from the locally made oak furniture to the homemade tiles round the pool. And what a pool! Temptingly curvaceous, with a jacuzzi and pebble beach for children. Furnishings are fresh, local, designed for deep comfort. Bedrooms are creamy-coloured, country-style with an elegant twist. The bar/living-room has a rustic fireplace, filled with flowers in the summer. The young Achards love to provide guests and their children with the very best and that includes lunches served by the pool; they also sell their own lavender and oil. Mas de l'Oulivié joins the *crème de la crème* of Provence's small country hotels – a stylish retreat.

rooms	27: 16 doubles, 7 triples, 2 quadruples, 2 suites.
price	€100–€245. Suites €290–€410.
meals	Breakfast €11–€15. Poolside lunch €7–€25. Restaurants in village.
closed	Mid-November-mid-March.
directions	From north A7 exit 24 for Les Baux. Mas 2km from Les Baux on D78 towards Fontvieille.

	Emmanuel & Isabelle Achard
tel	+33 (0)4 90 54 35 78
fax	+33 (0)4 90 54 44 31
email	contact@masdeloulivie.com
web	www.masdeloulivie.com

Map 16 Entry 325

Mas des Comtes de Provence

Petite Route d'Arles, 13150 Tarascon, Bouches-du-Rhône

Homesick for the south of France and looking for a life change after a frenetic professional career in Paris, Pierre fell for this historic hunting lodge and has settled in nicely after a huge restauration. The *mas* belonged to King René whose château is just up the road; some say the Germans blocked the underground tunnel that connected the two buildings. A massive, soberly, elegant stone exterior dating from the 15th century protects the big interior courtyard overlooked by grey-green shuttered windows. The rooms are regal and awesomely huge – the Royal suite measures a nice 100m2. The suite Roi René is in tones of ivory, brown and beige; Garance in brick and yellow; ironwork chairs and side tables add extra interest. The pool is well hidden from the house in the two-hectare park dominated by 300-year-old plane trees, twisted olive trees, cypress and a profusion of roses. Pierre & Elizabeth may prepare a barbecue by the pool, serve generous pre-dinner snacks to the adults while feeding the children. They can direct you to the best canoeing, hiking, cycling, or riding – all just minutes away.

rooms	9: 6 twins/doubles, 3 suites for 4-6.
price	€130–€200. Suites €220–€380.
meals	Breakfast €12. Lunch €25. Dinner with aperitif & coffee €37.50, book ahead.
closed	Rarely.
directions	Tarascon towards Arles on D35 'Petite Route d'Arles'. 200m after leaving Tarascon, take small road on left. Mas 600m on left.

	Pierre Valo & Elisabeth Ferriol
tel	+33 (0)4 90 91 00 13
fax	+33 (0)4 90 91 02 85
email	valo@mas-provence.com
web	www.mas-provence.com

Map 16 Entry 326

Hôtel Le Cadran Solaire

5 rue du Cabaret Neuf, 13690 Graveson, Bouches-du-Rhône

A soft clear light filters through the house, the light of the south pushing past the smallish windows and stroking Sophie Guilmet's light-handed, rich-pastelled décor where simple Provençal furniture, stencil motifs and natural materials – cotton, linen, organdy and seagrass – give the immediate feel of a well-loved family home. The simplicity of a pastel slipcover over a chair, a modern wrought-iron bed frame and a white piqué quilt is refreshing and restful – and the house stays deliciously cool in the summer heat. The solid old staging post has stood here, with its thick walls, for 400 years, its face is as pretty as ever, calmly set in its gentle garden of happy flowers where guests can always find a quiet corner for their deckchairs. You can have breakfast on the shrubby terrace, under a blue and white parasol, or in the attractive dining room where a fine big mirror overlooks the smart red-on-white tables. A wonderful atmosphere, relaxed, smiling staff all of whom are family. And really good value.

rooms	12: 8 doubles, 4 twins.
price	€60-€80.
meals	Breakfast €7. Restaurants in village.
closed	November-March, except by arrangement.
directions	A7 exit Avignon Sud for Chateaurenard. D28 to Graveson; signed.

	Sophie Guilmet
tel	+33 (0)4 90 95 71 79
fax	+33 (0)4 90 90 55 04
email	cadransolaire@wanadoo.fr
web	www.hotel-en-provence.com

Map 16 Entry 327

Mas de Cornud

Perire Roure des Baux (D31), 13210 St Rémy de Provence, Bouches-du-Rhône

Guest house, cookery school and wine courses combine in a typical farmhouse where two majestic plane trees stand guard and the scents and light of Provence hover. Nito, the chef and a nature-lover, cares about how colour creates feeling, how fabrics comfort: she and David, the *sommelier*, have done a superb restoration (hangings from Kashmir, old French tiles). Bedrooms are big and varied, all warm and simple. The atmosphere is convivial and open: you are a member of a family here, so join the others at the honesty bar, choose a book in the library, or have a swim in the big pool. The kitchen is the vital centre of Cornud: here you eat if the weather is poor – otherwise the garden has some lovely eating spots – and learn, if you have come for cookery lessons; though many stay without following a course. A country kitchen, with cast-iron range, long wooden table, wood-fired and spit-roast ovens, it also has a non-slip floor and granite worktops – very professional. Direct from local artisan growers come herbs, fruits and vegetables. Come and be part of Provence for a week. *Children over 12 welcome.*

rooms	7 + 1: 6 doubles, 1 suite for 2-5. 1 studio for 2 with kitchenette.
price	€100–€220. Suite €240–€395. Studio €580 (min. 1 week).
meals	Picnic €40 with wine. Lunch €21–€35. Hosted dinner €55–€65.
closed	November–week before Easter.
directions	3km west of St Rémy de Provence on D99 towards Tarascon. D27 for Les Baux 1km, then left at sign for Mas on D31.

	David & Nitockrees Tadros Carpita
tel	+33 (0)4 90 92 39 32
fax	+33 (0)4 90 92 55 99
email	mascornud@cs.com
web	www.mascornud.com

Map 16 Entry 328

Ateliers de l'Image

36 boulevard Victor Hugo, 13210 Saint Rémy de Provence, Bouches-du-Rhône

If you've slept under one too many flouncy coverlets with fabric-lined walls to match, here is a version of a top class hotel with, as the brochure says, "quality service without the la-di-da". The young staff may wear black T-shirts with the name of the hotel inscribed upon it, but they all seem to swim in their element and the smiles are genuine. Curiously, Philippe opened his first tiny hotel and a black and white film processing lab at the same time – thus bringing together his twin passions. People thought him quite mad, but the idea caught on and the place filled. Some came solo, some came in groups and brought their tutors with them, delighted to find such a friendly and favourable environment in which to learn new techniques. The Ateliers is just a bigger, grown-up version of that first tiny seed. The huge park that hides behind this centre-of-town hotel will save your sanity in the summer; a morning's meditation in a treehouse off one of the bedrooms will cure your soul. A photo gallery, taï chi, organic risotto, sushi… Philippe is a young man with a vision.

rooms	32: 26 doubles, 5 suites (1 for 4-5), 1 suite with treehouse.	
price	€165-€380. Suites €300-€600.	
meals	Lunch & dinner €15-€65.	
closed	January.	
directions	A7 exit Cavaillon to St Rémy de Provence; 'centre ville'. Main road through town on right.	

	Philippe Goninet
tel	+33 (0)4 90 92 51 50
fax	+33 (0)4 90 92 43 52
email	info@hotelphoto.com
web	www.hotelphoto.com

Map 16 Entry 329

Mas du Vigueirat

Chemin du Grand Bourbourel, 13210 Saint Remy de Provence, Bouches-du-Rhône

A small pool cascading into a larger pool, wisteria and honeysuckle, a walled garden with quiet corners, nothing to disturb the view but meadows, woods and grazing horses. You'll find it hard to leave this tranquil, scented spot although St Rémy – with its galleries and Van Gogh museum – is but three kilometres. Arles, Avignon, the lavender fields and olive groves of Baux de Provence are not much further. High plane trees flank the drive to this dusky pink, blue-shuttered Provençal farmhouse. Inside all is light, simplicity, gentle elegance. Bedrooms are uncluttered spaces of bleached colours, limed walls and terracotta tiled floors. Views are over the garden or meadows while ground floor 'Maillane' has a private terrace. The high-beamed dining room/salon is a calm, white space with a corner cosy with sofas and books. If the weather's warm you'll breakfast outside under the plane tree. After a dip in the pool and a doze over your book, enjoy one of Catherine's delicious lunches freshly made from the vegetable garden. No suppers, but the helpful Jeanniards will recommend local restaurants.

rooms	4: 3 doubles, 1 suite.
price	€85-€140. Suite €140-€180.
meals	Picnic available. Poolside meals in summer €5-€10. Restaurants nearby.
closed	Christmas.
directions	From Lyon A7 exit Avignon Sud to Noves. In St Rémy, right at 5th r'bout to Maillane. After 3km, right at sign for *pepinières*.

	Catherine Jeanniard
tel	+33 (0)4 90 92 56 07
fax	+33 (0)4 90 26 79 52
email	contact@mas-du-vigueirat.com
web	www.mas-du-vigueirat.com

Map 16 Entry 330

Le Mas des Carassins

1 chemin Gaulois, 13210 St Rémy de Provence, Bouches-du-Rhône

You'll be charmed by the gentle pink tiles and soft blue shutters of the *mas* turned hotel, which settles so gently into the greenery surrounding it. The garden is massive and bursts with oleanders, lemons, 100-year-old olive trees, lavender and rosemary. Carefully tended patches of lawn lead to a good pool with barbecue, and after a swim, there's *pétanque* and badminton to play. Or you could spin off on bikes – the charming town of St Rémy de Provence is no distance at all, down a peaceful road. This is Van Gogh country (he lived for a time nearby, following in the steps of Nostradamus) and an ancient land: the hotel lies within the preserved area of the Roman town of Glanum. Bedrooms are dreamy, washed in smoky-blue or ochre shades; dark wrought-iron beds are dressed in oatmeal linens and white country quilts; some have a light canopy. Ground-floor rooms open to small gardens with table and chairs. The young owners have thought of everything: they will organize collection from the airport or train, car rental, and tickets for local events. *Unsupervised pool. Children over 12 welcome.*

rooms	14: 12 twins/doubles, 2 suites.
price	€98–€128. Suites €165.
meals	Breakfast €11.50. Dinner €25, weekdays only. Restaurants 5-minute walk.
closed	January-February.
directions	From St Rémy de Provence centre, over Canal des Alpilles on Ave Van Gogh, then right into Ave J. d'Arbaud. Hotel entrance on left after 180m.

	Michel Dimeux & Pierre Ticot
tel	+33 (0)4 90 92 15 48
fax	+33 (0)4 90 92 63 47
email	info@hoteldescarassins.com
web	hoteldescarassins.com

Map 16 Entry 331

Hôtel Gounod Ville Verte

Place de la République, 13210 Saint Rémy de Provence, Bouches-du-Rhône

Madame and Monsieur Maurin are experienced and enthusiastic hoteliers, and are right to be proud of this latest project. Hotel Gounod is at the very centre of the lively artistic town of St Remy. It takes its name from the composer Charles Gounod, who wrote the famous opera Mireille here in 1863. Gounod informs the theme of the whole place: each of the 34 bedrooms – discovered through a labyrinth of corridors – has been decorated to represent a phase of the composerís life. His music plays softly in the comfortable communal areas and in the loos, and a statue of the Virgin Mary reflects his religious leanings. The effect is theatrical, colourful, diverting and at times marvellously eccentric, bordering on the kitsch. Beds are voluptuous. Brightly painted mannequins are dotted here and there. Some of the rooms look out onto the garden, an oasis of calm where you can laze by the pool, surrounded by palm trees. For a gastronomic treat, pad over to the salon de the, where Madame Maurin – an excellent patissiere – serves her masterful creations beneath the wooden-beamed ceiling.

rooms	34: 10 twins, 20 doubles (10 with terrace), 1 duplex, 3 suites for 3.
price	€115-€185. Singles €80. Suites & duplex €215-€230.
meals	Tea room for snacks from €11. Good choice of restaurants in town.
closed	20 February-20 March.
directions	A7 exit Cavaillon to St Rémy de Provence, follow signs for centre ville. On the main square in Saint Rémy opposite from church.

	M & Mme Maurin
tel	+33 (0)4 90 92 06 14
fax	+33 (0)4 90 92 56 54
email	contact@hotel-gounod.com
web	www.hotel-gounod.com

Map 16 Entry 332

Hôtel Restaurant Le Berger des Abeilles

Quartier du Rabet, RD 74e, 13670 St Andiol, Bouches-du-Rhône

You may spot and stroke a friendly horse, in the field next door to this welcoming inn. Nicole lends a plot of land to a local educational circus while growing organic vegetables and herbs on another. She knows everything about cross pollination, busy as she was with bees for 10 years before taking over the inn as the fifth generation to do so. As a tribute to her ancestors the bedrooms are all named after the mistresses of the farm: Alexia, Julie, Rachel, Anaïs… even Maya for herself, the ex-bee keeper. Light, fresh and rag-walled, they are of standard size with – except for the larger two on the ground floor – their own little patios and garden furniture. A vast green parasol of 200-year-old plane trees offers total shade for cool summer relaxing and there is a high-hedged sunny spot for dipping in the pool. Mediterranean and Provençal flavours dominate Nicole's fresh, simple and seasonal menus are served outside on the terrace or in her honey-golden dining room. Informal, relaxed and unpretentious, this is a great base for exploring Saint Rémy and the surrounding region.

rooms	8: 4 doubles, 3 twins, 1 family room for 4-5.
price	€72-€110.
meals	Breakfast €10. Lunch €25-€52. Restaurant closed Sunday-Tuesday.
closed	November-25 March.
directions	Exit Avignon Sud on N7 towards Aix en Provence for 6km to St Andiol. Left at crossroads in Cabannes for D74E.

	Madame Nicole Grenier Sherpa
tel	+33 (0)4 90 95 01 91
fax	+33 (0)4 90 95 48 26
email	abeilles13@aol.com
web	www.berger-abeilles.com

Map 16 Entry 333

Mas Doù Pastré

Quartier St Sixte, 13810 Eygalières, Bouches-du-Rhône

It's a charming place, gypsy-bright with wonderful furniture, checked cushions, colourwashed walls, fine kilims. Built at the end of the 18th century, this lovely old *mas* belonged to Grandpère and Grandmère: nine months were spent here, three up in the pastures with the sheep. Now Albine and her sisters have decided to turn the old farmhouse into a hotel and keep it in the family – she and her talented handyman husband, Maurice, have succeeded, brilliantly. Bedrooms have wooden or tiled floors, antique doors and comfortable beds; all are big, some with their own sitting areas. Bathrooms are original with stone floors and beautiful washbasins picked up at flea markets; a claw-foot bath peeps theatrically out from behind striped curtains. Breakfast is generous 'continental' and if you want a lie-in, light meals are served all day long. Chaises longues with their attendant awnings encircle the pool; long views reach to the Alpilles; Romany caravans sit in the back garden; shaitsu treatments are in the hamman – better book early. *Minimum stay three nights July & August. Unsupervised pool.*

rooms	13 + 3: 10 doubles, 2 twins, 1 suite for 4. 3 gipsy caravans for 2.
price	€115-€180. Suite €220.
meals	Breakfast €13. Light meals (1pm-8pm) €17-€21.
closed	15 November-15 December.
directions	From A7, exit at Cavaillon for St Rémy for 10km, then left for Eygalières. Mas on route Jean Moulin, opposite Chapelle St Sixte.

	Albine & Maurice Roumanille
tel	+33 (0)4 90 95 92 61
fax	+33 (0)4 90 90 61 75
email	contact@masdupastre.com
web	www.masdoupastre.com

Map 16 Entry 334

Mas de la Rabassière

Route de Corn llon, 13250 St Chamas, Bouches-du-Rhône

Fanfares of lilies at the door, Haydn inside and Michael smiling in his chef's apron – Rabassière means 'where truffles are found' – his Epicurean dinners are a must. Wines from the neighbouring vineyard, and a sculpted dancer, also grace his terrace table. Cookery classes using home-produced olive oil, jogging companionship and airport pick-ups are all part of his unflagging hospitality, always with the help of Thévi, his serene Singaporean assistant. Michael was posted to France by a multi-national, soon became addicted, and on his retirement slipped into this unusually lush corner of Provence. The proximity of the canal keeps everything green which means you can play on a croquet lawn, walk through a grassy olive grove or sit in the garden with masses of orange roses everywhere. Big bedrooms and drawing room are classically comfortable in English country-house style: generous beds, erudite books, a tuned piano, fine etchings and oils, Provençal antiques. Come savour this charmingly generous and individual house and sample Michael's homemade croissants and fig jam under the old beam covered veranda.

rooms	5: 2 twins, 2 doubles, 1 suite.
price	€125. Singles €75.
meals	Dinner with wine, €35, book ahead for first evening.
closed	Rarely.
directions	From A54 exit 13 to Grans on D19; right on D16 to St Chamas. Just before railway bridge, left for Corrillon, up hill 2km. House on right before tennis court. Map sent on request.

	Michael Frost
tel	+33 (0)4 90 50 70 40
fax	+33 (0)4 90 50 70 40
email	michaelfrost@rabassiere.com
web	www.rabassiere.com

Map 16 Entry 335

La Bastide de Voulonne

84220 Cabrières d'Avignon, Vaucluse

This bastide sits in splendid isolation in the lavender fields stretching beneath the ancient hilltop villages perched on the Luberon mountains. The heart of this 18th-century farm is an inner courtyard where you can breakfast to the soothing sound of the fountain. The Bastide has been open for guests since Sophie and Alain rescued it from years of neglect. They have done a fantastic job, sticking to natural, local colours, with tiled floors. The bedrooms are huge. The garden – more like a park – is vast, with a big pool not far from the house. It's a great place for children; Sophie and Alain have three. They grow vegetables in the garden and menus centre round local food. Breakfast is a buffet, in an airy, tiled breakfast room if it's too chilly for the courtyard. Dinner is served at one long table in a big dining hall where the centrepiece is the carefully restored old bread oven. There are loads of places around for a good lunch, or Sophie will prepare a picnic for you. *Two-day truffle courses in January & February.*

rooms	11: 9 twins/doubles, 2 family suites for 3-4.
price	€122–€145. Family €152–€168.
meals	Breakfast €11. Dinner €30, not Wednesdays & Sundays.
closed	Mid-November–mid December; open by arrangement only Jan & Feb.
directions	After Avignon A7 on N100 for Apt. At Coustellet x-roads to Gordes; at r'bout (Collège de Calavon) for Gordes. After 1km right. Bastide 600m on left.

	Sophie Poiri
tel	+33 (0)4 90 76 77 55
fax	+33 (0)4 90 76 77 56
email	sophie@bastide-voulonne.com
web	www.bastide-voulonne.com

Map 16 Entry 336

Château La Roque

Chemin du Château, 84210 La Roque sur Pernes, Vaucluse

The first-known stronghold dominating the valley from this craggy lookout held back the Saracens in the eighth century; ceded to the Papal States in the 13th century, it was again an important strategic outpost. In 1741 it settled into peace as a private household. The peace remains blissful, the only interruption coming from the bees buzzing in the acacias. The large square house and its ramparts are in mellow honey-coloured stone; have breakfast on a sunny terrace dappled by vines. Bedrooms are huge, simple bordering on spartan, but never cold. One has a big deep coral bed under high vaulted ceilings, with two antique chairs as bedside tables. Floors are terracotta, interspersed with polished ochre cement in some rooms. Bathrooms continue the theme: roomy, simple, each with big double basins – on old pedestals or perhaps set on tables. Chantal and Jean have a brilliant formula for dinner. Instead of offering a complicated menu, they buy top quality local meat or fish and grill it on request, with organic fruit and vegetables from the village. *Children 12 and over welcome.*

rooms	5: 2 doubles, 3 suites.
price	€90–€160. Suites €185–€210.
meals	Breakfast €15.
	Dinner €40, book ahead.
closed	Rarely.
directions	From Lyon, A7 exit Orange Sud for Carpentras; for Pernes les Fontaines; for St Didier; for La Roque 2km.

	Chantal & Jean Tomasino
tel	+33 (0)4 90 61 68 77
fax	+33 (0)4 90 61 68 78
email	chateaularoque@wanadoo.fr
web	www.chateaularoque.com

Map 16 Entry 337

Bastide Le Mourre
84580 Oppède Le Vieux, Vaucluse

Victorine fell in love with this old bastide years before it came on the market. Now she has her little piece of paradise, a blue-shuttered hamlet in the heart of the Luberon encircled by vines, olives, jasmine and roses. Attached to the house are the gîtes: the pigeonnier, the silkworm house, the wine stores, two barns and, at the top of the garden, blissfully secluded and shaded by an ancient oak, the little round Moulin for two. All have their own private entrance and terrace where breakfast is served, all are filled with light and colour, all will delight you. Imagine big sisal rugs on ancient terracotta floors, fine Provençal ceilings and painted wooden doors, open stone fireplaces and whitewashed stone walls, a piqué cotton cover on a baldaquin bed, a dove-grey dresser in a sweet, chic kitchen. Victorine was an interior designer and her love of texture, patina and modern art shines through. The pool is set discreetly on a lower level away from the house, the views will seduce you, the peace is a balm. *Minimum stay three nights.*

rooms	6 houses, each with kitchen: 2 for 2, 3 for 4, 1 for 5-6.
price	€130–€185 (€780–€1,550 per week).
meals	Breakfast €12. Restaurants 5km.
closed	Rarely.
directions	Avignon to Apt to Coustellet to Oppède Le Vieux. On route to Oppède Le Vieux, first right Chemin du Mourre. Big house with blue shutters on left.

	Victorine Canac
tel	+33 (0)4 90 76 99 31
fax	+33 (0)4 90 76 83 60
email	lemourre@ad.com
web	www.lemourre.com

Map 16 Entry 338

La Bastide de Marie

Route de BonnieuxQuartier de la Verrerie, 84560 Ménerbes, Vaucluse

Pale blue shutters wink from the vineyards surrounding the 18th-century farmhouse. Enter a vast lobby, lit by high windows, peppered with antiques and washed with a palette of white, beige and dove-grey. Smiling staff wear soft cream linen, high painted dressers are filled with country jars, books and *antiquités* and in the low-beamed dining room or on the dappled veranda, fresh, zingy Provençal food is brought to white-clothed square tables: sardine fillets marinated in herbs, ravioli of soft goat's cheese with pine nuts and basil, poached apples, cinnamon sorbet. Upstairs, each heavenly bedroom is different; one soft green and pink with an iron baldaquin bed, another exquisite with *terre cuite* floor, lime-washed beams, a big soft sofa. A claw-foot bath under the stairs, three lovely sketches of dancers, a gilt-edged armchair – all is enchanting. Outside, plant pots spill over with white flowers and a pool runs around two sides of the house. The air is scented with lavender, you are surrounded by cypresses and planes and nearby Ménerbes is perched on a hill. Captivating at every level.

rooms	14: 8 doubles, 6 suites.
price	Half-board only, €415-€515; suites €620-€715.
meals	Half-board includes tea, aperitif, lunch or dinner, wine & coffee.
closed	November-March.
directions	From Avignon, N100 to Apt/Coustellet. Right at Beaumettes for Ménerbes, 6km (do not enter Ménerbes); D103 to Bonnieux for 4km. Bastide is on right.

	Jocelyne & Jean Louis Sibuet
tel	+33 (0)4 90 72 30 20
fax	+33 (0)4 90 72 54 20
email	bastidemarie@c-h-m.com
web	www.labastidedemarie.com/index_uk.html

Map 16 Entry 339

Auberge du Presbytère

Place de la Fontaine, 84400 Saignon, Vaucluse

They say "when the wind blows at Saignon, tiles fly off in Avignon": the Mistral can blow fiercely down from the mountains to the Mediterranean. This 11th-century village of only 100 inhabitants lies deep in the Luberon hills and lavender fields; the Auberge du Presbytère sits deep in Saigon, half hidden behind an old tree near the village's statue-topped fountain. Unforgettable meals are served under this tree, or in a pretty terraced garden. The bedrooms are striking, a huge fireplace in one, the Blue, with its stone terrace, looks out onto the hills and the simplest of all the rooms, the little one, Pink, has sleigh beds. Lovely Italian stone blocks tile the big bathrooms. A log fire burns on chilly days in the smart but informal sitting area. Jean-Pierre, attentive, and with a disarming sense of humour, will make you feel at home and, though this is perhaps not an obvious choice with children, provides early supper specially for them. A secret, splendid place from which to visit the nearby hill towns. Or if you are fit, rent a bike and follow the cycling signs. Outstanding value and food.

rooms	16: 14 twins/doubles, 2 with private shower or bath & separate wc. Some rooms connect to sleep 3-4.
price	€55-€135.
meals	Breakfast €9.50. Lunch & dinner €26-€34. Restaurant closed Wed.
closed	Mid-November–mid February.
directions	From Apt N100 dir. Céreste; at r'bout with 1 olive & 3 cypress trees towards Saignon to start of village. Left on lane for 'riverains' to Place de la Fontaine.

	Jean-Pierre de Lutz
tel	+33 (0)4 90 74 11 50
fax	+33 (0)4 90 04 68 51
email	auberge.presbytere@wanadoo.fr
web	www.auberge-presbytere.com

Map 16 Entry 340

Le Clos du Buis

Rue Victor Hugo, 84480 Bonnieux, Vaucluse

The lovely village of Bonnieux has somehow avoided the crush of unchecked tourism. Le Clos sits up in its old heart, overlooking the town and the surrounding hills. Part of the structure used to be the town bakery; the owners have left the original store front as a reminder. Time and loving care have been given without restraint – Monsieur decided to return to his native village – and everything appears to have been here foverever: Provençal country cupboards that reach up to the ceiling, old cement patterned tiles; one stone staircase with a good iron bannister leads up to clean, uncluttered bedrooms, the other   down to the garden. One side of the house is 'in' town, the other is open to   stunning views of endless hills. Provence is here on all sides, from the green and white checked cotton quilts on the beds to the excellent food served by your host in the yellow ochre dining room. If wine or weather keep you from the hills (good hikes abound, and M. Maurin can drive to meet you with supplies), days can be spent browsing the book collection by the big stone hearth in the sitting room. Delightful.

rooms	7: 2 doubles, 4 twins/doubles, 1 family room for 3.
price	€102–€117.
meals	Many restaurants within walking distance.
closed	Mid-November–mid-February. Open for Christmas & New Year.
directions	From Avignon A7 to Aix exit 24; D973 to Cavaillon; left on D22 to Apt 30km; right on D36. In village centre.

	M et Mme Maurin
tel	+33 (0)4 90 75 88 48
fax	+33 (0)4 90 75 88 57
email	le-clos-du-buis@wanadoo.fr
web	www.leclosdubuis.com

Map 16 Entry 341

Le Mas des Romarins

Route de Sénanque, 84220 Gordes, Vaucluse

Michel and Pierre bought this hotel – overlooking one of France's most beautiful villages – in May 2002. Forget the buildings on either side: the secluded pool and garden make you feel away from it all and the hotel even has its own private path into town. The fabulous hilltop view of Gordes with its distant misty-blue mountains and surrounding plains encourages you to linger over a delicious buffet breakfast, usually taken on the terrace. Inside, the sitting room is comfortable without being over-lavish and the warmth of the open fire is always welcome on days when the chilly Mistral wind gets up. The bedrooms are done in ochres and smoky rusts to contrast with stone, oatmeal and cream for the two-toned painted walls. Parisian linens and soft furnishings are combined with traditional cotton prints. Rooms are small, but cool, comfortable and quiet. Join the other guests when the four-course *table d'hôtes* is served; otherwise they will book a restaurant for you and help you explore the local culinary delights (of which there are plenty) on your own. A happy spot, easy living, great walking.

rooms	12: 9 twins/doubles, 3 quadruples, some with private terraces.
price	€97–€160.
meals	Breakfast €10.50. Dinner €27 Monday, Wednesday, Friday. Restaurants 10-minute walk.
closed	12 Nov–16 Dec; 2 Jan–11 Mar.
directions	From Avignon, east on N7; left onto N100 for Apt; left to Gordes. Route de Sénanque on left on entering Gordes. Hotel 200m on right.

	Michel Dimeux & Pierre Ticot
tel	+33 (0)4 90 72 12 13
fax	+33 (0)4 90 72 13 13
email	info@hoteldesromarins.com
web	www.hoteldesromarins.com

Map 16 Entry 342

Le Mas de Garrigon

Route de St Saturnin d'Apt, Roussillon en Provence, 84220 Gordes, Vaucluse

Christiane, a writer and journalist, settled in the Luberon after years in Africa, bought the plot of land and built the *mas* from scratch in 1979, using local materials and tailoring the house to the hill. The idea was to build a really special place to stay — each room has its own terrace looking out to the wild beauty of the hills. We don't generally recommend piped music... but the classical music Christiane plays does add to the atmosphere. In palest terracotta with lightest blue shutters, the house sits among cypress, olive and almond trees and is perfect in summer, when you can lounge by the pool, and perfect in winter too, when you can settle down by a crackling fire, maybe with a book from the well-stocked library. Inside is in complete and striking contrast to the muted, natural tones used outside: bedrooms are a joyful riot of reds, yellows and blues. Don't worry: Christiane's mix of bold and simple, traditional and daring is never garish, it all works perfectly. Great welcome, great food.

rooms	9: 6 doubles, 2 twins, 1 family room for 3.
price	€105-€145. Family room €145-€180. Half-board mandatory Easter-October, €260-€286.
meals	Breakfast €16. Picnic lunch available. Lunch & dinner €45. Restaurant closed Mondays & Tuesdays mid-November-December.
closed	Rarely.
directions	From Cavaillon on D2 between Gordes & St Saturnin d'Apt.

	Christiane Rech-Druart
tel	+33 (0)4 90 05 63 22
fax	+33 (0)4 90 05 70 01
email	mas.de.garrigon@wanadoo.fr
web	www.masdegarrigon-provence.com

Map 16 Entry 343

Lou Granos

Chemin des Chavelles, Les Beaumettes, 84220 Gordes, Vaucluse

Slip down the garden path past a sea of lavender, wisteria, cherry blossom and olives to a hidden terrace and a chaise longue. Or wander round the potager and herbs – *le jardin de curé* – where Mohamet the gardener will smile a greeting. Surrounded by dry stone walls and views over the Luberon to Menèrbes, this place soothes with its beauty and timelessness. Built to Nicky's design, right down to the glass cupboard doors, the house is full of light and space, neutral colours and stylishly simple furnishings. Modern paintings and wall hangings – Nicky ran an art gallery in Paris – add colour to the bedrooms; most open to the garden or your own terrace. Bathrooms are luxurious with huge showers. Nicky cooks dinner by arrangement, perhaps duck preceded by chilled cucumber soup, with local wines and herbs and vegetables from the garden. Dine on the covered terrace, take brunch by the pool. For cooler days, there's a flower-filled sunroom and a chandeliered dining room. Throw in a gym, jacuzzi, meditation hut and masseur and you have a grand little place to de-stress.

rooms	5 + 1: 3 doubles, 1 twin, 1 suite for 4. 1 cottage for 4.
price	€120-€220. Suite €190-€260. Cottage €1,600-€1,900 per week.
meals	Breakfast €10. Lunch or picnic €24. Hosted dinner €38, except Sunday.
closed	Christmas.
directions	A7 exit Avignon Sud, left on D22. N100 to Apt. 4km after Coustellet right to Beaumettes; D103 to St Pantaléon & Gordes for 1.2km; 2nd road on right before bridge. Signed.

	Nicky Verfaillie
tel	+33 (0)4 90 72 49 01
fax	+33 (0)4 90 72 49 09
email	lougranos@lougranos.com
web	www.lougranos.com

Map 16 Entry 344

La Bastide Saint Joseph

Chemin St Joseph, 84400 Rustrel, Vaucluse

The delicious, cream-coloured bastide was a natural staging post for the 18th-century traveller and ultimately became a *relais de poste*. After a further spell as a convent, it was abandoned; by the 1950s, trees were coming through the roof. When Meta arrived, four years ago, it had been rescued by an architect... ripe for revival. Gentle smiling Meta, Canadian by birth and well-travelled, speaks perfect French and knows *everything* about her corner of the Lubéron. She has also created a sophisticated yet wonderfully relaxing place to stay. Beautiful big bedrooms have polished, honey-coloured boards and rush mats to soften the tread; bathrooms are as luxurious, if not more so: one has a bath for four! Candles line the elegant sitting room hearth, to be replaced, in winter, by logs. Meta, ever thoughtful, puts exquisite books and flowers in your room and serves you breakfast where you fancy: in the garden, the chapel room or courtyard. Stroll through the garden, planted with cypress and 400 lavender bushes, to the pool, perfect with towels and honesty bar. *Cash or cheque only.*

rooms	4 doubles.
price	€100-€160.
meals	Restaurants in village.
closed	Rarely.
directions	Avignon to Apt on N100 then D22 for Rustrel; 10 minutes to roundabout for Gignac. House 1 minute up on left, follow stone wall to blue gates.

	Mrs. Meta Tory
tel	+33 (0)4 90 04 97 80
fax	+33 (0)4 90 04 90 12
email	metat@attglobal.net
web	www.bastide-saint-joseph.com

Map 16 Entry 345

Hostellerie du Val de Sault

Route de St Trinit, Ancien chemin d'Aurel, 84390 Sault, Vaucluse

This landscape has been called "a sea of corn gold and lavender blue": from your terrace here you can contemplate the familiar shape of Mont Ventoux, the painter's peak, beyond. The charming, communicative Yves has gathered all possible information, knows everyone there is to know on the Provence scene and is full of good guidance. He creates menus featuring truffles or lavender or spelt, or game with mushrooms for the autumn perfectly served in the informal atmosphere of the light, airy restaurant. And… children can eat earlier, allowing the adults to savour their meal in peace. Perched just above the woods in a big garden, this is a modern building with lots of space inside and out; wooden floors and pine-slatted walls bring live warmth, colour schemes are vibrant, storage is excellent; baths in the suites have jets. Each room feels like a very private space with its terrace (the suites have room for loungers on theirs): the pool, bar and restaurant are there for conviviality; the fitness room, tennis court and boules pitch for exercise; the jacuzzi space for chilling out. *Locked shed for bikes.*

rooms	20: 11 doubles, 5 suites for 4, 4 apartments for 2 (no kitchen).
price	€145. Suites €175. Apts €280. Half-board only, May–Sept: €114–€195 p.p.
meals	Breakfast €11. Lunch & dinner €36–€40. Closed for lunch certain days April–Oct.
closed	11 November–March.
directions	D1 Col des Abeilles for Sault for 30km, then for St Trinit. After big bend, left by fire station. 1km on.

	Yves Gattechaut
tel	+33 (0)4 90 64 01 41
fax	+33 (0)4 90 64 12 74
email	valdesault@aol.com
web	www.valdesault.com

Map 16 Entry 346

La Barjaquière

17 Ancien Chemin de Ronde, 84330 Saint Pierre de Vassols, Vaucluse

There is much more to La Barjaquière than meets the eye. A watery and peaceful world awaits behind this 17th-century edifice set in a small village: blue sky and pots of bougainvillea reflect in a dream of a pool; a second courtyard beckons with another pool, heated this time, flanked by trompe l'oeil visions of terracotta vessels spilling with greens and reds. Antique doors, stencilled flowers over the staircase, a quiet sitting space and a book of poetry – Ghislaine has made it all sing with her sense of warmth and colour. Daniel explains that the original primitive structure with its beams, nooks and crannies, mezzanines and terraces inspired this maze of a Provençal interior. You'll even find a sauna on the ground floor. Soleillant has a beaded curtain and a terrace overlooking the village; apricot floor tiles reflect in the pale yellow, waxed walls. The shimmering ochre walls of Le Parc seem to hold a hundred layers of light which contrast well with a carmine sofa and quilted bedspreads. Add the engaging hospitality of inventive hosts; you will find it very hard to leave. *Minimum stay two nights mid-June-mid-September.*

rooms	5: 3 doubles, 2 suites for 2-3.
price	€120-€160. Suites €180-€210.
meals	Dinner with aperitif and wine, €40, book ahead.
closed	Never.
directions	A7 exit 22 Carpentras; D950 then D13; left at 2nd aqueduct on D974 to Bedoin & Mont Ventoux for 7.7km. At St Pierre left on D85 to village church. House opposite.

	Ghislaine André & Daniel Poncet
tel	+33 (0)4 90 62 48 00
fax	+33 (0)4 90 62 48 06
email	welcome@barjaquiere.com
web	www.barjaquiere.com

Map 16 Entry 347

Le Château de Mazan

Place Napoleon, 84380 Mazan, Vaucluse

The father and uncle of the Marquis de Sade were born here – an unexpected connection, given the luminosity of the place. Though the infamous Marquis preferred Paris, he often stayed at Mazan and organized France's first theatre festival here in 1772. The château is in a charming village at the foot of Mont Ventoux. Ceilings are lofty, floors are tiled in white-and-terracotta squares that would drown a smaller space, windows are huge with the lightest of curtains. This is a family hotel, despite its size, and Frédéric, who speaks good English, ensures you settle in. His mother, Danièle, is in charge of décor. Ground-floor bedrooms have French windows opening to a private sitting area; first-floor rooms are elegant, with pale tones, antique mirrors and appliqué quilts. Rooms on the top floor, the old servants' quarters, could get hot in summer. There are palms outside, posies within, and secluded spots in the garden – doze in the shade of the mulberry trees. There's a large terrace for dinner. Do eat in: the young chef has worked in Michelin-starred restaurants and is keen to win his own.

rooms	30: 14 doubles, 2 suites for 4, 14 family rooms for 3-4.
price	€90–€255. Suites €400.
meals	Breakfast €15. Lunch €30-€55. Dinner €55-€65. Restaurant closed Tuesdays January-September; Mondays October-December.
closed	January-February.
directions	In Carpentras for Sault & Ventoux then Mazan. In Mazan, 1st right near Mairie, then left.

	Danièle & Frédéric Lhermie
tel	+33 (0)4 90 69 62 61
fax	+33 (0)4 90 69 76 62
email	chateaudemazan@wanadoo.fr
web	www.chateaudemazan.fr

Map 16 Entry 348

Les Florets

Route des Dentelles, 84190 Gigondas, Vaucluse

The setting is magical, the food imaginative, the greeting from the Bernard family is from-the-heart warm and the walks are outstanding. Les Florets sits just below the majestic Dentelles de Montmirail – a small range of mountains crested with long, delicate fingers of white stone in the middle of Côtes du Rhône country. Over 40km of paths wind through here so appetites build and are satiated on the splendid terrace under the branches of plane, chestnut, maple, acacia and linden trees; the low stone walls are dressed with impatiens and hydrangeas (and the peonies were blooming in March!). You'll also be sampling some of the wines that the family has been producing since the 1880s. Bright blue and yellow corridors lead to rooms which are simply and florally decorated; all have big, sparkling, tiled bathrooms. We liked the tiny 50s reception desk dressed with a huge bouquet from the garden; a wonderful ceramic *soupière* brightens one corner, a scintillating collection of delicate glass carafes stands in another. Book well ahead, people return year after year.

rooms	15: 14 doubles, 1 apartment for 2-4 in annexe (no kitchen).
price	€95–€130. Apartment €125–€150.
meals	Breakfast €12. Lunch & dinner €24.50–€52. Restaurant closed Wed April-Oct; Mon eve & Tues Nov-Dec.
closed	January-March.
directions	From Carpentras, D7 for Vacqueyras. Right on D7 to Gigondas for 2km. Signed.

	M & Mme Bernard
tel	+33 (0)4 90 65 85 01
fax	+33 (0)4 90 65 83 80
email	accueil@hotel-lesflorets.com
web	www.hotel-lesflorets.com

Map 16 Entry 349

Domaine le Vallon

Chemin de Serres, 84810 Aubignan, Vaucluse

Standing on the doorstep of the *petit château* all you hear is the wind ruffling the majestic trees and distant tractor rumble. Just three bedrooms here: one deep orange with high celings, another cream with a canopied bed, another with *oeil de boeuf* windows; all come sprinkled with choice antiques, prints and interesting etchings. Floors are sweeping ancient parquet or terracotta, bathrooms are large and well-stocked. Dutch Fred and French Michèle are lovely hosts living their dream and with three languages between them conversation flows. Dinner is *grand gastronomie*: son Eddy's cooking is a treat, delectable wines are poured into engraved glasses, cookery courses are planned. Breakfast is a relaxed affair; in winter on the glass-covered veranda, in summer at pretty little tables outside. Warm scents (rosemary, jasmin, thyme), crisp lawns, an orangerie, roses and a curved seat for two, a 'bassin' pool and a summer kitchen. Beyond, two hectares of vines and all of Provence.

rooms	4: 3 doubles/twins, 1 studio.
price	€90–€145.
meals	Dinner €28–€48 twice weekly, book ahead.
closed	December–January.
directions	From Lyon A7 exit Bollene, D7/D8 to Carpentras. 1 km after Aubignan, sharp left opposite sign "Cuisine St. Luc". Follow Chemin de Serres 600m, through the crossroads. Le Vallon 700m on left.

	Michèle & Fred Vogt
tel	+33 (0)4 90 62 71 27
fax	+33 (0)4 90 62 62 51
email	vogt@vallon-provence.com
web	www.vallon-provence.com

Map 16 Entry 350

Château Talaud

D107, 84870 Loriol du Comtat, Vaucluse

Lavish and elegant – a stunning place and lovely people. Hein has a wine export business, Conny gives her whole self to her house and her guests. Among ancient vineyards and wonderful green lawns – an oasis in Provence – the ineffably gracious 18th-century château speaks of a long-gone southern way of life. Enter, and you will feel it has not entirely vanished. Restored by the owners to a very high standard, the finely-proportioned rooms have been furnished with antiques, many of them family pieces, and thick, luxurious fabrics. The big bedrooms mix old and new, Directoire armchairs and featherweight duvets, with consummate taste and bathrooms are old-style hymns to modernity. The swimming pool is an adapted 17th-century irrigation tank: one goes through an arch to the first, shallow cistern, leading to a deeper pool beyond – ingenious. Guests may laze in the lovely gardens but Conny is happy to help you plan visits in this fascinating area. Then return to one of her delicious meals where guests all sit together. An exceptionally fine, well-kept guest house.

rooms	5 + 3: 3 doubles, 2 suites. 2 apartments for 3; 1 cottage for 5.
price	€160–€195. Apartments & cottage €1,200–€1,400 per week.
meals	Dinner with wine €45, twice-weekly.
closed	1-13 January; 17 February-3 March; 15-31 December.
directions	D950 for Carpentras, then D107 at Loriol du Comtat; at r'bout right for Monteux. Château 1km on right.

	Conny & Hein Deiters-Kommer
tel	+33 (0)4 90 65 71 00
fax	+33 (0)4 90 65 77 93
email	chateautalaud@infonie.fr
web	www.chateautalaud.com

Map 16 Entry 351

Domaine de Bournereau

579 chemin de la Sorguette, 84170 Monteux, Vaucluse

Pick your spot in the garden: under the 250-year-old plane tree, by the fountain, in a flowery bower or around the pool with views to white-capped Mont Ventoux. Klaus and Hermann, two delightfully sweet Germans who opened the hotel a couple of years ago, keep you happy with refreshing drinks. These two farm buildings, all creamy plaster and blue shutters, have been vigorously restored. Inside, the style is light and modern, with polished terracotta floors, smart wicker furniture, flowers from the garden and striking paintings. (Some of these Hermann's, as he will shyly admit.) Original artwork is a feature of the bedrooms too, taking the edge off the 'new hotel' feel of these simple spaces so neatly decorated. The wheelchair-friendly ground-floor room has a terrace; another room has a window opening into the branches of the magnificent plane tree. Breakfast on the terrace, dine smartly by candlelight – a local chef brings the freshest produce from the markets three times a week. There's great hiking trails in the Dentelles mountains, history in the Pont du Gard, Van Gogh in the museums.

rooms	12: 5 doubles, 6 twins/doubles, 1 suite for 2-4.
price	€95–€170. Suite €190.
meals	Dinner €29 three times a week, book ahead. Wine €18–€35.
closed	November–January.
directions	A7 exit Avignon Nord. D942 to Carpentras for 10km. Follow signs for Monteux centre; first right after 20m; first left after 500m.

	Hermann Mayer and Klaus Haug
tel	+33 (0)4 90 66 36 13
fax	+33 (0)4 90 66 36 93
email	mail@bournereau.com
web	www.bournereau.com

Map 16 Entry 352

Auberge de Reillanne

04110 Reillanne, Alpes-de-Haute-Provence

The solid loveliness of this 18th-century house, so typical of the area, reassures you, invites you in. And you will not be disappointed: you'll feel good here, even if you can't quite define the source of the positive energy. Monique clearly has a connection to the spirit of the place and has used all her flair and good taste, making all the curtains and bedcovers herself, to transform the old inn into a very special place to stay. Bedrooms are large and airy, done in cool, restful colours with big cupboards and rattan furniture. There are beams, properly whitewashed walls and books. Bathrooms are big and simple too. Downstairs, the sitting and dining areas are decorated in warm, embracing colours with terracotta tiles, white tablecloths and flame-coloured curtains. This would be a place for a quiet holiday with long meditative walks in the hills, a place to come and write that novel or simply to get to know the gentle, delicate, smiling owner who loves nothing better than to receive people in her magical house.

rooms	6: 3 doubles, 3 triples.
price	€70–€75. Singles €55. Half-board €68 p.p.
meals	Breakfast €8.50. Dinner €23.
closed	20 October–March.
directions	N100 through Apt & Céreste. Approx. 8km after Céreste, left on D214 to Reillanne. Hotel on right.

	Monique Balmand
tel	–33 (0)4 92 76 45 95
fax	+33 (0)4 92 76 45 95
email	monique.balmand@wanadoo.fr

Map 16 Entry 353

Mas du Pont Roman

Chemin de Châteauneuf, 04300 Mane, Alpes-de-Haute-Provence

A land of treasures: Ligurian *bories* – igloo-like dry-stone huts – squat camouflaged in the landscape; Roman churches sit quietly as if time had not passed; a stunning 12th-century Roman bridge spans the river on the edge of this property, a recently renovated 18th-century mill at the end of tree-lined boulevard on the outskirts of a village. Marion graciously watches over your creature comforts while Christian, a most hospitable and jovial host, knows everybody and everything about the immediate area and the intriguing market town of Forcalquier. The sitting/drawing room, with a crackling fire on cool days is an ideal spot to enjoy an aperitif before dinner; Christian will help you pick out your restaurant. An indoor swimming pool and two sauna rooms complement the spanking new bedrooms with their stone quarry tiles, pristine tiled bathrooms and flowery bedspreads. Beautiful grounds, stunning views, flowing water and an outdoor pool and terrace complete the picture. Organise your nightwatch for shooting star extravaganzas at the nearby St Michel Observatory.

rooms	9: 3 doubles, 4 twins, 1 single, 1 family suite for 4.
price	€75–€90.
meals	Breakfast €8 (included out of season). Light meals available during summer. Two restaurants in village, 2km.
closed	Rarely.
directions	From Marseille A51 exit Forcalquier; N100 for Apt 3km. Enter village; left, hotel on right at end of avenue of trees.

	Christian & Marion Vial
tel	+33 (0)4 92 75 49 46
fax	+33 (0)4 92 75 36 73
email	info@pontroman.com
web	www.pontroman.com

Map 16 Entry 354

Le Moulin du Château

04500 St Laurent du Verdon, Alpes-de-Haute-Provence

A sleepy place — come to doze. Your silence will be broken only by the call of the sparrow-hawk or the distant rumble of a car. This 17th-century olive-mill once belonged to the château and stands at the foot of an ancient grove; the vast pressoir is now a reception area where modern art hangs on ancient walls. The Moulin is a long, low, stone building with lavender-blue shutters and the odd climbing vine, and stands in its own gardens surrounded by lavender and fruit trees. In the bedrooms light filters though voile curtains, and shadows dance upon the walls. The feel is uncluttered, cool, breezy, with vibrant colours: turquoise, lilac, lime — luminous yet restful. This is an easy-going 'green' hotel where the emphasis is on the simple things of life — and the organic, Mediterranean cooking is a treat. Boules is played under the cherry tree, poppies grow on an old crumbling stone staircase and views stretch across fields to village and château. There are bikes for gentle excursions into the countryside, and further afield are the Cistercian abbey of Le Thoronet, the Verdon Canyon and Digne Les Bains.

rooms	10: 5 doubles, 2 twins, 1 quadruple, 1 triple, 1 suite.
price	€75–€100.
meals	Breakfast €8. Picnics €10. Dinner €31, not Mondays & Thursdays. Restaurants nearby.
closed	2 November-February.
directions	From Gréoux les Bains D952 until Riez, then D11 for Quinson; head towards St Laurent du Verdon; take road after château. Signed.

	Edith & Nicolas Stämpfli-Faoro
tel	+33 (0)4 92 74 02 47
fax	+33 (0)4 92 74 02 97
email	info@moulin-du-chateau.com
web	www.moulin-du-chateau.com

Map 16 Entry 355

La Bouscatière

Chemin Marcel Provence, 04360 Moustiers Ste-Marie, Alpes-de-Haute-Provence

If you ever had a dream of dramatic Provence, this must be it. The cliffs rise indomitably, the water tumbles down, the old village looks as if it grew here. This enchanting vertical house, firmly fixed to the rock since 1765, was originally a wood store then an oil mill. Its lowest level, in the village centre, houses the oil press; its highest, seventh level opens through the lush secluded garden with its tiny, ancient chapel (now a delicious bedroom with heavily-carved Spanish bed and little terrace) to the top of the village and its perfect Romanesque church. Inside, all is country elegance and supreme comfort against a backdrop of exposed rock, white limewashed walls and original beams. This is a tiny preserved corner of old Provence; all rooms feel as though one is in some time honored and adored family house, with a vase of flowers here, an antique mirror there, and everywhere the scent of lavender and linen dried in the fresh air. The biggest bedroom is pretty grand, another has a tracery alcove, all are softly attractive. Guests are honored friends, to be cared for and spoiled. Perfect.

rooms	5: 2 twins/doubles, 3 doubles.
price	€115-€190.
meals	Breakfast €5-€15. Dinner €30, book ahead.
closed	Rarely.
directions	A8 from Nice exit 36 to N555 for Draguignan; D557 to Aups. D957 to Moustiers Ste-Marie. Follow road to highest point of village to parking area. Do not drive into village.

	Geneviève and Joel Calas
tel	+33 (0)4 92 74 67 67
fax	+33 (0)4 92 74 65 72
email	bonjour@labouscatiere.com
web	www.labouscatiere.com

Map 16 Entry 356

Villa Morélia

Vallée de l'Ubaye, 04850 Jausiers, Alpes-de-Haute-Provence

Villa Morélia has a fascinating history: far from isolating themselves in this village deep in the Alps, the inhabitants exported their textile skills first to Flanders, then to the Caribbean and in the 19th century to Mexico, where some 60,000 descendants still live. Many, however, returned and put their money and taste for things foreign to good use, building exotic villas in their valley. With its imposing height, asymmetric façades and coloured chimneys, the Villa Morélia, designed by a renowned Marseilles architect, Eugène Marx, stands out from the rest. Now Robert and Marie-Christine have opened it as a hotel and established an award-winning restaurant. This charming couple know quite a bit about cuisine, music, dogs and a relaxed style of living. You will love everything inside: high airy ceilings, walnut windows and doors, beautiful tiles and big bedrooms which manage the trick of looking both elegant and welcoming. On top of this, you can ski, go rafting or canyoning, the chef comes from the Eden Roc in Antibes and Robert will pick you up if you don't want to drive.

rooms	8: 3 doubles, 1 single, 3 family rooms for 3, 1 suite.
price	€140-€170. Single €110. Family rooms €185-€210. Suite €280.
meals	Breakfast €14. Picnic lunch available. Dinner from €45-€75.
closed	November-26 December.
directions	7km from Barcelonnette on D900 Gap-Cuneo road. In centre of village.

	Marie-Christine & Robert Boudard
tel	+33 (0)4 92 84 67 78
fax	+33 (0)4 92 84 65 47
email	rboudard@aol.com
web	www.villa-morelia.com

Map 16 Entry 357

L'Auberge du Choucas

Monêtier les Bains, 05220 Serre Chevalier 1500, Hautes-Alpes

In an eternity of pure blue air and pure white glaciers, drenched in sunshine 300 days a year, the Alpine village and its old inn, just behind the Romanesque church, pander to your terrestrial appetites. The lush garden is ideal for summer breakfasts with the birds; the sitting room suggests cosy fireside tea – friendly cat and modern pictures – the stone-vaulted dining room with its great open fire is the place to be bewitched by the young chef's magic – "the art of cookery lifted into the realm of poetry," said one guest. But you are summoned by ski slopes, dramatic ice caves, soul-nourishing walks and natural hot springs. Then return to open one of the beautiful doors, painted by an artist friend of Nicole's, into a panelled, carpeted cottagey bedroom with a snug little bathroom. Those with balconies are blissful in the morning sun, duplexes have two (bigger) bathrooms. A brilliant show, led by the amazing whirlwind Nicole who also nurtures a passion for Latin and Greek. Seconded by her charming daughter, Eva, they attend to the minutest details, anxious that it should all be perfect for you.

rooms	12: 8 twins/doubles, 4 duplexes for 4-5.
price	€100-€270. Half-board €100-€215 p.p.
meals	Breakfast €17. Lunch €19-€42. Dinner €33-€67. Restaurant closed mid-April-May; mid-Oct-mid-Dec.
closed	3 November-6 December; May.
directions	14km from Briançon on N91. Hotel in village, behind church in front of town hall.

	Nicole Sanchez-Ventura
tel	+33 (0)4 92 24 42 73
fax	+33 (0)4 92 24 51 60
email	auberge.du.choucas@wanadoo.fr
web	www.aubergeduchoucas.com

Map 12 Entry 358

Hôtel du Vieux Château

Place de la Fontaine, 83630 Aiguines, Var

Aiguines sits like a belvedere on the flank of Mount Magrès overlooking the Lac de Ste Croix. Once an *oppidum* (hill fort) on the Roman road linking Fréjus to Grenoble, it has never stopped being a place of constant passage. The eye travels unhindered over the lavender-covered Plateau de Valensole towards the blue mountains in the distance. Frédéric, affable and smiley, was born in Aiguines and came home to roost after a busy and peripatetic youth. He is taking his time restoring the hotel, once part of the village's castle. "I want to get it right," he says. Getting it right means no fuss and frills, but a crisp refreshing simplicity. A good sense of colour marries yellow, blue and old rose with Provençal or tartan-patterned curtains; very right in the bathrooms with rich hued Salernes tiles, deep turquoise, royal blue, salmon, grass-green. Rooms at the front have those views over the rooftops to the lake, others catch a glimpse of a castle. Bedrooms at the back, looking over a village street, are naturally quieter and may well be cooler in a searing summer. A place with 'soul', intrinsically French.

rooms	10: 8 twins/doubles; 2 twins/doubles with separate wc.
price	€55-€75.
meals	Lunch & dinner €21.50-€26.50. Restaurants in village.
closed	October-April.
directions	From A8, exit for Draguignan, then D557 through Flayosc & Aups for Moustiers Ste Marie to Aiguines.

Frédéric Ricez

tel	+33 (0)4 94 70 22 95
fax	+33 (0)4 94 84 22 36
email	contact@hotelvieuxchateau.fr
web	www.hotelvieuxchateau.fr

Map 16 Entry 359

Auberge du Lac
Rue Grande, 83630 Bauduen, Var

Hard to imagine, as you gaze on the blue-green waters of its lake, that the auberge, an inn for hundreds of years, once stood on the old Roman road from Fréjus to Riez. They changed its name in 1973, when the Sainte-Croix Lake was created for the national electricity company, the EDF. The auberge feels genuinely old; the clean smell of beeswax wafts through its maze of corridors, and the rooms are filled with polished Provençal pieces. The young Monsieur Bagarre worked as EDF inspector in Paris but a taste of life in the city persuaded him to return to the peace of the auberge, which he runs with his mother. Enjoy breakfast in your room, perhaps by the window overlooking the lake, or on a terrace under the vines. Or, on cooler days, in the dining area, again looking onto the lake; this is a series of beamy, white-walled rooms whose little tables are dressed in warm local colours. Monsieur steps in as chef when needed. A lot of thought has gone into the bedrooms, full of pictures and flowers. Some rooms have balconies, bathrooms are colourful, and there are enough towels for an army.

rooms	11: 3 doubles, 1 twin, 7 family rooms.
price	€48-€75.
meals	Breakfast €6.90. Lunch & dinner €24-€45.
closed	11 November-15 March.
directions	A8 to Le Muy then N555 for Draguignan; D557 for Flayose then Aups; D957 for Aiguines; after 7km, D49 to Bauduen.

	M & Mme Bagarre
tel	+33 (0)4 94 70 08 04
fax	+33 (0)4 94 84 39 41

Map 16 Entry 360

Une Campagne en Provence

Domaine le Peyrourier, Route de Bras, 83149 Bras, Var

Water gushes and flows throughout Martina and Claude Fussler's 170-acre estate; springs, streams and rivers abound. In the 12th century the Knights Templar created a myriad of irrigation channels through which the water bubbles around the house. It retains its massive fortress-like proportions and many original features. The owners love their Campagne and it shows; it is utterly immaculate but with a sociable relaxed family atmosphere. The main house is arranged around a central patio, with stairs leading up to the bedrooms. Simple Provençal furnishings are lit by huge windows, with cosy 'boutis' quilts and sumptuous linen and towels. The bathrooms are cleverly worked around architectural features, while the fixtures are plush. The well-stocked apartments Paloma and Papillon have knockout views across the vineyards. Dinner can be arranged, with the accent on local produce and wine from their own vineyards. Restive teenagers can relax in the media room, others may prefer the sauna and Turkish bath. An isolated paradise for Templar enthusiasts, overseen by two geese and a very old dog.

rooms	6 + 3: 4 doubles, 2 twins. 3 apartments for 3, weekly rental.
price	€85–€115. Apartments €550–€850 per week.
meals	Hosted dinner with wine, €30.
closed	Never.
directions	A8 exit St Maximin-La St Baume to centre. At 2nd r'bout, D28 toward Bras. At 9km follow signs.

	M & Mme Fussler
tel	+33 (0)4 98 05 10 20
fax	+33 (0)4 98 05 10 21
email	info@provence4u.com
web	www.provence4u.com

Map 16 Entry 361

Les Quatre Saisons

370 montée des Oliviers, Route du Brûlat, 83330 Le Castellet, Var

For those hooked on the Da Vinci Code, the Sainte Baume mountain range with its walks and legends revolving around Mary Magdalene is an easy drive. Or the hill villages of La Cadière d'Azur and Le Castellet with Templar connections may tempt; but you will rejoice upon your return to this lovingly run hideaway on a hill with its thick walls, warm yellow stone and cooling breezes. Didier and Patrice, with previous lives in the catering and hotel worlds, will take good care of you. Only built 20 years ago, with careful recuperation of old doors, beams and stone, the main house and annexe cradle the pool mirroring a more southern architectural tradition. The main house, where winter guests can have pre-dinner drinks, has an impressive sunken circular area round a fireplace and a succession of spacious elegant rooms furnished with good Louis XVIII pieces. All rooms have their own private outdoors sitting area, be it a terrace or small sealed-off patio beneath a vine-clad trellis. Care and thoughtfulness, attention to detail, this is a dream of a place. Thor, the French bulldog, welcomes other well-behaved dogs.

rooms	6 + 1: 4 doubles, 2 suites for 2-3. 1 apartment for 2.
price	€90-€110. Apartment €120-€130; €600-€700 per week.
meals	Lunch €15-€25. Dinner €33-€35; book ahead.
closed	15 days in January.
directions	A50 exit 11 to Le Beausset. Left at big r'about onto D26 to Le Brûlat-Castellet. Right after 1.5km, straight on small road until gate. Ring.

	Patrice Darras & Didier Marchal
tel	+33 (0)4 94 25 24 90
email	reservation@lesquatresaisons.org
web	www.lesquatresaisons.org

Map 16 Entry 362

Hostellerie Bérard

Rue Gabriel Péri, 83740 La Cadière d'Azur, Var

"It was one of the best meals I have ever had in this region," said our inspector. René is Maître Cuisinier de France, Danièle is a qualified expert in the local wine and their son Jean-François now shines in their bistro, Le Petit Jardin. The emphasis is on Provençal food, using only organic, seasonal produce and herbs from their garden. Madame and Monsieur are true belongers: they grew up in this ancient village, opened in 1969 and have lovingly, respectfully restored this complex of highly evocative buildings: an 11th-century monastery; a blue-shuttered bastide; an old village *maison bourgeoise*; a painter's hideaway. The views from the dining room and the bedrooms are superb: framed visions of olive groves, of vines in their seried choreography and Templar strongholds on mountain tops in the distance. Each is a surprise: a delicate wrought-iron four-poster, with checked counterpane and toile de Jouy curtains is a favourite. Daughter Sandra, full of friendly enthusiasm, handles the day-to-day. A true family affair, bags of atmosphere, culinary delights; it doesn't get much better.

rooms	40: 36 doubles, 4 suites for 4.
price	€83–€162. Suites €223–€256.
meals	Breakfast €18. Lunch à la carte. Dinner €45–€130.
closed	2 January–12 February.
directions	A50 towards Toulon, exit 11. Follow signs to Cadière d'Azur. Hotel in centre of village.

	The Bérard Family
tel	+33 (0)4 94 90 11 43
fax	+33 (0)4 94 90 01 94
email	berard@hotel-berard.com
web	www.hotel-berard.com

Map 16 Entry 363

Le Logis du Guetteur

Place du Château, 83460 Les Arcs sur Argens, Var

A vertical rabbit warren of renovated old stones around a cobbled courtyard at
the top of a medieval village, beneath the keep – the Watchman's House has
intimacy, good taste and incomparable views from most of the bedrooms. Below
the courtyard, the summer dining room is one of the loveliest stone-flagged
terraces we know, delicious, original food with whiffs of the Mediterranean is
served on perfectly-dressed tables. Along a secret passage, the winter restaurant in
the stone-walled, 'medieval'-furnished vaults is just as cosy as you'd wish in a
snowstorm. The accent is on food here so bedrooms are comfortable with all
you'd expect for the price. Each one is different: an elegant wrought-iron bed
here, generous red velvet drapes there, gauzy white canopies, faux tapestry
counterpanes, compact bathrooms. The curvaceous pool has more panoramic
views. Astoundingly, in the 1960s this little village was a heap of red-grey stones
about to be bulldozed to make way for skyline blocks, then saved by a group of
caring Parisians. Avoid the cheaper rooms and ask for one with a view.

rooms	13: 8 doubles, 2 twins, 2 suites for 3-4, 1 apt for 4-5 (no kitchen).
price	€108-€130. Suites €139-€159. Apartment €175-€195.
meals	Breakfast €15. Lunch & dinner €34-€76. Restaurant closed 20 January-February.
closed	February.
directions	A8 exit 36 Le Muy. N7 for Le Luc 3km; right into Les Arcs. Le Logis & Vieille Ville signed at far end of Les Arcs. (5 mins by taxi from station.)

	Max Callegari
tel	+33 (0)4 94 99 51 10
fax	+33 (0)4 94 99 51 29
email	le.logis.du.guetteur@wanadoo.fr
web	www.logisduguetteur.com

Map 16 Entry 364

La Maurette Roquebrune

83520 Roquebrune sur Argens, Var

Don't look for signs, there are none, Wolfgang doesn't want to "make it look like a hotel". La Maurette stands in splendid isolation, at the very top of a hill looking straight at a World Heritage site, the rock of Roquebrune, which in some way resembles Australia's Ayers Rock. Red earth, rock, mediterranean vegetation, the place has an amazingly mysterious feeling about it. Built of the volcanic stone, La Maurette melds with its surrounding like some ancient settlement; it consists of a main house, several annexes and a castle-style gatehouse housing two rooms. Once past the entrance gate, visitors are greeted by a larger-than-life statue of a seated Rhodesian Ridgeback; the Blumbergs are among the world's best breeders. That and their hospitality activity are both undertaken with gusto and passionate commitment. Bedrooms all have quarry tiles and a Provençal style but are otherwise very different in size, colour and design; they also each have their own terrace and a bottle of wine waiting for their occupants. More a place for a honeymoon than with the children.

rooms	11 twins/doubles, 7 with kitchenettes.
price	€85-€156.
meals	Breakfast €11. Village restaurants 2km.
closed	Mid-November–March.
directions	A8 exit 37 for Fréjus & Roquebrune or to N7 then D7 at Le Pont du Prieur for Roquebrune sur Argens. Over Argens river, right, then left, left again, pass tree in middle of road. Well signed.

	Dr. Christine & Wolfgang Blumberg
tel	+33 (0)4 98 11 43 53
fax	+33 (0)4 98 11 43 52
email	info@lamaurette.fr
web	www.lamaurette.fr

Map 16 Entry 365

Hotel de la Verrerie

Chemin de la Verrerie, 83600 Les Adrets de l'Esterel, Var

No frills but so much to praise! La Verrerie may lack the patina of age but it has a matchless site. Glorious views stretch to the distant Alps from large well-proportioned windows and a lush garden that tumbles down to the river. Hardworking John and Debbie, lovely hosts, have swapped corporate travel for a densely wooded valley and a garden full of roses, palms, lavender and fruit... Join in with the pruning in autumn and you may get a free night! Bedrooms are large, peaceful, sunny, their chintzy furnishings being replaced by a fresh simplicity and excellent linen. One room, sky-lit, is beautifully cool in hot summer; practical, spotless bathrooms are en suite. A shared fridge in the kitchen keeps picnic foods fresh, the internet keeps you in touch and the baker delivers scrumptious croissants for breakfast. Just perfect for sightseers wanting a restorative base – on the edge of the ancient village of Les Adrets yet a few kilometres from the coastal road linking Provence and the Riviera. Bliss for inveterate walkers, and for families: a huge lake for swimming and watersports lies down the road.

rooms	7: 5 doubles, 2 family rooms for 3-4.
price	€45-€70.
meals	Breakfast €8. Restaurants within walking distance.
closed	Never.
directions	A8 exit 39 to Les Adrets; right at roundabout; signed.

	John & Debbie Orfila
tel	+33 (0)4 94 40 93 51
fax	+33 (0)4 94 44 10 35
email	reservations@laverrerie.com
web	www.laverrerie.com

Map 16 Entry 366

Centre International Marie Eugénie Milleret

37 avenue du Commandant Bret, 06400 Cannes, Alpes-Maritimes

A convent in Cannes! This unlikely establishment offers the best of two totally different worlds: the peace and quiet of a secluded *maison d'accueil* and, 20 minutes away, the worldly sophistication of the film festival town of Cannes. It is run with the dedication and warmth one would expect from 'the best kind of nuns' who, without promoting their faith, simply allow it to inform everything they do. The rooms, once the cells of the 60-odd nuns who lived here before France became a secular state, are plain but perfectly comfortable, many with views over to the sea; breakfast, which you can have in the somewhat austere dining room or take out to the rather more inviting terrace, is both copious and delicious. Lunch (which can be a picnic if you order in advance) and dinner are unfussy, homely affairs, but at this price you could treat yourself to an occasional blow-out in Cannes. This is a place for refreshment of the soul, whether you find it lying in the sun on the beach, under the trees in the garden, or in the chapel. *Subscription of 8 p.p. to CIMEM Association usually requested.*

rooms	65 doubles.
price	Half-board €45-€54 p.p. Full-board €53-€62 p.p.
meals	Restaurants in town.
closed	Never.
directions	Cannes Centre Ville. At top of Bvd Carnot, left (opp. Hôtel Amarante) into Bvd des Anglais, then right into Bvd de la République. At 2nd T-junc. left into Ave du Commandant Bret; 500m up hill on left.

	Reservation service CIMEM
tel	+33 (0)4 97 06 66 70
fax	+33 (0)4 97 06 66 76
email	contact@cimem.com
web	www.cimem.com

Map 16 Entry 367

Hôtel Le Cavendish

11 boulevard Carnot, 06400 Cannes, Alpes-Maritimes

Some people have it and some don't. Madame Welter has more of it than most, and her talents show in every niche of this splendid rebirth of a Napoleon III edifice. Subtle are the modern comforts and splendid are the rooms, many with balconies or terraces. Sensuous, exuberant and almost edible is the choice of fabric and colour: crunchy rasberry taffeta, tasselled pistachio green, golden apricot silk, twilight mauve – yet never over the top. On the contrary, one feels as though one is a guest in the grand home of a *grand homme*, such as its namesake, Lord Cavendish. How convivial to have a complimentary open bar for guests in the evening, how attentive to offer leaf teas for breakfast, how sexy to dress the curvy Carrara marble staircase with candles at dusk, how elegant to slip between the lavender-scented sheets of a turned down bed at night. Freshly baked croissants, cakes and crumbles, baked apples, homemade jams and a cheery staff make mornings easy, especially if you are attending one of the events at the Festival Hall, only 10 minutes away. Superb. *Private beach nearby. Valet parking 20.*

rooms	34 twins/doubles.
price	€130–€295.
meals	Breakfast €20.
closed	Never.
directions	From Nice A8; left at roundabout on Boulevard Carnot; follow signs for Palais des Festivals.

	Christine & Guy Welter
tel	+33 (0)4 97 06 26 00
fax	+33 (0)4 97 06 26 01
email	reservation@cavendish-cannes.com
web	www.cavendish-cannes.com

Map 16 Entry 368

Val des Roses

6 chemin des Lauriers, 06160 Cap d'Antibes, Alpes-Maritimes

You could drive here, park the car and not touch it until you leave: a sandy beach with a view to old Antibes is a minute away, the old town and market 10 minutes and the shops five. Frederik and Filip are Flemish, in their twenties and found the Val des Roses a short while ago after searching for the 'perfect place'. Filip has all the necessary diplomas; both brothers are charming and sure to make this venture a happy one. They do everything themselves and put on an excellent breakfast, which you can have in your room, on the terrace or by the pool. They will also do light lunches. For dinner, they will recommend a place; phone ahead and make sure you get a good table. Or if it's Friday, there is a BBQ on the terrace. A definite find: not cheap, but well worth it. The gracious white house, with white shutters, is enclosed in its garden by high walls in a quiet little road. Inside, fabrics and walls are mostly white, cool and tranquil. Interestingly, the bedrooms are open plan, with a large oval bath giving a sybaritic touch. Many guests are return visitors. *Children over 14 welcome.*

rooms	4: 3 suites for 2-3, 1 suite for 4.
price	€140-€190.
meals	Breakfast €14.
	Poolside snacks available.
closed	Rarely.
directions	From Antibes towards Cap d'Antibes, *les plages*, to Salis Plage. Keep shops on right. Immediately after Hotel Josse, at old stone archway, Chemin des Lauriers on right. Ring bell on gate.

	Frederik & Filip Vanderhoeven
tel	+33 (0)6 85 06 06 29 (mobile)
fax	+33 (0)4 92 93 97 24
email	val_des_roses@yahoo.com
web	www.val-des-roses.com

Map 16 Entry 369

Bastide Saint Mathieu

35 chemin de Blumenthal, 06130 Grasse, Alpes-Maritimes

The contrast between rustic simplicity and contemporary elegance is truly impressive. A massive stone edifice, the bastide overlooks fields and hills of olive and lemon trees. Retreating here from Malawi as their children grew older, Inge and Arie restocked the grounds with 3,500 plants: 60 new olive trees, lemons, grapefruit, figs, cherries, almonds. This is Arie's domain: he will show you his hands to prove it. Inside is Inge's work and everything is just as she likes it. In one room, the huge canopied bed is placed right in front of the window to catch the early sun. In spite of the luxuries of CD player, internet connection, cashmere blankets and drinks tray, you feel you are staying with a friend – a very attentive one! Bathrooms are decadently gorgeous but never flashy. Choose your soap from Molinard, Fragonard or Galimard: Inge tries to be fair to all the old Grasse houses. Breakfast is as late as you like, watched over by an old painted angel by the fireplace. The pool is huge, or you can settle under an old plane tree with a coffee.

rooms	5: 3 doubles, 2 suites.
price	€255-€375.
meals	Good choice nearby.
closed	Rarely.
directions	A8 exit 42 Grasse Sud; 2nd right before MacDonald's; left at r'bout; at Elephant Bleu car wash r'bout for St Mathieu to Moulin de Brun; left at T-junc.; immed. right into Chemin de Blumenthal (towards St Jean).

	Arie & Inge Van Osch
tel	+33 (0)4 97 01 10 00
fax	+33 (0)4 97 01 10 09
email	info@bastidestmathieu.com
web	www.bastidestmathieu.com

Map 16 Entry 370

La Grande Bastide

Route de la Colle, 06570 St Paul de Vence, Alpes-Maritimes

This 18th-century bastide has been turned into a country-house hotel which provides calm luxury, plus the most fantastic views through a sea of palm and olive trees of one of the jewels of Provence: St Paul de Vence. This is not simply an enchantingly 'typical' village, it is also an important artistic centre, still frequented by musicians, writers and painters following in the footsteps of Matisse, Daudet and Pagnol. Despite its proximity to the main road (ask for one of the quieter rooms), the gardens manage to keep the exterior world at bay. From the welcoming entrance, along the 'outside corridors' which look out over the gardens, to the rooms, decorated in Provençal style – painted furniture, pretty cotton prints, pastel painted walls – you feel the personal touch of the owners. The pool is overlooked by the terrace where you can eat a breakfast worthy of the setting. You may just want yogurt and honey, or perhaps the full English with a sophisticated French spin appeals? Whatever you choose, a warm welcome and truly painstaking attention to your comfort are guaranteed.

rooms	14: 11 doubles, 3 suites.
price	€145–€206. Suites €190–€290.
meals	Breakfast €16. Informal lunch at poolside.
closed	22 November–26 December; 10 January–mid-February.
directions	From A8, exit 47 for St Paul de Vence. After La Colle sur Loup, hotel signed on left.

	Heinz Johner
tel	+33 (0)4 93 32 50 30
fax	+33 (0)4 93 32 50 59
email	stpaullgb@wanadoo.fr
web	www.la-grande-bastide.com

Map 16 Entry 371

L'Hostellerie du Château

Le Bigaradier, 6,8 place Francis Paulet, 06620 Le Bar Sur Loup, Alpes-Maritimes

What do you do after a long and successful career as an international opera singer? You undertake a huge renovation of a château, of course (the foundations of which date from Roman times) and open a hotel and restaurant. Then you hunt out the perfect antique for each bedroom, make sure fine linens dress top bedding, and choose soft curtains to frame dreamy views. Love at first sight - that's how Véronique Von Hirsch describes her first visit to Le Bar sur Loup many years ago. You understand how her heart was captured when you meander around this authentic perched hill town, gaze over the ramparts to the long views over the valleys and, in the main square, follow the slow clickety-click of boules from the hotel's terrace café. Peace reigns; the hordes on the coast are left miles behind. A talented chef whips up inventive meals in the glassed-in 'Bigardier', named after the Seville orange so prevelent in the area. Oh, yes, Madame also founded an art school and is now artistic director of a vocal ensemble; we are sure evening concerts and weekend festivals will follow in no time at all.

rooms	6: 3 doubles, 2 twins, 1 triple.
price	€90-€150.
meals	Breakfast €8. Lunch €15-€30. Dinner €45.
closed	Never.
directions	From Grasse toward Nice on D2085; left on D2210 to Le Bar Sur Loup. L'Hostellerie on main square.

	Madame Véronique Von Hirsch
tel	+33 (0)4 93 42 41 10
fax	+33 (0)4 93 42 69 32
email	info@lhostellerieduchateau.com
web	www.lhostellerieduchateau.com

Map 16 Entry 372

Un Ange Passe

419 avenue Jean Léonardi, 06480 La Colle sur Loup, Alpes-Maritimes

Serenity, forests and tropical views. The Deloupys had just put the finishing touches to their previous Special Place in the old part of Nice but when they saw this hidden treasure they leapt in with their eyes wide open. Now they've moved from the hum of the city to the jingle of goats' bells and the splash of the stream. The old sheepfold, with its original roof tiles and steep stairs, is palm-lush on the outside, freshly modern within: open-stone walls, polished terracotta, plants, cushions, gliding glass doors to a floodlit pool. Airy, air-conditioned bedrooms have tree-top views, showers have floating glass basins and each has its own private terrace and bathrobes for the pool. You are on the edge of the village, five minutes from St Paul de Vence, but it feels as though you are at the end of the world or at the beginning of time. Surrounded by over 100 hectares of protected parkland, you can take time to explore on foot, horseback or by kayak. Martine and Bernard are warm, cosmopolitan people who delight in sharing their knowledge of the area. *Minimum stay two nights.*

rooms	5: 2 doubles (one with kichenette), 1 family room for 3, 2 family rooms for 3-4 (one with kichenette).
price	€75-€105.
meals	Restaurants 1km.
closed	Rarely.
directions	Ask for map for full directions. Antibes A8 exit Cagnes sur Mer; 1st r'bout to Colle s Loup; over 2nd r'bout; 3rd r'bout to Colle s Loup; 4th r'bout towards Bar s Loup & Colle s Loup; do not go into St Paul.

	Martine & Bernard Deloupy
tel	+33 (0)4 93 32 60 39
fax	+33 (0)4 93 82 45 29
email	contact@unangepasse.fr
web	www.unangepasse.fr

Map 16 Entry 373

Villa Saint Maxime

390 route de la Colle, 06570 St Paul de Vence, Alpes-Maritimes

A modern gem, on a site facing St Paul de Vence – a retreat of vast white spaces. The house was built by a British architect during the first Gulf war. In an echo of the inner courtyard of eastern dwellings, the main atrium has a retractable roof allowing a cooling breeze to waft through in summer. Bold sweeping lines, marble and terracotta, a blue-parasoled pool and, in the central stairwell, a broken-glass garden that sparkles like Ali Baba's jewels. Each air conditioned room has a balcony or terrace to make the most of the view; bath and shower rooms are spectacular. Ann and John spent their early married life in this ancient, fortified village so beloved of Marc Chagall, and have deep emotional roots here. Ann collects modern art; there's a piece or two in your room, more in the famous Maeght Foundation down the road. Breakfast, with champagne if you wish, is any time at all, while a delicious homemade orange aperitif sets the mood for dinner. Immaculate restaurants and bars are a step away. *Children over 12 welcome. Unsupervised pool.*

rooms	6: 4 doubles, 2 suites.
price	€140–€195. Suites €170–€360.
meals	Many restaurants within walking distance.
closed	Rarely.
directions	A8 exit Cagnes sur Mer for Vence then St Paul. Nearing village, left at blue sign for villa. At end of road, blue gate, on left.

	Ann & John Goldenberg
tel	+33 (0)4 93 32 76 00
fax	+33 (0)4 93 32 93 00
email	riviera@villa-st-maxime.com
web	www.villa-st-maxime.com

Map 16 Entry 374

Hôtel Cantemerle

258 chemin Canta Merle, 06140 Vence, Alpes-Maritimes

How appropriate: 1930s sophistication on the doorstep of the Maeght Foundation and Saint Paul de Vence. Much of the furniture came from the old Palais de la Mediterranée in Nice and the feel is pre-war ocean liner – first class, of course! The hotel was built in 1985 in the gardens of Madame Dayan's mother's house, itself the mildly eccentric creation of an Englishman reputedly related to royalty. Rooms are ochre-roofed cottages half concealed by luxuriant garden; the older, duplex quarters have a large private terrace leading to the pool, the newer are on one level, and look to umbrella pines and hills beyond. Colours are muted, relieved by the odd bright kilim or Persian rug and some engravings from the Maeght; the feel is clean but sumptuous. Some rooms have an ethnic touch: nothing heavy-handed, just the odd statue or spear leaning in a corner. A great place for a visit in cooler months: as well as the outdoor pool there's a covered one with luscious green tiles, Moroccan lamps and a hammam. Breakfast is lavish and whenever you like. Lunch or dine in the Art Nouveau restaurant, or outside.

rooms	26: 9 doubles, 17 duplex suites.
price	€180-€200. Suites €205-€225.
meals	Breakfast €15. Lunch & dinner €30-€60. Restaurant closed Mondays September-June.
closed	Usually October-March.
directions	A8 exit Cagnes sur Mer for Vence. At r'bout (with musical instruments & petrol station) right for 100m.

	Madame Christine Dayan
tel	+33 (0)4 93 58 08 18
fax	+33 (0)4 93 58 32 89
email	info@hotelcantemerle.com
web	www.hotelcantemerle.com

Map 16 Entry 375

Hôtel Windsor

11 rue Dalpozzo, 06000 Nice, Alpes-Maritimes

A 1930s Riviera hotel with a pool in a palm grove and exotic birds in cages? All that… and much more. Bernard Redolfi-Strizzot has brought the Thirties into the 21st century by asking contemporary artists to do a room each. The result? So many gifts of wit, provocation, flights of fancy, minimalist sobriety and artistic creation: Joan Mas's *Cage à Mouches*, Jean le Gac's blue figures, cosmopolitan Ben's writing on the walls. The other rooms are far from plain, with Antoine Beaudoin's superb frescoes of Venice, Egypt, India – all our travel myths – and Tintin. Plain white beds have contrasting cushions or quilts; furniture is minimal and interesting; delightful little bathrooms, some directly off the room, are all individually treated. All clear, bright colours, including the richly exotic public areas: the much-travelled owners chose an exquisitely elaborate Chinese mandarin's bed for the bar; panelling and colourful plasterwork for the restaurant; a fine wire sculpture, stone and bamboo for the hall. Light filters through onto warmly smiling staff. And there's a stunning Turkish bath, sauna and fitness centre.

rooms	57 twins/doubles.
price	€75–€155.
meals	Breakfast €10. Dinner à la carte €28–€38. Restaurant closed Sundays.
closed	Rarely.
directions	In centre of Nice, 10min walk from train station. A8 exit Promenade des Anglais. Left at museum on Rue Meyerbeer. Right on Rue de France & 1st left Rue Dalpozzo.

	Odile Redolfi-Payen & Bernard Redolfi-Strizzot
tel	+33 (0)4 93 88 59 35
fax	+33 (0)4 93 88 94 57
email	contact@hotelwindsornice.com
web	www.hotelwindsornice.com

Map 16 Entry 376

Hôtel Les Deux Frères

Place des Deux Frères, 06190 Roquebrune - Cap Martin, Alpes-Maritimes

Only the rich and famous have this view so go ahead, be brave, get up at the crack of dawn and wonder at the beauty of the light coming up over the ocean and the along the coastline. All terrace tables have views but you will be able to pick a favourite for hot coffee and croissants and linger even more. Willem, the young Dutch owner who combines Provençal comfort with an exotic flavour – down to the seven languages he speaks and his restaurant's innovative dishes – is full of ideas. There is now a little snack bar next door for refreshments and he has added two refurbished apartments. You can either sleep in the old village store, 'L'Alimentation', with its bright yellow façade and vintage scale in the window, or in the 'Four', the old bakery. And there are views of the coastline, mountainside or the old village square from every small, sparkling hotel room. Choose between an oriental blue and gold ceiling, a stylish lime green or a nautical blue. After parking in the village you will follow a short, fairly steep path. Ideal for the young and fleet of foot and excellent value for the area.

rooms	10 + 2: 10 doubles. 2 apartments for 2 (only microwave & fridge).
price	€100-€110. Single occupancy €75.
meals	Breakfast €9. Lunch from €24. Dinner from €45. Restaurant closed Mon & Tues noon in summer; Sun eve; mid-Nov-mid-Dec; 1 week in March.
closed	Never.
directions	A8 exit 57 for Menton then Roquebrune Cap Martin. Left at Roquebrune & Vieux Village. Stop at municipal car park & walk 50m.

	Willem Bonestroo
tel	+33 (0)4 93 28 99 00
fax	+33 (0)4 93 28 99 10
email	info@lesdeuxfreres.com
web	www.lesdeuxfreres.com

Map 16 Entry 377

General De Gaulle signed the initial legislation for the creation of its National and Regional Parks in 1967. Forty national and regional nature parks in France now represent 11% of its landmass. Most are off the beaten track and are often missed by the foreign visitor. The motorway network is such that one swishes by huge patches of beautiful countryside without even realising it.

The National and Regional Parks charter promotes:

- Protection and management of natural and cultural heritage

- Participation in town and country planning and implementation of economic and social development

- Welcoming and informing the public, raising environmental awareness

There is a ban on hunting, camping, building and road construction in the six national parks: Cévennes, Ecrins, Mercantour, Port-Cros, Pyrénées and Vanoise. Access can be difficult but the rewards are considerable.

There are regional parks to be found in the mountains of Queyras (Hautes Alpes), the plains of Vexin (Ile de France), along the coast of Camargue (Provence), in the woodlands in the Northern Vosges (Alsace-Lorraine), in the wetlands of Brière (Western Loire) and off-shore in Port-Cros (Côte d'Azur).

All are ideal for rambles. Serious walkers can choose from the sentiers de Grandes Randonnées (GRs for short) which range through the parks and all park offices can provide maps of local walks.

There are grottos and museums to visit along with animal parks roaming with bison, yak, greater kudu and a pack of wolves. Activities include: horseriding, cycling and bike rentals, canoeing and kayaking, canal boating, sailing, fishing, spa treatments, wine tours, bathing, rock climbing, handgliding, ballooning. There are packhorses in Livradois-Forez (Auvergne) and donkeys for hire in Haut-Languedoc (Languedoc). A range of activities make them ideal for children and a multitude of crafts are to be observed: clog-making, silk weaving, glass working, stone working in the Morvan (Burgundy), cheesemaking and pipe-making in the Haut Jura (Franche Comté).

www.parcs-naturels-regionaux.fr

This central web site links to all the other parks. All have English language versions.

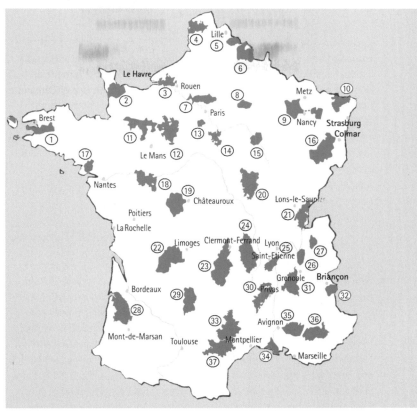

1. Armorique	14. Gâtinais français	27. Massif des Bauges
2. Marais du Cotentin et du Bessin	15. Forêt d'Orient	28. Landes de Gascogne
3. Boucles de la Seine Normande	16. Ballons des Vosges	29. Causses du Quercy
4. Caps et Marais d'Opale	17. Brière	30. Monts d'Ardèche
5. Scarpe-Escaut	18. Loire-Anjou-Touraine	31. Chartreuse
6. Avesnois	19. Brenne	32. Queyras
7. Vexin français	20. Morvan	33. Grands Causses
8. Montagne de Reims	21. Haut-Jura	34. Camargue
9. Lorraine	22. Périgord Limousin	35. Luberon
10. Vosges du Nord	23. Volcans d'Auvergne	36. Verdon
11. Normandie-Maine	24. Livradois-Forez	37. Haut-Languedoc
12. Perche	25. Pilat	
13. Haute-Vallée de Chevreuse	26. Chartreuse	

Cycling and walking in France

Cycling in France

France offers rich rewards to the cyclist: plenty of space, a superb network of minor roads with little traffic, and a huge diversity of landscapes. Choose the leafy forests and gently undulating plains of the north, or the jagged glacier-topped mountains of the Alps. Pedal through wafts of fermenting grapes in Champagne, resinous pines in the Midi, or spring flowers in the Pyrénées. Pedal slowly, stopping in remote villages for delicious meals or a café au lait, or pit yourself against the toughest terrains and cycle furiously.

Bikes are an important part of French culture and thousands don their lycra and take to their bikes on summer weekends. The country comes to a virtual standstill during the three-week Tour de France cycling race in July and the media is dominated by talk of who is the latest maillot jaune (literally 'yellow jersey' – the fellow in the lead). Cycling stars become national heroes and heroines.

Mountain bikes are increasingly popular. They are known as VTTs (vélos tout terrain) and there is an extensive network of VTT trails, usually marked in purple.

When to go

Avoid July and August, if possible, as it's hot and the roads are at their busiest. The south is good from mid-March, except on high ground which may be snow-clad until the end of June. The north, which has a similar climate to Britain's, can be lovely from May onwards. Most other areas are suitable from April until October.

Getting bikes to and through France

If you are using public transport, you can get your bicycle to France by air, by ferry or via the Channel Tunnel. Ferries carry bikes for nothing or for a small fee. British Airways and Air France take bikes free if you don't exceed their weight allowance. If you travel by Eurostar, you should be able to store your bike in one of the guards' vans which have cycle-carrying hooks, with a potential capacity of up to eight bikes per train. To do this you need to reserve and pay extra.

Some mainline and most regional trains accept bikes, sometimes free, most for a fee. Some have dedicated bike spaces, others make room in the guard's van. Information is contradictory on timetables and ticket agents may not have up-to-date information. Trains indicated by a small bike symbol in the timetable may no longer accept bikes,

some without the symbol do.
To be absolutely sure, check out
the train at the station the day
before you depart. Insist on a
ticket *avec réservation d'un
emplacement vélo*. If you are two or
more make sure the réservation is
multiple.

In the Paris area, you can take bikes
on most trains except during rush
hours. Certain central RER stations
forbid bikes on trains.

Maps

The two big names are Michelin and
the Institut Géographique National
(IGN). For route-planning, IGN
publishes a map of the whole of
France showing mountain-biking
and cycle tourism (No. 906). The
best on-the-road reference maps
are Michelin's Yellow 1:200,000
Series. IGN publishes a Green Series
at a scale of 1:100,000. For larger
scale maps, go for IGN's excellent
1:25,000 Top 25 and Blue Series
(which you will also use for
walking). You can buy maps at
most Maisons de la Presse
newsagents in France, or at
Stanfords in the UK.

A new map of Paris showing bike
routes, one-way streets, bus sharing
lanes, rental facilities, week-end
pedestrian and bike only streets is
available at some bookstores.
www.media-cartes.fr

Bike rental
Maison Roue Libre
Affiliated to Paris's public transport
system RATP
www.rouelibre.fr (0)1 44 76 86 43
Mike's Bike Tours-Paris
www.mikesbiketoursparis.com
(0)1 56 58 10 54

Bike tours designed with the
English-speaking tourist in mind;
day and night tours of Paris; day
trips to Versailles and Monet's
Garden at Giverny. Also organise
Segway (self-balancing motorized
scooter) tours of Paris and Nice.

Walking in France

With over 60,000km of clearly
marked long distance footpaths, or
sentiers de Grandes Randonnées
(GRs for short), and a fantastic
variety of landscapes and terrains,
France is a superb country in which
to walk. Hike in the snow-topped
glaciers of the Northern Alps, walk
through the lush and rugged
volcanic 'moonscapes' of the
Auvergne, or amble through the
vineyards of Burgundy, Alsace or
Provence.

Stroll for an afternoon, or make an
odyssey over several months. Some
long-distance walks have become
classics, like the famous GR65, the
pilgrim road to Santiago de
Compostela, the Tour du Mont
Blanc, or the 450km long GR3

Sentier de la Loire, which runs from the Ardèche to the Atlantic. Wild or tamed, hot or temperate, populated or totally empty: France has it all.

Wherever you are staying, there will almost certainly be a GR near you. You can walk a stretch of it, then use other paths to turn it into a circular walk. As well as the network of GRs, marked with red and white parallel paint markings, there's a network of Petites Randonnées (PRs), usually signalled by single yellow or green paint stripes. In addition, there are sentiers de Grandes Randonnées de Pays (GRPs), marked by a red and yellow stripe, and any number of variants of the original GR route which eventually become paths in their own right.

The great reward for walkers is the discovery of rural France in a way not possible by car. You'll see ruined châteaux, meet unforgettable country characters and encounter a dazzling variety of flora and fauna if you look for it: golden eagles, griffon vultures and marmots in the Alps and Pyrénées, red kites and lizard orchids in the Dordogne, and fulmars and puffins off the rocky Brittany coast. There's no room for complacency, however, as hundreds of species are threatened with extinction: 400 species of flora are classed as

threatened and about 20 species of mammals and birds are vulnerable or in danger of extinction.

When to go

The best months for walking are May, June, September and October. In high mountain areas, summers are briefer and paths may be free of snow only between July and early September. In the northern half of France July and August are also good months; southern France is ideal for a winter break, when days are often clear.

Maps

As mentioned in the cycling section, the two big names for maps are IGN (Institut Géographique National) and Michelin. IGN maps are likely to be of most use for walkers. A useful map for planning walks is the IGN's France: Grande Randonnée sheet No. 903 which shows all the country's long distance footpaths. For walking, the best large-scale maps are the IGN's 1:25,000 Serie Bleue and Top 25 series.

Books

The FFRP produces more than 180 topo-guides – guidebooks for walkers which include walking instructions and IGN maps (usually 1:50,000). Most of these are now translated into English so it's worth buying one before you leave.

ALASTAIR SAWDAY'S
SPECIAL ESCAPES

Home · Search · Hotlist · Owners · Links

Shutters on the Harbour, St Ives

Cornwall, England

You'd never guess that this 1875 former fisherman's cottage in the belly of the old town is the lap of modern luxury inside. Georgie and Janin have cleverly renovated this tiny dwelling into a funky palace with lots of surprising touches. Originally pilchards were pressed in the old lounge and shipped to Tuscany – now the only remaining sign is the wooden grooves in the stone walls. From the neutral stone-floored lounge with sheepskin rugs on the rattan chairs, scamper into the shower/washing room to wash off the sand – perfect for surfers. Up to a suspended floor with the kitchen with round table, built-in benches and all mod cons and a second chill-out space – both look down to the lounge. A spiral stair leads up to the bedrooms. Here Janin's furniture-design skills were brought in to create wacky bedside tables using driftwood and stylistic shapes. There are painted wooden floors, funky light sculptures, neutral colours and portholes leading to the bathroom - separated by a vibrant sari curtain. It has a beach-house style with a modern homespun element and they have carefully made the most of the limited space; it can be tight in some corners but somehow that adds to the fun. An ideal spot from which to make the most of St Ives.

'Shutters on the harbour' Belhesda Hill

Owner's Notice Board

BEAUTIFUL ST IVES

Last week of September and all of October still available. STUNNING CONVERSION OF FISHERMAN'S COTTAGE IN HEART OF ST IVES

Note: This information has been provided by the owner or is an element of Shutters on the harbour and is not verified or endorsed by AW.

Bedroom 1

Details for Shutters on the Harbour

Contact Georgina Lenain	**sleeps:**
tel: +44(0)7770 431558	**rooms:** 2 doubles with shower; shower room.
fax: +44(0)20 8877 0700	**price:** £550.00 – £960.00. In winter short breaks negotiated
@ Send E-mail Enquiry	**closed:** Never.
	changeover: Saturday- negotiable.

? Details Explanation

Currency Converter

Sitting room with winter rugs

♦ ✗ 🧺 🍴 👟   ? Symbol Explanations

Why Come Here?

Checklist	**Points Of Interest**
✓ Dishwasher	◆ Eden Project 1-hour drive.

Views on Porthminster Beach

Now what?

A whole week self-catering in Britain with your friends or family is precious, and you dare not get it wrong. To whom do you turn for advice and who on earth do you trust when the web is awash with advice from strangers? We launched Special Escapes to satisfy an obvious need for impartial and trustworthy help – and that is what it provides. The criteria for inclusion are the same as for our books: we have to like the place and the owners. It has, quite simply, to be 'special'. The site, our first online-only publication, is featured on www.thegoodwebguide.com and is growing fast.

www.specialescapes.co.uk

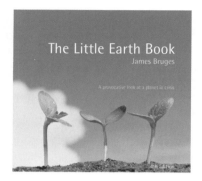

The Little Earth Book
Edition 4, £6.99
By James Bruges

A little book that has proved both hugely popular – and provocative. This new edition has chapters on Islam, Climate Change and The Tyranny of Corporations.

The Little Food Book
Edition 1, £6.99
By Craig Sams, Chairman of the Soil Association

An explosive account of the food we eat today. Never have we been at such risk - from our food. This book will help clarify what's at stake.

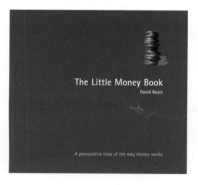

The Little Money Book
Edition 1, £6.99
By David Boyle, an associate of the New Economics Foundation

This pithy, wry little guide will tell you where money comes from, what it means, what it's doing to the planet and what we might be able to do about it.

www.fragile-earth.com

Order Form

All these books are available in major bookshops or you may order them direct.
Post and packaging are FREE within the UK.

British Hotels, Inns & Other Places	£13.99
Bed & Breakfast for Garden Lovers	£14.99
British Bed & Breakfast	£14.99
Pubs & Inns of England & Wales	£13.99
London	£9.99
French Bed & Breakfast	£15.99
French Hotels, Châteaux & Other Places	£14.99
French Holiday Homes	£11.99
Paris Hotels	£9.99
Ireland	£12.99
Spain	£14.99
Portugal	£10.99
Italy	£12.99
Mountains of Europe	£9.99
India	£10.99
Morocco	£10.99
Turkey	£11.99
The Little Earth Book	£6.99
The Little Food Book	£6.99
The Little Money Book	£6.99
Six Days	£12.99

Please make cheques payable to Alastair Sawday Publishing. Total £

Please send cheques to: Alastair Sawday Publishing, Yanley Lane, Long Ashton,
Bristol BS41 9LR. For credit card orders call 01275 464891
or order directly from our web site www.specialplacestostay.com

Title   First name   Surname

Address

Postcode   Tel

Fh4

If you do not wish to receive mail from other like-minded companies, please tick here ☐
If you would prefer not to receive information about special offers on our books, please tick here ☐

Report Form

If you have any comments on entries in this guide, please let us have them. If you have a favourite house, hotel, inn or other new discovery, please let us know about it. You can e-mail info@sawdays.co.uk, too.

Existing entry:

Book title: _____

Entry no: _____ Edition no: _____

New recommendation:

Country: _____

Property name: _____

Address: _____

_____

_____

_____

Tel: _____

Comments: Report:

_____

_____

_____

_____

_____

_____

_____

_____

Your name: _____

Address: _____

_____

_____

Tel: _____

Please send completed form to ASP, Yanley Lane, Long Ashton, Bristol BS41 9LR or go to www.specialplacestostay.com and click on 'contact'. Thank you.

À l'attention de:
To:
_____

Date:
_____

Madame, Monsieur
Veuillez faire la réservation suivante au nom de:
Please make the following booking for (name):

Pour	*nuit(s)*	*Arrivée le jour:*	*mois*	*année*
For	night(s)	Arriving: day	month	year
		Départ le jour:	*mois*	*année*
		Leaving: day	month	year

Si possible, nous aimerions	*chambres, disposées comme suit:*
We would like	rooms, arranged as follows

À grand lit	*À lits jumeaux*
Double bed	Twin beds
Pour trois	*À un lit simple*
Triple	Single
Suite	*Appartement*
Suite	Apartment

Nous sommes accompagnés de enfant(s) âgé(s) de ans.
Avez-vous un/des lit(s) supplémentaire(s), un lit bébé; si oui, à quel prix?
We are travelling with children, aged years.
Please let us know if you have an extra bed/extra beds/a cot and if so, at what price.

Nous aimerions également réserver le dîner pour personnes.
We would also like to book dinner for people.

Veuillez nous envoyer la confirmation à l'adresse ci-dessous:
Please send confirmation to the following address:

Nom: Name:
_____

Adresse: Address:
_____

_____

Tel No: Email:
_____

Fax No:
_____

la réservation – Special Places to Stay

Quick reference indices

Cookery

Cookery lessons and visits to markets organised by owner or third party. Check for dates, language and conditions.

Mushroom hunting

Mushroom hunting, sometimes followed by cookery lessons in the kitchen.

Health & beauty

Spa, sauna, massages, skin care, yoga, thalassotherapy, aromatherapy...

Art
Courses in painting, pottery, sculpture...

Horses
Equestrian activities: accompanied rides, riding/jumping lessons, dressage...

Rent the whole house
Getting married? Mum's birthday? Entire property can be rented; catering services provided

Seminar facilities
Meeting room with refreshments available

Languedoc - Roussillon 275 • 276 • 277 • 279 • 282 • 284 • 285 • 286 • 289 • 291 • 295 • 298 • 299 • 300 • 303
Rhône Valley - Alps 305 • 307 • 309 • 311 • 312 • 313 • 314 • 315 • 316 • 317 • 318
Provence - Alps - Riviera 321 • 323 • 325 • 326 • 329 • 330 • 331 • 333 • 334 • 335 • 338 • 341 • 342 • 346 • 347 • 348 • 355 • 359 • 361 • 363 • 364 • 367 • 368 • 369 • 372 • 373 • 374 • 375 • 376

Gardens
Extraordinary garden on site or nearby
The North 3
Alsace 23 • 26
Burgundy 30 • 31 • 34 • 41 • 45 • 46
Normandy 75 • 76 • 78 • 87 • 91 • 97 • 99
Brittany 102 • 104 • 110 • 113 • 115 • 116 • 117 • 124
Western Loire 129 • 132 • 134 • 135 • 136 • 137 • 142 • 145 • 146
Loire Valley 154 • 155 • 160 • 165 • 166 • 168 • 169 • 170 • 175 • 179
Poitou - Charentes 180 • 183 • 184 • 187 • 191 • 192 • 193
Aquitaine 203 • 206 • 208 • 209 • 213 • 215 • 218 • 219 • 221 • 224 • 230 • 232
Limousin 233
Auvergne 238
Midi - Pyrénées 242 • 243 • 244 • 248 • 249 • 253 • 258 • 259 • 261 • 265 • 266 • 268 • 270 • 272
Languedoc - Roussillon 274 • 279 •

280 • 281 • 288 • 289 • 291 • 293 • 295 • 303
Rhône Valley - Alps 307 • 313 • 317 • 318 • 320
Provence - Alps - Riviera 323 • 324 • 329 • 330 • 332 • 338 • 344 • 348 • 352 • 356 • 361 • 363 • 366 • 367

Heated pool
Heated pool on the premises

Burgundy 30 • 34 • 37 • 40 • 42
Normandy 78 • 85 • 87 • 97
Brittany 101 • 104 • 111 • 112 • 115 • 116
Western Loire 125 • 126 • 129 • 136 • 137 • 139 • 144 • 148 • 149
Loire Valley 152 • 153 • 154 • 155 • 157 • 158 • 159 • 163
Poitou - Charentes 181 • 184 • 190 • 196
Aquitaine 207 • 213 • 215 • 232
Auvergne 237 • 238 • 240 • 241
Midi - Pyrénées 245 • 249 • 255 • 256 • 259 • 260 • 261 • 264 • 269
Languedoc - Roussillon 279 • 286 • 298 • 299 • 302
Rhône Valley - Alps 309 • 311 • 317
Provence - Alps - Riviera 321 • 334 • 336 • 344 • 345 • 346 • 347 • 354 • 357 • 363 • 371 • 375

Cycling
Cyclists welcome; bike storage available
Picardy 8
Champagne - Ardenne 11 • 13
Alsace 26
Burgundy 30 • 32 • 37 • 39 • 41 • 45 • 46 • 47 • 48

Fishing

May be salt or fresh water, on site or within walking distance

Ski trails

Ski trails less than an hour away

Secure parking

No car?
Transport organised from airport
or train station

Up in the air
Ballooning can be arranged by
the owners

Water sports
Kayaking, canoeing and/or sailing
available on site or very nearby.

Little ones
Particularly child friendly

Quick reference indices

Wifi
Wireless internet connection available

Index by property name

Index by property name

Index by property name

Index by town

Index by town